"It ain't what you don't know that gets you into trouble.
It's what you know for sure – that just ain't so."
~ Mark Twain ~

If everybody's SCREAMING, who's *listening*?

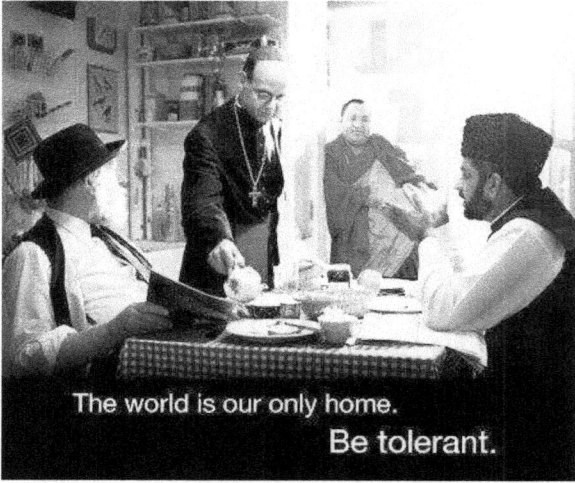

The world is our only home.

Be tolerant.

Briefly Deconstructing "Jihad" *

To most Muslims, and according to the Holy Quran, there are three levels of "Jihad":

"Jihad e Akbar," or the "Greatest Jihad," which is the lifelong personal struggle to resist temptation and be an honest, moral person – in all respects and at all times. Think "Do the right thing;"

"Jihad e Kabeer," or the "Great Jihad," which is to extend those values to family, neighbors and community, essentially live by "The Golden Rule;"

"Jihad e Asghar," or the "lesser jihad," emphatically the jihad of last resort – to physically defend yourself/family/community, justified only to the extent of neutralizing the threat(s) to yours and all monotheistic religions.

In this book, we are delving into humanity's individual and collective "Jihad" (struggle) over who we are, and what we stand for, in a world that is conflicted at so many levels.

*Quran material above condensed by Dan Sockle with assistance from Muslim contributors.

America's Jihad

Joining Humanity's Struggle with Jihadists, the Far left, the Far Right, and other Extremists since 9/11

Second Edition

Compiled and edited by
Dan Sockle

America's Jihad
Second Edition

Copyright © 2017 by Dan Sockle

Website: http://AmericasJihad.com

Email for more information:
dan@americasjihad.com

ISBN: 978-1-893471-29-0

Library of Congress Control Number:
2016949511

1. Peace   2. History   3. Politics

4. Middle East 5. Culture   6. Religion

7. September 11, 2001 (9/11)

Published in the United States by AYWN Publications,
Vancouver, WA

Cover art by Brian "Bush" Bashant

"If man does find the solution for world peace, it will be the most revolutionary reversal of his record we have ever known."
~ General George C. Marshall ~

"Until the latest of our world conflicts, the United States had no armaments industry. This conjunction of an immense military establishment and a large arms industry is new in the American experience. In the councils of government, we must guard against the acquisition of unwarranted influence, whether sought or unsought, by the military industrial complex. The potential for the disastrous rise of misplaced power exists and will persist."
~ President Dwight D. Eisenhower
in his Farewell Address, Jan. 17, 1961 ~

"It isn't enough to talk about peace. One must believe in it. And it isn't enough to believe in it. One must work at it."
~ Eleanor Roosevelt~

"I alone cannot change the world, but I can cast a stone across the waters to create many ripples."
~ Albanian-born Anjeze Gonxhe Bojaxhiu ~
(better known as Mother Teresa)

Let us hope this book might do the same . . .

Dedication

To the many brave people of all faiths who have stood up to the violence and oppression perpetrated by radicals, extremists, ideologues, governments and criminals who have falsely claimed that their atrocities were directed by their god or holy scripture.

To our military and their families who have sacrificed so much – not just for America, but often for the safety and freedom of so many strangers in far off lands. Global political motives might not always have been clear or pure, but, for the vast majority, the American soldier's heart and belief in purpose has been, first and foremost, to protect, defend and, ultimately, liberate the innocent.

To all who have fought for what they believed in. To be fair, throughout the history of guerilla or asymmetric warfare it has generally been accurate to say, "One man's terrorist is another man's freedom fighter." In 2003, this adage has never been more true than in the days and weeks that followed the ill-advised decision to essentially fire what remained of the Baghdad government and virtually all of the Iraqi military. In the name of "debaathification," almost overnight our "liberation" of Iraq effectively became, in the eyes of the Iraqis, an "occupation" - unleashing 500,000 well-armed, organized and patriotic countrymen who ultimately, with prompting and support from Al-Qaeda, became America's worst nightmare. What an incredible calamity America's political "leadership," Republican and Democrat, has inflicted upon our own military – and the Iraqi people.

To the Chaplains of the world who set aside their ordained faith in order to provide spiritual support to those of all ethnicities and beliefs, focusing first on our commonalities as humans - not to our too-often contrived or invented differences.

Acknowledgements

A special thanks to my wife, Susan, and to the twenty-five other contributors and co-contributors to this book. I sincerely thank all of you for believing in this unique undertaking. We might have different experiences and perspectives, and certainly different opinions and ideas, but we are all sufficiently humble to strive to learn and grow every day of our lives. If we can open a few minds and plant a few seeds through this book, the website, our individual and collective endeavors, then we just might help to turn the tide on fundamentalism and radicalism around the world. "World Peace" is a noble goal, "love" is a wonderful word, but the reality is that humans have too many frailties and flaws to ever achieve a world totally devoid of hate, greed, mental illness, or the various levels of conflict that can be triggered for the wrong reasons, or even no reason at all. Let us strive to better understand and respect one another, identify our shared values and common interests, and see where we can go from there.

Setting our political and religious differences aside, let us also acknowledge that flawed decisions of both Presidents Bush and Obama, in 2003 and 2011, caused or significantly contributed to the growth of the "Islamic State" (aka: DAESH) and what has ultimately led to what has arguably become the greatest refugee crisis of modern times - over 65 million refugees and internally displaced persons spanning north/central Africa across the Middle East to central/south Asia. Let us acknowledge that American policies and actions, driven by politicians, contributed to this crisis. We must strive to find that all important balance between security and compassion in helping our fellow human beings who have essentially lost everything.

Introduction:
Why this book? Why Now?

America has dug itself into a hole. Our relative isolation, educationally speaking, has resulted in an often-dysfunctional foreign policy going back decades. Our public education system, including much of "higher education," public and private, has generally subordinated or ignored other world languages, cultures and religions. Further, we Americans have been raised to avoid talking about politics or religion. Political Correctness, or hyper-annoyance and narcissism, has come to dominate and intimidate public discourse, impeding open, honest, meaningful and constructive confrontation of our greatest challenges. We are at a point in history where political and religious fundamentalism and extremism have brought the world to dangerous crossroads. Sadly, as evidenced by the increased suffering of innocents, most notably the worst refugee crisis since World War II, America is ill-prepared to effectively and compassionately sort it all out.

Meanwhile, our legal system is built upon an adversarial process for resolving disputes. Like many of the tribal cultures we strive to understand, our own criminal justice system is generally retributive, not restorative. Our media thrives on the most extreme, outrageous, and bloody. Pundits and talking heads model shouting matches with little or no effort towards compromise and solutions. Politicians' rhetoric is theater as they pander to their party bases and special interests and exploit misunderstanding, misperceptions and fear for the sake of attracting financial support and/or votes. Political campaigns are increasingly comparable to open warfare.

"Black Lives Matter," "Blue Lives Matter," "All Lives Matter." Today's visceral arguments over expressions that are <u>all</u> true is but one example of today's *Divided* States of America. What happened to those words that touched and inspired so many of us back in July 2004, so eloquently spoken by then Illinois US Senator Barack Obama?:

> "…there is not a liberal America and a conservative America, there is a United States of America. There is not a Black America, and a White America, a Latino America, an Asian America - there is a <u>*United States of America*</u>…"

We are an instant gratification society with far too many impediments to constructive conversation about the issues that should matter most. Our "Greatest Generation" is dying and our "all volunteer" military has resulted in a miniscule percentage of our population ever having served any kind of cause greater than themselves. This further reduces our exposure to, understanding of, and respect for both our own disparate cultures across fifty states, and, of course, the multitudes outside our borders – about which we understand so very little.

There is no one "magic bullet," no one "expert," no one "leader," and certainly no easy answers to save the day, unite the world, achieve World Peace, or even bring forth the ultimate truth. Every single person has developed his or her own truth and view of the world around them based upon their individual life experiences and journeys. Hopefully, most humans share a willingness, perhaps even a desire, to do right by those who are suffering, dying, or otherwise in distress or disadvantage through no fault of their own. Unfortunately, there are also those who would exploit nearly any situation (even prey upon someone's sympathy) for personal gain – perhaps driven by their nature or, more likely, a feeling that humanity's pursuit of true justice and fairness amounts to a futile or even foolish pursuit of the impossible dream. How often have you heard, "Life isn't always fair" or "It's only politics as usual?" Today, it seems that there are too many justifcations for disillusionment and distrust.

Indeed, humanity's struggle to find truth and accountability in our leaders, elected or not, in politics and/or religion, does appear to be a cruel exercise in futility. Given the untrustworthiness of both major presidential candidates in this 2016 campaign, Hillary Clinton and Donald Trump, this is more evident today than ever. Bernie Sanders has arguably tapped into the "Occupy" dissenters, while Donald Trump appears to have tapped into the outrage of the "Tea Party" and others similarly frustrated with "politics as usual." I submit that the "Occupiers" and "Tea Partiers" have more in common than differences, but each movement has been co-opted by the extremists on the "Left" and "Right," leaving no room for compromise or collaboration. There is no "win-win" effort afoot; instead, we find only "win-lose," which is sadly a "lose-lose" for the American people.

This book's intent is to take a definitive step towards gaining a better understanding and respect for those coming from backgrounds and places much different from your own. You will read about the lives of twenty-four people from various parts of the world, but also very much like you in their hopes and dreams for a better tomorrow.

You will agree with many and disagree with some, but the key is to gain a better understanding of how they have come to their views of the world around them – and their visions for a better future, for themselves, their children, grandchildren and future generations.

Arising from my career in communications intelligence, criminal and civil investigations, mediation and an attempt to apply all of this experience during a year in Iraq, it is ultimately my hope that your own "journey" through the pages of this book will enable you to more willingly engage others, prevent or resolve conflicts more effectively, and simply gain a healthier understanding and respect for your fellow human beings and the world around you.

I wish you a most fruitful journey of your own, and sincerely hope that you will also discover more constructive and meaningful ways to engage with others – from those beside you to the many wonderful people on the other side of the globe. We are all humans. We are increasingly in this world <u>together.</u> Let's make the most of it.

Dan Sockle

Foreword

Written by Jim Moody, veteran of the Korean War with
continued service in Southeast Asia

* * *

Back to the Future:
Are We Destined or Condemned to Keep Repeating
Our Mistakes of the Past?

It was the suddenness of the attack -- that and the American deaths involved -- that brought the country together in demanding retribution. Some even dared to call it revenge. And so we went to war. After our military mobilized an overwhelming force in the area, we attacked, promising the indigenous people that we were going to help them build a new nation: a democratic nation based on individual freedoms. The war that followed was over very quickly. The Secretary of State called it a "splendid little war." The President proclaimed our victory.

At the beginning of the war, we imported a new leader, a man who had been in exile abroad. He led his forces, as best he was able, in support of our troops and, at the same time, began to try to form a government, and create a new central authority. With our help, he hoped to establish a new nation, to bring American style democracy to the area - but tribal conflicts made a unified government difficult to realize. And, at the same time, American corporations began to move in, lured by rich prospects of profit and visions of future expansion. The President decided that he would not relinquish American sovereignty just yet; it was too soon. The country wasn't ready. And that was when the real trouble began.

In areas far from the capitol, distant areas that had had only the most tenuous of connections with the central government, neither victory nor control came easily. An insurgent movement, resentful of what they saw as simply further instances of colonial exploitation, began to resist, gaining strength as time passed. A document written by our own President stating that a major factor in the decision to attack and conquer the country was the economic opportunities that American control offered our corporations exacerbated the situation by seeming to confirm that we were not there to free the country but rather were intending to create a kind of colony. As the situation in the outlying areas deteriorated we attempted to consolidate our control by establishing military garrisons - outposts - in the more distant areas. These far flung outposts were difficult to supply and defend, even with our overwhelming military superiority. They became targets for hit-and-run attacks. American troops died. Costs escalated, and, at home, dissenting voices began to be heard.

It was a militarily difficult situation. Our troops were fighting a kind of unconventional war, an asymmetric war that was unfamiliar to them. They were working in difficult terrain, a kind of terrain with which they had little or no experience. And they were fighting an enemy that they didn't understand, a fanatical Muslim enemy willing to die to defend his village, or his family, or his religion, or even his personal honor. Our forces began to experience hit-and-run encounters and suicide attacks. As American casualties mounted so did our troops desire to "get some payback." A Brigadier General was later court-martialed for telling his junior officers, "I want no prisoners. I want you to kill and burn - the more you kill and burn, the better it will please me. I want all persons killed who are capable of bearing arms in actual hostilities against the United States." When questioned as to what age would be deemed capable of bearing arms, he replied, "The age of 10." And his troops complied, killing thousands of Muslims - men, women and children, and burning villages to the ground. Local anger and belligerence grew. The situation continued to get worse.

The military commander told the President that the key to the solution was more troops, and so a "surge" of new troops was sent in. Only our overwhelming military and technical superiority kept the situation even marginally under control. Rumors of atrocities committed by American troops began to appear in the American and world press; stories of women and children - collateral damage - dying, of unwarranted killings, or outright murder. Reports of torture and water-boarding became more frequent. Our troops were baffled and confused, and increasingly angry. They had little understanding - or appreciation - of the local culture, and so they found themselves unwittingly being dragged into centuries-old tribal conflicts. They didn't seem to understand that in the Muslim world any death of a family member, or even a distant relative, demanded, as a matter of honor, the death of one of the perpetrators: "blood demands blood." Local hostility was met with contempt and derogatory names for the local inhabitants such as "Niggers" and "Googoos".

As the war dragged on for year after year, support at home waned. More and more voices were heard questioning our very presence. The war became a wedge issue to be exploited for political gain. It divided the nation into bitterly opposed camps. In the military, reputations were gained and lost, soldiers were court-martialed. Even General Officers were put on trial and convicted for various "improprieties" such as ordering that no prisoners were to be taken.

It all sounds depressingly familiar. If you're thinking "Iraq," or even "Afghanistan," you're wrong. What I've just described is a military action that was first a part, and then a continuation, of the Spanish-American War. The war against the Moro's, the Muslim population that had inhabited the outlying areas of the Philippine archipelago for hundreds of years, dragged on long after the Peace Treaty ending the war was signed in Paris in 1898. The conflict has since come to be known to historians as the Philippine-American War, or the Moro War. It's considered by some historians to be our least honorable war, with the possible exception of our war with the American Indian Tribes. It was a war marked by massacres, concentration camps, torture, ignorance, arrogance, and death on a large scale.

Philippine Muslims, who had lived in accordance with the beliefs and norms of their own Muslim culture for hundreds of years in virtual isolation, saw no reason to change their lifestyle at the request of foreigners: Be they American or Spanish outsiders. Protected by distance, almost impassable dense jungle, lack of roads and poor communications that protected them from these influences, intrusions, or invasions, the Moro's had evolved an effective traditional tribal society. When attacked, these tribal Muslims did what they had always done, what they had done during centuries of tribal conflict: they fought back. The Moro War that lasted for a decade or more beyond the signing of the Paris Treaty of 1898 - the treaty that gave America sovereignty over the Philippines (not to mention Guam and Puerto Rico) - was characterized by ignorance, callousness and great cruelty. It is a matter of historical record that the troops took few, if any, prisoners. Their letters home show that while some of them were appalled at what was happening, many were not. Many apparently killed without mercy. It is a war that Philippine Muslims have never forgotten.

This was probably our first serious, long-term conflict with Muslims. It occurred over 100 years ago. And that wasn't the end. We are fighting there still. In 2015, approximately 500 Special Operations troops that had been stationed for some time in the Philippines "training" the local Filipino special operations forces, left the Philippines, but not before commanding one last operation in which more than 40 of the local troops were killed.

Most Americans have forgotten about this savage conflict - if they ever even knew about it. It isn't part of the curriculum taught in our schools. The only reason that I had any interest in it was because my Great Grandfather, Edward Valentine Moody, fought there as a Sergeant in Battery A of the California Volunteers Heavy Artillery. As a boy, I read the letters he wrote home about the conflict. His discharge certificate hangs on my wall. This personal connection whetted my appetite for military history, and may have influenced my own decision to enlist in the military. More seriously, while most Americans might have forgotten (or never known about) the war with the Moro's, the Muslim world has not forgotten.

In our current conflicts in the Middle East we seem to have forgotten whatever lessons we learned in the dense jungles of Mindanao. We launched our campaign in the Middle East with, at best, a rudimentary knowledge of the culture and society in which the conflict would take place. The American public, if not the troops, were amazed and shocked by the determined resistance we encountered from local militias and insurgents. Didn't they know they were defeated? We were baffled by suicide attacks, something that our soldiers in that long ago war learned about the hard way. Americans were chagrined when we learned of some of the actions taken by American troops. We seemed surprised and a little angry that our military might didn't bring about an immediate surrender.

There were those who, in the midst of that long ago war with the Moro's, wrote reports stating that it would be impossible to get Muslims to accept our laws, our form of government, because that would require them to give up their religion and their culture in order to do so. The authors understood the power that a culture based on religious belief exercises over a people. But those lessons seem to have been lost; we have apparently repeated the same tactical and strategic mistakes that we made in the Philippines so long ago.

In Afghanistan and Iraq, in our zeal to "liberate," bringing the "gift" of democracy, to build a nation in our image, we failed to recognize that, without a long period of education, a Western-style democratic government would be a difficult, maybe even impossible, concept to establish in the Muslim world. We relied too much on overwhelming military superiority in our attempt to achieve victory, seemingly oblivious to the fact that military might had not prevailed in previous asymmetric conflicts in which we had participated: the Philippines, Viet Nam, etc. Despite "crash courses" and quick-reference culture/language cards, our troops by-and-large were ill-equipped for effectively engaging with the various ethnicities, cultures, languages, and historical complexities spanning hundreds of years. Despite noble efforts at unit levels, our overall ignorance relative to the indigenous populations ultimately transformed "liberation" into "occupation" – resulting in insurgencies being fought, in many instances, by former military turned "freedom fighters."

What's the point? Perhaps it's put best in the Bob Dylan song when he asks, "….. When will they [we] ever learn, when will they [we] ever learn?" Or, in a more philosophical vein, Edmund Burke's quote: "Those who do not know history are doomed to repeat it." If we can't understand Muslim culture and society, perhaps we can, at least, learn the lessons of history.

Twenty years of conflict. Nearly a trillion dollars spent. And, most important of all, 5000+ American lives lost, tens of thousands wounded, and an estimated 400,000 Iraqi and Afghan deaths - and to what end? When will we ever learn? *Will* we ever learn?

Edward Valentine Moody

"The farther backward
you can look, the farther
forward you will see"
~ Sir Winston Churchill ~

Religions/Belief Systems Around the World
(2005/2015)

1- Christians - 2,116,909,552 [2.2B] (which includes
      1,117,759,185 Roman Catholics, 372,586,395
      Protestants, 221,746,920 Orthodox, and 81,865,869
      Anglicans)
2- Muslims - 1,282,780,149 [1.6B] (Approx. 85% Sunni/15%
      Shi'a/Shi'ite)
3- Hindus - 856,690,863 [1.1B]
4- Chinese "Folk" – (not in CIA stats) [1B]
5- Buddhists - 381,610,979 [500M]
6- Sikhs - 25,139,912 [28M]
7- Jews - 14,826,102 [14M]
8- Others - 814,146,396
9- "Non-Religious" - 801,898,746
10- Atheists - 152,128,701

(First figures according to About.com, citing *CIA World Factbook/2005* estimates; with 2015 estimates in [brackets] - according to Wikipedia: "Major Religious Groups")

"This is my simple religion:
There is no need for temples
No need for complicated philosophy
Our own brain, our own heart, is our temple
The philosophy is kindness"
~ The Dalai Lama ~

"7 Deadly Social Sins:
Politics without principle
Wealth without work
Commerce without morality
Pleasure without conscience
Education without character
Science without humanity
Worship without sacrifice"
~ Mahatma Gandhi ~

Table of Contents

Note: Each contributor to this book was asked to write about his or her "journey" from the attacks of September 11, 2001 to the present day. Thus, each chapter represents individual experiences, conclusions, opinions and perspectives. Each essay is his or her "truth," which should be considered as such, independent of the other twenty-three contributors to this book or the overall project (website, etc.).

Chapters

Appendices

Chapter One

Operations Enduring and Iraqi Freedom
Unintended Consequences
and Lessons Unlearned

Dan Sockle

My journey since 9/11 has been heavily influenced by my thirty-five years of government service, over twenty-five of which were in criminal and civil investigations, and six of which were in communications intelligence, mostly in West Berlin and Augsburg, West Germany, during the Cold War. When later pursuing my masters degree in Public Administration, I was drawn to an elective, "Conflict Resolution," which ultimately led me to work as a volunteer community mediator – helping people at earlier stages of conflict in the hope of helping them to avoid the civil and/or criminal justice systems. In 2008-2009, I spent a year in Kirkuk and Baghdad, which significantly influenced my current path and, ultimately, this book.

More recently, in addition to working with the local mediation community and organizations supporting our veterans and military families, I have concurrently and increasingly reached out to and engaged our area's Muslim communities. Most encouraging is that while I have become involved in these profound challenges of our time, I also discovered and joined Rotary International. In doing so, I have jumped in with both feet to help this global organization find a realistic approach to its foundational Area of Focus, "Peace and Conflict Prevention and Resolution." Shortly after joining Rotary, 2012/2013 President Sakuji Tanaka declared his theme to be "Peace Through Service," or, as we called it at the district and local levels, "Building Peace – One Community at a Time."

This chapter is about how I got from twenty-two years in the Army, and these many years of criminal and civil investigations, to joining what I have discovered to be a constructive and viable effort to help all parties to achieve higher levels of effective communications, mutual understanding and respect – enabling them to transcend ethnic, religious, cultural and/or political divides.

1

Throughout my career in criminal and civil investigations, and mediation, I often reflected on the frequency of breakdowns in both individual responsibility and organizational accountability. I am not making excuses for the "bad guys," but there were plenty of lapses, particularly in property and economic crime cases ("Fraud, Waste and Abuse"), where the levels of government negligence frequently influenced the government attorneys not to prosecute the case.

Prelude to 9/11/2001

In 1991, as an active duty warrant officer and special agent/ criminal investigator, I deployed to Saudi Arabia and Kuwait as part of Operation "Desert Storm." In late March/early April, due to the insistence of our regional "Coalition" partners, our forces stopped short of removing Saddam Hussein from power. This was over concerns about unleashing the "Kurds" in northern Iraq, and the "Shiites" in southern Iraq, viewed as likely to create chaos for the bordering countries (Saudi Arabia, Syria, Jordan, Turkey, Iran and Kuwait), Generally speaking, there was little-to-no mention of the "Sunni's" or the Baath Party regarding the cultural, ethnic and religious dynamics of the country or region. I would venture to say that many or most of us, there in theater and back here at home, thought that the Kurds and Shiites were either two sects of Islam or two ethnic groups who somehow represented trouble. (I will get back to these two groups later in this chapter.) All we knew for sure is that it would be problematic for the region if either or both were "freed" from the tyrannical control of Saddam Hussein's regime. (For more detail about these dynamics, with focus especially on the Kurdistan region, Operation "Provide Comfort," and how the Kurdish people grew to love America, I highly recommend the book *Invisible Nation* by Quil Lawrence).

Regarding potential "powder kegs" of ethnic or religion-based clashes of cultures, one need look no further than the former Yugoslavia and Marshal Josip Tito's dictatorial control of the various ethnic and religious groups that comprised that complex country. The former Yugoslavia gradually deteriorated after Tito's death, eventually resulting in the civil war among Croats, Serbs, Bosnians and the former Yugoslavian military/security forces, which included the genocide charges eventually brought by the United Nations against Slobodan Milosevic. Much of that violence and bloodshed involved Muslims vs. non-Muslims.

During the "Cold War," having been a part of the intelligence community monitoring Soviet and Warsaw Pact military and political communications, we had a unique-though-qualified respect for Tito. While part of the Warsaw Pact alliance of (mostly) Communist countries aligned against the North Atlantic Treaty Organization (NATO), Tito often acted independently, seemed to run a "tight ship," and was generally seen as a weak link or "Maverick" in the Soviet-led Warsaw Pact alliance.

Thus, I would have to say that the handling of Iraq's invasion of Kuwait in 1990, Operations "Desert Shield" and "Desert Storm," not only effectively relied upon our intelligence and lessons still being learned from Yugoslavia/Bosnia/Croatia, but was a model of effective diplomacy and coordination across many cultures and belief systems. Unfortunately, unknown or unrecognized for its significance at the time, Western intelligence failed to recognize the emerging issue of "Infidels in Muslim Lands," especially involving Saudi Arabia, Osama bin Laden's country of birth – and focus.

September 11, 2001

Exercising just before going to work as a state investigator in Olympia, Washington, I was watching the news at 5:46 AM, as local programming was interrupted for "breaking news" - attention being upon the North Tower of the World Trade Center, into which some kind of aircraft had just crashed. Along with the rest of the country I'm sure, I was mystified by the clear blue skies and pondering how in the world this could have happened by accident. Of course, when United Airlines Flight 175 flew into the South Tower, it was instantly clear that America was under attack. I went to work reflecting on my military service, including sixteen years as an Army CID Agent, and started making inquiries as to how I could join the Federal Aviation Administration as a Federal Air Marshal… which quickly became an exercise in futility since the Office of Personnel Management (OPM) had age cut-offs relative to armed federal law enforcement positions.

As it turns out, at fifty-one, I was fourteen years beyond the maximum age, unless I had previous federal civilian law enforcement experience. My military service, wearing civilian clothes and carrying a sidearm for over sixteen years, did not count as previous civilian federal law enforcement service. I would venture to say that this policy prevented America from being able to almost instantly put into the air experienced and qualified former agents from the Army's Criminal Investigations Division (CID), Air Force Office of Special Investigations (AFOSI), and the Naval Investigative Service - now the Naval Criminal Investigative Service (NCIS), which also serves the Marine Corps.

Alas, this was not my first frustration involving the world of criminal investigations and/or intelligence and matters of national security. Prior to 9/11/2001, particularly our federal (including military) intelligence and investigative agencies were not very good at sharing information or resources. In fact, especially within the intelligence community, it was common practice to control access to classified information not only relevant to the individual's level of security clearance, but his or her "need to know." This compartmentalization was based upon a historical position that no one person should have access to all pieces of the puzzle – except, of course, at only the highest levels. Particularly during the "I Spy" days of the Cold War, where undercover operatives and informants were constantly probing for vulnerable targets, this practice minimized the damage that might occur as individuals were compromised and flipped to reveal or obtain classified information, certain documents, and even highly sensitive equipment.

Having worked in both the intelligence and criminal investigation worlds, by mid-day on September 11, it was easy for me to imagine how such a complex attack on the United States could have happened – even despite the best efforts of individuals in either or both professions. To its credit, the Bush Administration almost immediately recognized this vulnerability or flaw, creating the Department of Homeland Security and realigning our various intelligence and law enforcement agencies. This included a change in philosophy that lead to the de-compartmentalization of intelligence to better facilitate "connecting the dots." While the intent was valid, not all of the problems have been remedied. Sadly, DHS has become a bureaucratic monster and, potentially, more of a threat than a protector of American citizens.

Unfortunately, several years later, this de-compartmentalization and resultant interconnectivity between various government systems contributed to PFC Bradley Manning, from his low level position of access, being able to obtain and share classified and sensitive communications of the US military and even Department of State to Julian Assange and "WikiLeaks." Thus, in "fixing" our ability to share information and "connect the dots," we find unintended consequences of another sort.

Back to 2001-2002, my greatest consolation over being "too old" to re-enter armed federal service was mitigated by working with and for two retired AFOSI agents as we continued to share that frustration and console one another as we continued to serve the state taxpayers

4

relevant to liability claims of bodily injury or property damage. I was also concurrently pursuing a Masters in Public Administration at The Evergreen State College, a very liberal campus where the government, especially at the federal level, was generally distrusted and often the target of various protests. Thus, in a much different way, I frequently found myself defending our country - albeit on another level. I was, and still am, quick to acknowledge the many flaws and dysfunctions of our government, and often lamented how such shows as "The X-Files" sadly created a generation or two firmly convinced that no one in the federal government, well, except perhaps Agents Fox Mulder and Dana Scully, could be trusted... I suspect that this otherwise terrific drama influenced many of those "Truthers" who have created or supported the various theories that the Bush Administration plotted to take down the Twin Towers in order to benefit the Military Industrial Complex and/or the big oil corporations.

Unfortunately, in March 2003, after the easier-than-anticipated successes over the Taliban and Al Qaeda following our invasion of Afghanistan, the Bush Administration somehow convinced itself that it was time to go into Iraq and finish the job that was not completed in the First Gulf War. Perhaps having all of the logistics and personnel already in the region made it too easy to selectively "cherry-pick" their sources (especially Ahmed Chalabi) and the assertions that Saddam Hussein had weapons of mass destruction (WMD's). Whatever the case, Secretary of Defense Donald Rumsfeld appeared to set aside the intelligence and lessons earlier cited (from the First Gulf War), and the war-gaming (and planning) scenarios prepared by the Pentagon between 1991-2002. Somehow, Vice President Dick Cheney, Secretary Rumsfeld, CIA Director George Tenet and a reluctant Secretary of State Colin Powell convinced themselves and President Bush that we would be greeted by the Iraqi's as "liberators." It was also predicted that we would be in and out of Iraq in 12-18 months.

As depicted in the excellent 2007 film, *No End in Sight*, we actually came close to realizing that original expectation. Indeed, the majority Shi'a population initially welcomed us with flowers and flags, believing that we were delivering democracy, and thus "majority rules," to this country that was previously ruled by the minority Sunni. Had it not been for incredibly poor planning, the elusive Saddam and his sons (Uday and Kusay) retaining some remaining support and hope for a return of the old regime (mostly out of fear, some out of loyalty), and pressure from the Grand Ayatollah Ali al-Sistani on the U.S. to purge all Baathists, i.e. those most associated with the Hussein regime, the essential governmental infrastructure of the country might have remained intact and capable of an effective transitional government. Unfortunately, as Ambassador L. Paul Bremer replaced retired General Jay Garner, implemented "Debaathification" and ultimately "fired" the Iraqi military (500,000 well-armed, organized and patriotic Iraqis), the "Liberation" turned into an "Occupation" and cost thousands of Coalition and Iraqi lives over the subsequent eight years. At the same time, as a power vacuum was created, Shi'a and Sunni Muslims turned on one another, and radical Muslims turned on the country's minority ethnic and Christian populations, mostly Assyrian and Chaldean, – similar in some ways to what happened in Yugoslavia after Tito's death.

That "firing" of the entire Iraqi military, to the dismay of both our Generals and senior officers – as well as the Iraqi leadership in both the military and highest levels of the government, will go down in history as one of the worst tactical and strategic decisions of all time. We have all heard the adage, "One man's terrorist is another man's freedom fighter." One can hardly blame the Iraqis for the "insurgency" that followed, even a tacit, survival-driven alliance with elements of al Qaeda, as the former Iraqi military fought not only for their families, but for their pride and country.

Eighteen months with the Human Terrain System (HTS)

In April 2008, I finally got my opportunity to directly engage in the "War on Terror" and head for Iraq - to help "fix what we had broken," to quote Colin Powell. My greatest motivation was that my youngest son, an Army infantryman, was on his second combat tour in Iraq, this time as a part of the "Surge." The "Human Terrain System" emerged out of the *Counter-Insurgency (COIN) Manual* co-created by General David Petraeus. Dubbed "CORDS for the 21st Century," HTS was modeled after and compared to its Vietnam predecessor (*Civil Operations and Revolutionary Development Support*). In 2006, the HTS concept arose to create, train and field teams of from five to nine personnel co-led by military officers and anthropologists or social/political scientists, bringing cultural insights to the battlefield. The intent was to more effectively (and non-lethally) engage the indigenous populations to reduce and minimize casualties on all sides, and improve our image and relationship with the people of Afghanistan and Iraq. The first team arrived in Afghanistan in 2007. Their successes led to an almost immediate demand for one Human Terrain Team (HTT) for every Army Combat Brigade or Marine Regiment. The scramble was

6

on and, yes, haste does make waste.

Unfortunately, the American Anthropological Association (AAA), drawing upon their belief that the CORDS program had betrayed the non-lethal targeting concept by ultimately targeting innocents, quickly and aggressively spoke out against HTS, pointing to how the military had betrayed anthropologists and related advisors in Vietnam and Cambodia. No matter how hard the HTS leadership tried to convince AAA that those incidents were exaggerated and this program had learned and adjusted from those lessons, training and directing all team members accordingly, the AAA would not relent in what amounted to, in my opinion, an unfair and biased protest of the wars in Afghanistan and Iraq by "Academia." I believe their position was more an extension of anti-Bush sentiments than fact based – at least as their assertions pertained to the current and evolving HTS doctrine. Ultimately, however, their opposition and related criticism of those anthropologists who "crossed the picket line" did result in many highly qualified and quality folks steering clear of the program – lest they might jeopardize their reputations and careers for the long term.

Another unfortunate byproduct of the AAA's opposition was the extent to which the HTS leadership bowed to and promised anthropologists or acceptable equivalent "recruits" that they would have increasing leadership authority over "their" team and, ultimately, be allowed to control and publish the results of their field research. Going into a combat environment, Combat Brigade Commanders were not too receptive to the notion of longer term research or studies to be conducted in their Areas of Operation (AO's). During training, the "Rapid Ethnographic Assessment Protocol" (REAP) was put forth as the optimal compromise. REAP's essentially reduced what might be a year-plus research project to 30-60-90 days. Unfortunately, once deployed and interacting with a commander who would have to divert some of his troops from other missions to escort and protect our teams, those serving as a senior social scientist (anthropologists, when we had one) had to justify their proposed missions (research) by attempting to develop reliable information that was actionable within a 24-48 hour window. A difficult, if not impossible task, this was nevertheless the reality of being in a combat zone where distinguishing between the good guys and the bad guys was a matter of life and death – for both the Coalition forces as well as the Iraqi citizenry.

The most successful social scientist I had the honor to observe and work with was Nancy St.Claire, whose degree was in psychology and vocation was counseling. Her philosophy was to get out into the

7

field and engage the local population. With no experience in the military, she was a courageous "trooper" that we sorely missed when she left. Unfortunately, her successor, quite the opposite, arrived intent to reduce or eliminate our interaction with our supported brigade's intelligence elements. It was as if she was carrying the AAA banner as she attempted to exercise control over all tasks and treat everyone on the team, particularly the Iraqi Americans, as second-class citizens of little importance. I contended from the onset of training in Leavenworth, KS, that these individuals most familiar with the local cultures were arguably the most important element of both the individual teams and the program in general. Instead, more often than not, in a program that was supposed to be all about cultural sensitivity and awareness, our Arabic and Kurdish linguists were often treated with little respect.

Chaplains and Opportunities Lost

In the bigger picture, as we initiated a community outreach to reconnect local Turkmen (Shi'a and Sunni) with two cemeteries and a shrine within the secured perimeter of the Kirkuk Air Base (cut off during base expansions under Saddam Hussein), I soon learned of restrictions that had been placed particularly on our Army Chaplains not to engage with local religious leaders. The concern that apparently originated at high levels of the military and/or State Department, was that the US and Coalition forces did not want to be misperceived as being on a "Crusade" to impose Christianity on a Muslim nation. Contacts with the local Religious Affairs Council for the Kirkuk Province, and subsequently with area religious leaders, revealed their frustrations at not being engaged, heard, and afforded the opportunity to be a part of the solution to bring peace and security to their people. Fortunately, the US Air Force Chaplains, the USAF and Iraqi Air Force Base Commanders, and the local Provincial Reconstruction Team (PRT) all supported this outreach initiative, which was ultimately and primarily facilitated by the USAF Chaplains. In May 2009, when the restored "Saqi Shrine" and two cemeteries were availed to local families, political and religious leaders. Even an Emissary from Ayatollah Sistani was present to witness firsthand this significant demonstration of respect and outreach for a better relationship between the base and the surrounding populations – be they Arab, Kurd or Turkmen, Sunni or Shi'a. That project was the highlight of my tour in Iraq – seeing so many good people come together to connect particularly the more peaceful times of that Shrine with the desire on all sides to restore a similar sense of peace and good will to today's Kirkuk. (See Appendix E)

8

During the Saqi Shrine outreach project, I had the pleasure of getting to know several dedicated Chaplains, both Army and USAF. One of them was Army Chaplain (LTC) Timothy Bedsole, the newly-designated "World Religions" Chaplain at the Multi-National Coalition-Iraq (MNCI) headquarters in Baghdad. Among his tasks was to explore how brigade and battalion-level Chaplains could in fact better support not only their assigned unit(s) but the overall effort to build better relationships with local religious leaders. Both of us lamented that only at this late stage in OIF were we beginning to realize that if only we had been training and modeling the Chaplaincy concept to Iraqi Security Forces (military and police), the future of Iraq might be much brighter. In fact, when Chaplain Bedsole had first learned of the emerging Human Terrain System back in 2006, he attempted to initiate a dialogue and potential working relationship between HTS and the Chaplain Corps – noting that Chaplains were trained and naturally pre-disposed to mediate interpersonal conflicts and overcome differences among people of varying ethnicities, faiths and cultures. Unfortunately, that potential collaboration did not materialize.

Things we should have known

Sadly, by 2008/2009, seventeen years after "Desert Storm," we had only progressed to the point of identifying the Kurds and Arabs as ethnicities who hated one another, the Sunni and the Shi'a (aka: Shi'ites) as the two major branches of Islam, and that Saddam's political party and power base, the Baath Party, was predominantly (if not exclusively) Sunni. We also learned that Sunni Muslims comprise 80-85% of the Muslim population worldwide, while the Shi'a are in the minority at 15-20%. In Iraq, Iran and only a handful of other countries, those ratios are reversed. Upon entering Iraq in 2003, particularly Shi'a Muslim Iraqis did in fact wave flowers and flags, greeting American and Coalition forces as their liberators. This was because they understood that America represented "democracy," and to them, this meant "majority rule," which would clearly flip Iraq's governance on its ear and put them in charge. If only it was more broadly recognized and understood that there are over one hundred sects of Islam (just as there are over six hundred versions of "Christianity"), we might have had a much different and more effective policy for not only engaging our Chaplains, but in recognizing the value of integrating this role into the Iraqi Security Forces – and, perhaps into the highest levels of government in Baghdad as well.

It is also worth mentioning that about 90% of Kurds are Sunni

Muslims – yet a far more moderate and tolerant interpretation of their faith – as evidenced by the Kurdish Peshmerga leading the ground fight against ISIS/DAESH today – *and* the fact that so many non-Muslims have found safe refuge in the Kurdistan region of Iraq.

Meanwhile, in Iran, the Ayatollah Khoumeni, the Supreme Council, former President Mahmoud Ahmadinejad and now President Hassan Rouhani have no doubt looked at US-led Coalition forces on both their western border (Iraq) and to the east (Afghanistan and Pakistan). Is it any wonder that Iran has been training and arming those who are fighting against Coalition forces in both Iraq and Afghanistan?

How my world changed after returning from Iraq

By now, in late 2009, I had seen Dr. M. Zuhdi Jasser on CNN and FoxNews. As a practicing physician in the Phoenix area, an eleven-year veteran of the US Navy, and proud American Muslim, Dr. Jasser was saying those things that we had been longing to hear from the Muslim world since 9/11/2001. Founder of the American Islamic Forum for Democracy (AIFD) and American Islamic Leadership Coalition (AILC), Dr. Jasser was straightforward in his criticism of both the violent "Jihadists" and those who were more subtly promoting what he called political Islam. I cannot overstate how refreshing it was to see and hear an emerging and assertive voice calling out much of the American Muslim leadership or spokesmen who represented groups like the Council on American-Islamic Relations (CAIR) and the Islamic Society of North America (ISNA).

Dr. Jasser gave me hope that very soon more of the mainstream American media would start picking up his messaging – that especially CAIR representatives were, at a minimum, misleading in their claims to speak for the majority of not only American Muslims, but Muslims (and Islam) worldwide. As he and some of my Muslim friends have indicated, CAIR and similar Muslim organizations have consistently been taking a "victim" position – first and foremost, claiming that Muslim Americans have been unfairly singled out for discrimination, oppression and/or "profiling" at some level. Arguably, CAIR has become the ACLU (American Civil Liberties Union) for Muslims – claiming that any criticism or scrutiny of any Muslims of any age or gender, amounted to prejudicial "profiling" that only perpetuates Islamophobia.

[Dr. Jasser has appeared before Congress several times, serves on the U.S. Commission on International Religious Freedom, and authored *A Battle for the Soul of Islam*. His own struggle to influence American Muslim leaders to speak out against 9//11 and radical Islam was featured in the 2008 film "The Third Jihad," which stirred CAIR to convince the *New York Times* that the film promoted Islamophobia. CAIR additionally called for (then) NY Police Commissioner Ray Kelly to resign or be fired due to his use of the film in support of training for his police force, particularly his Counter-Terrorism officers. I encourage everyone I know to watch this important film which Rudy Giuliani dubbed a "Wake-up call to America."]

In March 2010, I was invited to share my experiences in Iraq, and with the HTS program, with the Columbia River Chapter of the Military Officers Association of America (MOAA). That led to giving a presentation to the Rotary Club of Vancouver, which led to a nice (and mostly accurate) article, "Bringing Human Touch to a War Zone," in the local newspaper (*The Columbian*) as well as opportunities to teach/facilitate classes at the local community college (Clark College's "Mature Learning" program). It was during that time that I started reaching out to members of the area Muslim communities, seeking guest speakers willing to address the complexities of their faith, and their own concerns about the radical extremists who seemed to have hijacked Islam to serve their personal and political agendas.

By January 2012, after the classes and several local area presentations with Harris Zafar and/or Arif Humayun, authors of chapters in this book, I approached them about bringing together perhaps 8-10 Muslims and non-Muslims, military veterans and members of "Academia," women and men, each of them telling of their personal journeys spanning 9/11/2001 to today. I proposed the name America's "Jihad", to bring attention and clarity to how especially Osama bin Laden (and al Qaeda) extended this word into an un-Quranic version of "self defense" that justified this aggressive "Holy War" so long as non-Muslims ("Infidels") occupied predominantly Muslim lands. As you can now see, this collaboration that originally envisioned about 8-10 contributors grew to over twenty and became a much larger undertaking that included the creation of a website (http://americasjihad.com/) through which our readers might connect with the writers and continue the much-needed "conversation."

"When you ain't got nothing, you got nothing to lose"
Bob Dylan (from "Like a Rolling Stone")

In my most recent class at Clark College, focusing on how AQI (al Qaeda in Iraq) "evolved" (more like devolved) into ISIS (Islamic State of Iraq and "Sham," Arabic for Syria), or ISIL (Islamic State of Iraq and the Levant), into today's "Islamic State," I used this lyric (and astute observation) by Bob Dylan to provide the context through which mostly young and disenfranchised Muslim boys and men are targeted and recruited. They have flocked to Syria and Iraq to enlist into this growing army of fighters who seem to have no limits when it comes to killing even fellow Muslims or even strapping on a suicide vest – or driving an explosives-laden vehicle into a given neighborhood market, police station or checkpoint, or army base. When there is no hope for a better life, no basis for imagining or dreaming of a better tomorrow, death with honor becomes appealing – especially as it might elevate your "worth" or status – and bring both honor and perhaps money to your family – not to mention a better afterlife in "paradise" with those "72 virgins."

Of course, when you consider the beheadings of not just soldiers, but reporters and other innocents, one has to ask how this honors one's God with shouts of "Allah u Akbar" ("God is Great") as the victims are slaughtered. Yes, beyond the appeal to those of low self-esteem, one must also consider that there are many in the realm of sociopaths and psychopaths. Why not join today's "Foreign Legion" of like-minded zealots for whom there is great satisfaction to be had when imposing your will on others without limitation or fear of prosecution? The appeal of such total power and control over others, including women and children, is certainly resonating with those "criminal minds" that are, sadly, a part of every ethnic group and religion (or belief system) around the world--most certainly not limited to Muslims.

So where's the GOOD NEWS?

As you will read in the last chapter, it is my hope that this overall effort will serve to bridge some of the unnecessary divides arising from ethnic, religious, cultural and/or political differences. A fairly common notion in management is to never bring forth a problem without at the same time, presenting options - potential solutions to the issues(s) at hand. There are arguably more problems than there are answers - especially when you consider the millions who have been displaced from their homes over the past two decades or more. As many world "leaders" wrestle with the outright violence and barbarism of Abu Bakr al Baghdadi and the "Islamic State," or "DAESH," perhaps the even greater challenge revolves around the mostly non-violent byproduct of this terror and uncertainty that is forcing so many Syrians, Iraqis, Libyans, and others to run for their lives, abandoning their homes, and homeland, for a safer, if not better life for their families - as so many thousands have done as both Internally Displaced Persons (IDP's) and outright refugees who have fled the onslaught in favor of the unknown - mostly in Europe, but similarly in parts of Southeast Asia.

As you will find, each contributor shares some of his or her ideas for turning the tide on radicalism or otherwise helping the world to be less conflicted. While some of my ideas might be implied in elements of the preceding pages, I have drawn from my fellow contributors and added my own ideas, including a little "Mediation 101," in the final chapter of this book and in Appendix K.

(Note: Dan's photo and background are at the end of the book)

"You can either curse the darkness or light a candle."
~ Chinese Proverb ~

"One cannot and must not try to erase the past merely because it does not fit the present."
~ Golda Meir ~

"Some of the best lessons are learned from past mistakes. The error of the past is the wisdom of the future."
~ Dale Turner ~

"Blowing out someone else's candle doesn't make yours shine any brighter."
~ unknown ~

Chapter Two

Tribalism and Arab Culture

Jim Moody

Jim Moody, PhD, joined the Air Force immediately after graduating from Lowell High School in San Francisco, CA. He was trained as a Korean and Chinese linguist and served in Korea in the 6922nd Radio Squadron Mobile, then in the 6004 Air Intelligence Service Squadron. After his discharge from the United States Air Force, Jim attended the University of California, Berkeley, majoring in Oriental Languages and Linguistics. He graduated Magna Cum Laude and was recruited into the Central Intelligence Agency. After leaving the CIA he returned to UC Berkeley to take up graduate studies in Anthropology, receiving a PhD in Anthropology and Linguistics with a Far Eastern area specialty. He has taught undergraduate and graduate level Anthropology at Lawrence University, the Queen's University of Belfast, University of Otago Medical School and Clark College in Vancouver, WA. Jim is also active in advocating for veterans.

Prelude

On 9/11, I was just in the process of making an egg sandwich for breakfast after reading the newspaper, when my wife called me and told me that I'd better turn on the TV -- something terrible had happened. I tuned in just in time to see the second plane crash into Tower II. I sat, horrified and mesmerized by the falling bodies, the close-ups of desperate people trying to escape the flames, and finally by the terrible, impossible, apocalyptic fall of the towers. It was a vision of hell on earth.

Over the next days as the identity of the perpetrators was revealed I was dumbfounded, confused. I'm a trained anthropologist and my training, particularly as a cultural anthropologist interested in the world view of members of other societies, made me ask, "Why?" It made me desperate to understand how and why a group of Arab

Muslims would carry out such an act. What kind of a view of the world would justify or make such a brutal and indiscriminate act understandable or meaningful?

I turned to books - mostly ethnographies - and articles on Arab culture and society. I searched out scholarly articles. I read news articles and analyses from newspapers from all around the globe. And slowly a sense of what had happened and some ideas about why it took place began to take shape.

I'd lived and studied in tribal societies. I'd written about them, and some of the dynamics that I began to discern were familiar. Gradually I was beginning, just beginning, to understand the "why."

As an anthropologist, I tried to remain objective, though it was hard. After all, my "tribe" had been attacked. But I convinced myself that looking for some understanding of Arab culture was necessary and important. I rationalized that 'understanding' a societys' culture doesn't mean 'accepting' or 'approving' of it. No, it simply means what it says; understanding the 'logic' or the 'meaning' of what happened in terms of the world view of those who carried out the act, not in terms of my American world view. As an anthropologist, I believe that if we're to have any chance of reaching a solution to the problems in the Middle East, we need to communicate effectively in a manner that the opposing party understands, using a language that is meaningful to them. And in order to do that we need an understanding of that group's Culture.

I still have hope, a faint hope, but hope all the same, that a non-violent solution can be found. And so I've dedicated myself to trying to give others an understanding of what I have come to call "Arab Culture." This short chapter is a first step towards that end.

Introduction

In his recent book on the events leading to the failure of U.S. policy in Afghanistan, *88 Days to Kandahar*, Robert Grenier, the former CIA Chief-of-Station in Islamabad, Pakistan, describes the problem as one of "overwhelming overreach." He then goes on to say:

"In the process we overwhelmed a primitive country, with a largely illiterate population, a tiny agrarian economy, a tribal social structure, and nascent national institutions. We triggered massive corruption through our profligacy; convinced a substantial number of Afghans that we were, in fact, occupiers; and facilitated the resurgence of the Taliban."

One of the most crucial terms in this short excerpt is the term "tribal." In reports from the Middle East it appears again and again in everything from news reports - tribal militia, tribal fighters, tribal chiefs, etc. - to academic works attempting to either describe or understand events in the area.

It all seems clear in hindsight that there has been, and still is, little understanding in the Western world of just what "tribal" implies. It's clear that many of the customs, actions, attitudes and etc. of tribal groups - the savagery of ISIL, the apparently subservient role of women, the meaning of Jihad, and much more - baffle, confuse, and even frighten members of Western society. For many, what we don't understand - we fear.

In the hope that a clearer understanding of Arab culture, "tribal culture," will enhance our ability to understand what is taking place in the volatile area I would like to offer a short overview, an anthropological overview, of Middle Eastern tribal culture - what some writers have identified as "Bedouin" culture. It should become clear that there are very deep and fundamental differences between the culture - the world view - of the Arab world vs. that of the West. The secularism of the West stands in sharp contrast to the religiously-oriented cultures of the Middle East, and the group-oriented culture of the Arab world is the antithesis of the individual-focused culture and society of America.

I am emphatically not creating a stereotype of Middle Eastern tribal societies. It's clear that within that broad category there will be, for example, many regional differences in how the Arab worldview is structured and realized. Urbanization also has an effect on how the traditional values of Arab culture are expressed. Still, those working and doing research in the Middle East (ME), both Western and Arab scholars, agree that there are some factors common to all the ethnographic areas, a set of values and ideals that is common and generally accepted across the broad spectrum of Middle Eastern cultures and societies. I would like to examine just a few of those factors in the hope that it might make some of the events taking place in that area more understandable, even if sometimes not more acceptable.

Full Disclosure

I think that it's appropriate before I begin to point out that my "data" has been gleaned from many sources: ethnographies, academic papers, and etc. I don't speak Arabic and so although some of the material I consulted was written by Western researchers and some by Arab scholars, I have read all of it either in English, or in English translations of Arabic texts. Based on that data I'll try and outline a few of the cultural characteristics of Arab culture that may in part explain some of the events that now are newspaper headlines. The analysis, time and space-limited, will not be exhaustive, but I hope that it will be, at least, informative.

Tribal Society

Just what is "tribalism"? The term has been defined in many ways depending on what group is doing the defining; there is no single "best" definition. In his book *Muslim Society*, Ernest Gellner defines the tribe in a more expansive definition than that originally put forth by early anthropologists: as a social, political and cultural unit based on *solidarity and common identity* (my italics), identified by kinship, either real or fictive, a common lineage, or, in some cases, self-defini- tion. According to Gellner, tribalism implies a framework of solidar- ity and loyalty that can exist even in modern societies. In the Middle East (ME) the tribe might be based on genealogy or territory. In some urban settings, for example, "tribes" are formed based on the area of origin, with families from a particular town or area congregating in a neighborhood and forming a more or less cohesive and cooperative group, a "tribe." It's commonplace in some societes for Sunni and Shia populations in urban areas to create enclaves of co-religionists.

But as you might expect, the notion of "tribe" can, and has been, put to various uses depending on who is doing the defining. Dominant tribal leaders, for example, have used the concept to establish alli- ances, achieve political position and authority, and so on.

In everyday tribal life the concepts of Arab culture, though not specifically delineated, are realized in the actions, the everyday inter- actions, within each tribal group, and in their contact with other social groups. The tribal cultural values are expressed in everyday actions: the forming of alliances, the negotiation of marriages, dispute settle- ment, and in various aspects of patronage - the patron/client relation- ship that is a part of tribal life.

How strong an influence is Arab culture on the daily activities in ME society? A few commentators make the point that education and urbanization seem to have some effect on the extent to which Arab culture influences the daily lives of everyday Arabs. But there seems to be a general consensus that for many Arabs the basis for the cur- rent culture is the culture of the Bedouin, the culture of the desert. Despite the fact that Bedouins, people of the desert or bawd or badiya, now constitute a relatively small portion of the Arab population, many modern Arabs, even educated urban dwellers, still take pride in claiming Bedouin origins in much the same way that some Americans trace their ancestors back to the Pilgrims, or to the romanticized American frontier with its emphasis on individualism and independence. In Arab society the Bedouin ethos is still an ideal to be emulated. And in outlying areas in particular, areas distant from the urban centers and the rudimentary and generally distant state apparatus and institutions, the Bedouin world view still informs and shapes the behavior of the local Arab population.

In the harsh environment of Afghanistan and similar areas organizing into a tribe was and still can be crucial for survival. Some historians and anthropologists state that the culture that identifies Arab society today is a clearly a Bedouin cultural adaptation that was shaped and grew in a period called the *Jehalla*, "The Time of Ignorance," *before the advent of Islam*. In this harsh environment nomadic tribes raided and fought with other groups in search of livestock and other sources of wealth, and in such an environment, a strong, structured group unquestioningly obedient to the directives of experienced leaders was essential for the group's very survival.

In 621 AD, the Prophet Muhammad had the first of his visions and over the next centuries the Qur'an, the Holy Book of Islam, was assembled from his revelations, stories of his life, and sayings recorded by his followers. The Qur'an changed the Bedouin ethos in some ways - it spoke against female infanticide, for example - but it generally institutionalized the male-dominated, patriarchal, patrilineal culture that was already in existence.

East and West

There are many differences between Western culture and the culture of the Middle East. But there are two major and important differences that, in my view, set the two cultures apart and, in all probability, contribute to their inability to understand one another.

Western society, with some exceptions, is what has come to be called secular; Middle Eastern culture - Arab culture - is by contrast religiously oriented. We'll return to this topic a little later, but it's important to keep in mind that secular culture generally attempts to exclude religion from the political arena. It focuses on the individual and his capabilities (and his rights and responsibilities) and tends, ideally, to tolerate individual diversity within a society. It resists basing its' institutions on a single set of religious principles. Individual rights and responsibilities are paramount and are established and protected by civil law.

Religious societies in general are what might be called "collectivist." They tend to focus on the collective, the group as a whole, and to downplay the importance of the individual. The laws, Sharia law in Muslim society, for example, are religiously based and an individual's rights are determined by how devoutly he adheres to spiritually-based principles and laws.

Western culture is, then, generally secular. Diverse religions, political groups, and etc. exist side-by-side and the bedrock for this diversity is found in each country's civil laws. The American Constitution, for example, creates inalienable rights for individuals that are not specifically based on the principles of any single religion.

Arab culture's laws are firmly rooted in Islam. The law, Sharia law, is overtly and specifically Islamic. For each group, secular and religious, the opposite group's actions and attitudes can be difficult to understand, even incomprehensible. And because of this many of the culturally-based attitudes and actions that follow are similarly incomprehensible.

Arab Culture and Society

Arab culture emphasizes the collective, the family, the lineage, the tribe. In placing the emphasis on the family, concomitantly Arab culture de-emphasizes the individual. Each individual family member must contribute to the success of the family, to the maintenance of the family's honor. If the family fails, if its honor is lost and it loses the respect of the community, all the individual family members fail with it. And the relative strength and wealth of the family is crucial to the success of the individual members. A strong family, one that is respected, a family whose honor is intact, will be respected and, as a result, have a better chance at success. Every family member, particularly the male members, must aggressively protect the family's honor, both by exhibiting exemplary behavior and by responding aggressively to any evidence of disrespect. The successful family, the respected family, will be able to make successful alliances with other families or lineages, arrange marriages for its members, form beneficial political and economic alliances, provide a living for its male members and so on. A family without honor and respect will fail. A common statement is that an Arab without a successful family has no chance of surviving.

In anthropological terms, the ideal Arab family is patriarchal, patrilocal, and patrilineal.

The Arab family - an extended family, one with many sons or male members - is the ideal. Often in the more rural settings a set of parents, their children, and occasionally a married son or sons with their families, live together in a single compound under the absolute authority of the father. A group organized under the authority of the eldest male member is termed patriarchal: governed by the patriarch. The Arab family is also, ideally, patrilocal: the family dwells together in a group focused around the eldest male member, either the father or, in his absence, the eldest son. In a patriarchal family elder males are honored and obeyed and are usually, either as individuals or as a council of elders known as the Shura, responsible for governing both the family and, with the cooperation of the village religious leader, the tribal village.

What's in a Name?

Arab tribes are also, as stated, patrilineal: the family origins and its connection to other families, is traced through a long line of patriarchs or elder males. The naming traditions in Arab society express the importance of familial relationships and the importance of family generally. An Arab has his "first" name as his own. This will be followed by his father's name, his grandfather's name and so on: a string of names listing ancestors on his father's side. Women, who remain members of their father's lineage rather than becoming members of the husband's patrilineage, will have a string of masculine names after their own name. A man might include ibn - son of - in his name so that Abdul Ibn Saud would mean: Abdul, Son of Saud. The inclusion of Al also indicates family. Bou - father of - might also be included. Zai - as in Hamid Karzai - also indicates "son of." But whether or not an individual includes or excludes various parts of the name depends on circumstances, or context, or sometimes just whether or not he feels like it. If the string of names gets too long all may be dropped except for the father's name. As one ethnographer wryly points out, all this makes the use of telephone directories in Arab society a bit of a puzzle for non-Arabs.

Some names - Abdel - might indicate a religious affiliation. Abdel-Rahman, Servant of the Merciful, would indicate a Muslim, for example. The important point to note is that family connection, the collective, is emphasized, particularly if the family is well respected, successful, and powerful. But all names eventually inform about that

21

most important information of all in Arab culture: who are your people, your family? Nearly every aspect of Arab society will hinge on the reputation and status of your family and your patrilineage.

Childhood

From early childhood Arab children are taught to respect and obey the older males in the family. They are taught to be polite and deferential. Several ethnographers use the term "modesty" to describe the ideal male behavior within a family. The term, in this context, seems to mean "deferential." Disobedience or disrespect can bring harsh physical punishment. A disrespectful or disobedient child brings dishonor on the family.

Almost from infancy, male and female children are treated differently. Studies of very early childhood tell us that female children are weaned earlier and, while still quite young, take their place with other females of the family in the women's area within the house or compound. There they learn, from a very early age, to perform the traditional woman's role: running the day-to-day business of the home and caring for the family's male members. Male children, weaned later, are often allowed to continue to breast feed, even to be fed on demand in response to their cries. Their transition at puberty into a more adult role is later than is the case with female children. In some areas females are considered marriageable at puberty. Male children, at puberty, are encouraged to be in the company of the elder males of the family, learning deference and respect. They learn the appropriate behavior for a male member of the family. And they are encouraged at a relatively early age to monitor the "honor" of the female members of the family.

In Arab culture, as previously mentioned, the family's honor is paramount. Family honor is the responsibility of every family member. Anything that "blackens the face" of a family member reflects on the family as a whole and influences the respect that the family can command from others. But while a male who transgresses and "loses face" has a variety of ways in which he can "whiten his face" again, not so the female members of the family.

The Commoditization of Women

There is an Arab saying that "women carry the honor of the family." Not only that, but the young daughters of the family can be an economic benefit as well. One author quotes an Arab proverb that points out that there are three sources of wealth: women, gold, and land. However, if a woman loses her honor, or is even, in some cases, merely accused of losing her honor, it cannot be restored. From being of value to the family as a potential source of wealth or respect through her exchange in marriage, an arrangement that includes the exchange of a negotiated "bride price," she now has a negative effect. She is now a drain on the family economically and a detriment to the family honor. There is no way that that effect can be altered. In some Arab communities the "honor killing" in which a family member murders the accused woman is still practiced as a means of re-establishing the family's honor. In order to protect against such difficulties daughters and wives are secluded and protected in the women's quarters in the family compound, and from an early age, the family sons are taught to guard the honor of their family's women zealously.

Women in Arab culture have been and generally still are perceived as weak and libidinous, and so, traditionally, measures were, and in some areas still are, taken to control the females libidinous impulses, reduce the level of temptation that they place before males, and limit opportunities for transgression. In some Arab areas, mostly in Africa and in Yemen, some young women are still subject to genital alteration (clitoridectomy or infibulation) in order, apparently, to reduce their libido and prevent them from engaging in any behavior that will darken their honor and, by extension, that of the family.

In more traditional areas women who move about in public are expected to wear burqas - a dark garment that covers them entirely – or, at the very least, a hijab: a veil and a cap that covers their hair. A female's hair is considered a symbol that has sexual connotations just as the beard is a symbol of male potentcy.

Marriages generally are arranged. They are contracted between families, not individuals, and are expected to benefit the family, the collective, rather than the individual. Without the family backing arranging a marriage is difficult financially. To marry the daughter of a high status family can be very expensive. Individual desire or love is not of primary concern. Young girls barely past puberty are sometimes married to men they have never met before their wedding. In some situations, particularly in the more remote areas, a young girl can be married to an older, sometimes much older, male. The wedding, remember, is a family alliance, not a love match, and the benefit to the family is directly proportional to the prestige of the two families involved.

Marriage is a contractual relationship, and not unexpectedly, it's also a financial one. The groom's family is expected to pay a bride price that can include goods, dwellings, and other objects of wealth. A contract is signed and if, for any reason, the marriage fails - if the bride doesn't eventually produce male offspring, for example - the return of some or all of the wealth exchanged is detailed in the marriage contract. But to be marriageable at all, a woman must have her honor intact. There are many ways she can lose her honor. If a woman is raped, for example, her honor is irrevocably lost. She may be killed by her own family in order to restore the family honor. Although such cases are rare, they still occur from time to time.

Arab culture is somewhat unique in that some marriages are endogamous: a young man, rather than contract marriage with another family or lineage, will contract to marry a female cousin: his father's brother's daughter. Given the cultural logic in place this makes perfect sense. All of the benefits - money, property, children, the wife - stay within the same patrilineage. They aren't lost to "outsiders." This strengthens and enlarges the family. Furthermore, any doubts about the new bride's loyalty to the family are erased. As a first cousin she is, unlike a female from another lineage, already a member of the lineage through her father.

Sexuality

Sexuality is, according to many authors, an Arab cultural concern. The moral standards for women and for men are quite different. Male sexuality is less controlled. Men are free to have up to four wives. It's expected that young men will want to roam, to be sexually adventurous. For married men roaming is not encouraged under Islam. But in some areas men are able to make time-limited marriage contracts for a number of days, or even hours. These contracts are complete with payment clauses and specified time limits. The contracts make provision for any children that might result from this very time-limited "marriage." They allow a man to have a sexual relationship with a woman that is of short duration, but not a sin according to Sharia law.

Patron-Client

Arab culture, in addition to being family-oriented, is male dominated. Younger males obey and respect older males. Older males, in turn, exist in a hierarchy. They will subordinate themselves to older or even more respected males: the lineage elder, the Imam, or the tribe chief. Younger males learn that they must obey and respect older men if they expect to be assisted in marrying or making a living, etc. Even in business in more urban environments the Patron/Client relationship is an important one. This pattern of exchanging loyalty or favors for assistance is common in Arab business relations, and even affects the faculty/student relations.

Conflict

Tribal society was conceived in conflict. In the ME+ alliances are formed and dissolved depending on the context of the conflict. As another Arab proverb states, "Me against my brother, my brother and I against my cousin, and all of us against the world." Alliances and relationships between families, lineages and tribes coalesce or dissolve depending on the level of conflict or opposition. Within the family it's brother versus brother, but if the level of conflict or competition changes to the lineage level, then it's cousin versus cousin, and finally, if the lineage or tribe is under threat all the elements will come together in defense. Local disputes will be set aside in the face of a greater threat.

Within the family there is a premium placed on male offspring. Not only does having many male children protect against the possibility that sickness or conflict will result in the elimination of a family's male line, but having more males in a family makes the family stronger in the event of some interfamily or intertribal dispute. It also is beneficial in agrarian environments in which hand labor is the means of production to have more hands to do the work.

The brothers in a family conflict might attempt to better their status as each male member struggles to rise above his siblings and cousins in the family hierarchy. Family versus family, or lineage versus lineage: intratribal disputes can, on occasion, become violent. Where violence occurs another aspect of Arab culture that is difficult for Westerners to comprehend comes into play: revenge killings.

"Blood demands blood" - or words to that effect - is another common saying in Arabic. If a member of a lineage or a tribal group is killed the family's strength has been diminished and their honor has been attacked. In such a situation every male relative of the victim who falls within five degrees of kinship (relationship that can be traced through five male relatives) is honor bound to kill a male member of the offenders' group in order to restore the offended family's honor and restore balance. Alternatively, in some situations the conflict can be resolved by paying the victim's family an agreed amount of "blood money," but if that doesn't happen, revenge is required.

For every Iraqi, every Afghan, every Arab that American or Coalition forces killed in the course of our longest war, there is potentially a family waiting to even the score by killing one of us. That amounts to, at the very least, more than 200,000 individual honor debts waiting to be collected. And for every Arab male humiliated and caused to lose face by having his family's female quarters invaded by patrolling troops, being thrown to the ground or manhandled in front of his family and neighbors, there is probably an individual with a burning desire to restore his self-respect, and the honor of his family, by evening the score.

There is no time limit on these debts. One of Hamid Karzai's young relatives was killed in an honor killing some twenty years after the original offense took place. The young nephew hadn't even been born when the original offense was committed. The collective is all-important; the honor of the lineage or the tribe, depending on the level of conflict, is all-important, and "blood demands blood."

Authority and Authoritarianism

There are a number of other features mentioned by most authors that would bear discussion in a larger context as part of a more complete picture: Arab fatalism, subjectivity, violence, male domination. This is not the place to write a complete ethnography of the Arab world. We can only sketch some outlines that might help us understand what is happening in the Middle East.

But some features of Arab culture and society bring up more vexing questions. What are some of the features of Arab culture and society that might be important in increasing our understanding of the events taking place in the Middle East? What characteristics can we see?

1. The Importance of the Collective: The family, the lineage, the tribe, the Umma (Arab Nation), are all more important than the individual member(s). Individuals theoretically should be willing to sacrifice anything and everything on behalf of the honor of the collective.
2. Submission to Authority: The Arab family teaches its members unquestioning submission to authority.
3. Group honor: Individual prestige and success is linked to and

dependent on the success of the collective. The individual who depends on his own personal activities or abilities to achieve success will, according to various commentators, inevitably fail. Rewards accrue to the individual who protects the honor and prestige of the group and helps the collective succeed.

4. Conflict: Alliances between families, lineages, and even tribes, are made and broken in response to the level of challenge being encountered. Family battles family, unless the challenge becomes Shi'a versus Sunni. And Shi'a and Sunni will be in conflict unless the conflict is perceived as being Muslims against the world, the rallying cry of ISIS /ISIL.

5. Aggression: There is no limit to the level of violence that can or should be directed against sanctioned groups that offend against Islam. Some of the violence is described in the Qur'an and is required and not subject to adjudication.

6. Unquestioning Obedience: Unquestioning adherence to the values and beliefs perceived as being endorsed by authority figures.

7. Fatalism: The belief that individual activities have less to do with outcomes and events than the will of God: "Insha Allah."

In another context this list of traits would be a rough definition of what the social sciences have come to call Authoritarianism.

Authoritarianism

There are a number of authors who have written about Middle Eastern authoritarianism. What is meant by Authoritarianism? The term refers to a syndrome characterized by at least three major traits:

First, authoritarians submit and surrender their individual autonomy to those they perceive and acknowledge as legitimate authorities. Authoritarian leaders expect and demand absolute obedience to their commands and edicts. This style of authoritarian control characterizes the leadership of virtually every State in the Middle East with the possible exception of Israel. In some cases the tribal aspect was obvious. Saddam Hussein controlled Iraq by playing on tribal loyalties, pitting Sunni against Shi'a. Tribal societies in the Middle East are not democratic, and even when they begin democratically they tend to devolve into autocracies. Changes in leadership move from one autocrat to another usually through assassination or revolution rather than through democratic processes. Leaders like Saddam and Gaddafi have claimed tribal leadership in order to use their power in that role to suppress opposing tribes. They've rewarded those who have assisted them and acknowledged their authority, a classical tribal nepotism that we in the secular West have labeled corruption.

Second, authoritarian leaders demand absolute acceptance and adherence to the values and beliefs which they endorse. In sharp contrast to secular governments that ideally encourage and protect conflicting subcultures, authoritarian leaders punish and eliminate competing philosophies and religions. There has been a spate of genocidal ethnic "cleansings" over the past twenty years, many of them involving Muslims either as perpetrators of the violence or as its victims. Attempts to stamp out any competing attitudes, religions, and etc. that might threaten the absolute authority of the leader are endemic in the ME.

This relates directly to the third characteristic of an authoritarian regime: aggression towards sanctioned target groups. The actions of ISIL and various tribal militias in murdering groups of Middle Eastern Christians, Sunnis, Shi'a, Yazidis, Kurds and others fall in this category. The true authoritarian demonstrates his total commitment, obedience and loyalty by the ferocity of the violence he commits on perceived opponents, transgressors and apostates.

Fatalism in the "true believer," in the authoritarian, stems from his lack of confidence in his own ability to achieve his goals individually. If an individual has been taught blind obedience and reliance on the authority and wisdom of more powerful figures without the opportunity to develop confidence in his own capabilities, his own personal achievement, that individual often comes to believe that all outcomes are literally in the hands of God. As mentioned previously, a phrase that is often heard in Arab discourse is "Insha Allah" – "God willing."

This might be, at least in part, a reason why America's experiments in what was to be "nation-building" and the establishment of participatory democracy have failed. A number of authors point out that a large percentage of Middle Eastern Arabs, in some areas as much as 80%, angry at the years of exploitation that the Middle East has suffered under various colonial regimes, now feel that the invasion of Afghanistan, followed by Iraq, was simply another example of Western colonialism in action. They don't believe that the goal of the coalition was to establish democratic government, to "nation-build," or to otherwise truly benefit them in any way. Even if they did, the fact that they are tribal precludes them from believing that it's possible to peacefully share power with opposing groups that have contradictory or antithetical values. Subsequent events and actions, military and otherwise, have lent credence to their perceptions.

28

In addition, feeling shamed and dishonored by the actions of Western governments, particularly the United States, actions for which they are honor-bound to seek revenge, ISIL communiqués and bulletins say clearly that they are convinced that the only solution is the establishment of their own Islamic nation, The Caliphate, under the leadership of a strong and autocratic, even authoritarian, Caliph. The Arabs of the Middle East, with the memory of hundreds, in some cases thousands of years of colonial exploitation and humiliation; with the memory of more recent bloody conflict with other families, lineages or tribes, and with a lifetime of loyalty and obedience to strong, authoritarian leaders, are poor material for experiments in nation-building.

What about Democracy?

The failure of democratization in the Middle East is a given. Almost all nations in the ME are ruled by Autocrats. There are several possible explanations. The first and most obvious is that the Middle East has always been authoritarian and that no viable institutions - unions, business organizations, etc - have developed to challenge the power of the authoritarian regimes.

Other authors suggest that the authoritarian regimes in the ME have avoided a transition to more democratic institutions by using some traditional tribal processes in a non-traditional way. The Patron/Client authoritarian relationship, it has been suggested, has been used to perpetuate a new strain of authoritarianism. The new "tribal" leaders have privatized various industries and commodities and used these in a predictable tribal way to reward other tribal heads and secure their cooperation - if not their loyalty. Loyalty is a difficult commodity to obtain in a tribal environment. The leader must always be aware of the ambitious rival who wants to overthrow the patriarch and take his place - and his authority.

The so-called "Arab Spring," the attempted overthrow of autocrats and dictators, hopeful at the start, was quickly subverted and turned into power struggles between autocratic groups. There's little apparent difference between being killed by, for example, Assad's minions and being beheaded by ISIL. In either case, individuals stand helpless in the face of violent, authoritarian regimes of one kind or another.

A further explanation might be found in the Qur'an which says, to paraphrase, that a poor leader is better than chaos. Anything but chaos. So many feel that even a relatively ineffective autocrat is better

29

than anarchy or chaos.

In the end, it might be that for many Arabs their culture simply hasn't prepared them for democracy. Socialized in what is essentially an authoritarian environment they have learned from a very early age that obedience and loyalty are the path to success, not individual achievement.

Is Secularism the Answer or the Problem?

A major stumbling block in establishing any kind of communication or accommodation with ISIL, with what has come to be known as "radical Islam," is Western, and particularly American, secularism: our insistence that organized religion has no place in governmental institutions. We are, as previously stated, a secular nation. Arab culture is equally militant about Arab society, including its laws, being based on Islam.

Is there any way out of this dilemma? Why don't we here in America have the same accommodation that seems to be working in Southeast Asia? Islam and other religions seem to be able to exist in relative harmony there. What's so different about the two environments?

There are at least two different approaches to secularism. When we talk about secularism, do we mean positive secularism - insuring a place for alternative religious views in our society - or negative secularism - using the law to guarantee that there is no religious input into our civil society and governance?

American foreign policy has largely been negatively - and often naively - secular. We've objected to any religiously-oriented political regime. By supporting secular dictatorships and attempting to institute the American brand of negative secularism in other countries, have we unwittingly encouraged the growth of religious radicalism?

It might be too late for us to reverse course in the Middle East. Honor, revenge, cynicism about the West's true motivation in encouraging a democratic state, might all have combined to render even a quasi-peaceful solution to the crisis in the Middle East impossible.

We've been strangely blind to the fact that in some nations, most notably in Southeast Asia, a positive secularism - guaranteeing all religions the right to participate in civil society - while not perfect, has been relatively peaceful. Could this be the model we need to encourage? Turkey has seen successes and was once a good example of positive secularism, in this case in a predominantly, but not exclusively, Muslim environment, with economic growth and progress leading to what might still be a peaceful integration of Muslims and non-Muslims in a functioning and effective society.

So… what's your tribe?

It might be that the era of secularism, particularly negative secularism that seeks to exclude religiosity from civil society, is over. Of greater concern is the possibility that tribalism, if we use the more expansive definition, is not confined to the Middle East. An argument can be made, for example, that the conflict in Northern Ireland was a religiously-based tribal war. The two sides to the conflict saw no possibility of compromise, a characteristic of tribal conflict. Each sect, Protestant and Catholic (or Loyalist and Rebel) was determined to drive the other "into the sea." The violence and viciousness there matched anything now occurring in the Middle East, though on a smaller scale. It was, in my personal view, rampant tribalism.

Violence in Europe between Muslims and non-Muslims clearly has elements of tribalism.

Even here in America, as Robert Reich wrote in a NY Times editorial called "The New Tribalism and the Decline of the Nation State;" it might be that the idea of the Nation State is deteriorating in a rebirth of tribalism. Are we "One Nation, Under God," or are we intransigent Democrats and Republicans vowing that our enemies will never have a victory and that we won't be content until they, whoever 'they' are, go down to total defeat? Are we tribal? Income inequality has divided America into separate classes. Mitt Romney's unguarded comment about the "47%" seems to indicate the presence of two "tribes," two separate and not equal "nations" here in America. Red states and Blue states. Different races, different tribes. And, in a conflict between tribes, there is no compromise, only absolute victory and defeat.

America's Middle Eastern Policy, by framing the conflict in the Middle East as a "tribal conflict," has created two obstacles to a peaceful conclusion. First, we create a situation where victory or defeat are the only options, prolonging the bloodshed and violence. Second, we make it impossible to achieve a positive secular solution like that in place in other nations in which there is a mixture of "tribes," a secular solution achieved by guaranteeing all religious, and non-religious groups access to the political process.

The probability of defeating all Muslims in a global conflict is slim at best. The problem is probably made worse by forces in America that are trying to move our nation from being a Democracy to being a Christian Theocracy. If that occurs, then some form of tribal war and destruction will almost inevitably follow. Such an act would inevitably turn the present conflict irrevocably into a tribal war: Christians versus Muslims. There are an estimated 1.8 billion Muslims worldwide, about 24% of the world population. The likelihood of driving them all down to defeat, even if this was judged to be a worthwhile goal, is less than zero.

A more attractive alternative might be to guarantee all religions, Muslims included, peaceful access to equal status as citizens and human beings - and equal access to political power. This might seem an unlikely and unpopular path in the light of ISIL's violent and intransigent bid for power and territory. But there seems to be few alternative possibilities except letting the tribal conflict in the Middle East resolve itself and then engage with the victors as they attempt to re-establish a viable society among the ruins. The cost of that solution in human suffering and death is unimaginable. Either solution will require a willingness to truly engage other people, other religions.

We would do well to attend to the words of the astrophysicist Geoffrey Marcy, writing in the *New York Times*:

> "The challenge of any person's or species' life is to learn others' truths without giving up your own."

In the end, we must try to find a solution that restores honor and respect to all ethnicities, all races, all religions and all cultures.

"A people inspired by democracy, human rights and economic opportunity will turn their back decisively against extremism."
~ Benazir Bhutto ~

"I am a firm believer in the people. If given the truth, they can be depended upon to meet any national crisis. The great point is to bring them the real facts."
~Abraham Lincoln ~

Chapter Three

United We Stand: My decade-long personal journey since 9/11/2001

Arif Humayun

Arif Humayun manages an international technology licensing business and devotes his free time towards explaining Islamic teachings. His first book, *The Summit of Religious Evolution,* (pub 1992) establishes the common bonds between the three Semitic faiths. *Islam and the US Constitution* (pub 2002) was his response to the 9/11/2001 terrorist attacks to highlight the contradictions between Islamic teachings and the radicals' actions. In *Connivance by Silence* (pub 2011), he includes and addresses the "Munir Commission Investigation of Scriptural Basis of Demands" and urges his fellow Muslims to reject the radicals' misinterpretation of Islam. He has authored several papers on Radicalism among Muslims, Sharia, Jihad, Blasphemy, Apostasy, etc. Arif is an avid supporter of separation of religion and politics, and co-founder of the Circle of Peace. Website: http://www.circleofpeaceonline.org/

The United States is an exceptional nation As a people, we are not bound by blood, nationality, ethnicity or religion. Instead, our entrepreneurial spirit and intellectual freedom connects us to the core belief that, irrespective of our past, we can shape our future together. This has made America a "melting pot" where people from around the world have come together to make this an exceptional and unique country. A perfect example of that unity was demonstrated in the immediate aftermath of the September 11, 2001 terrorist attacks; a decade later, however, several attempts to divide the country along political, economic, and religious fault lines have dented that unity. The challenge for all of us is to understand and resolve the issues that have been exploited by vested interests and defeat their objective to polarize society. The strength of our country is in its unity.

This is my personal journey, as an American Muslim, to identify the concerns that cause Muslims to be viewed as radicals or "anti-American" and explain that the religion of Islam does not sanction or support radical ideologies. Political and cultural ideologies of Muslim immigrants are the root cause of these issues. And radicalism is not the exclusive monopoly of Muslims; radicalism exists among Christians, Jews and other religious and secular groups in America (and around the world) and should be defeated jointly by better understanding and communications among all communities.

Needless to say, 11 September 2001, or "9/11" as it came to be commonly known, demonstrated this unique American spirit. As we began the day on the West Coast, an early morning phone call from the East Coast broke the terrible news of the plane crashing into one of the Twin Towers in Lower Manhattan, NY. Before we could tune in to the news channels, another caller updated us that the event was being billed as a terrorist attack by Muslims. Urging caution, the call ended with the advice that the family stay home and check developments before venturing outdoors. Unfathomable images of the chaos underway in Manhattan were being telecast. The short-lived assumption of the possibility of an accident was soon shattered when another plane struck the second tower and reports of additional hijackings and crashing into the Pentagon and in Pennsylvania were confirmed.

Naturally, the thought of mass internment of Japanese-Americans in the aftermath of the Pearl Harbor attacks during the Second World War (WW II) came to mind when our national rationality yielded to war hysteria and President Roosevelt authorized their internment. Subsequent acknowledgement[1] and corrective action by President Ronald Reagan in 1998 also resonated in my mind. Having discussed these thoughts, my wife and I decided to follow our normal routine. Dropping off our two kids at school, I went to the office.

In addition to feeling depressed at the terrible national loss of life and property, we carried an additional burden – the perpetrators of this horrible crime were our co-religionists who had not only distorted and monopolized our faith but were justifying their attack on our country as a religious obligation. This thought was intolerable. I decided to reach out and share my grief with colleagues, acquaintances, and people I met during the days and weeks that followed; I refuted the terrorist's justification that Islam somehow allowed this or any other act of senseless killings, violence and destruction. I recall the strong

---

1 President Ronald Reagan apologized for the internment on behalf of the U.S. government in 1998 acknowledging that the internment decision was driven by "race prejudice, war hysteria, and a failure of political leadership" and disbursed about $1.6 billion in reparations to Japanese Americans who had been interned and their heirs.

urge to buy a US flag, which due to high demand, had suddenly disappeared from stores. A colleague gave me a flag and holding it gave me a feeling of strength and patriotism that cannot be described.

While picking our daughter up from school that day, one of her friend's mother asked me if Islam justified such attacks acknowledging that her friends and extended family were openly condemning Muslims. Accepting my refutation, she requested to be "educated" to be able to rebut the negative assertions. We invited her to our home and explained the Islamic teachings and practices and how ideological and geopolitical events have enabled radical groups to hijack Islam by misrepresentation and "engineering" certain doctrines to justify their nefarious designs. Armed with this knowledge, she began her mission to dispel the misconceptions about Islam.

We greatly appreciated her initiative for trying to ascertain the facts from reliable sources. This one example of independent thinking was representative of the American society. The majority's reaction, which unfortunately did not get much public attention, was exemplary and further demonstrated the strength of our country. A section of the media did play on the hysteria and stereotyped Muslims as terrorists; a few Muslims were killed. One Sikh – mistaken as Muslim because of his turban – was also killed. Additionally, some mosques were firebombed while others received hate mail and threats. Against a few threats, one mosque in Portland, Oregon, was overwhelmed by messages of support; several hundred people left flowers outside the mosque and some even offered to guard the mosque property or accompany members for grocery shopping and other outdoor activities to give them an additional sense of security. This positive reaction, sadly, did not get much media attention.

Such examples of instantaneous positive reaction far outweigh the very limited negative reaction to a great national tragedy. Having witnessed uncontrolled and widespread rioting in Pakistan in 1979 when the US was falsely accused of occupying the Kaa'ba[2] in Mecca, the reaction against the Twin Tower attacks was negligible; the 1979 riots in Pakistan, fueled by national hysteria, destroyed the American Embassy in Islamabad and the Consulate in Lahore.

2 Sacred Mosque in Mecca where Muslims perform Hajj (obligatory pilgrimage). The attackers turned out to be Saudi extremists who were opposed to the Saudi monarchy

President Bush's ill-advised initial reference to the Crusades[3] on 9/11 was unfortunate; it did not help American Muslims because of the negative connotations of those historic battles between Christians ideologues and Muslims; if anything, the comment reflected poorly on his knowledge of Islam. The President did quickly clarify his comment and differentiated between the religion of Islam and the radicals' agenda of monopolizing the religion. Terming Islam as a religion of peace, he condemned the terrorists for attempting to achieve their goals from behind its façade. Many leaders stepped forward with this differentiation which was carried by electronic and print media. I vividly recall Karen Armstrong's[4] books on Islam, which upheld the peaceful credentials of Islam, being highlighted along with her and other experts' interviews refuting the al-Qaeda and Taliban's interpretation of Islam. These swift actions of strong leadership, public debate, education and effective law enforcement kept this difficult situation from getting ugly. This was the example of a united country brought together by a national tragedy.

The lack of knowledge about Islam, and the instantaneous desire of non-Muslim Americans to understand this faith, was an eye opener. It demonstrated the Muslims' failure to have effectively communicated their beliefs within their adopted societies. I undertook researching and writing articles to explain the religion of Islam and highlighting its key teachings. My articles vehemently rejected any association between Islam and violence under any guise (including Jihad, Sharia, Blasphemy, Apostasy) that radicals' used to justify violence. Rejecting the radicals' objective for establishing an "Islamic" government, my articles argued that Islam did not sanction any particular form of government; rather the Qur'an stipulated peace, equality and justice as the principles of governance. Furthermore, I explained

---

3 The historic roots of this anti-Islam discourse can be traced to the 11th century when Pope Urban II called for a crusade against Muslim Empires. Islam's portrayal as a barbaric and oppressive faith became part of a larger Western discourse, in which the religion was depicted as obscurantist. The traditional Western narrative of Islam and science, in which Muslim scientists are considered mere transmitters of Greek and Latin knowledge but rarely thinkers in their own right, remains widely unchallenged and Western scientists and philosophers played down the achievements of their Muslim counterparts. Those behind the anti-Islam discourse have rarely been interested in truth or accuracy, which can be easily established through available evidence

4 Author of several books on Islam e.g., *Islam: The Short History, Muhammad: The Prophet of our Times,*

that legislative Sharia was: (1) the first formal system of legislation that served the growing Islamic empires of the time, (2) a human effort and not a scriptural requirement, (3) developed by the Abbasid Caliphate in the 8th-9th centuries when the global economy was agrarian, (4) is inapplicable in today's industrial economy, and (5) constitution-based governments comply with the Qur'anic principles of peace, equality, and justice and evolved into effective models for good governance.

A section of the media continued to vilify Islam and I took it upon myself to counter this negative portrayal of my faith. Several weeks of conversations brought two vivid realizations: the widespread confusion among Muslims' understanding of their religion which naturally resulted in gross misunderstandings about Islam among non-Muslims, and the lack of availability of good English-language publications on Islamic teachings by Muslim authors to refute this prevailing and growing negativity. In the aftermath of the 9/11 terrorist attacks, disparaging comparisons between the Islamic teachings and the US Constitution were made in which the religion of Islam was incorrectly and unjustifiably condemned. Having researched and published a book on the evolution of Semitic religions in 1992,[5] I decided to cross reference the US Constitution with the Qur'an. The research was enlightening and showed remarkable consistency between the two documents; my second book, titled *Islam and the US Constitution* was published on July 4, 2002. The selection of Independence Day 2002 for this publication was deliberate because I expected the patriotic spirit to be heightened that day. Due to time constraints, I published the book electronically. The book's website had very heavy traffic and was frequently cited in other publications

The dynamics of the Constitution writing process, the refinements through the various amendments, and the balance this document

---

5 My interest in religion began in 1989 while living in Australia. A work colleague, who was Christian, made comments against the Prophet of Islam which I could not ignore. Instead of starting an argument without any solid data, I was upfront and admitted to him that I did not understand my religion well enough to respond to his comment but was willing to research that and some other topics that came up in our conversation. We identified the topics and thus began my three-year research which enabled me to refute every assertion made by my colleague. We met six times during my three-year stay in Australia. Each session began after dinner and ended the next morning; a specific topic was covered in depth till my colleague could not provide any further scriptural data to support his point. That research formed the basis of my first book *Islam: The Summit of Religious Evolution* that was published in 1992. This background provided a good overview of comparative religions and facilitated research for the second book.

created between the various organs of the government to safeguard the intent and spirit of the Constitution was simply amazing. Also remarkable was the separation of religion and politics as a matter of policy. This experience brought a fundamental change in my personality; rather than shrugging aside any discussion on religion, I welcomed the opportunity to discuss how misconceptions, based on failed regional reformation movements became part of the local culture and traditions. Immigrants from the Muslim world brought their 'religious' traditions to their adopted homeland not only caused more confusion but also prevented any debate about their origins. These distortions were thus allowed to become part of the Muslim faith in the US and other Western countries where Muslims settled.

Publishing detailed White Papers[6] on Islamic topics like Radicalism, Sharia, Apostasy, Blasphemy, Islamic Government, etc., enabled me to speak publicly on these topics. As awareness grew, I was invited to speak at schools, universities and to other groups. The White Paper on Radicalism was in response to the terrorist attack in Mumbai (India) in 2008. During my routine business travels to India, I was a frequent guest at both the Taj and Oberoi Hotels. My wife and I stayed at the Oberoi and had meals at the Taj that summer. We watched the live TV coverage of the attacks and could visualize the restaurants where we had savored the excellent cuisines. Our hearts went out to those that were mercilessly killed by the attackers under the name of Islam. The White Paper on Radicalism was widely distributed throughout the USA.

The overbearing influence of the extremists' literal and selective [mis]interpretation of the Qur'an comes from the Wahabbi or Salafi interpretation which is adopted by terrorist groups like the Muslim Brotherhood, Jama'at-i-Islami, al-Qaeda, Taliban, etc. Rather than abiding by the Qur'anic injunctions, these groups cherry-pick and, when unable to rationalize Qur'anic teachings with their desired interpretations, declare them abrogated! [7] Similarly, they reinforce their interpretation by selective references to the Prophet's exhortations[8] and

---

6 Can be viewed and downloaded from www.CircleofPeaceOnLine.org

7 Report of the court of inquiry constituted under Punjab Act II of 1954 to enquire into the Punjab disturbances of 1953, p 223-4

8 Collected and collated approximately 200 years after the Prophet's death by a process which allowed incorrect events to be attributed to him. Although some "corrected" versions are now available, the contradictions within and among collections exists. These must be subordinate to the Qur'an and the rule of thumb is to reject any exhortation that is contrary to the Qur'an which is the primary source for Islamic teachings

juristic opinions from legislative Sharia.[9] While the legislative Sharia development was terminated in the 10th century, it did serve as a useful form of legislation for a diverse and growing Abbasid Empire. This system had a built-in separation of religion and politics because, while the legislation was developed by the Caliphate[10] , its implementation was left to independent political entities, which were part of the Caliphate. This system of governance allowed Muslims to control large empires, become prosperous and progressive, and attracted knowledge from people of all faiths. The Abbasids encouraged education, promoted sciences and arts, and encouraged development. This made the Caliphate the center of excellence and an unrivaled repository of knowledge from around the world.

I continued research to better understand the dynamics of the rapid ascent, gradual decay and the termination of effective Muslim rule from the 7th – 18th centuries. I realized that historical facts were very different from what I learned growing up in Pakistan; those facts had been distorted! Muslims were naturally disillusioned when the three great Muslim empires[11] were defeated and colonized by European (Christian) powers in a relatively short time. As their world crumbled around them, Muslims sought explanations for some very difficult and 'unexpected' questions.

One fundamental change that caused the decline of Muslim dominance was the change in the global economic base from agrarian to industrial. This 3-4 centuries long European-driven initiative, generally known as reformation and renaissance, was indeed difficult. It transformed Europe through education and technical developments, which brought about the industrial revolution. The Muslim Empires during this period enjoyed the fruits of their earlier victories, had become complacent, and did not realize the tectonic changes that were underway. When the Ottomans realized this fundamental change, it was too late for them to catch up.

Additionally, the Muslims' religious beliefs were also challenged by European missionaries who actively sought to proselytize

---

9 A system of legislation developed by the Abbasid Caliphate to develop laws around Qur'anic principles of equality, peace and justice but drawing heavily from secondary and derived sources. Abu Fad'l (Great Theft) discusses the development of legislative Sharia in detail.

10 A system of governance developed after the Prophet's death in 632 CE. Caliph literally means successor. The first four Caliphs were elected (or selected) by Muslims. Later, Caliphate became hereditary and the victor of the way became the Caliph and kept it within their dynasty.

11 Saffavid in Iran, Ottoman in Turkey, and Mughal in India

them. In India, in addition to Christian missionaries, Hindu missionaries also mounted an aggressive assault on Islam to bring back those Hindus who had become Muslims during the Mughal rule. These multi-faceted attacks against Muslims, the defeat and disintegration of the Ottoman Empire into some three dozen countries, the termination of the Ottoman Caliphate, in addition to the colonization of the three Muslim Empires, gave birth to the Muslim Brotherhood in Egypt in 1928; the Muslim Brotherhood's foundational demand was the re-establishment of an Islamic State and the reestablishment of the Caliphate. This remains their battle cry even to this day.

The radicals' goal – the re-establishment of the Islamic State – is a mirage because it had actually never existed in history.[12] Radicals point towards the period when the Prophet was the overall leader in Mecca and Medina and the subsequent "Righteous Caliphate" that lasted for some 30 years after his death. According to their revised history, that was very peaceful period and all citizens – including the Caliphs – were equal before the law and justice was promptly delivered to the victims. While that may be partially true, that three-decade period was also a very turbulent – of the four caliphs, the last three were murdered. This caliphate ended during the term of the fourth caliph, Ali, who was defeated; this began the new phase of Caliphate where the caliphate became political; the victor became the Caliph and it stayed within their dynasty.

The Muslims' failure to lead the transition away from the agrarian economy resulted in the colonization and ultimate disintegration of their empires. And Muslims' refusal to adopt the new educational standards and practices required for the industrial economy did not help. Rather, Muslims blamed their plight on non-Muslim Westerners and some still consider themselves to be victims. This major reversal in fortunes of the Muslim empires created a leadership vacuum which was filled by politicized clergy who classified their defeats as divine punishment for the Muslims' departure from their faith; they urged the faithful to revert to the pristine teachings and practices of Islam as was done during the time of the Prophet and the righteous Caliphate that followed. That is when revisionist Muslim history and such untenable demands were born. They engineered doctrines by misrepresenting facts, selectively quoting from the Qur'an and the Prophet's traditions to assert that legislative Sharia, Jihad, Apostasy and Blasphemy will be the foundations of the mythical Islamic State which has never

---

12 A recent book, *Illusion of an Islamic State,* Ed. H. E. Kyai Haji Abdurrahman Wahid (former Indonesian President) discusses this in great detail.

existed in history, and will never become reality in the future. This concept of an Islamic State gave rise to political Islam and catalyzes radicalism today.

I came to the realization that every individual Muslim has the responsibility to research, understand and refute the divisive doctrines that have been engineered and sadly accepted by Muslims as part of the faith. Those who chose to remain silent were actually empowering the radicals. Thus my third book, *Connivance by Silence*,[13] was published in November 2011. This book relies heavily on the findings of a high-powered independent judicial commission's report published by the Pakistan Government in 1954. Commonly known as the Munir Commission Report, it analyzes and refutes every radical doctrine that serves to justify violence under the name of Islam. *Connivance by Silence* relates the report's analysis and recommendations to current terrorist events like the Fort Hood shooting by US Army Major Nidal Hasan, the failed Times Square bombing by Faisal Shazad, and the famous "underwear bomber," Umar Farouk Abdulmutallab. Not only that, this book will empower any individual, irrespective of faith, to ask probing questions to refute any doctrine supported by radical Muslims. This phenomenon, catalyzed by excessive enthusiasm with limited knowledge, is well characterized by Haji A. Mustofa Bisri, [14] an Indonesian Muslim scholar:

> *"Efforts to transform Islam into an ideology, and to create an Islamic state, are generally prompted by an excess of religious enthusiasm unsupported by sufficient knowledge of Islam itself. Excessive enthusiasm may lead a person to absolutize the knowledge he or she has attained, despite it being quite limited and partial. As a result, he or she brands other forms of knowledge as erroneous and rejects them."*

Appreciating the enormity of this project, I sought partners with whom to form alliances to share my findings with other Americans. The polarization within the US had grown over the decade to alarming proportions based on revenge for some despicable acts between Muslim and Christian extremists vying for political clout within their

---

13 A. Humayun, *Connivance by Silence: How the Majority's Failure to Challenge Politically Motivated [Mis]interpretation of the Qur'an Empowered Radicals to Propagate Extremism*, www.Xlibris.com

14 Kyai Haji A. Mustofa Bisri, Never Cease Learning, Epilogue, *The Illusion of an Islamic State*, p. 250 (2011)

communities. An extreme example of such polarization, promoted by Christian radical groups, was the "International Burn a Koran Day" announced by a theologically belligerent Florida pastor of a small church, Terry Jones.[15] Through Facebook messages, Jones urged people around the world to burn copies of the Koran on September 11, 2010. His refusal to abandon the plan, despite appeals and warnings from all quarters, caused this event to become the center of an international conflagration between Christianity and Muslims. Clamoring for notoriety, Jones used the title of his book, *Islam Is of the Devil,* to create anti-Islamic hysteria by citing his belief that Islam promotes violence and that Muslims want to impose Sharia law in the United States. Jones was exploiting his excessive enthusiasm which lacked knowledge to drum up support for this un-Christian act. Jones' actions mirrored al-Qaeda's and the Taliban's because they also play on the same sentiments. Like Jones, other extreme right wing Christian and Jewish groups have fanned hatred against Muslims and, without understanding, have created national hysteria by opposing the implementation of the inapplicable Sharia as a national law. Right wing politicians have tried to capitalize on this divide and use it as an electioneering tool as well.

The majority of Americans condemned Jones' belligerence and openly demonstrated their support of their Muslim neighbors. One bright example was demonstrated by a Christian friend who started an online campaign to distribute two Qur'ans for every one burned by Jones. Another example was observed at a mosque in Portland, Oregon, which had organized an interfaith seminar on peace. Representatives from all religions were invited to speak about peace in their respective tradition. The large attendance overwhelmed the organizers who had to arrange for over 500 attendees when a much smaller number had been expected. The parking lot, sidewalks and every flat area around the small mosque was used by attendees. This standing-room-only event received extensive coverage by the local media.

A Caucasian American reached out and complimented the event emphasizing that such events should become more frequent. In the ensuing conversation, he welcomed my offer to send him some of my articles. He shared those with his friends and soon we met to form a non-sectarian interfaith group called the Circle of Peace[16] whose membership traversed any doctrinal restrictions. Treating each other as human beings and respecting and honoring each other, we decided

---

15 http://abcnews.go.com/US/terry-jones-pastor-burn-koran-day/story?id=11575665
16 www.CircleOfPeaceOnLine.org

to remove intellectual barriers by discussing religious concepts openly, especially the ones that were used by radicals to justify violence,
and which had created confusion and fear among the people.

Through the Circle of Peace, I contacted the American Islamic
Leadership Coalition (AILC) and the American Islamic Forum for Democracy (AIFD). With a mission to "advocate for the preservation of
the founding principles of the United States Constitution, liberty and
freedom through the separation of mosque and state,"[17] these two
groups are actively educating the American people about Islam and
differentiating it from the radical strain (Islamism) that clamors for
the establishment of the Islamic State and Sharia. AIFD's founder, Dr.
M. Zuhdi Jasser, had narrated a documentary titled "The Third Jihad,"
where he had highlighted the radical's agenda to form an Islamic State
and implement Sharia. The New York Police Department (NYPD) had
used this documentary for training officers to enable them to identify
potential radicals who believe in these objectives. Self-proclaimed
Muslim civil rights groups like the Council of American Islamic Relations (CAIR) and the Islamic Society of North America (ISNA),
along with New York Times (NYT), started a high profile campaign
to condemn the film and malign Dr. Jasser. On March 5, 2012, AIFD
and AILC held a press conference in Manhattan to show support for
NYPD for their anti-terrorism activities, which were condemned by
several Islamist groups like CAIR and ISNA who 'claim' to represent
all Muslims.

Through these alliances, I have made several presentations to
explain Islam and its teachings to various groups including school and
university students, church groups, law enforcement and the Army.
These presentations differentiate between the fundamental teachings
of Islam and the politically driven engineered doctrines, which are
contrary to the teachings of Islam. This information is readily available through the Circle of Peace and AILC-AIFD websites.

While my efforts during the past decade were focused on pro-
jecting the proper teachings of Islam to the American people, the re-
luctance of many Muslim groups to unequivocally condemn any association of violence with Islam was frustrating. The best these groups
did was to offer qualified condemnations and linked them with political conflicts in the Middle East and South Asia. Radical Islamic
groups fanned anti-American and anti-Western sentiments amongst
Muslims by exploiting torture, prisoner abuse, and the desecration of
Qur'ans at the Guantanamo Bay Detention Center in Cuba, and

17 http://www.aifdemocracy.org/; http://americanislamicleadership.org/

Bagram Detention Center in Afghanistan. Additionally, the Danish cartoon controversy and other similarly unfortunate events, whose images were flashed across the electronic media, added fuel to the growing anti-American and anti-Western sentiments in the Muslim world. Without reference to the inhumane treatment of prisoners by al-Qaeda and the Taliban, the Muslim world largely accepted the narrative and gave an immense boost to the radicals' propaganda war. Some events in the Muslim world provided additional propaganda boosts to the radicals. For example, the Palestinian Intifada, Israeli-Lebanon War, the Red Mosque event in Pakistan, all provided further justifications for indoctrination by the radicals who branded their political differences as religious differences that pitched Islam against Christians and Jews.

Al-Qaeda and the Taliban cleverly focused their rhetoric towards Muslims living in the West to gain their support. This was evident by the frightening trends in surveys[18] where young Muslims in Europe and North America identified themselves as Muslims first; their citizenship of the state was secondary. Likewise, young Muslims supported the implementation of Sharia in their adopted countries, viewed al-Qaeda and the Taliban as furthering the cause of Islam and justified suicide bombings as a legitimate tool against innocent victims. "Home grown" terrorists, responsible for attacks or attempted attacks in the US and Europe, can be understood in that light. Scratching the surface reveals political connections, ideologies, and overseas funding for groups that support the radicals' view of re-establishing an Islamic State. This background explains how many Middle Eastern and South Asian political entities have exploited and attempted to monopolize Islam for accomplishing their political objectives. Such politically-driven (Islamist) groups hide behind the democratic and secular laws in the US and Europe to further their objectives.

As already mentioned, the engineered doctrines that have led to radicalism among Muslims are a recent phenomenon and their resolution lies in public discussion and refutation of those doctrines. That was actually done in Pakistan in 1954 when a high-powered and independent judicial commission examined those doctrines. Generally known as the Munir Commission, this two-member commission was headed by the country's Chief Justice and another Supreme Court judge to investigate the cause(s) of the clergy-led rioting in Pakistan. This Commission exposed the fact that the power struggle between two political parties was the underlying cause of this rioting. The

18 http://pewresearch.org/assets/pdf/muslim-americans.pdf

provincial government of Punjab exploited the politicized clergy to debase the prime minister who hailed from the former East Pakistan (now Bangladesh). That report cleverly investigated and refuted every engineered doctrine of politicized Islam (or Islamism) that was used by the provincial government against the prime minister in the 50's and is currently being used by al-Qaeda, the Taliban and similar radicalized Muslim groups. To varying degrees, the more than two dozen so-called scholars could not agree on a simple definition of a Muslim! That report holds the key to confronting Islamism today. Unfortunately, any reference to that report is avoided in Pakistan and the Muslim world. Instead, governments in so-called Muslim countries have sharpened their rhetoric, entrenched themselves deeper into their political position, funded the construction of mosques and propagation of their version of Islam, and even supported militant groups to further their political objectives. The fundamental geopolitical and ideological divide has two aspects – Arab and Non-Arab, and between Sunni and Shi'a Islam – the pole bearers of which are Saudi Arabia and Iran respectively. Each group is further subdivided into competing factions for whom these religious and geopolitical divides are a source of sustenance.

What became a very United States of America immediately after the attacks on September 11, 2001, now stands polarized today. Sadly, Islam and "Islamophobia" are now front and center in the "global war on terror," one of the many political footballs during every election season. To bring the country back together and defuse this explosive situation, the following steps must be undertaken:

1. First and foremost, Muslims have to resolve the ideological divide amongst themselves by understanding Islam as a religion and rejecting the engineered doctrines that claim the religion to be a political system. Moreover, they must also learn and understand history, and remove any misconceptions.
2. Muslims must denounce all violence perpetuated by radicals under the guise of Islam, uphold human rights, educate their fellow citizens about their religion, and remove any misconceptions.
3. American Muslims must educate their fellow citizens about their religion. Americans have to work together in uniting the country by understanding the issues and not allowing political rhetoric to divide them.

"There is nothing more dangerous than sincere ignorance."
~ Dr. Martin Luther King, Jr. ~

"I've learned that people will forget what you said,
people will forget what you did, but people will never
forget how you made them feel."
~ Maya Angelou ~

"Too many of us are not living our dreams -
because we are living our fears."
~ Les Brown ~

"It is not necessary to change. Survival is not mandatory."
~ W. Edwards Deming ~

Chapter Four

In the Wake of Iraq's Dissolution

Stories of those trying to save it, those trying to tear it apart, and those trying to survive it

Benjamin Sockle

Benjamin Sockle (shown here with son Geiger, named after Wayne Geiger) served in the U.S. Army Infantry from April 2001 to August 2014. He served two tours in Iraq: Mosul (2004-2005), and during the "Surge" in Baghdad and Muqdadiyah (2007-2008). He served in Command Centers (S-3), Liaison in a variety of roles and functions, including Brigade for Iraqi Security Forces, and as a Stryker Squad Leader. These different levels of interaction with the coalition forces and Iraqi nationals gave him a unique perspective on the war in Iraq and its fallout. With his contribution to this book, he hopes to broaden perspectives on the lives people are forced to live (and find ways to survive) in a country that is being torn apart from within. In America, land of the free and most fortunate, we take far too much for granted – and, sadly, have no clue regarding the suffering of others. The next time you see the grave marker of a fallen soldier, take a moment to reflect on those he or she left behind.

9/11/2001

On September 11, 2001, I was at a friend's house. Just four days earlier, I had graduated basic training and advanced individual training to become an infantryman. One of my drill sergeants told my class, "Every ten years there is a conflict. You will go to war." I didn't expect things to happen as quickly as they did. I woke up that

47

morning with my friend's mom yelling "We're going to war!" This was not exactly how I planned on waking up. I was in complete disbelief that something like this was happening. I thought maybe it was an accident. I sat like everyone else and watched. I saw the second plane hit and realized my friend's mom was right. I knew then that my life was going to change. I would have to deploy somewhere. No one ever knows how war will affect them. It was never something I really thought about beforehand. But now, thinking back, it gave me a new and unique perspective on life.

After spending two tours in Iraq, I noticed that there is much more to the story than most people see. You don't realize how much of a struggle day-to-day life can be for people there. These men that work for networks such as Al Qaeda or ISIS don't have any regard for whose lives they screw up. Their mission is about instilling fear and becoming more powerful. There is no concern for the general population whether they be Muslim, Christian, male, female, young or old. The chaos that they cause far exceeds what is reported by the media. Just like in our own country, the overriding storylines are those that are most abrasive to us. You see that they are kidnapping and beheading people from Coalition countries that are there as journalists or humanitarian support and no one likes it. Those things stick with you because you consider them to be a threat to your own safety at some level. When ISIS executes over a thousand college students in Iraq, it hardly makes the news and, worse yet, we hardly seem to take notice of just how impactful this is on a society and culture. We don't seem to get it. We are talking about normal people, arguably like you and me, living in a country and region being torn apart by people who have no regard for humanity. Left in the wake of their actions are these once "normal" people, now struggling to survive and make sense out of a life that presents no hope. We attach our understanding to the easiest thing we can conceive, which is about all Muslims hating all non-Muslims, which simply is not the case. In my time there I realized that we were trying to hold together a dream for a nation of people who were living a nightmare. I hope that these stories that I share will help more to realize that extremists do not represent an entire race, religion or country.

A Hope, a Bond, a Sacrifice

My first story will be the one most impactful on my life. I remember standing by myself, staring at the moon. I don't remember what I was thinking. This had been one of the worst days of my life.

One of my good friends and fellow soldier had been killed in an Improvised Explosive Device (IED) attack. There were seven more casualties at Baghdad General and we weren't sure of their status. We had just returned to our base and it was around 0200 (2 AM). Maybe I just wasn't ready to walk back to my room yet - my roommate was one of the injured. Who wants to just go sit alone in a room with no one around after something like this happens? I don't remember what it was or what I was feeling - if anything at all. Then I felt a hand on my shoulder, it was Nelson. He looked at me and said, "I'm really sorry, man. They were good guys." He took a long breath and shook his head and added, "It just sucks, man." I thanked him, shook his hand and walked back to my room.

I took off all my gear and sat down on my bunk. I looked over at my buddy's empty bunk, pulled out a cigarette and lit it. He was one of those severely injured in the IED, and alive when we dropped him off at the hospital. Usually, after we got back from our missions, we would pick out a show to watch or play something on an X-box we shared. That night I just sat in silence by myself. He was a good friend of mine. I knew his wife and kids. We had been friends for three years and already through one deployment together. You can't help but feel for them. This bombshell is about to be thrown in their lap. You wish that you could warn them, help prepare them or do something to make what they are about to hear easier. I stayed up most of the night and

Ben's Platoon and 2 Strykers in Germany just before deploying to Iraq

into the morning. Eventually, my mind calmed enough to go to sleep, but not without reliving the event over and over again.

We had set out on the evening of 18 October 2007, to do some "presence patrols" in our area of operations (AO), the Dora district of southern Baghdad. Basically, we were supposed to go around to a few neighborhoods and talk to the local populace about any activity in the area that concerned them. This consisted of a wide range of topics. Most of the time, we inquired about terrorist activity.

But the citizens of Iraq had more concerns than that. We would talk to them about government corruption, displaced families, damage to property, medical needs, water and electricity issues. Things had started to die down in our AO over the preceding week or two. When we first made our push into the area, there was a significant amount of resistance. There was a lot of small arms fire and IEDs. After a few weeks of our battalion maintaining a significant force in the area, the enemy had moved primarily to IED's as their weapon of choice.

The patrol had set off like normal. We convoyed from our Operating Base to the Dora district without incident. We started talking to locals in the area, but weren't getting any substantial information. This wasn't a big deal for us. Sometimes you just like to sit and hear about the concerns people have outside of war-related issues. It helped us remember that we weren't just there to fight a war. We were there to establish hope and protect a foundation for a new government. As we were maneuvering around the neighborhoods, one of our Strykers (2-1) got a flat tire. "2-1" was a number for one of the vehicles. We were third platoon, so our four vehicles were labeled 2-1, 2-2, 2-3 and 2-4. I believe we had six Strykers out on patrol that night. A determination was made that two of the vehicles would escort the one with a flat to a base nearby to get fixed. The other three, along with a dismounted group, would remain in sector and continue the presence patrol. I was with the group of three that would stay in sector. I remember being jealous that they were going to a base during chow hall hours.

After a couple hours, we heard the other group of vehicles call over the radio that the tire was fixed and they were on their way back to link up with us. They would be taking a pretty direct route back out. I believe it was the same route they took to the base for the repairs. I think everyone expects something to happen when you're there. You can't fight the over-riding feeling that you are in a place where people want to kill you and have the means to try. It affects all of us in different ways and some more than others. Honestly, that day, I just didn't see it coming.

A sound like fingernails on a chalkboard and static rang out over our radios. I knew immediately there was something wrong. It was unlike anything I'd ever heard before over our radios. Another transmission came over the radio shortly after that. Sounds of screaming, yelling and static, none of it made sense. Then one of the other Strykers came over the radio and gave a report, "2-1 just hit an IED. They're still moving." Our standard operating procedure was to push through the "kill zone" to a safe area to assess casualties and damage, to avoid a potential ambush. We immediately loaded up our dismounted personnel and started heading towards their location. "60th and Yohomama" was the intersection where we would meet them.

My Platoon Sergeant was in the Stryker with me. I kept yelling at our driver that he needed to go faster. It was probably only ten city blocks away, but it felt like an eternity. While en route we started getting the reports of the casualties. "One expected" - my heart sank after hearing that. What an indescribable feeling to hear someone is going to die. We are trained day in and day out to never give in. Then we heard who it was. "It's Geiger!" someone shouted. As soon as we got there, I jumped out with our medic to help treat casualties. All of the casualties were already separated and prioritized by the significance of their injuries. Under the light of headlights from one of the Strykers, they were strewn out across the street. A few of them were screaming in pain while getting worked on by the doc and others. I rushed up to them to see if I could help with any of the treatment. Blood everywhere, people screaming, others trying to calm them down and put on tourniquets. It looked like complete chaos but it was under control. Everyone was doing exactly what they had been trained to do. Another set of hands wouldn't help anyone so I moved on to assess what else needed to be done. I couldn't help but think of where Geiger was. I started looking around for him. He wasn't there. I asked the medical vehicle (MEV) that was there and they said they had already loaded him up.

I went back to our lieutenant and asked him what he needed. "We need security. Just make sure we have security." He seemed a little shocked by the situation. He was in the Stryker when it was hit by the IED. He had a torn meniscus and a few other non-life-threatening injuries, but he was still doing his job. I did as he instructed. I went around and checked to ensure that security was set up like it needed to be. Everything was in order. I checked on the guys pulling security to see if anyone was shook up. Everyone was okay. Someone called over the radio that all the casualties had been loaded and were ready to be transported to Baghdad General Hospital. Our Stryker and another loaded up our dismounts quickly to provide escort for the MEV.

We went as fast as we could. The whole drive all I could think was that I hoped Geiger would pull through. Maybe if we had gotten to them quicker. Maybe if we can get to the hospital quick enough. You can't help but think about these things. Next thing I know we're pulling up to the hospital. The medical vehicle pulled up to the emergency entrance and we spun around and parked on the other side of the hospital. The Platoon Sergeant and I dropped our helmets and ran inside. We got to the emergency room and our First Sergeant was standing there. "You two stay back!" as he waved us away. I knew Geiger was gone. I could just feel it. I know that he wouldn't have told us to stay away unless there was something we shouldn't see. It hurt, but I knew he was protecting us.

We waited around until we were given the official word on everyone we brought there. It was a long walk back to our Stryker. Everyone was going to be looking to us for the word on who made it and who didn't. It wasn't a responsibility that I enjoyed. Seeing everyone's faces drop when you have to say "He's gone." God it was tough. We only took three vehicles to the hospital. This meant we had to go back into our AO and continue to pull security while we waited for the assets necessary to move the damaged Stryker back to our base. When we got back to the scene, a few guys that had been on the ground pulling security near the damaged Stryker, loaded up in my vehicle. I was standing out of the back pulling security when I heard one of them say "Man, I hope Geiger is all right." We had already put out over the radio that one was KIA (Killed in Action). I guess, somehow, they just didn't hear it. I leaned down into the Stryker and the eight guys in the back all looked at me. My heart sank as I told them he was gone. "He didn't make it. I'm sorry." I didn't know what else to say after that. Honestly, I just hoped that everyone else knew so that I wouldn't have to tell anyone else. It was becoming increasingly painful to have to tell all our guys. Geiger was someone that everyone loved. His loss was a heavy blow to everyone who knew him, but especially tough for us.

Finally, hours after 2-1 was hit by the IED, it was on a recovery truck and ready to move. We took it back to our base and put it in an area with the rest of our Strykers. Our battalion assigned a detail of a few guys from another platoon to help clean it out so our guys didn't have to do it. The platoon sergeant, a few other guys, and I went over to the Stryker to see it in better light. It was a mess. The IED that was used is called an EFP (Explosively Formed Projectile). There were three different projectiles that impacted 2-1. One hit the rear, one hit the middle and one the front of the troop compartment. This is the area where everyone, except for the driver, ride in the Stryker. Two of the projectiles came almost clean through the armor (the front and middle impacts) and the other hit the back corner of the Stryker, shattering into thousands of fragments of shrapnel. There were two soldiers in the back that had their legs and torso shredded by shrapnel. Both men have since been through surgery after surgery to repair the damage, but at least they are alive. Five other soldiers in the troop compartment were hit by smaller pieces of shrapnel, and had various other non-life-threatening injuries. Geiger was sitting near the middle of the troop compartment. Somehow, of the three rounds to hit the Stryker, two of the rounds hit him. I never saw him, but everyone told me it was instant. From what I heard, he didn't look like the same person anymore. Part of his face was missing and a hole in his chest. I'm almost thankful I never saw him. I will never have that image stuck in my head that the people inside his Stryker will. They also said he was telling jokes when it happened, which was exactly what you'd expect from him. He always wanted to cheer people up - it was just how he was.

Back at our base, once everything was pretty much wrapped up, there were only a few of us from the platoon still at the Stryker. One by one we kind of peeled off to go back to our rooms. I probably made it thirty feet from 2-1 before I stopped and looked up at the moon. When Nelson put his hand on my shoulder I was really taken aback. He was one of the last guys remaining out there, checking on people and offering his condolences. He didn't have to be, he had no obligation to even care. He was our interpreter. He grew up in Baghdad and was educated to be an engineer. But, after the war started, he decided to help Americans try to fix his country. Though I always knew he was a good man, I never expected this. He wanted to help us talk to people and figure out what we could do to make their lives better. On this night, he took the time to make sure we were okay. He was a brave and extremely intelligent guy. Usually when we were out on patrols he would be the first to tip us that someone was acting outside of the norm. There was a woman that we had sitting in a room when we were searching a house that he realized was holding her arm weird. He came up to us and said that she had to be hiding something and she was acting nervous when he asked if she was okay. We brought in a female soldier to search her and she had a purse under her dress that had a pistol in it. It was his passion and attention to detail that assisted in us being successful in our operations. I don't know where he is now, but I always hoped that he would end up with a better life. When we left Iraq he gave me a knife that he bought as a token of our friendship. He told me that we were one of the best groups of guys he had ever worked with. I told him we felt the same way about him. We were lucky to have him during our deployment.

Live by Your Hopes, Die by Their Sword

Too often we heard about stories of an Iraqi policeman opening fire on a group of soldiers or an Iraqi army soldier doing the same. It's not often that you hear about the ones who are sacrificing themselves to make a difference. Some, like Nelson, impacted people beyond their own country and dedicated themselves to the entire process, not just for their own benefit. There are people all over the world who aren't as narrow minded or extreme, like the media portrays. In a previous deployment I was in Mosul, Iraq. I worked at a compound called the Joint Coordination Center. Two Americans would work there as liaisons to the Iraqi Army, Police, National Guard, Commandos and Kurdish Peshmerga. The purpose of the compound was to allow us to work in conjunction with the Iraqi's when coordinating missions and basic civil service. This helped us pass along normal police (civil) situations that we would encounter to them. It also served as a way to gather intelligence. The Iraqi police monitored a tip line that was a good source of information. The main person we worked with was an Iraqi Policeman who went by the name of "Sam."

Sam was a very driven individual. He was also a devout Muslim. Whenever there were emergency situations that would arise like IED's or firefights, Sam would direct his people to take charge and get the job done. There were several times, when he was not around, that other Iraqi's would insist that the Americans do it for them. He had a real belief that if they would just plant their feet and take a stand, that Iraq would be a better place. I saw him tell people day after day, "We have to do this for us!" I also saw him get phone call after phone call from terrorists telling him that they were going to find him and kill him. He would explain after he hung up on them that he just wished he could get through to them. "They're tearing everything apart. They're killing their own people. We could be better than this. We could prosper. All they want to do is create destruction." He was so intelligent and so dedicated to addressing Iraq's problems for the good of his people. He was a person that had the ability to make an impact and to get Mosul, at least, on the right track. Shortly before the end of our deployment in

54

2005, Sam was found executed and left on the side of the road. He had been shot in the head nine times. It was heartbreaking and extremely disappointing to see someone with so much to offer being executed. He was a special person that could have helped so much. Instead, he was struck down by ignorance. I can't help but think, knowing Sam, that he was defiant of their stupidity to the very end.

Treading Water in an Empty Pool

These are the stories you don't hear about in the news. These are the people who are sacrificing and dedicating themselves for hope, peace and prosperity. They have families, they are Muslim, Christian, Kurdish - they are Iraqi. Yet none of this prevails because the over-riding story line is no longer about hope, it's about despair. We don't understand that all these people are trying to do is survive in a country that is in extreme disrepair. No choice is simple. Everyday life was becoming increasingly hard for these people. There were so many people that lost jobs and weren't able to do anything. Think about our own recession. How many people said, "A college degree will only get you so far." Now, add to that, your government has been dissolved and you have extremists plotting and executing plans to slow or reverse the progress of your government's reconstitution. How do you start over when you can't be an engineer anymore? Or when your house has been leveled by terrorists or coalition forces? In these most extreme circumstances I believe people turn to one of two things. You try to please God and insure your passage to the next life, or you stop at nothing to provide for your family.

Dying to Survive

A short time before Geiger was killed, my platoon was called to track down a person who was believed to have just set off a House Bourne Improvised Explosive Device (HBIED). We had been told that a drone was tracking a man on a scooter as he fled from the area of the HBIED. Eventually, we were led to a house where we would find the man who fled. I don't remember if we knew at the time how many soldiers from our sister company were killed or injured in the explosion, but we knew that it had at least caused a few to be evacuated to Baghdad General. I think people always expect some dirtbag with a beard and a head wrap to be standing around with an RPG over his shoulder, waiting for some American to show up so he can blow them to smithereens. Truth is, some of the people that were carrying out these kinds of attacks, were the furthest thing from that stereotype.

My platoon entered the front gate and quickly confirmed the presence of a green scooter. Two of our squads went inside to search for a military aged male. I began looking around the scooter and yard for any signs that there had been any bomb or homemade explosive manufacturing. We also searched for any remote equipment that could have been used to detonate the HBIED. It was confirmed over the radio that a military aged male had been found in the house. I had the pleasure of being responsible for gathering all evidence, sworn statements and processing all detainees into detention facilities. So, my next step was to try to confirm that this guy had some involvement with detonation of the HBIED. While they continued searching the interior of the home, I tested the scooter for explosive related chemicals using an "Expray kit." Basically, you use a wipe and rub it on different surfaces, then spray them with different chemicals that will change colors to confirm the presence of explosive chemicals. I wiped the grips and area on the back where there were straps to hold stuff on the bike. The areas tested positive for nitrates. I tested another vehicle there to see if it had been used at all but tests came back negative. At this point my search outside was complete and the tests were done on the scooter.

I moved inside to see if I could complete the explosives testing on the guy we had tracked down. I was really kind of shocked when I saw him. He was short, pudgy, little mustache and had a comb-over. He had a wife and a few kids that were sitting in one room bawling their eyes out. He kept apologizing to his family and saying goodbye to his kids. His hands were shaking like crazy and sweat was pouring down his face. I tested his hands with the Expray and they also came up positive for nitrates. We cataloged the things that he had in his pockets, took pictures and loaded everything up in evidence bags. We let him say goodbye to his family then we loaded him up in our Stryker.

We were about an hour away from the detention facility to which we were directed to take him. I think he cried almost the whole ride. He explained over and over again that he had lost his job because of the war. He couldn't find work in the Mahallah (neighborhood) that he lived in because Al Qaeda controlled everything there. His family was starving and he couldn't do anything about it. Someone approached him and said if he detonated a bomb after Americans went in that they would give him the equivalent of seven hundred dollars. He got paid and did his deed. What a twisted place where someone can be put into a position where, out of necessity, they take other people's lives to feed their family. He didn't believe in an Islamic State or Caliphate or some extreme divine literature. He was acting on a primal instinct to survive and care for his family. I can't help but think that if I was in similarly dire straits I could say, "I'm just going to do this one thing. It'll get us by until we can figure something out."

When we arrived at the detention facility it was late. I was hungry. I was hoping it wouldn't take forever to get him processed in. I compiled all the paperwork and made sure all the statements and evidence were in order. The personnel from the detention facility frisked him and took him inside to the holding area. I stood out front and waited for another person to come out and sign for all the evidence. When he showed up, I started going through things so they could write out the evidence inventory. When we got to his wallet I figured it would be empty (they usually were). Inside I saw all of the money there - fresh, still somewhat crisp bills. I was in disbelief. This man just killed American soldiers, who were there to protect and make his life better. Meanwhile, he didn't have any way to provide for his family. Instead, he is in jail, along with the money he had been paid. To say that no one was better off would be the ultimate understatement. His family, now without their father and husband, would be left to figure it out on their own.

In the End, Life is Relative and Far Too Short

Every person's life is not a simple script. We can't go on every day thinking that everyone has the same simple choices that we might face. We can't assume that because of what we've been through, or what decisions we make, everyone else's should be the same. These men I worked with, detained or fought against were all Muslim. All of them led very different lives and supported different causes. All of them acted on the belief that what they were doing was necessary. Some for God, some for their country, and some for their families. Surviving in different parts of a complex country and region, all overrun by varying levels of chaos and despair. Their lives were based off of events set in motion, some prior to their own lives, even from thousands of miles away, that set them on a course to fight for their lives – and for those they love. All of this in a setting where dreams aren't allowed or even possible to imagine, where children witness murder and life is just surviving. I hope that at some point we can get beyond the natural labels that exist. I hope that we can discern the difference between who people really are instead of who we assume them to be.

Often these days I see and hear people saying that they should still be getting credit for going on deployments and what they've been through. I don't think that any of us should have done anything on deployment for merit or recognition, and especially asking for it years later. But, everyone is different. I personally can say that nothing that I went through was anything that I could compare to the pain that Corporal Wayne Geiger's parents (Randy and Kim Geiger) had to deal with in the loss of their son. I would like to dedicate my chapter to them and to the memory of Wayne. After his death, they have been so amazingly strong and dedicated to remaining a part of our lives as we try to live life in a manner that would make him proud. I will be eternally grateful for their love and sacrifice for our nation and hope that we "Wolfpack" boys can help keep a fraction of who he was alive. A part of Wayne Geiger will live on in so many of us whose lives he touched.

CPL Geiger with his mother and sister

CPL Wayne Marshall Geiger,
June 10, 1984 – October 15, 2007

———————————

"First, we had the land and they had the Bibles. Now we have
the Bibles and they have the land."
~ Chief Dan George ~

"Freedom is never more than one generation away from
extinction. We didn't pass it to our children
in the bloodstream. It must be fought for, protected,
and handed on for them to do the same."
~ Ronald Reagan ~

"Prejudice is a burden that confuses the past, threatens the
future and renders the present inaccessible."
~ Maya Angelou ~

———————————

Chapter Five

American Born and Raised:
Life and Challenges as a Muslim in the United States

Harris Zafar

Harris Zafar is the National Spokesperson for Ahmadiyya Muslim Community (America's oldest Muslim organization), Harris not only presents the community's nationwide efforts (such as the "Muslims for Peace" initiative) but also encourages Muslims to speak out about the true, moderate teachings of Islam to counter the incorrect image caused by extremists across the world. He is a frequent lecturer, writer & news commentator about Islam, including topics such as Shariah, Jihad, women's rights, interfaith, freedom, etc. When debunking misunderstandings of Islam – even confronting other Muslims as well – Harris goes to the source of Islam to uncover the true teachings. In June 2014, Harris's new book, *Demystifying Islam; Asking the Tough Questions,* was released. Harris has appeared on various media as a reasoned and moderate voice for Islam, including CNN and FoxNews.

Growing up in America

Growing up as a Muslim in America was not so different than growing up as any other kid in this country. There really weren't many Muslims in my school. Even if there were, I suppose I wouldn't know since we didn't talk about such things in school. So I spent my time with average American kids from a variety of backgrounds. I knew I was slightly different, but so was everyone else.

For me, growing up as a Muslim child and teenager meant simple things:
- I couldn't lie; I had to be honest, trustworthy, and have integtty
- I treated my parents with respect
- I had to treat others with respect, especially teachers and anyone older than me
- I would go to the Mosque every Friday for prayer services and

61

Sunday for education classes
- I had to be incredibly hard working
- I couldn't drink alcohol
- I couldn't eat pork
- I couldn't gamble
- I couldn't go out on dates

This changed when I graduated high school and left home to attend college in 1997. This is why I began searching for what it truly meant to be a Muslim. I sought to understand my faith in depth and not perform habitual practices. It is here that Islam began to take a new significance in my life. I studied it, questioned it and challenged it. I came away with a newfound love, admiration and appreciation for the values, guidance, morals and spirituality Islam inculcated within me.

After graduating in 2001, I enjoyed being home once again and taking part in religious dialogues at the Mosque. A few months later in September, tragedy struck that changed the landscape of Islam in America. Tuesday, September 11th, 2001, is a day that still lives fresh in my mind. I was a 22-year-old recent college graduate, who was awakened early that morning to news that two planes crashed into the twin towers in New York.

I turned on the TV just in time to watch the second tower collapse. I went numb. The remainder of the day, I was glued to the TV, as were millions of other Americans that day. I felt a mixture of shock, utter sadness, anger and confusion. The footage of people jumping out of a burning building from 90 stories high is one of the most horrifying images I have ever seen in my life. As I thought of those people jumping and their families, my heart ached and I could not hold back my tears.

As the day went on, news outlets increased their estimates of the number of people missing, feared dead and confirmed dead. I kept wondering how something like this could happen. Why would anyone do something like this? I always knew there were bad people in this world, but this was beyond just a bad act by a bad person. To me, only pure evil could have driven anyone to do something like this.

Soon, images of Osama bin Laden began to appear on the television airwaves. Later, images of bin Laden were joined by discussions about groups called Al-Qaeda and the Taliban. For many Americans, this was the first time they had heard of bin Laden and these groups, but for many of us Muslims, these names were rather familiar. We had known about bin Laden and these groups for some years, with a growing frustration and resentment of their behavior and public statements. As their names and faces became associated with the loathsome acts of 9/11, little did I know how long-lasting of an impact this would have on my life.

In the immediate aftermath of the attacks on 9/11, I took notice of the reaction that many Muslims had feared: people began building much anger towards Muslims and Islam in general. Many began blaming Islam as a sort of threatening ideology that calls for death and destruction. They would claim that Muslims and their faith are not compatible with the United States of America and wanted Muslims out.

From around the nation, we heard reports of Muslims and Arabs being targeted, attacked or insulted. The day after 9/11, six bullets shattered the windows of a Mosque in suburban Irving, Texas.[1] That same day, a group of at least 300 people tried to march on a Mosque in suburban Bridgeview, Illinois, while chanting "USA." One of the teen marchers was quoted as saying, "I'm proud to be American and I hate Arabs and I always have."[2] A Mosque in Alexandria, Virginia, was also attacked by bricks bearing anti-Muslim handwritten notes.[3]

Two weeks after 9/11, a female Muslim graduate student at Harvard was on her way to prayers when four men approached her and tried to physically take off her hijab while reportedly saying, "What are you doing here? Go home to your own country."[4] Four days after 9/11, a Sikh man wearing a turban, Balbir Singh Sodhi, was mistaken for a Muslim and fatally shot at the gas station he owned in Mesa, Arizona. When the suspect was arrested and was being handcuffed, he reported stated, "I stand for America all the way." [5]

These are just a few of a large number of similar attacks and incidents. My local Mosque is the first and oldest Mosque constructed in Portland, Oregon, and we received a few phone calls containing threats and some full of obscenities with the message that we need

---

1 Dallas area Mosque target of shooting", *The Battalion*, September 12th 2001
2 "Crowd in Ill. demonstrates at mosque as backlash", *USA Today*, September 13th 2001, http://www.usatoday.com/news/nation/2001/09/13/backlash.htm
3 "AFTER THE ATTACKS: RELATIONS; Arabs and Muslims Steer Through an Unsettling Scrutiny", *New York Times*, September 13th 2001, http://www.nytimes.com/2001/09/13/us/after-attacks-relations-arabs-muslims-steer-through-unsettling-scrutiny.html
4 "Grad Student Assaulted in Alleged Hate Crime", *The Harvard Crimson*, October 1st 2001, http://www.thecrimson.com/article/2001/10/1/grad-student-assaulted-in-alleged-hate/
5 "Sikh Owner Of Gas Station Is Fatally Shot In Rampage", *New York Times*, September 17th 2001, http://www.nytimes.com/2001/09/17/us/sikh-owner-of-gas-station-is-fatally-shot-in-rampage.html

to go back where we came from. All of these incidents led President George W. Bush to visit a DC-area Mosque and bravely state, "Those who feel like they can intimidate our fellow citizens to take out their anger don't represent the best of America. They represent the worst of humankind. And they should be ashamed of that kind of behavior."[6]

In this state of fear where Muslims found themselves, we saw changes in Muslim behavior. Muslim men who had worn beards for years suddenly shaved them off so as to minimize the chance of being identified as a follower of the Islamic faith. Muslim women who would typically cover their head in public suddenly refrained from doing so in order to liberate themselves. They sought liberation not from any oppression from Muslim males; rather, from the same verbal and physical attacks as experienced by the female student at Harvard and other women who reported similar harassment.

It was a very tense moment in our history, but, at the same time, I saw glimmers of hope. When I would arrive at my local Mosque, I would see the entrances lined with flowers, cards and messages of support. It was a completely unexpected yet incredibly warm gesture. Even though we had received those few threatening and harassing phone calls, we literally received hundreds of calls of support from average Americans - who were complete strangers to us - saying they are with us and know that we had nothing to do with the atrocities of 9/11. Some would offer to do our shopping for us in the event we did not feel comfortable going out ourselves. One gentleman who was a security guard at the mall offered to do security at our Mosque for free.

We graciously declined all such offers, however, as we refused to live as prisoners in our own hometown. This was the biggest lesson we chose to take away from this experience. This was our home, and we had been here for years. Our own neighbors came to our support in large numbers by rejecting the notion that Islam or all Muslims were to blame for 9/11. Far from hiding or fading into the background, we took an active role within the community. Our Mosque was inundated with requests from various institutions and schools requesting for either a Muslim speaker to come speak to their group or for their group to visit the Mosque and learn about Islam. In the first few months after 9/11, we spoke to thousands upon thousands of people about Islam.

I was asked to deliver several lectures and presentations as well by the Mosque leadership. Here I was, just 22 years old, going out

---

6 "Bush: U.S. Muslims should feel safe", CNN.com, September 17th 2001, http://articles.cnn.com/2001-09-17/us/gen.bush.muslim.trans_1_muslims-islamic-quran?_s=PM:US

speaking as a representative of the Islamic faith. Thus began a major shift in my life as an American Muslim. Since there was such a heightened awareness and interest in Islam, people sought Muslims to answer any question they had about this faith.

During these first few years after 9/11, I felt that we were all united as simply Americans. There was a renewed patriotism across the religious spectrum. We even began to proudly hang the American flag outside of our house. It felt as if people understood that we were all attacked on 9/11 and, thus, the dialogue was very healthy. New interfaith groups were sprouting all over the country; people continued to have an interest in learning about Islam; and most made concerted efforts to refrain from judging all Muslims based on the actions of a select group of lunatics. The number of lectures steadily increased.

By and large, what we were asked to speak about the most was terrorism, violence and the topic of "Jihad." And as time went on and additional acts of violence were perpetrated by savages calling themselves Muslims, we continued to be asked to speak about terrorism, violence and Jihad.

Some Muslims complained about being put in a situation where they felt that all Muslims in the United States were expected to represent Islam. Surely that is unfair for a normal member of a group to have to answer for the actions of other members of that group. Just as it would be absurd for anyone to expect every Jew in America to answer for examples of Israeli aggression in the occupied territories, it would be similarly absurd for every Muslim to have to answer for the violent actions of these self-proclaimed Muslims.

For me, yes, I did begin to yearn for the opportunity to speak on deeply spiritual and meaningful matters, but I understood that violence in the name of Islam was the primary point of interest for those who knew little about Islam. So it was important for us as Muslims to provide the education that was so desperately needed on the subject of Jihad, which was being grossly misrepresented. Being a member of that community which has had a consistent definition of Jihad for the entire 120+ years of its existence, it was imperative to demystify this subject.

"Jihad" is one of the most commonly misunderstood concepts in Islam, both by Muslims and non-Muslims. Often translated as "holy war" by pundits in the media – a wholly inaccurate and incomplete translation of this word – Jihad is simply an Arabic term which means to strive or to struggle towards an effort. It refers to the act of making an endeavor in a noble manner. According to Islamic teachings, the greatest Jihad (the Arabic of which is "Jihad-e-Akbar") is defined as the act of struggling or striving within or against one's evil tendencies to improve one's character. This is a struggle waged against our lower selves, with the aim of purifying ourselves.

The Holy Quran – Islam's holy scripture – states: *"He it is Who has raised among the Unlettered people a Messenger from among themselves who recites unto them His Signs, and purifies them and teaches them the Book and wisdom, although they had been before, in manifest misguidance"* (62:3).[7]

This verse tells us that the Prophet Muhammad came with the message for us to purify ourselves by following the wisdom found in our faith. Islam provides us with the tools and teachings from God that we need to purify ourselves. This is our greatest struggle; to rid ourselves of indecency and vice. Everyone has vices they can stand to do without, and our Jihad is to continue to strive to overcome those vices.

This guidance is not just found in the Quran. The Prophet Muhammad is also quoted to have said, "the mujahid (striver) who is exalted above other Mujahideen (strivers) is the one who strives against his own self."

Some Muslims chose to take this new interpretation of Jihad post-9/11 – perhaps seeking to appease those who legitimately attacked the previously understood notion of Jihad as a violent tool used to spread Islam. The Ahmadiyya Muslim Community, however, has always maintained a consistent view of Jihad as taught by the Founder of the Community, Mirza Ghulam Ahmad of Qadian, whom we accept as that Promised Messiah and Reformer whose coming was foretold by the Prophet of Islam. In the late 1800's, he emphatically declared that the doctrine of violent jihad goes against the teachings of the Holy Quran and the practice of the Prophet Muhammad. In its place, he taught his followers to wage a bloodless, intellectual "Jihad of the pen" to defend Islam. This is why rational discourse and interfaith dialogue are at the core of the Ahmadiyya Muslim Community.

The fact is that Islam does not condone terrorism of any kind. Rather, Islam sets an expectation on Muslims to establish peace and order in society and not to disrupt this peace and order. The Quran states, "And create not disorder in the earth after it has been set in order."[8] When looking at the permission granted to Muslims to

---

7 Holy Quran, chapter 62 verse 3, http://www.alislam.org/quran/search2/showChapter.php?ch=62&verse=3
8 Holy Quran, chapter 7 verse 57, http://www.alislam.org/quran/search2/showChapter.php?ch=7&verse=57

engage in a physical resistance, it becomes clear that the intention is never to create chaos and disorder. Rather, Muslims can only turn to a physical altercation in order to defend the right to freedom of religion.

In this regard, the Quran states, "And fight them until there is no persecution, and religion is professed only for God. But if they desist, then remember that no hostility is allowed except against the wrongdoers."[9] Fighting only continues as long as people (any people, not just Muslims) are being persecuted for their faith. Islam teaches us that physical resistance becomes necessary because if God did not repel unjust people by means of just people, then the unjust people would wreak havoc.[10]

But let's be honest; there are many Muslims in the world who do not live up to these Islamic teachings, and, after a few years had passed since 9/11, the discourse began to shift, as I felt there was an increasing number of people who were becoming antagonistic against Muslims and Islam. No longer were they as careful to not judge all Muslims by the actions of the lunatic fringe. Somewhere around 2005-2006, the unity we all had felt since 9/11 as fellow Americans began to dissipate. There was more finger-pointing, frustration, hurt feelings and even bitterness. As the war in the Middle East continued to drag on and acts of terrorism also continued, I felt more agitation on all sides of the political spectrum.

There were repeated instances of violence, murder and threats from Muslim individuals and groups, which made the lives of Muslims like me increasingly difficult. I had been actively speaking about Islam's true and peaceful teachings and condemning violence, but my words were being drowned out by calls for violence, and acts of violence by radicals. The past few years bear testimony to that sad reality.

In November 2009, Major Nidal Malik Hassan opened fire at the Fort Hood Army base, killing 13 people and wounding 29 others.[11] Six months later, 30-year-old Pakistani American Faisal Shahzad attempted to blow-up a car at Times Square, New York. Shahzad's attempted terrorism had a strong impact on me because, on paper, the description of Faisal Shahzad sounds a lot like me. Early 30's ... American citizen ... Pakistani ethnicity ... American education ... working

9 Holy Quran, chapter 2 verse 194, http://www.alislam.org/quran/search2/show-Chapter.php?ch=2&verse=194
10 Holy Quran, chapter 22 verses 40-41, http://www.alislam.org/quran/search2/showChapter.php?ch=22&verse=40
11 "Soldier Opens Fire at Ft. Hood; 13 Dead", CBS News, November 6th 2009, http://www.cbsnews.com/stories/2009/11/05/national/main5539067.shtml

a normal 9-to-5 job ... from an educated family. He was the average American Muslim in the eyes of his friends, neighbors and co-workers, but ended up becoming a terrorist. This suddenly caused some to become suspicious towards all of us average American Muslims.

At this point, there was a growing allegation that there was a missing concerted voice from within the American Muslim community that condemns all acts of terrorism and violence. Some called this a "deafening silence." On the other hand, Muslims who had been loudly speaking out against violence, aggression and terrorism were growing tired of not only having to answer for each and every act of violence by a terrorist but also having their voices go unheard. There were indeed both Muslims and non-Muslims who hated one another due to ignorance, intolerance, and an absence of love and peace. Recognizing this state of disharmony, the Ahmadiyya Muslim Community — as the oldest Muslim organization in America — took it upon itself to start the healing through a grassroots education initiative called "Muslims for Peace," aimed at spreading the message of peace and tolerance.

The "Muslims for Peace" initiative (www.MuslimsForPeace. org) provided a powerful voice to answer the oft-asked question, "Where are the moderate Muslims?" After Faisal Shahzad's attempted bombing in New York's Times Square, our community identified the prevailing allegation of a missing unified voice condemning violence. Thus, we formally launched the "Muslims for Peace" grassroots campaign in July of 2010.

Our goal was simple: debunk the myth that Muslims do not stand up against terrorism and that Islam promotes violence instead of peace. It was the Ahmadiyya Muslim Community's simple way to spread the message of Islam one person at a time in order to give everyone the opportunity to learn what Islam truly preaches.

As the 9-year anniversary of 9/11 approached, people became distracted by news of a sole Pastor in Gainesville, Florida, threatening to burn hundreds of copies of the Holy Quran due to his belief that the Quran and Islam were entirely evil. This was incredibly disappointing. At a time when we were actively meeting with people in order to build bridges of understanding, here came this man to tear them apart.

That same month, the editor in chief of the magazine entitled *The New Republic* looked down at Muslims so much that he wrote about Muslims on the magazine's blog: "I wonder whether I need honor these people and pretend that they are worthy of the privileges of the First Amendment."[12] Of course, there was also the story of a

12 *"The New York Times* Laments 'A Sadly Wary Misunderstanding of Muslim-

Muslim cab driver in New York having his neck slashed by a passenger who hurled anti-Muslim abuses at him as he attacked.[13]

With all of these events unfolding around us, my community at the Portland Rizwan Mosque decided to counter the hate and intolerance with an interfaith prayer vigil at our Mosque on September 11th, 2010 – the 9-year anniversary of the terrorist attacks - and the same day Florida Pastor Terry Jones scheduled to burn the Qurans and thus further the divide between people. Leaders from about a dozen different faith groups came together that day at our Mosque with a message of peace and reconciliation.

Over 500 people poured into the humbly-sized Portland Rizwan Mosque that day to hear words of inspiration from the esteemed panel of leaders who spoke about the need and importance of inter-religious harmony. I was honored to be the speaker on behalf of the Muslim community of Portland. We were reminded that we are all children of the same one God. This teaching of respect and love for one another is common among all of the world's faiths. The Quran honors the books and prophets of other faiths when it states: *"Say ye: 'We believe in God and what has been revealed to us, and what was revealed to Abraham and Ishmael, and Isaac, and Jacob and his children, and what was given to Moses and Jesus, and what was given to all other Prophets from their Lord. We make no difference between any of them; and to Him we submit ourselves.'"* [14]

Just two months later, Portland was rocked the day after Thanksgiving when news quickly spread that a young Muslim teen allegedly attempted to set off a bomb at the Christmas tree lighting ceremony in Portland's downtown Pioneer Square.[15] Fortunately, the alleged terror plot was foiled, but this hit close to home.

Incidentally, earlier that same day, I led a group of Muslims around downtown Portland to meet with our fellow Portlanders and give them our "Muslims for Peace" flyers. A day that began with Muslims spreading the message of peace and understanding ended with a

---

Americans.' But Really Is It 'Sadly Wary' Or A 'Misunderstanding' At All?", *The New Republic,* September 4th 2010, http://www.tnr.com/blog/77475/the-new-york-times-laments-sadly-wary-misunderstanding-muslim-americans-really-it-sadly-w
13 "N.Y. man charged with stabbing cab driver for being Muslim", *USA Today,* August 25 2010, http://www.usatoday.com/news/nation/2010-08-25-cabbie-stabbing-muslim_N.htm
14 Holy Quran, chapter 2 verse 137, http://www.alislam.org/quran/search2/show-Chapter.php?ch=2&verse=137
15 Attempted Terrorist Attack in Portland", *Examiner,* November 27 2010, http://www.examiner.com/article/attempted-terrorist-attack-portland

single Muslim attempting to take the lives of thousands of innocent people.[16] The next morning, we quickly went back to the site of the attempted bombing not only to hand out more "Muslims for Peace" flyers but to also be clear with our fellow Portlanders that we whole-heartedly condemn all such acts of terrorism.[17]

Six months later came the news that millions of Americans had surely been waiting for. Osama bin Laden – public enemy #1 – had been killed in a raid in Pakistan. For so many people, it was the clos-ing of a chapter that began 10 and a half years earlier. But while some Americans danced in the streets, celebrating the death of Osama bin Laden, we were among those who were aware that the death of bin Laden does not usher-in an era of peace and unity, nor did it signal the end of our war on terror. I knew we still had our work cut-out for us to free the minds of both Muslims who had fallen prey to the radi-cal ideology and non-Muslims who had been convinced that such an ideology is synonymous with Islam.

Upon the death of bin Laden, our community was invited to participate in a public event, organized by a Christian group at Mult-nomah Biblical Seminary, entitled "Osama – A Christian Response." For this event, I was asked to deliver a presentation on the topic of "Osama – A Muslim Response." It was a wonderfully organized event with many powerful moments. One moment, however, stood out to me. One of the Christian leaders speaking made a statement that he is Christian first and American second. As I reflected on those words, I questioned how it would be received if I were to say that as a Muslim. How would people react if I were to publicly state that I am Muslim first and American second? I could imagine the outrage some would manufacture and the allegation that my loyalties to this nation could not, therefore, be trusted.

This is a challenge still facing Muslims in America. Our loyal-ties are often in doubt by those who do not trust Islam. This is why the Ahmadiyya Muslim Community launched a second initiative entitled "Muslims for Loyalty" in order to educate people that Islam has as one of its teachings a requirement that Muslims must remain loyal to the country in which they reside and must obey the authority of the land. I have been born and raised in this country and am an Ameri-can through-and-through. Yet, for some people, I am not American

16 Local NBC footage of Portland bomb scare, YouTube, http://www.youtube.com/watch?v=ghFxy1UJYng
17 Local ABC footage of Portland bomb scare, YouTube, http://www.youtube.com/watch?v=XsEmR7whuW4

enough because there are still many who define American as being non-Muslim. I cannot even count the number of times I have heard the sentiment that Muslims should go back to the Middle East.

To be honest, though, I do not get too bothered by this because this is an unfortunate trend in the United States to target a specific group and vilify them as being different, foreign and untrustworthy. As Professor Stephen Prothero once rightly put it, "The United States has survived a series of culture wars in which Catholics, Mormons and members of other religious minorities were anathematized as un-American." [18]

Yes, I have heard people claim that we Muslims are un-American, foreign, "not like us," with loyalties that cannot be to the United States. As hurtful and dangerous these statements may be, those are the same types of things that were said in this country about Catholics in the 19th century and about Jews in the 20th century. This will be a great challenge for Muslims going forward to determine the right manner in which to deal with antagonism. Responding in-kind will not serve to improve relations with non-Muslims at all. Muslims must not allow themselves to be baited into quarrelling in an unbecoming manner. The Quran tells us to argue in a manner that is best. As the Quran tells us, we cannot let anyone's enmity towards us cause us to act in a way that is not just.

Going forward, there are many challenges the Muslim world will face. The greatest will be to re-claim their faith, which has been misunderstood, misrepresented and misapplied. Muslims must admit and identify that there is a segment of our population that has become – or is becoming – radicalized. We must not have a knee-jerk reaction and play the victim role. There are Muslims across the world who have disgraced the name of Islam by performing vile and barbaric acts that they unfairly attribute to Islam. There is a radicalization problem within the Muslim community around the world. Fortunately, a tiny yet vocal minority is currently radicalized, but if it isn't confronted and countered, the tiny minority will grow. This is a Muslim problem that requires a Muslim solution. We must take responsibility for cleaning up our own house.

In order to re-claim our faith, Muslims must also re-discover our faith. Far too many Muslims – however moderate and modern they may be – believe in fantastical stories and lose sight of

---

18 "How 9/11 changed religion in America", *USA Today*, September 10 2011, http://www.usatoday.com/news/opinion/forum/story/2011-09-10/911-religion-islam-christianity/50354708/1

the essence of Islam's teachings. Whether you believe that the punishment for apostasy is truly death, or that the dajal is literally a one-eyed giant monster, or apply literal interpretation to metaphorical parables in the Quran, or do not apply rationality and reasoning while interpreting Islam's teachings – you must re-discover the true nature of your faith, as your misunderstandings will prevent you from properly living and representing your faith.

The greatest challenge facing non-Muslims is to discover the teachings of Islam. Just like Christianity, there is much diversity of thought within Islam. So do not judge the entire Islamic faith system based on the views or actions of a few. See Muslims for who they are as humans and individuals. If you must judge anyone, let your judgment be based on that individual's own actions; not based on the actions of another Muslim you saw on television. Refrain from over-simplifying matters, as religious teachings are nuanced.

All of us must discover and remain firmly grounded on the path towards peace, justice and reconciliation. We are all human and desire the same things: peace, security, justice, fairness, economic stability, safe neighborhoods and freedom to worship (or not worship) as we see fit. But the world is currently heading down the path of self-destruction, with many countries driven by enmity and/or greed. To establish peace, we must first establish justice and fairness in our land and across the world.

We should not malign one another. Let us discuss our differences within the confines of respect and understanding. The true nature of interfaith dialogue is to learn what makes someone else different and to respect it, even if you do not agree with it. As the Promised Messiah and Founder of the Ahmadiyya Muslim Community once wrote, *"We belong to the same denomination of God's species and are referred to as humans. Furthermore, as inhabitants of the same country, we are mutual neighbors. This requires that we become friends to each other, with purity of heart and sincerity of intentions."*

———————————————

"The individual has always had to struggle
to keep from being overwhelmed by the tribe."
~ Friedrich Nietzsche ~

"If you want peace, you don't talk to your friends.
You talk with your enemies."
~ Desmond Tutu ~

"Instead of building walls, we need to build bridges"
~ US Navy Admiral James Stavridis ~

———————————————

Chapter Six

The American Tribe

Rod Coffey

Rod Coffey is a recently retired Army Infantry Colonel with wide-ranging experience in counter-insurgency and counter-terrorism theory and practice. With tours in Kosovo and Iraq, and extensive practice creating counter-IED training solutions for Afghanistan, his additional work as a trained historian has led to a decades-long study of Islam itself, political Islam and Middle Eastern "tribal" societies.

9/11/2001

As the attacks on 9/11 took place I was flying over Europe returning to Kosovo from a planning session in Germany. My three days in Germany were seen as a break my bosses offered me for hard work while serving as the Deputy Operations Officer for the U.S. Task Force in Kosovo. With about ten NATO officers I landed back in Skopje, Macedonia, where we would then transfer to a bus that would take us back into Kosovo. During the wait for the bus a British officer came toward me from a building nearby and said, "A plane has just crashed into the World Trade Center in New York City." I stared at him, "No, no way - I don't believe it." "You may want to go upstairs," he said pointing to the building he had just exited. "There is a TV up there and it's all they are covering."

When I arrived in the room with the TV I stayed standing there staring at the scene of devastation in downtown Manhattan multiple times. The loop was showing two planes crashing into the towers; one plane attacking each tower.

I had not served in Panama or "Desert Storm." The part of 10th Mountain Division I was in did not deploy. We had thought violent extremist Islamists would confine their attacks to the Islamic world, the "near enemy." There seemed to be little doubt it was not them, but I wondered why now? I felt anger for the most part, a steely focused, ice cold determination, and a realization that 14 years of training and military service had now come to this. My generation would see the elephant.

As I boarded the bus for a quiet, somber drive back into Kosovo I worked my way to the rear. As one of two U.S. officers on board, I could feel the wondering glances and unnaturally hushed mood in our group. "This is Pearl Harbor; these sons-of-bitches have no idea what they've done; we will hunt them down and kill them no matter how long it takes." Every face in the bus turned to me and then slowly turned away. I said nothing the rest of the trip, and no one else did either.

In the weeks, months and years after 9/11 a somewhat haphazard study of Islam, Islamic culture, Arab culture and history intensified for me. So did a deep foray into the literature on counter-insurgency ultimately affirmed by the U.S. Army and U.S. Marine Corps joint publication of a counterinsurgency manual. Nagl, Galula, Kilcullen, the British in Malaysia, the more creative Abrams vice Westmorland era in Vietnam, the South American and African insurgencies, the Philippines both in the early 1900's and later, became the air I breathed. The counterinsurgency reading led to anthropological study of tribal societies. I read the Koran five times, and many of the Hadith.

In counterinsurgency theory, the long-ingrained focus on destroying the enemy army is altered to seeing the local population, its security and well-being, as the military center of gravity. Their co-operation, if not loyalty, is what is decisive. Leveraging and finding ground for mutual cooperation with them is how one wins. It is actually nothing new, and we Americans, contrary to criticism asserting otherwise, have in fact become very good at it.

Conventional fighting and killing, and dying, still has to be done, but the organizing, design and objectives of operations change in counterinsurgency. This altered way of operating requires a sometimes difficult change in organizational culture. For my men I told a simple story as a means of understanding the change in focus between conventional operations and counterinsurgency. This story came from a published account of the interrogation of an Iraqi insurgent who had detonated an IED on an American vehicle:

As the interrogator deepened his research on the pattern of U.S. activity around the IED strike he realized almost daily a dismounted patrol had passed the same location. Seeing as the insurgent had the IED in place for two weeks before detonating it on a vehicle patrol, why he did not do so against the foot patrol might reveal something about target priorities for this particular insurgent force. Could the insurgents possibly be thinking that serious damage to a vehicle and wounding some U.S. soldiers was more impactful than killing one or two on foot?

When the American asked, "Why didn't you detonate the IED on the foot patrol?" the Iraqi responded, "Oh, we knew those Americans."

Such is the influence of tribal alliances and relationships in much Middle Eastern culture. The dismounted Americans belonged to a unit that had helped or treated kindly members of the insurgent cell opposing them or perhaps their relatives. Consequently, they were honor bound not to treat them as an enemy.

In Iraq we understood and leveraged these dynamics by entering into the gradual socialization and favor and alliance exchange of the Iraqi tribal system. We built relationships through sharing meals, drinking tea and addressing the local concerns for economic well-being and security.

Invariably, an understanding of the recent past in Iraq, and of Islam, aided in this endeavor. Initially in the deployment we experienced five solid weeks of often intense urban guerilla combat, especially during the first three weeks in an area of East Rashid, Baghdad, known as the Hadar neighborhood.

The sections of Hadar bore the Mulhalla or neighborhood designations Mechanics, Ossia and Shurta. The most serious fighting we endured took place in Mechanics where we lost five men, two by small arms fire and three by booby-traps located in buildings, a sixth, Corporal Wayne Geiger, was lost on a road bordering Mechanics to an explosively formed projectile (EFP) IED, meaning the last soldier certainly died from the activity of an Iranian-resourced extremist Shi'a militia rather than the extremist Sunni movement of Al Qaeda in Iraq (AQI), which later became the Islamic State of Iraq (ISI), better known as ISIS/ISIL or "DAESH" today. So full of life (and humor), Corporal Geiger was a heartbreaking loss to his brothers-in-arms, family and friends. Like the "Sinsil 7," the US Army, and America, lost some quality human beings.

On the other hand, over fifteen insurgents were killed by us with over 300 detained. They were successfully identified and detained with the cooperation of other Iraqis friendly to the Coalition.

These friendly Iraqis were primarily "Sons of Iraq," or Sahwa. Counterinsurgency doctrine calls for raising an indigenous local, essentially paramilitary force. There are several reasons for this:

- One critical reason is the knowledge a local force will have in regard to "who's who" in the neighborhood or village. If insurgent extremists thrive on being able to operate almost invisibly by mixing in the local population then information from that population is one of the best means to deny extremists the anonymity they seek.
- An additionally salient reason is the ground force intensity needed to secure the local population and protect them from extremist threat, coercion and/or persuasion

Although this ground-intensive approach has its critics, in my view, such criticism is misguided. You cannot drone strike or bomb your way to a defeat of extremists attempting to dominate a population. Of the Iraqis we worked with, there is no doubt some of them were low-level former anti-US fighters. Iraq possessed a large array of groups with diverse motivations for fighting, and complex relationships among power players of all stripes.

We increased this presence and acknowledged those locals who were willing to take up arms to keep extremism at bay. In our initial approach to the area we used loudspeaker messages stating, **"We realize Al-Qaeda does not represent Islam."** This was one of the most effective ice-breaker themes we had based on later feedback from the neighborhood. Another approach we would use for those Iraqis knowledgeable about the history of Islam is telling them we understood Al Qaeda behaved like the Khawarij. Briefly put, the Khawarijites were an early puritanical Islamic sect who held themselves justified in killing other Muslims for disbelief – they were extremists. What messages such as this did is build immediate bridges of understanding between us and the local Sunnis.

The assistance of the Sahwa was, of course, not without controversy. It was not always easy for our own men to stomach following leads from men who clearly had fought Americans in the past. However, this was not the case with all of them and, in fact, some had not

77

been involved in past action against US forces. There were two equally important reasons why some Sunni Iraqis were willing to work with the Americans in the Sahwa formations. First was Sunni feelings of marginalization and isolation as a result of the overthrow of Saddam. Many Sunnis leaped at the opportunity to, in effect, form an armed political and social structure which could interact with the US authority - over the heads, if you will, of the Shi'a-dominated Iraqi government. Second was in fact a genuine disgust with the extremism of Al Qaeda in Iraq. The creation of terror, the murder of other Muslims, the opportunism and the predilection to murder innocent people for effect created its own backlash in the Sunni population. It is important to remember this. In all the cases I am aware of, an Islamist Extremist attempt at violent influence is eventually met with a counter-reaction within the Muslim population. In the case of Iraq in particular however, not only did Al Qaeda in Iraq explicitly aim to incite sectarian violence between Sunni and Shi'a – the very existence of the sectarian split created fertile ground for their growth.

I used to consistently point this out to the Iraqi leaders I worked with. AQI wants you to collapse into sectarian violence. It is the easiest way for them to justify their existence and recruit. In more than one instance I would discuss with Sheikhs and Iraqi military officers, and politicians, the view that *both* sects were beset with extremists. In those times Muqdata al-Sadr and his Mahdi Army and associated groups possessed elements within them who were just as terroristic and extremist on the Shi'a side as was AQI on the Sunni.

In our operations in Hadar, Baghdad, one could see the effect of the extremists on both sides and the diverse permutations in between. It was not hard to find capable local leaders willing to risk their lives for the sake of ending extremist domination of their neighborhoods. What was difficult was attempting to heal the Sunni-Shi'a divide - the very existence of which provided fertile ground for the extremists of each side to grow or develop.

One area where we pushed out Al Qaeda was a Sunni enclave bounded by Shi'a on three sides. The police had positions and stations just outside the area and were Shi'a dominated. The Sunni population inside the neighborhood swore up and down that Shi'a police would not protect them and would often shoot indiscriminately into their neighborhood. The police, on the other hand, unwisely labeled most Sunnis as terrorists.

Before we left Hadar we had authorized three new groups of Sahwa. One of the last major security efforts we worked on was essentially negotiating between the Shi'a police and new Sahwa groups to clear up misunderstandings and find a way for both to contribute to stability. The fact we had cleared the area of Al Qaeda gave us enormous clout. We were the dominant tribe one had to ally with, or at least not oppose, in order to flourish.

In addition to the fighting we did, the most significant means we had to push out the extremists and, more importantly, keep them out, was the building of relationships. We exerted most of our efforts making sure the locals "knew those Americans." The point here is, at least in my experience, extremism took root in places where local authority and civil society had broken down. A situation of chaos or uncertainty and fear would develop where just enough people were motivated at some level to dominate others through fear.

By December 2007 we had moved to Diyala province to clear out another Al Qaeda enclave in an area the Americans had somehow termed Iraq's "breadbasket." It was a rural area filled with about a dozen or so villages bounded by canals and the Diyala River, as well as the city of Muqdadiyah. The area was a haunting microcosm of Iraq's divisions with Sunni and Shi'a enclaves in close proximity to one another, and less than twenty miles from where the Kurdish population began to the east.

Clearing out the area involved more raising of local forces or Sahwa and, above all, the establishment of trusting relationships between the locals and partnering elements of our battalion. Ironically, though we had seen much more actual combat in Baghdad, it was in rural Diyala where we shed our blood alongside Iraqis who were also fighting extremist Muslims. One of the worst days of my life was when we lost seven men in a house booby trapped with explosives. When I arrived at the site, the house looked like a scene from a bombed out World War II city, huge blocks of buildings collapsed upon one another as if a giant had crushed an adobe hut. Nothing can erase from my mind the brief conversation I had with the company commander who had already arrived, I asked Captain Dave Gohlich, "How many?" he replied, "Seven." In disbelief, I exhaled, "Seven?!"

One of those seven was a young Muslim Iraqi interpreter nicknamed "Roy." Mohammed al Latefe, his real name, had joined the Americans as an interpreter after witnessing Al Qaeda kill two of his school mates. At the memorial service, the way in which we also paid respect to Roy convinced several of the other interpreters, who were planning to return to Baghdad, to instead stay with us.

Because it explains so much about who we were and are, how

the American soldier has faced down extremism, I'll offer the eulogy I gave at their memorial:

On behalf of all the soldiers of 3rd Squadron, 2nd Stryker Cavalry Regiment, we thank you for coming to pay tribute to our fallen brothers in arms.

We are here to honor the memory and service of seven men, seven of our brothers in arms.

There is a story about loss in war where one character comments to another, "We are ready for the occasional empty chair, the fond farewell for comrades lost. But we are never, never ready for so many."

I cannot, as your commander, in anything I say today, diminish the impact of losing these men all at once. In fact, because we lost them so quickly, it all seems like a bad dream -- that we will wake up tomorrow and they will all be back again.
Each of us, whether present at the scene that day or not, will remember when we first found out. We will remember our inner anguish when we got up the nerve to ask, "Who was it?" Others will recall the steeled strength it took to calmly and professionally report and verify the battle roster numbers, knowing full well we owed them this calmness and professionalism, so their families would be taken care of.

Others of us will never forget rescuing the four wounded that day and getting them to a helicopter as fast as we could. All these things are true. All these things will be seared in our memories. It was a terrible day and we cannot change that.
We are not alone in mere personal grief, or our desire to honor the fallen. The presence of the general officers here is their effort to acknowledge the sacrifice of this unit and the bravery of these men. Although I have not been able to access every news report, the ones I have read indicate the nation supports us, mourns with us and honors the men we have lost in the recon platoon.

The governors of the states of Virginia and Nevada, Wisconsin and Oregon, and New Mexico, have ordered the flag of the United States of America and the flags of their respective state flags be flown at half-mast on the day of our men's funerals. We are not alone in honoring them. Again, I don't have news stories for all of our men yet but those I have read indicate hundreds have attended their funerals.

And why this reaction? Why hundreds of people at funerals? Why governors issuing decrees for flags to be flown at half mast?

Because we are all in awe of their great sacrifice, courage and devotion to duty and each other. These men, our men, are fallen on the field of battle. Forever more that is their legacy. Their names are now enshrined on the scroll of America's hallowed dead. And where they died, where they shed their blood, is sacred ground to us.

We still cannot help think why. Why do we have to lose such good men? Part of the answer is only good men like these volunteer to serve and defend their country. Here's two brief examples of their motivations:

SPC Davis had his car packed and had been admitted to the University of Oklahoma when he changed his mind and decided to enlist in the army. His family believes he did so out of pride for his father who had served in the military and had passed away in 2003. There he was -- the excitement and opportunities of college life and getting a degree ahead of him -- and he heard that call, the call to defend and serve his country. At the last moment he could not go through with the easy choice. He chose the harder life of a soldier in a time of war.

Of SSG Gaul, his stepmother noted, "Being a soldier was his life. It was what he truly wanted to do."

I could mention every one of them and tell a similar story. I wish I knew more about Roy's story, for the courage and guts displayed by our interpreters on a daily basis was an inspiration for us all.

It is still a natural human instinct to ask....But what did they die for? Wasn't it a waste?

There are several answers to that question but the most basic and simple is they died for us. They entered that house so you and I wouldn't have to. At that moment they saw it as their duty to clear that house and they acted with discipline, courage and bravery. The character of our fallen heroes in the recon platoon is revealed by the actions of the living that day.

As many of you know, they were essentially lured to the house by someone that we later discovered had ties to Al Qaida. One of the members of the platoon, on the roof when the blast occurred and the building collapsed -- and wounded himself -- ran down the local who had had lured them to the house. And then, when he found him, did nothing more than detain him.

That professionalism, that discipline, that honor and self-sacrifice speaks of extraordinary nobility of character in the entire platoon. Another soldier, the senior squad leader at the scene, with calmness and strength, took over the role of platoon sergeant as if he had been doing the job for months.

I could go on and on about the enormous character demonstrated by that entire platoon and entire company that day - a strength and determination that continues today.

And then there is the unfeigned determination of the recon platoon. It's not put-on. It's not fake. They are not trying to be something they are not and failing to express their emotions about this. But the speed with which they have rebounded and insisted to me that they go out on missions again is awe-inspiring.

I do not know where such men come from, except to say they are the kind of men who have made America great and will continue to preserve it.

The act of going in first, the act of willingly doing your duty in a dangerous environment, is by its very nature an act of heroic self-sacrifice for the sake of others. These men we honor today had that spirit of self-sacrifice and devotion to duty to an awe-inspiring degree.

And so I need to speak of what else they died for, and what I believe our honored dead would now expect of us.

I'll begin by saying what they would not want. They would not wish to be seen as victims of a misguided war, victims of stop loss - or victims of anything else for that matter.

We know we are fighting extremism here in a thousand ways. And as the hometown news articles are getting written, several of these fallen heroes are on record stating they believed the war in Iraq is a noble cause.

For those who want to support us by getting us out of Iraq as soon as possible, without a victory, I have but one comment. You're too late. We have sacrificed too much and all we ask of you is the necessary time to finish the job.

Our children and yours, our grandchildren and yours will be safer for it.

This squadron and the formations on its left and right have, in the balance sheet of history, already achieved far more than extremist reckless hatred will ever accomplish.

SSG Dozier once asked his father Carl, "Is it weird to really want to do this?" His father Carl, filled with pride at what his son had become, said, "No, this is what you're trained to do."

On another occasion, this brave man, SSG Jonathan Dozier, told his father he was prepared to die, "But," he said, "I don't want to die for nothing."

So I ask you, Wolfpack, to make this promise with me: SSG Dozier will not have died for nothing. We owe him a victory. We owe him a win. We owe him our own lives if necessary.

If the enemy comes out to fight, he will be met with a disciplined lethal ferocity he has never before endured. If he plays

the sly game of intimidating, beheading and torturing the in-
nocent people of Iraq when he thinks we're not looking, he
will be met with a cunning, a sophistication and a relentless-
ness that will lead to his utter defeat.

At the end of the memorial service, my sergeant major and I proceeded to march in step and salute the assembled photos of the fallen. This ritual would be followed by every soldier in the assembly. While it is often customary to have the most senior officers follow the unit commander to render this honor, General Petraeus insisted on the recon platoon following next.

I had kept my composure during the eulogy. As I raised my hand in salute, I lost it. The tears rolled down as I proceeded around the seated guests and toward a receiving line. I managed to control myself again before I had to speak with anyone. First Sergeant Bowman came up and said, "Oh Sir..." "I know," I replied. That was all we needed to say.

Upon leaving this memorial service, we still had nine months to go in a fifteen-month deployment. However, these were the last deaths we suffered. The reason they were the last deaths we suffered is because we were good at counterinsurgency. Why? Because of the inherent decency and self-sacrificing discipline of the American soldier. Because, in fact, we and the Iraqis who helped put down Al Qaeda are the good guys. Commentators who blame the rise of Islamic extremism primarily on Western policy are poor historians and even poorer citizens. Moreover, they are complicit in condemning the Muslim world to an even longer cycle of hopeless violence. They are enablers.

There are unresolved issues within Islamic and Middle Eastern culture against which many Muslims (though not enough) are struggling themselves. They deserve our enthusiastic support -- not a misguided self-flagellation that discredits the very values good Muslims are courageously fighting for.

We cannot thank these men enough for their sacrifice. I'll mention again the man who detained the Iraqi he witnessed lead his buddies to their deaths. Were he an extremist, he would have decapitated the man when he cornered him. He was an American soldier – he detained him. Sergeant Joseph Weeren went on to earn a commission in the U.S, Army and marry the cousin of one of the fallen from that day.

But, we had nine more months...

One of the pieces of advice American soldiers received before deploying to Iraq was to never speak about religion. This was bad advice and I did not follow it. Never proselytize - yes of course, but to never reference God to a religious culture made no sense. One of our most successful negotiations was between Shi'a Big Barwana and Sunni Little Barwana. During that discussion I cited the fact we all knew God would judge us one day and he would judge us on whether or not we stopped the killing.

This brief account of my experience may make it sound too easy to uproot Islamic extremism. I do not mean to leave that impression. A conversation I had with one Imam may serve to reveal the difficulty. This Imam admitted he had done whatever Al Qaeda asked him to do when they controlled his village. He told me how Al Qaeda was "crazy." They would kill anyone for the smallest reason. He, on the other hand, a good Muslim, would only kill someone for one of only three reasons. If they murdered someone, if they had sex with someone they were not married to, or if they left the Muslim faith.

Therein lies the problem - a lack of acceptance of the progress society has made over the centuries in asserting certain freedoms and rights. We must never apologize for asserting the rights and freedoms we have always and will always fight for. The fight against this type of extremism is generational, and it is not "Western Imperialism" to oppose blasphemy laws that invoke the death penalty. It is decency.

We cannot evade our moral responsibility in this struggle by a pivot to the Pacific. (The current administration, in my view, has dangerously made all of us less safe by trying to focus our military deterrence on the Pacific, motivated more by hopes of avoiding future ground combat than sound strategy.)

As an Iraqi judge told me when I asked him why he was so brave in taking on the insurgency, "It's raining outside, and I am already wet."

No amount of war-weariness will make the rain go away.

We in the U.S must do as we have always done when confronted by the false comfort of murderous autocracy.

Remind them how free men fight.

With permission from each of their families, COL Coffey ends this chapter with a photo tribute to the "Sinsil 7:"

SINSIL 7

SSG Jonathan Kilian Dozier
30 September 1977

SSG Sean Michael Gaul
25 June 1978

SGT Christopher Alan Sanders
30 April 1985

Mohammed Al Latefe

SFC Matthew Ignatius Pionk
10 October 1977

CPL Todd Edward Davis
7 March 1985

SGT Zachary McBride
16 October 1987

9 JANUARY 2008

"Am I not destroying my enemies
when I make friends of them?"
~ Abraham Lincoln ~

"I object to violence because when it appears to do good, the
good is only temporary. The evil it does is permanent."
~ Mahatma Gandhi ~

"A better world shall emerge based on faith
and understanding."
~ Douglas MacArthur ~

Chapter Seven

Shalom Alechem/Salaam Alekum
Peace be upon you

Rabbi Debra Kolodny

Rabbi Debra Kolodny is a veteran of several social justice movements, bringing a spiritual perspective to worker's rights, racial and economic justice, women's, enviromental, peace and LGBTQ issues for over 30 years. She is the Executive Director of Resolutions Northwest, a Portland based non-profit that does racial and Restorative Justice work as well as community mediation, facilitation and conflict resolution. Prior to that, she was the Executive Director at Nehirim, rabbi at P'nai Or in Portland, and Executive Director of ALEPH: Alliance for Jewish Renewal. Founded by Rabbi Zalman Schachter-Shalomi (may his memory be a blessing), a fundamental tenet of Jewish Renewal is Deep Ecumenism: the imperative to connect to the deep well of truth shared by all traditions. Rabbi Debra has brought that vision to hundreds of venues, teaching on spirituality and sexual orientation and gender identity, environmentalism, mysticism, healthy community, prayer, Torah study and more.

9/11/2001

On September 11, 2011 I lived right outside of Washington DC near Takoma Park, Maryland. I was riding my bicycle that morning. At exactly the moment the first World Trade Center Tower was felled I took a spill on my bike. Nothing caused it. I just lost my balance and fell. I had raced in triathlons, ridden centuries (100 mile rides), regularly cycled for 18 years, and had never had an unprovoked spill. It was minor. I was not hurt. But when I found out about the Tower I realized that the crash's reverberation had reached me hundreds of miles down Interstate 95. Later that day I sat in my home, overwhelmed by

88

military jets and helicopters filling the air space. Living so close to the Pentagon I too was at Ground Zero. The attack's reverberations now raged around me.

Forty-four days later I made pilgrimage to New York and visited the rubble of the Twin Towers. A poem came through me, inspired by the site, by those mourning all around me and by Torah.

Pilgrimage, October 25, 2001

Have you been to 911?
Made pilgrimage to place undone,
Seen plumes of smoke rise to the sun,
Felt heat from crematorium?

Tasted ash and rancid air,
Read poster board, "New York: We care."
Smelled flowers pushed through leaning fences,
There to block heartbroken entrance,
Deeper into gaping wound,
Where heroes toil, where lives were ruined.

Have you heard our anthem sung?
By ministering angels, 5 voices strong?
Breathtaking harmony they are gifting
To New York's finest: eyes soft, hearts lifting
At makeshift alters have you prayed?
Seen candles, photos, pain displayed
And there, beneath the lily's glory...
A baby shoe. What is her story?
Is it parent or her own life
Stolen 'way by aerial knife?

Have you seen the tall crossed bars?
Found comfort in this sign of G-d?
Or do you see midst rubbled ground
To stir your faith, what I have found?

There's Jacob's ladder, stairs and all
Steel beamed tower, skeletal
Reaching upward, grounded deep
The path from there to here is steep

Yet, in this place, I did not know
G-d's calling card, it just said, 'YO!'*

You know what's next, the story's clear
We've had our dream, may time be near,
To wrestle angels, one and all,
Then limp, transform, and live G-d's call.

Embrace our siblings, long estranged,
Share our wealth, with gift exchange,
Build an altar, pitch our tents
Make peace our lasting covenant.

Note: "Yo" is a greeting found in Philadelphia and New York City. It can mean "Hello", "Hey" or just be a term of familiar connection saying "Pay attention!"

Before 9-11, I had done a considerable amount of interfaith activism and peace-building, teaching, advocating and partnering with Muslim activists and friends. After 9-11 and that October visit to New York, I began to devote my personal teaching and prayers to peace-building. My divrei Torah (sermons) on Shabbat more frequently looked to inspire a shift in global consciousness towards love, compassion, healing, wholeness. I devoted my meditation practice to opening hearts and inspiring love between Israelis and Palestinians. I organized a meditation group to work on this collectively.

In 2011, I partnered with a dear friend, a Sufi Sheikh, Dr. Ibrahim Farajaje, to teach a week-long course filled with Sufi and Kabbalistic text, prayer and practice, a week designed to help open gates of understanding, heart connection and love, not just for those who attended, but for all who could feel the resonant vibration of our prayers. We hoped to help create a different reality on the planet—one that would reverberate for peace, that would clear the pain and strife away, that would open gates for a new way.

In January of 2015 I created and co-led an Abrahamic prayer, practice and learning community in Portland, Oregon, for several months called "Bosom of Abraham." Sufi Teacher Arifa Byron, Pastor Jennifer Brownell and I invited people to: Open gates to Oneness through a song-drenched, glorious evening of chanting, prayer, zikr, whirling and dance. Join us as we merge into the Beloved and become Peace. Short teachings will spice and deepen our holy adventure.

I am convinced that gates to wholeness and peace that are unavailable through activism, conversation or other change technologies can open through shared prayer and practice.

Below is an example of a teaching I have given on this theme. To all who read this, Shalom Alechem, Salaam Alekum: Peace be upon you. Bimherah v'yameinu. Speedily and in our day.

***

Many scholars say that the word *Ivrit*, or *Hebrew*, comes from the root of the word *avar,* to cross over. Imbedded in the core identity of the Jewish people is the invitation, the expectation or perhaps even the mandate, to cross over - to always be heading some place better. An invitation to transcend our current status and seek something deeper, something higher, to find the bridge between here and there, to BE the bridge between here and there. To be brave enough to cross boundaries that might seem impossible to pass through. To be faithful enough to recreate the kind of world imagined at the beginning of Creation - a world we once had, and we can have again. Whether that gorgeously balanced, lushly landscaped, Spirit drenched place called Gan Eden is mythological does not even matter, because the state of wholeness, the experience of the intra-connectivity of 'all that is' is NOT mythological. It is in fact the truest thing that is.

Our Torah calls us to cross the boundary between what our broken hearts settle for and what our essential consciousness feels and yearns for: Heaven here on earth.

What does it mean to be a boundary crosser? To answer that question it helps to enter a liminal space, a place between what is and what could be. A space where we can see the light of the Divine in ourselves, in one another and in all of Creation. If we take that invitation, crossing over the boundary between what is now and what is possible, we can change the world.

Faithful Jews look for guidance on how to do this, and frankly, on all matters, to our Torah. I have always looked for Torah to provide teachings on peace, but in the wake of 9/11, all the more so. In the wake of 9/11, I feel an imperative, an unshakeable deployment to be a spiritual healer for the planet, a spiritual warrior for peace.

One place I find guidance is with our third of patriarch: Yaacov or Jacob. The Torah teaches that Yaacov left Beer Sheva and went towards Charan to find a wife. Rashi calculates his age as 63, when he did this. Sixty-three. Yaacov was already a mature man.

91

On this journey Yaacov dreams of a ladder with angels ascending and descending. YHVH (G-D) stands above declaring, "Ani Adonai, Elohei Avraham avicha, v'Elohei Yitzchok" ("I am Adonai, the G-d of Abraham, your father, and the G-d of Isaac"). And then G-d promises Yaacov the land upon which he lays his head. And what's more, Torah tells us: V'hinei anochi imach, ushmarticha bchol asher telech...And behold, G-d said to Yaacov, "I am with you, and will guard you wherever you go..."

Yaacov awoke from his dream and he said: "Yesh HaShem b'makom haze, v'anochi lo yadati." ("There is G-d in this place and I did not know it.")

We are told in this moment: Ayn ze ki im bet Elohim, This is none other than the house of Elohim, v'ze sha'ar hashamayim, and this is the gate of heaven.

So, let's unpack all of this.

First, we are taught that the gate to heaven is the place where one dreams. How do we cross over from our current chaotic, often unhealthy, weather weirding, violent material world into a world in balance, in right relationship with the precious earth and all of her Creatures, a world of justice and fairness and beauty, where all can be safe and healthy and educated and honored and whole?

We dream. Being a boundary crosser means being a dreamer. And through those dreams we enter the gate to heaven. And when we enter the gate of heaven, we are promised safety. But no promises before we dream. First, we must have the courage to let go of control and allow inspiration to come in. Even when we have no idea that G-d is with us, G-d is still here in this place. Yesh HaShem b'makom haze. When we take the first step, when we dare to dream, we are rewarded. A glimpse of heaven is given and safety is ours. So being a boundary crosser means being brave, taking the initiative, letting go and opening to possibility.

At 63, already an age when one might expect wisdom and spiritual development, Yaacov knows enough to be brave and let go. But he still has more waking up to do before he can fully manifest his boundary-crossing role. What else has to happen to Yaacov? What else has to happen to us before WE can become spiritual warriors for peace, the spiritual planet healers that we are called to be?

When Yaacov was 99-years old, he had another encounter with G-d. This is one where Yaacov gets his name, Yisrael. He wrestles with a man or an angel and he prevails. And what happens after that wrestling? Yaacov reconciles with his long-estranged brother, Esav, with whom he's had enormous enmity. Yisrael fears violence might erupt at this meeting. Instead love and peace emerges.

From this we learn that with sufficient spiritual development the potential for violence, even war can be averted and peace can prevail. From boundary-crosser to peacemaker. How did that happen?

Let's explore the story and see!

There is a period of 36 years between Yaacov's two Divine encounters. Thirty-six years. In gematria, Jewish numerology, 36 is twice chai. Chai means life. So two lives were lived between the time when Yaacov first leaned into G-d consciousness and his actual wrestling with Source. Two lifetimes since he left home fearful that his brother Esav would kill him because he had stolen his birthright. Two lifetimes since deceit and theft prompted him leaving his birth home. Two lifetimes during which midrash tells us that he studied Torah, developed a relationship with many wells of water, wells which are the gateway to Ruach HaKodesh, the Holy Spirit, bursting forth from within the earth. Two lifetimes during which he married, parented, learned what it meant to provide for a family, and so perhaps, with all of this living, Yaacov had fully experienced the Divine law of midah c'neged midah, which means, 'like begets like', or what you might call Karma. Perhaps during those 36 years Yaacov's debt toward his brother was paid back. Perhaps it was balanced by Laban's deceit towards Yaacov. Perhaps those years rendered Esav able to receive Yaacov with kindness.

But more than just the spiritual growth took place during those 36 years. Also pivotal to the story of how Yaacov encountered Esav are the choices Yaacov made upon that meeting. He sends his two wives and two concubines along with their retinue and gifts ahead of himself, hoping to appease Esav before he even sets eyes upon Yaacov. Yaacov remains alone in the rear. Is this a sign of his fear, sending others ahead of him? Some say yes, he is a coward.

But is that what was really going on? Was he cowardly or was he wise in the ways of reconciliation, so wise that he knew that he needed another encounter with the Holy before he was ready to greet his fear.

Perhaps Yaacov knew that he had to be his highest self for the most terrifying moment of his life. After all, the future of the Israelite people was at stake. Was Yaacov wise enough to know that two lifetimes might have made him a different man, but not man enough to heal the breach that his own deceit had created?

Let's say that this is what happened, that Yaacov sent his family ahead out of Divine wisdom or intuition, and not cowardice. What happens next in this story? Yaacov does not sleep that night. This was not a night for dreaming, but for awakening. Yaacov had matured from being able to see the Divine to being able to dive into an actual physical encounter with Mystery. He throws his whole being into hand-to-hand engagement for hours with this man, or is it an angel of G-d?

And just what IS that engagement with this man/G-d representative? Vaye'avek is the verb that is used. It is almost always translated as 'he wrestled.' But that verb, aleph, bet, kuf, also means embrace. Yaacov engaged in the most intimate struggle possible-embracing that which challenged him instead of casting it away. Embracing instead of attacking. Embracing instead of trying to change. Embracing and wrestling at the same time.

When the experience is over, the ish, the man that Yaacov embraces, wrestles, dances with says: Yaacov, ki sarita im Elohim v'im anashim vatuchal, "You have contended with G-dly beings and with men and you have won."

Ha Rav Aharon Solevechik has a gorgeous analysis of Yaacov's struggle. He says that the being that renames Yaacov doesn't use the word nilchamta, you have fought, when he describes Yaacov's engagement. He uses the term sarisa - you have striven.

Nilchamta is from the same root as milchama, war. It implies violence and struggle in order to defeat and control or destroy.

Sarisa, on the other hand, suggests a striving towards authority and influence, followed by efforts to inspire good, noble and spiritual qualities inherent in one's adversary.

Yaacov, he says, struggled with that man/angel in a way that maintained his own personal integrity and at the same time did not diminish the integrity of his adversary.

And then what happens? What I noticed is that Yaacov leaves this striving with a limp, with the name Yisrael and a blessing. Yaakov names the place Peniel, G-d's face, and declares, Ki raiti elohim panim el panim vatinatzel nafshi, Because I have seen G-d face to face and my soul has survived. And then the sun shines on him. Yaacov sees the face of G-d and then he literally sees the Light. Yaacov experiences enlightenment.

What I love so much about Rav Solevechik's teaching is that it foreshadows EXACTLY the way I see Yaacov behaving on his way to reconcile with Esav. Yaacov strives with Esav in the same exact way that he strove with that angel/man. Yaacov honors both his own and his brother's integrity, inviting Esav into his highest self.

How did he do this—honor both his brother and himself? Yaacov led with gifts and with sublimation of his own authority, the subordination of his wealth, of his power, of any ego he might have. He prostrates seven times before his brother. He nullifies himself.

When Yaacov saw his brother, what did he see? The very thing he saw in his moment of enlightenment after his wrestling. Torah tells us that Yaacov saw the face of G-d in his brother Esav, Pnei Elohim. So, we learn: once enlightened, it is possible to see G-d's face in everyone one encounters, even those we fear the most. Even those we think are going to kill us.

And after this, after seeing G-d's face in his long estranged brother, Yaacov repeatedly refers to Esav as my master, Adoni, a form of the word Adonai, which is a name for G-d. Yaacov sees the face of G-d. Yaacov honors the G-d in Esav repeatedly. Yaacov gives Esav a blessing. A blessing a long time in coming.

Torah calls us to cross the boundary between what our broken hearts settle for and what our essential selves feel and yearn for-heaven right here on earth.

What does it take to be a boundary crosser who becomes a peacemaker?

Be brave. Dream. Open to possibility. Open to enlightenment. Allow grace to fall upon us. Know when to submit. Make amends. Heal wounds you have created. Honor the other-especially those who scare us. Lead with gifts. See that of G-d in everyone.

When we cross over the boundary between what is now and what is possible, we can change the world.

"We need to move beyond the idea that girls can be leaders,
and create the expectation that girls should be leaders."
~ Condoleezza Rice ~

"The heart never knows the color of the skin."
~ Chief Dan George ~

"No one is born hating another person because of the color
of his skin, or his background, or his religion.
People must learn to hate, and if they can learn to hate,
they can be taught to love – for love comes more naturally to
the human heart than its opposite."
~ Nelson Mandela ~

Chapter Eight

Changing Attitudes towards Muslim Women: Pre and Post 9/11

Dr. Shanaz Tejani-Butt

Dr. Shanaz Tejani-Butt is a global lecturer who has authored numerous publications on the neurobiological basis of stress disorders. As National President for the Women of the Ahmadiyya Muslim Community (2000-2010), Shanaz mobilized 68 chapters across USA to dispel myths about Muslim women through education and community volunteerism. Her passion for justice shaped several initiatives for underprivileged women and children. The Khadijah Scholarship provides adult women an opportunity for economic self-sufficiency. Her work against domestic violence led to Annual Bike-a-Thons to Break the Cycle, in partnership with CSW and Erie County of NY. She directed the "Feed the Hungry in America," program under Humanity First USA, to adopt food pantries that catered to the needs of the poor and hungry. Shanaz is frequently invited to speak on social and religious justice at various interfaith venues. She was a recent invited participant at the First United States of Women Summit, June 2016, hosted by the White House. Shanaz received her BS and MS degrees from the University of Bombay, Ph.D. from the Virginia Commonwealth University and post-doctoral training from the University of Pennsylvania. She is a tenured Professor at University of the Sciences in Philadelphia and currently pursuing her MBA in Pharmaceutical Business and Healthcare.

September 11, 2001

With the explosion of communication technology, the world has literally become flat and feels much smaller than ever before. And whether we like it or not, we are all emotionally connected to each other regardless of the color of our skin or our ethnic, cultural, economic and educational backgrounds. Throughout the world, manmade and natural disasters are occurring with alarming frequency, with no resolutions in sight. One such shocking event that haunts us even today occurred on September 11, 2001. On that Tuesday morning, I watched with horror and disbelief at the images of the planes crashing into the Twin Towers of the World Trade Center Complex in New York City. I recall a numb sadness enveloping me when I heard that these plane crashes were no freak accidents. It felt as if all of America had come to a total standstill; paralyzed with shock and grief as fear and terror reverberated in New York City and echoed throughout the whole world.

At that time, I did not fully comprehend the lasting impact that 9/11 would have on my life as a Muslim woman living in America. 9/11 brought out the best and worst in all of us. There were helpful, supportive and understanding Americans – and those who were suspicious, negative and skeptical. I was concerned about repercussions against my children (ages 10 and 12 at that time) because of their Muslim names and being a minority in school. However, the teachers were very understanding and continued to treat us with the same regard as before - and so did my colleagues and friends.

When the enormity of the incident sank in, I became both ashamed and outraged at reports alleging that a group of Muslims had claimed responsibility for these vicious attacks against innocent Americans. Prior to 9/11, my family practiced Islam in the privacy of our home. However after 9/11, there was an urgency to get out of my comfort zone, to apologize and offer condolences on one hand, and defend Islam and Muslims on the other. I wanted to shout out to the world that these heinous acts should not be attributed to Islamic teachings. I wanted people to understand that we were not only "good" Muslims, "kind" Muslims, but also compassionate, loyal and trustworthy Americans.

Right after 9/11, several Muslim women were afraid to wear their head scarves for safety measure as it is the first form of identity of a Muslim woman. In my case, I felt a stronger opposing urge to inform my community that I was proud to be a Muslim. My reasoning was that if more people identified me and observed my behavior, I played a positive role in removing some of the misconceptions aimed at Islam and Muslims. If I did not explain my beliefs, the media and politicians would do so instead. Already, the 'Islam' practiced by Al-Qaeda and Taliban was being accepted by many as the gold standard. Thus, amidst the misrepresentation of Islam, post 9/11 forced the "coming out" of many Muslim voices and opinions. Suddenly, Islam became a very public religion intermingled with political agendas, ignorance, fear and media frenzy that continues to add to the misgivings and doubts about Islam even today.

(Mis) Understanding Islam

Until 9/11, Muslims were well accepted in America. Other than a faint curiosity about the way we dressed, or celebrated our religious holidays, Americans mostly discounted us as foreigners who practiced a culture different from their own. However, 9/11 brought a wave of almost fanatic urgency for Americans to understand Islam. I recall attending an interfaith event shortly after 9/11 at which the discussion centered around the meaning and concept of Jihad. The curiosity and interest in Islam, its people, culture, beliefs and habits rose significantly and continues to remain an important topic for many Americans. More Qur'ans have been sold and more books about Islam have been written in the last 15 years than any other decade. In an interview shortly after 9/11, Karen Armstrong described the rising misconceptions about Islam, "Sadly, the events of September 11 are going to confirm for many people a vision of Islam that is unjust. Islam does not preach violence, it does not preach vicious holy war, it certainly does not condone terror, suicide bombing or anything of that sort. Like all of the great world religions, it preaches compassion and justice, and that is why it has been a success." (*Newsweek* October 29, 2001). So true!

Google the word "Islam" or "Muslim," and you will find numerous links and sites that either speak for or against Islam. Further proof of the immense interest in Islam is the new jargon used to describe Islam and Muslims. These new descriptors not only portray our utter confusion but also succeed in creating all types of strange mental images as we try grope to understand who these Muslim people really are! What do Muslims really believe? Is Islam a violent or a peaceful religion? What or who is an Islamist? A Jihadist? What is Radical or Moderate Islam? With the media portraying Islam as an extreme religion of oppression and violence, Americans had also begun to question the status of Muslim women in Islam.

Anti-Muslim campaigns and anti-Islamic rhetoric by political candidates and religious leaders have heralded a new era of Islamophobia; widening the chasms of misunderstanding and misconceptions even further. The controversy of building an Islamic Center near Ground Zero did not help matters for Americans, and at the same time, the banning of the Hijab in France and Belgium created further rifts for Muslims. The cartoons depicting Prophet Muhammad in Danish and Norwegian newspapers, the book *Jewel of Medina* by Sherry Jones, and the burning of the Holy Qur'an by Terry Jones are just a few examples of countless major incidents that have occurred since 9/11. These events have added fuel to the fire on both sides; igniting emotions, conflict and hostility on American soil as well as instigating violent protests against the provocative and disrespectful representation of Prophet Muhammad's character and Islam. The invasion of Iraq and Afghanistan post 9/11 has further increased the mistrust and misgivings between the Muslim world and the "West."

What is Islam?

The word 'Islam' literally means 'Peace' and 'Submission to the will of God.' In practical terms, Islam is a way of life, a code of conduct that is guided by four basic principles: peace, equality, justice and service. God has empowered humans to differentiate between right and wrong, and given us the freedom to choose without force or oppression.

> There is no compulsion in religion. Surely, the right way has become distinct from wrong
> (Holy Qur'an, 2:257).

My role in dispelling misconceptions about Islam, Prophet Muhammad and rights of Muslim women has grown considerably after 9/11. Whether individually or in public forums, I find myself explaining and reiterating that Islam stands for peace and submission, and that Muslims are enjoined to greet each other with "Assalamo Alaikum," which means, "Peace be upon you." The frequent repetition of this phrase is an external demonstration of desiring peace for oneself and for others. And through this greeting, Islam inculcates a feeling of peace in the hearts of those who greet as well as those who are greeted, "Wa Alaikum Salam!" "And peace be upon you too." While Muslims are enjoined to believe in and accept all the Prophets of God, we believe that Prophet Muhammad is our spiritual and political leader, whose character and life examples are emulated by Muslims around the world. During his final pilgrimage to Mecca in 632 AD, Prophet Muhammad told his followers that God has made the lives, property and honor of every person sacred, and that the shedding of innocent blood is prohibited. The Prophet exhorted Muslims to treat all people with equality and justice, regardless of nation, tribe or position, and to treat all women with kindness and respect. Followers of Islam were told to practice righteousness and show compassion to the slaves, orphans, needy, women and children (Holy Qur'an 2:178). I hope that non Muslims will be able to distinguish between these guiding principles of compassion, equality and justice versus the misinterpreted teachings that extremist groups use to justify the killing of innocent people.

Against such a backdrop of myths, controversies and confusion, this chapter draws attention to a sensitive and difficult topic, in an effort to delineate facts from fiction regarding the struggles of all women. My chapter is not intended to paint a dire and hopeless picture. Rather, it is intended to break through the barriers of ignorance and apathy, and build bridges of mutual understanding, respect, cooperation and hope.

Struggling for Women's Rights

Throughout the centuries, women have struggled for equal treatment and basic human rights. In the ancient past, Christians and Jews considered women to be physically, mentally and spiritually inferior to men. While Greeks and Jews considered females to be unlucky, Christians and Hindus preferred to identify women and girls by their male family members (fathers, husbands, brothers or sons); a practice that still exists in many parts of the world. Before the advent of Islam, Arabs viewed girls as a burden and buried them alive. Women had no right to an education, to free speech, or to owning property. A woman was the property of her husband. She had no rights as a mother and had no say in the upbringing of her children. Birth of a daughter was a curse and a great loss and humiliation for the family. Even today, in many cultures, patriarchal societies control their womenfolk. Religious and tribal leaders oppose the education of girls and women, and deceitfully turn control and male dominance into an obligation and duty.

Events of the past 100 years in the West validates the ongoing struggles that women face for their rights, irrespective of beliefs or faith. It was only as recently as the 1920's that women in the United States were given the right to vote. Following President Kennedy's Commission on the Status of Women in the 1960's, women began to gain positions of power and leadership in education, business and politics. The Equal Pay Act of 1963 and the Civil Rights Act of 1964 prevented employers from discriminating against race, religion and gender. In 1979, the UN general assembly adopted the Convention to Eliminate All Forms of Discrimination against Women; now viewed as an International bill of rights for women. As recently as 1995, Hilary Clinton asserted that women's rights are human rights! In 2008, a global campaign was launched to end violence against women, and in 2010, Women's Equality day was observed. Interestingly, in 7th century AD, Islam gave women the same rights as men in the pursuit of secular and religious knowledge, and in financial, public and social matters. These Islamic rights are compatible with UN's Universal Declaration of Human Rights which came into existence approximately 70 years ago. In her book, *Paradise Beneath Her Feet,* Isobel Coleman questions whether Islam and Prophet Muhammad were ahead of the times in extending these rights to women almost 1500 years ago!

Global Bondage in the 21st Century

Fast forward to the present times and observe the struggles of women today. On one hand, there is a tremendous push to recognize and improve the rights of women and children. On the other hand, acts of violence and discrimination continue unabated, snatching away the rights of women irrespective of national and religious boundaries. Who said that slavery has been abolished? It has been replaced by a more immoral and depraved form of bondage in the 21st century. Today, in every corner of the globe, regardless of race, religion, ethnicity, or education, women are denied their basic human rights, beaten, raped, killed or sold. This persistent oppression and cruelty to women is a moral and ethical dilemma for all concerned. Why does this inequality and oppression continue to persist?

Domestic violence is the leading cause of injury to women, ages 15-44 in the US. Battering occurs among people of all races, ages, socio-economic classes, religious affiliations, occupations, and educational backgrounds. The cost of intimate partner violence exceeds $5.8 billion each year in the US, for medical and mental health services. Human trafficking is a disgraceful 32 billion dollar industry worldwide, with more than 27 million people enslaved. Such mass atrocities against women and children do not discriminate against race, religion, education or economic class, and have become one of the fastest growing crime sectors where there is no value or respect for human dignity. Interestingly, these dreadful acts against women are not labeled as faith based events. Have the media ever prescribed a specific religion to domestic violence or sex trafficking in the USA?

It saddens me to observe the indifference and growing acceptance of these immoral practices against women and children in the most developed countries of the world. Domestic violence and sex trafficking are not simply statistical data points to be submitted to a funding agency or included in an annual report. These are real, painful, degrading social injustices that contradict the values that America stands for and contrasts with the freedoms that this country espouses. Many of us know of families who have lost everything; lost their voices, their hopes, their will to survive, and have forgotten what it means to be free to enjoy some of the basic human rights that many of us take for granted. As fathers, mothers, husbands, wives, brothers, sisters, sons and daughters, we must change our attitude from apathy and indifference to compassion and sympathy. We may be of a different color on the outside, but when we hurt, we all bleed the same color!

Distorted Images of Muslim Women

In television, films, books, newspapers and magazines, Islam is presented as a backward and barbaric religion. The media presents Muslim women as weak and submissive to a faith that oppresses and dominates them. Muslim women who choose to cover themselves are pitied, and are thought to be victims of their beliefs. Invariably, the mental picture conjures up images of Muslim women as being oppressed, backward, downtrodden, inferior and voiceless beings.

Nearly fifteen years have passed since 9/11. And yet, many Americans stereotype Muslims as terrorists, fanatics or extremists when they see a woman with a head cover or a man sporting a beard. Whenever Islam is in the news, I can sense a silent reproach or sometimes even sympathy from my colleagues and friends because of my Muslim identity. While I believe that through my behavior, actions and words, I am able to convince those around me that I am a peaceful Muslim woman and desire the same comforts and opportunities from life as they do, I am not certain that they are convinced that Islam is a religion that provides men and women equal rights in all aspects of human and spiritual endeavors. Part of the reason could be the frequency with which we hear of brutality linked to some Muslim group, state or person. Part of it could be due to misinterpretation of the Shariah (Muslim law) by Muslim groups who use these laws to suit their own personal, tribal or political gains. Since 9/11, we have also witnessed an uprising of fundamental Islam which has imposed additional restrictions on women, preventing them from access to education, freedom to work or pursue a public office; or other restrictions that sharply contradict Islamic teachings.

Islam is the fastest growing religion in the world today and is the faith of over a billion people, half being women around the world. How can Islamic teachings repress 50% of the Muslim population? Prophet Muhammad said that women are the twin halves of men. The Holy Qur'an clearly states that both men and women will be equally judged through their moral attributes and good deeds.

> Surely, men who submit themselves to God and women who submit themselves to Him, and believing men and believing women, and obedient men and obedient women, and truthful men and truthful women, and men steadfast in their faith and steadfast women, and men who are humble and women who are humble, and men who give alms and women who give alms, and men who fast and women who fast, and men who guard their chastity and women who guard their chastity and men who remember God much and women who remember Him - God has prepared for all of them forgiveness and a great reward (33:36).

> I will suffer not the work of any worker from among you, whether male or female, to be lost. You are from one another (3:196).

Over the years, I have questioned why the Muslim world is in such a turmoil today. When the Qur'an lays a strong emphasis on seeking knowledge (20:115), equally for both genders, why do we have such a large number of uneducated people in the Muslim communities? Prophet Muhammad stressed the acquisition of knowledge as a duty of every Muslim man and woman. Prophet Muhammad also said, "A mother is a school; if she is educated, then the whole people are educated." Similarly, when the Qur'an gives equal status to men and women, why are Muslim women deprived of their basic human rights? Thus, it is not the teachings of Islam that are gender limiting; rather, it is the repressive cultural practices that restrict women around the world. Most of the bias against Muslims and Muslim women in particular, is based on the cultural lenses through which the

West views Islam. Islam is a culturally diverse religion with American Muslims hailing from countries all over Africa, the Middle East, Asia, Europe. Even in Arab states, they differ economically, socially and politically and have unique cultural and traditional situations that impact the status, rights and freedom of women. Even countries with traditional Islamic societies that follow the Islamic law are found to have different approaches in the way their women and girls are treated. While some groups of women in Afghanistan may be denied access to an education, dramatic progress has been seen in Jordan, Kuwait, Bahrain and the United Arab Emirates in regard to access. Although there is a huge gender gap, it is important to appreciate that such gender gaps and disparities also exist in developed countries in the Western Hemisphere.

Nobel Peace Prizes to Notable Muslim Women

Since 9/11, I have observed an ironic but growing dichotomy. On one hand, the status and rights of Muslim women remain an unsolved mystery and a highly disputed topic for many non-Muslims. On the other hand, noteworthy events celebrating Muslim women show great promise of hope, change and understanding. In 2003, the Nobel Peace Prize was awarded to Shirin Ebadi who became the first Iranian and the first Muslim woman ever to receive such a prestigious award. (Shirin's story: http://www.nobelprize.org/nobel_prizes/peace/laureates/2003/)

As a lawyer, judge, lecturer, author and activist, she has voiced her struggles for the rights of women and children. Shirin Ebadi says, "It is not Islam that oppresses women; it is a working interpretation of Islam that oppresses women. Women are the first victims of extreme poverty. In addition, they face discrimination in law and in practice in many countries in the world. We have to struggle against a patriarchal culture." In 2011, the Nobel Peace Prize was divided among three women, Ellen Johnson Sirleaf, Leymah Gbowee and Tawakkul Karman for their non-violent struggle for the safety of women and women's rights. This award to Tawakkul Karman, the first Arab woman from Yemen, boldly acknowledges that the Arab Spring could not have been possible without the full participation of their women: (Story:http://www.nobelprize.org/nobel_prizes/peace/laureates/2011/press.html#)

On July 12, 2013, the first ever Youth Takeover of the UN took place. Hundreds of young advocates supporting education arrived from around the world, including Malala Yousafzai from

Pakistan. (Story:http://www.huffingtonpost.com/ban-kimoon/malala-united-nations_b_3558563.html?utm_hp_ref=tw)

In her inspiring speech, Malala told the world to wage a global struggle against illiteracy, poverty and terrorism through books and pens. Her words continue to echo in my ears; "... one child, one teacher, one pen and one book can change the world. Education is the best weapon through which we can fight poverty, ignorance and terrorism." The world certainly paid attention to her struggles, and in 2014, the Nobel Peace Prize was shared by Malala Yousafzai from Pakistan and Kailash Satyarthi from India for their untiring efforts to provide rights to children. (http://www.nobelprize.org/nobel_prizes/peace/laureates/2014/)

It is significant to note that Malala Yousafzai is not only the youngest person, but also the youngest Muslim woman to receive this highest honor. With the 2014 Nobel Peace Prize being shared by a Muslim woman and a Hindu man, we can also hope for greater understanding and cooperation between Hindus and Muslims as they work to improve human dignity and respect.

The Pen is Mightier than the Sword

While differences in economic, social, political, cultural, religious, racial and traditional conditions will continue to impact the status of women around the world, I am encouraged and motivated by the honor and tribute given to these strong and brave Muslim women. Their courage and effort conveys a strong reminder to women who tend to forget or underestimate just how wide their sphere of influence really is. As a collective body of concerned and caring human beings, we should unify our efforts and voices to alleviate the pain, suffering and inequities that are so easily committed in the name of religions. By combining secular and religious values which do not compromise our core beliefs, and by providing access and opportunity for education, support and mentorship, we can bring positive change and lasting transformation for these women and their families. Nelson Mandela wisely stated, "Education is the most powerful weapon which you can use to change the world." And, research has confirmed that investing in women creates smaller and healthier families, better educated and productive children, reduced poverty and stronger civil societies.

As American Muslims, we have the opportunity to raise our voices and lend support to the cause of other women because we do not face the same risks and dangers that our sisters face in some parts of the world. Non Muslim Americans can help by tempering their judgment and criticism of Islam as an oppressive and suppressive religion. Americans on the whole, can advocate for positive change by holding government officials accountable when they support dictatorial regimes in Muslim countries to satisfy their political agendas.

Women and Peace

In reflecting over the past decade, I am in total awe of the rapidly growing advances in telecommunication, health and education, all of which have brought greater comfort and convenience in our lives. However, at the same time, I am deeply concerned by the high frequency with which human life is denigrated, devalued and destroyed. Natural and manmade disasters are leaving intense despair and sadness in their wake. Each year, about 10 million humans are added to the list of individuals affected by these types of adversities, with an increasing population experiencing not only a general dissatisfaction with life but also suffering from anxiety, insomnia, depression, post-traumatic stress disorder or suicidal tendencies.

For many of us, a common worry is the absence of peace and security. We all long for peace regardless of faith, cultural background, or geography, but it seems to allude us. Is peace even possible today? If we try to understand the root causes, I am reminded of a saying by Prophet Muhammad that we should like for our brother what we like for ourselves. Is it possible that peace has been severely compromised because of the high level of selfishness, deprivation, oppression and injustice that prevails in the world today? Peace and harmony cannot coexist with hopelessness and despair, with poverty and injustice, with lack of education and unemployment or when a person's faith is ridiculed or misinterpreted. Dr. Martin Luther King Jr. said, "Peace is both a journey and a destination." How true! We have been endowed with a choice to adopt or reject the path of peace of our own free will. Experiencing and sustaining peace is a dynamic process. It is a struggle, a journey of self reflection and self reformation. It is a Jihad of the Self aimed at elevating our emotional, moral and spiritual levels. In this regard, the Holy Qur'an guides us:

> And everyone has a goal to which he turns his whole attention. To vie with one another in doing good works. (2:149).

In almost every aspect of our lives, we establish short term and long term goals and compete with others to reach some level of excellence or promotion; whether it is in school, college, jobs, careers, homes or in the community. However, the teachings of Islam guide us that goodness above all else must remain the ultimate goal, the object of our competition. Truly attainable peace lies in the realization, appreciation and acknowledgement of the inherent goodness and beauty in all human beings.

Love for All, Hatred for None

The Ahmadiyya Muslim Community (http://www.alislam.org/), of which I am a member, has upheld the sanctity of all life and lives by the motto, Love for All, Hatred for None. At an Annual Peace Conference in the UK, the Head of the Worldwide Ahmadiyya Muslim Community, Hazrat Mirza Masroor Ahmad said, "If we want true peace and if we want to save the world from destruction, then we must act with justice, integrity and be faithful to the truth." Since 2010, the Ahmadiyya Muslim Community has launched its "Muslims for Peace" campaigns in both the USA and the UK, followed by the "Muslims for Life" campaign, during which blood drives are initiated all over the country on the anniversary of 9/11.

Dalai Lama XIV said, "All major religions carry the same message of love, compassion and forgiveness." For the past decade, through interfaith seminars and external outreach efforts, I have experienced closer ties of friendship and understanding between communities of various faiths. By sharing our religious wisdom, we have begun to appreciate the commonalities of our faiths rather than emphasize our cultural and too-often contrived differences. Through these dialogues and working with non-profit organizations, I have witnessed firsthand the dire conditions of women and children, regardless of their race, ethnicity or religion. I have also realized that many of the challenges that Muslim women and their families face in America result from a lack of secular and religious knowledge. As a practical solution, the Khadijah Scholarship Fund was created seven years ago to help women achieve economic self sufficiency. This scholarship fund is made possible through the auspices of the Women's Auxiliary of the Ahmadiyya Muslim Community (http://www.lajnausa.net/web/), and provides adult Muslim women the opportunity to go back to school to learn new employable skills. Through "Humanity First" (http://usa. humanityfirst.org/), members volunteer their time and expertise to build schools and hospitals, construct water wells, organize medical camps and other undertakings to improve the lives of humanity in developing countries, and bring relief to disaster struck areas around the globe.

In Conclusion

Based on the experiences of the past fifteen years, Islam continues to be a misunderstood and feared religion. However, it offers greater opportunities for Muslims such as myself to prove otherwise. Even though approximately 20,000 Americans are accepting Islam each year, it is hard for an average American to understand how Islam could be called a peaceful religion. Thus, the need to dialogue and connect with each other to replace inequality and injustice with justice and compassion is more urgent now than ever before. Retaliation and revenge is not the answer. As we witness rising extremist tendencies and increasing intolerance to Islam in the USA and the world, I am drawn even closer to the teachings of Islam to define and identify my personal journey. When I set out to defend my faith post 9/11, I would not have predicted that I would embark on this beautiful journey of self-reflection, accountability, advocacy and truth. This journey, this effort, this struggle, this jihad so far has enriched my soul and drawn me nearer to God and His people. My passion to serve the less fortunate and build peaceful communities will continue, Insha Allah (God Willing). I close with this promise from God: I will suffer not the work of any worker from among you, whether male or female, to be lost. You are from one another (Holy Qur'an, 3:196).

Extremism can flourish only in an environment where basic governmental social responsibility for the welfare of the people is neglected. Political dictatorship and social hopelessness create the desperation that fuels religious extremism."
~ Benazir Bhutto ~

"It has been said, 'Time heals all wounds.' I do not agree. The wounds remain. In time, the mind, protecting its sanity, covers them with scar tissue and the pain lessens.
But it is never gone."
~ Rose Kennedy ~

"Kindness is the language which the deaf can hear, and the blind can see"
~ Mark Twain ~

Chapter Nine

"Assyria, The Work of My Hands"
Isaiah 19:25

Johny Sargon Jacob

Dedicated to the memory of my dear brother,
Digol Baijan Jacob, who also served with the Coalition
forces in Iraq for four years.

Johnny Sargon Jacob, one of two native Arabic speakers on this project, is Chairman of the Assyrian Democratic Movement in San Diego, a Staff Electronics Engineer, and former Intelligence Analyst for the US military. Passionate about the plight of particularly Assyrians and other Christians in Iraq and around the globe, Johnny served in Iraq with the US Army for ten years as a linguist, cultural advisor, Human Terrain Analyst and in various other capacities. Johnny generated a variety of assessments, reports and recommendations to military staff regarding Iraqi political, social, economic, cultural, religious and tribal issues. Johnny prepared numerous presentations on culture awareness for US and Coalition forces. He is currently involved in assisting Assyrian Christians and other Iraqi and Syrian refugees through the Assyrian Aid Society-USA.

9/11/2001

September 11, 2001, for me was unlike any other day that I have ever experienced before. I remember that morning getting up and turning on the TV to listen to the morning news, just as I did every morning. What I saw unfolding that morning, however, was so bizarre, unbelievable, and unpredictable that I felt myself transfixed as if I were in a trance watching everything that was happening on the screen, in slow motion. I saw the first plane hit and reacted in disbelief, then the

111

second one, which jolted me a little closer back to reality. Gradually, logic and reason struggled to take hold of my mind, trying to make sense of what I just saw. Instinctively, from that moment onward I knew, in my gut, that this was an attack by radical Islamists. Then, as news reports rapidly followed about what was happening, it confirmed my worst suspicions. Ever since that awful, fateful day though, I have never ceased to wonder in amazement at the continuing denial of western civilization's reaction to the unremitting escalation of Islamic terrorism throughout the world.

I would like to look back now, through my own unique window of time, as a Christian Assyrian, born and raised in Iraq, later leaving there for England, Australia, and America, and returning to Iraq, for a few years, to serve with the coalition forces before coming back to America. This is especially important at this time, because, the Christian Assyrians are the indigenous people of Iraq and their survival is at a critical juncture now. They are on the precipice of extinction; their language, culture, history and religious heritage in the Middle East, could disappear forever, unless they are guaranteed a safe haven in their ancestral homeland where they can live in peace, freedom and security.

My story begins in Baghdad, Iraq, where I was born on April 15, 1952. I grew up in a suburb of Baghdad called Al Dora, which is approximately 15 kilometers south of Baghdad. At that time, Al Dora was about 95 percent Christian Assyrians. We had our own clubs, churches, and government schools. Although the schools were controlled by the government, and most of the students and teachers were Assyrian, the subjects were taught in Arabic instead of our neo-Assyrian Aramaic language. At that time, we enjoyed a great deal of freedom. Much of this, however, was attributable to the fact that we were living in a kind of self-imposed ghetto. Even so, for the most part, we were relatively happy, secure and free from persecution.

In 1952, Prince 'Abd al-Ilah was still Regent for his nephew Faisal, the last Hashemite King of Iraq. I was too young at that time to be aware of any movement within the populace, military or government to overthrow the monarchy, which eventually occurred on July 14, 1958. During those intervening years between 1952 and 1958, there was turmoil in Iraq, but due to my still being quite young I remained, for the most part, unaware of what was happening. It was later, before entering my teen years, that I gradually became more and more aware that Assyrians did not enjoy the full benefits of the larger Arab Muslim population. Older friends and relatives may have discussed these matters before then, but until you begin to experience it yourself, it will not take a firm hold in your mind. Eventually, the innocent years of my youth left and reality set in.

During my teen years in Al Dora, even after the violent over-throw of King Faisal II, Al Dora remained relatively calm and peace-ful. There were no bombings or attacks on Assyrians. Al Dora con-tinued to thrive as a haven for Assyrians who preferred to raise their families in a pleasant suburb of Baghdad, where they could socialize with and live in community with other Assyrians. The only problems I remember were of a minor nature involving curious Muslims from the larger adjacent sections of the surrounding metropolitan area. There were times when curious strangers from those sections might venture into our Assyrian town of Al Dora. Whenever that happened, I remem-ber joining with other Assyrian youths to insure that our community and fellow Assyrians remained safe from thugs and troublemakers. We would follow anyone that we did not recognize or that looked sus-picious, confront them and inquire what business they had in Al Dora. If they seemed suspicious, the strangers would be physically forced out of town. Most of the time these strangers came to Al Dora to both-er our girls, which we would not tolerate. Occasionally fights broke out. Sometimes the police made arrests. When they did, the authorities always took the side of the Muslims. If anyone went to jail, it was the Assyrians usually for a day or two, after which, they released them.

Throughout my teen years, I never got involved in the type of politics that involved Assyrian Nationalism. It would have been very dangerous to do so. Anyone who did would have been risking the hangman's noose in the public square. That is not to say that we never thought about it or discussed it. We knew that we were different, because we were Christians living among a majority population of Muslims and we spoke our own language at home which was different from theirs. Also, our customs were different, our food was different, our history was different. We were always conscious of these facts, but we knew our place and we understood that to transgress those bound-aries would have been dangerous to us and to our loved ones.

My beloved Assyrian People are the indigenous people of Iraq. Our history spans a long time, going back more than 5000 years. We are unique because we are an ancient people that have survived every form of persecution you can imagine. We, unlike our Jewish cousins, are a people still without a country, a people in diaspora throughout the world, without any form of autonomy, without wealth, worldly power or any form of international support. We are small in number, approximately three million worldwide, and our language, Aramaic, has been kept alive down through the centuries, only by our people. If the Assyrians were to all vanish tomorrow, then their language would be as dead as Latin; the theologians, archeologists, philologists and historians would consign it to the dusty tomes of academia.

I have often wondered if anyone would care if the Assyrians become extinct. Other people have disappeared from the world's stage. Where are the Babylonians, Sumerians, Hittites, and Philistines? These other ancient peoples of the Middle East seem to have disappeared or now call themselves by another name. Why do the Egyptians, Assyrians and Israelites still stubbornly persist? Is it a coincidence that the great Hebrew Prophet Isaiah declared that one day these same three nations would be a blessing to the whole world? I cannot help today but wonder, in the light of the greatest ethnic cleansing and persecution that Assyrians have ever suffered, if this prophecy has merit. Perhaps time will one day answer that question for me.

Biblical prophecy aside, I have often pondered if anything can be done today to eradicate the petty jealousies, suspicion, fear and hatred of others who may differ from us? It can't be legislated, forced or bred into us through indoctrination, social engineering or biology. And why all the aversion to our differences? Didn't someone once say, "Variety is the spice of life?" Can't we just "live and let live"?

It is probably difficult for someone living in a pluralistic, democratic society like America or one of the Western European nations to imagine what it is like for a Christian Assyrian growing up in Iraq. Not just now, amidst all the chaos and turmoil of the two Gulf Wars and the current terrorism involving ISIS, but down through the halls of time, after the fall of the Assyrian Empire. To be even more specific, from the advent of the conversion of Assyrians to Christianity during the first century A.D. to the present. If you examine the history of the region where Iraq is located today, you will discover that during that time period it was more or less consistently vulnerable to periodic episodes of violence, oppression, discrimination and bigotry toward minorities, especially after Islam established its footprint. There were, to be sure, intervals of relative calm in the centers of population, and it is also true that Assyrian tribal regions did exist in more remote areas, where there was a degree of autonomy, preventing friction between opposing cultural backgrounds and religious beliefs. If one is interested in this period of our history, a lifetime could easily be devoted to its study, but that is not the purpose of this chapter.

Imagine for a moment, if you will, a large modern skyscraper overlooking a panoramic view of a vast metropolitan area in New York, Chicago or Los Angeles. In that, building, there are perhaps hundreds or maybe more than a thousand windows. If you were to take the time to look, out of every one of those windows, each one would give you a different perspective on the geography surrounding that building. While one may notice subtle changes in geography over time, observation of and reaction to geography is relatively static and passive. Nevertheless, ask ten people what they see out of the same window on the 18th floor and you will get a variety of descriptions and reactions.

Now take a group of ten people, each one from a different cultural, linguistic, racial, religious and ethnocentric background and throw them together for a period of one week of close social interaction in the same environment. At the conclusion of one week, you will still get a variety of observations and reactions to each person's experiences, but the difference is that now they are each reacting with nine other sentient human beings, like themselves, not static, passive, moribund objects. They have different personalities, they possess a unique sense of self, and each one has a different collection of experiences. Also, each of them have different sensitivities, emotional and psychological traits, different beliefs, different world-views, different aspirations and vocational pursuits.

During that week of interaction, some individuals may have bonded quite well with other members of the group, while gossip and rivalries may have developed among still others, maybe hostility, discrimination, or even violence. On the one hand, we can tolerate our differences fairly well when we are relating to inanimate objects, but when two or more egos are involved, it seems to be another matter. Nevertheless, even in the cosmopolitan milieu of a competitive American society, I find it strangely fascinating, how a singular event such as 9-11, can pull all of the disparate members of that society together. When everyone is facing a common threat, that old instinct for survival starts pumping adrenalin through the system and the human herd, without even thinking, will quickly pull together. Is there anything that we can learn from all of this? Can, for example, the global community of nations save the Assyrian people from extinction?

The community of nations must first care enough to act. If they care, then the answer is yes, they can save the Assyrian people and if they can succeed in that endeavor, then it is possible to save others in the future too. How you might ask? Well, I'm glad you asked me. It's really quite simple. We have already applied a solution to the animal kingdom that could be just as easily adapted to the human species. What do we do when we are confronted by an endangered species in the animal kingdom? We declare them endangered, and then we take positive steps to protect them, in a wildlife preserve perhaps, where we can watch them and attend to their needs, nurture them and encourage them to multiply until they become self-sustaining. Well, I'm not suggesting that we put Assyrians in a wildlife preserve, after all Assyrians are not a sub-species, in fact, Assyrians are a very well educated people filling just about every professional occupation you can think of, especially in the industrialized, developed nations throughout the world. All it would take is for the United Nations to establish an autonomous, sovereign state of Assyria in the Nineveh Plain, their ancestral homeland. The United Nations could then provide a military buffer zone around Assyria to protect them from foreign intrusions. Assyria would have its own language, government, police force, military, churches, laws, commerce, schools, universities, industry, arts and sciences. If the international community of nations has neither the will or the desire to protect its smallest, most vulnerable and defenseless of members, then the entire human race is in serious jeopardy.

It is time for the powerful to protect the weak. It is time for the wealthy to protect the poor. It is time to put an end to nepotism, cronyism, exploitation, domination and condescension. If the human race does not respect the dignity of its smallest, weakest members, then the entire human race has lost its dignity. The signs are already all around us. Man's inhumanity to man is reverting to the most savage, brutal, inhuman treatment and lack of compassion for others that the world has ever seen and hardly anyone bats an eyelash. "What doth it profit a man if he gain the whole world and lose his soul?"

If one cannot tolerate others with whom they differ, to the point where that group becomes a danger and a threat to everyone, then it is incumbent upon the majority to act as one to preserve the safety of all. The case in point here being the terrorists who would have no power to harm others if they hadn't received that power from America, Arab Gulf States, Turkey and other nations who supplied them with the weapons, training and financing they are now using in a most cowardly manner to brutalize the weakest, most defenseless members of society. Why weren't those weapons regulated? They have no factories to resupply ammunition or spare parts. They number a mere thirty thousand or so, and yet the whole world is trembling in fear and helpless to stop them? What is going on here?

I believe the world is war-weary and preoccupied with the

looming threat of a global economic downturn. That, coupled with the spreading violence in the middle east, is causing governments everywhere to reassess their priorities. So, how then can we: Save America; Save the Assyrians; Save the World?

In 2003, I returned to Iraq to serve with the Coalition forces. When I arrived there, I was shocked to see how drastically the Iraq I remembered had changed. It was not the same as I left it. It had changed dramatically for the worse. The consequences of the fall of Saddam Hussein was short-lived. Immediately after his fall, everyone was happy, joyful, friendly. Religious and ethnic animosities seemed to have disappeared. Everyone wanted to invite you to their home for tea, distribute candies, celebrate with you. That spirit soon took flight and another demonic spirit seemed to have taken its place. Sunni and Shia were at each other's throat and the Assyrians were caught in between. There was a Church in Al Dora, St. George, that I used to attend when I was growing up. The radical Muslims painted slogans against US forces on the walls of that Church. The Clergy wanted to remove the graffiti by painting over it, but they could not, because if they did the Muslims who were watching would have killed the Priests. That was not the worst part. One day, a column of American military observers drove through the streets of Al Dora. When they came to the Church, the American Commander seeing the graffiti on the Church walls had the Priest brought before him and in a humiliating manner, demanded that he remove the graffiti. The Priest explained that he wanted it removed, but was under threat of death if he did. That Commander told the Priest, "If you don't remove it, I will kill you." That Church was later destroyed by radical Islamists with a powerful car bomb. As of this writing, many Christian Churches in Iraq have been destroyed, Priests and parishioners (men, women and children), have been tortured, brutally killed, raped, kidnapped, crucified, burned, buried alive and the Western mainstream press has barely made mention of it.

The foregoing examples clearly illustrate that if super powers like the United States cannot find an advantage that serves their own selfish interests, they will not help the persecuted, oppressed Christian Assyrians of the Middle East. To complicate this matter the Western press has now become an organ of the political structure in the West. They are no longer unbiased and free. Their interests have become global in scope, to help erect the so-called New World Order. Morality and justice, for them, emanate not from Heaven, but from their atheistic secular humanist mindset. They consider themselves a law unto themselves.

One example of this bias of the Western Press is their program to promote sympathy for the Kurdish people prior to the Gulf Wars and since then. The chemical attack on a Kurdish village was indeed a crime worthy of journalistic reporting; however, that promotion left out the persecution, oppression and killing of Assyrians by Kurds and their assassination of His Beatitude Mar Benyamin Shimun XIX, the Assyrian Catholicos Patriarch of the East, and 150 of his bodyguards in 1918. It also left out the continuous systematic attempt by the Kurdish population of Iraq to appropriate the ancestral homeland of the Assyrians by any and all means possible. This includes interfering directly and indirectly through manipulation and subterfuge in the political affairs of the Assyrians by creating divisive puppet groups they control to prevent Assyrian autonomy. Voter fraud, creation of a pseudo-Chaldean Party, confiscation of Assyrian land and disarming Assyrian local fighters are additional tactics they employed. It should be also noted that the Kurdish people are not a Semitic people and are not indigenous to Iraq, yet the West has favored them based on their number alone, which in all justice has no merit, considering how much the Assyrian people have suffered over the past century to serve the interests of the great Western powers.

The larger picture now should be very clear, the Kurds and Sunni in the north and the Shia to the south. If justice prevailed, then the Nineveh Province and all of its environs should belong to the Assyrians. It was theirs from time immemorial and they have paid for it many times over in blood and treasure. Justice, until now however, has not prevailed. Brutal Islamic theology has proven itself over and over to be unworthy and untrustworthy of protecting the innocent and defenseless indigenous people of Iraq. This is true not only of Iraq, but all Muslim countries where non-Muslims reside.

The Muslims claim that their population worldwide is 1.5 billion and of this number 1.2 billion cannot read, write or understand the Arabic language. Now consider that the Muslim's Holy Book, the Quran, was written in Arabic and that this book was forbidden to be translated into any other language, by the order of Allah. However, in the late 1700's the Quran was illegally and unofficially translated into other languages; translations considered by Muslim scholars to be distorted and untrue. Then, isn't it logical to conclude from this, that 1.2 billion Muslims have their faith built on a book that they cannot read or understand and all of their teaching about Islam was passed to them through Mullahs and Sheikhs that themselves did not master the Arabic language. The teachings of Islam, therefore, have been disseminated and handed down apparently by men who did not read or understand the Quran.

From the beginning of Islam, Muslim invaders occupying foreign soil gave their inhabitants only three choices: convert to Islam, pay the jizya (a heavy tax) or be killed. This continues to the present day...ISIS being a primary example. Once a person becomes an adherent to Islam and its teaching, he will succumb to its violent inhumane verses. More than one hundred of these verses condone and encourage a Muslim to kill, behead, lie, steal, enslave, kidnap, rape, destroy, abuse children and force non-believers to convert to Islam. One who sincerely desires to be a good, faithful Muslim, must obey the teaching of Allah through the Quran. We can only imagine then what goes on in the mind of a Muslim when he reads the Quran and must choose between obeying Allah or obeying the laws of civilized humanity.

For the rest of the time I spent in Iraq, I made every effort to encourage the coalition forces to help the Christian Assyrians. After all, Assyrians served the Allied forces through two World Wars, two Gulf Wars and all to their own detriment. At the conclusion of those wars, the Assyrians were always seen as collaborators with the West and suffered one persecution after another, all of which has culminated in the greatest persecution of all which now threatens the very existence of the Assyrians throughout the world. There has not been any attempt by America or the Coalition Forces in general, to help Assyrians establish a safe zone for protection. They have lost their homes, land, personal property, and are languishing in refugee camps or drifting about homeless, without food or shelter. They cannot be exploited for oil, so the West has no concern for them; they are considered expendable.

Before the new government was formed after the fall of Saddam, Hussein, the Bush Administration appointed Lewis Paul Bremer as the Administrator of the Coalition Provisional Authority of Iraq. He served in this capacity from May 11, 2003 until June 28, 2004. During his tenure he did nothing to insure the rights, protection or preservation of the Assyrian Christian minority and tried unsuccessfully to prevent them from having any representation in the government. It was only due to the efforts of an Assyrian politician, Yonadam Kanna, a member of the Iraqi National Assembly, that Assyrian representation was finally attained. This was a disgraceful betrayal of Assyrian interests by Paul Bemer and the United States. Minorities like the Assyrians cannot depend on powerful nations alone like America and Britain. I believe that we must appeal to a much wider audience, like the United Nations, because if we simply align ourselves with one region or another, that tends to offend the interests of another region. We must understand that we are now part of a global community and the survival of one has now become dependent on the survival of all. We cannot afford to spread division and animosities by choosing sides, as if this is a sporting event. We must work together. If we do not, then we will all hang together.

In conclusion, I can only repeat that if the human race collectively cares enough, they can change this in short order. The only question that remains is: do we care enough to act - before it is too late?

Assyrian refugees

- Act with honor and integrity in everything you do
- Believe in a Supreme Being and keep faith in the center of your life
- Be tolerant and considerate of different religious, social and political views
- Strive to leave the world a better place than when you entered
- Practice mutual help – give and accept help when it's needed
- Uphold and maintain the principles of good government: oppose divisive and degrading influences, and be a good citizen
- Value self-improvement over financial success
- Remain good at heart
- Strive to live a brotherly life
  ~ Edicts common to Judaism, Christianity and Islam ~

"Forgiveness does not change the past –
but it does enlarge the future."
~ Paul Boese ~

Chapter Ten

Healing the Rift

Conrad Pearson and Bonnie Conger

Conrad Pearson has 30 years of experience as a licensed Broker-Dealer, currently through SII Investments, Inc. He earned a Bachelor of Arts degree in Political Science with a minor in Middle East Studies from Portland State University. He completed graduate work at Johns Hopkins University School of Advanced International Studies. Conrad traveled to more than 30 countries working for Shell Oil, Chase Manhattan Bank, and then established his own company, Risk Insights. He takes pride in fostering long-term relationships with clients and their families. He is a board member of the Planned Giving Council for the Oregon Health & Science University Foundation. In 1987 he received the Paul Harris Fellow Rotarian of the Year award and was President of the Tigard Rotary Club from 1989-1990. Conrad and Barbara Pearson were named First Citizens by the Tigard Chamber of Commerce in 1998. Conrad established the God of Abraham Foundation in 2012, continuing his life-long mission of bettering the lives of children and families in need. His charitable foundation includes the "100 STRONG" program.

Bonnie Conger is Director of Community Service at Pearson Financial Group in Lake Oswego, Oregon. In 2012 she joined forces with Conrad Pearson's effort to make the world a more loving place. After her husband lost his 19-year battle with Parkinson's disease in 2011 at age 65, she vowed to give back to the community by volunteering to help others in need. Bonnie joined the Tigard Rotary Club in 2012 where she supports their numerous local and international projects. She was named a Paul Harris Fellow in her first year in Rotary. Bonnie earned a BA degree in psychology at Portland

122

State University. She has been an active member of Murray Hills Christian Church in Beaverton since 1988, and served on the board. She asisted developmentally challenged young adults to learn activities of daily living. She worked for 34 years at Providence St. Vincent Medical Center in Portland in the Internal Medicine Residency Training Program, and is active with "100 STRONG."

Conrad's Journey

My awareness that a "better tomorrow is possible" began over forty years ago as an undergraduate student at Portland State University (PSU). At that time, PSU had the only undergraduate program in the country that offered a degree in Middle East Studies. I had the opportunity to actually travel to the Middle East as a student, and studied the Palestinians. That was a real eye opener!

I continued my Middle East studies at Johns Hopkins School of Advanced International Studies (SAIS). After SAIS, my career path led me back to the Middle East numerous times. I visited for my work at Shell Oil, Chase Manhattan Bank and, eventually, my own consulting firm called Risk Insights.

During my travels and while doing business that took me to over thirty countries, I was immersed in different cultures and philosophies. I saw tremendous diversity. It was during this period of time that I felt God calling me to help make the world a better place. I met very loving people on both sides of the Middle East conflict, and became aware of how much they shared in common that never seemed to get talked about. The discussions always appeared to center around how the sides were different.

After ten years, I got burned out on international travel and decided to come back to Oregon. I wanted to engage in my other area of interest, in addition to international travel, that fascinated me since early childhood. Being the kid who played Monopoly until the wee hours of the morning, I entered the financial planning field.

I realized at that time that I was very tired of just paying lip service to "serving God by being a more loving person." I wanted to actually practice what God is calling us to do: Love God above everything, and love your neighbor as yourself. I listened and watched for direction.

The message I received was clear. It could not be denied. What I was to do reminded me of a short-order cook, receiving order tickets on the rotating cylinder above the counter in a restaurant's kitchen. I had specific directions, such as to call this person or contact that person. I was instructed to ask what they needed and how I could help.

There were also more general directions. For example, don't pass by a beggar on the street without giving that person something. No matter how little I had to share at certain meager times in my life, this directive still applied. I needed to make things happen at any level, even if it was for only one person at a time. The important thing was to make a difference.

Over time, I continued to develop the ways I could make a difference. I looked for problems where I thought I might be able to help make an important contribution.

9/11

Then September 11, 2001, happened. That moment in time highlighted some bigger needs. Since then, I have wrestled to find ways that people of the Jewish, Christian, and Muslim faiths in my own neck of the woods could be brought together in ways that would help heal the rifts between them.

Eventually, a concept began to form in my mind. The approach that I originally thought would work was the one that I, and many others, had used before. I developed a plan based on this "standard" approach, but with some new twists, based on my experience.

I have been one of the main sponsors at two annual events at the Oregon Convention Center. The formula is the same for each one. We book exciting speakers, provide good music, and, of course, serve food. By the end of the event, the attendees leave feeling really jazzed. The feedback is good from these events.

I wanted to do the same for the three faiths, so the following plan was made: The event was to be called the "God of Abraham Celebration" because the Jewish, Christian, and Muslim faiths all believe in the same God that Abraham believed in. Three dynamic speakers, one from each faith, were to be featured. Each one of these thinkers was to be a leading speaker on actually practicing love. A special intra-faith youth choir would sing. People would be asked to sign up to receive daily one-minute downloads reminding them to practice love each day.

This daily message would be the key piece to how this event would be different from the standard formula. I made the observation that with the other two annual events, as well-received as they were, it seemed like the message wore off faster than I preferred. To make a bigger difference, people need to have a daily reminder to do acts of loving kindness in their life every day and by their own choice. That was the idea, anyway.

Pastor Dr. Gary Chapman was one of the people who agreed to speak at the "God of Abraham Celebration" event. Pastor Chapman is the author of numerous books, including *The Five Love Languages: How to Express Heartfelt Commitment to Your Mate*. It has sold over seven million copies, according to a November 2011 article in *The New York Times*.

When I described the event to Pastor Chapman, he expressed interest in the whole concept. However, a surprising revelation for me was when Pastor Chapman warned me, "The group that will probably be hardest to get to come to the table will be the Christians." Despite the very firm directives from Jesus in word and deed to love even our enemies, I discovered that Pastor Chapman's warning turned out to be embarrassingly true. Two of the most recurring criticisms I received about the event concept were that the Muslims were not worshipping the same God as the Christians, and the Muslims were really on a war campaign and could not be trusted.

With that experience fresh in my mind, I decided to change tactics. I observed that adults tend to be much more set in their ways than children. Therefore, I changed the focus to be more on youth. Children are more open, and the shelf life of the investment would be decades longer.

I also changed the order to the reverse of the previous approach. Before, there was to be a big event, the "God of Abraham Celebration," to kick off this effort. Now the effort would start with grass roots getting the word out, with a planned event after spreading our message to select audiences. With those changes to a new approach, "Operation Genesis" was born.

Testing the Concept

The Oregon Episcopal School (OES) in Portland, Oregon, was established in 1869. It is the oldest Episcopal school west of the Rocky Mountains. The school serves more than 840 children from the Northwest and around the world in pre-kindergarten through 12th grade. It includes both day and boarding programs. OES provides the next generation of global leaders with the skills needed to thrive in a changing world. It encourages global experiences across six continents through exchange programs, trips, and curricular connections.

Every year the 8th-grade journalism class at OES chooses to interview global citizens in the Portland community. These are people who are defined as making a positive change locally and around the world. The students spend most of the academic year working on this task. They research interviewees from a list of community projects, write questions to use in interviews, conduct individual interviews, and publish a book titled *Profiles from a Global Perspective.*

In 2012, Operation Genesis was selected as one of the projects. Two students came to interview me on a Friday afternoon after school. One was an atheist; the other a believer. They arrived 20 minutes early and seemed reluctant to leave after almost two and a half hours.

Before the students began interviewing me, I told them that I wanted to interview them. I asked who would like to go first. The boy, who is the atheist, answered that he would go first. I then asked the girl to take a blank paper, a pen, and a clock with a second hand and make a mark for every three seconds that her classmate spoke. When he finished, I instructed her to hand the paper, pen, and clock to him in order to repeat the process.

When the girl finished talking, I asked how many total marks there were. The young man carefully added them up. He reported that there were 159 slashes. I said, "That's how many people died of starvation since we began our discussion. Of those deaths, 80 percent were defenseless children under the age of five. In biblical times, there was not enough food. Today there is abundant food. Yet, people are still dying of starvation." I then asked the two students, "If children were dropping dead outside my window, would you be taking time to interview me? Hopefully, not!" They confessed that they would rather be out trying to solve the problem. I then remarked, "That is exactly what Operation Genesis is all about."

Getting Back to Basics

I believe that true healing between and within the Jewish, Christian, and Muslim faiths requires getting back to the basics. You cannot get more basic than going back to the very beginning. A major element of Operation Genesis is a discussion of three stories from the Book of Genesis. These stories are shared by all three Abrahamic faiths. They illustrate why we need to be more accepting of each other, and should motivate us to do daily loving acts to help those around us.

The three stories are "The Creation Story," "Abraham, Sarah, and Hagar," and "The Tower of Babel." The Creation Story shows that there is a higher power, God, out there who has communicated with humans. Scientists of the caliber of Albert Einstein have supported this concept. However, people believe in many competing "gods," as was also the case during the time of Abraham.

So which God is "The One"? It is defined here as the God who Abraham worshipped and is the subject of the second story. If there is truly only one God, then why is there not just one faith? The story of the Tower of Babel shows that God inspired wisdom in multiple approaches to our understanding of the One God that Abraham worshipped. It illustrates the wisdom in having more than one approach to understanding God. Humans are not ready for just one approach and a unified world.

All of these stories have variations in the details from different points of view and at different times in history. I am trying to use the core of the stories, those I see are in common, to illustrate my points.

The Creation Story – There is a God

I will begin with an overview of the first story from Genesis – that of Creation itself.

- Dark
- Light
- Firmament
- Water, land, and plants
- Eventually, animals and humans
- And, finally, rest

Everyone seems to know the basic story, even if we do not remember the actual sequence. The key question is how could humans have known this story and the basic sequence of how the Earth actually evolved before scientific knowledge developed sufficiently to observe it? Remember, this is thousands of years before telescopes and microscopes were invented. So how could this story be written correctly if a higher power, God, was not out there communicating this knowledge to us? The Creation Story is very ancient, and was oral tradition before it was finally recorded about 1,000 BCE.

For those who are concerned that people of different faiths are not worshipping the same God, there needs to be the equivalent of a longitude and latitude, i.e., a common directional faith location system to use for reference. Our reference point is the God who Abraham worshipped. This is the God of Abraham, Moses, Jesus, and Mohammad, all of whom added very distinct and important dimensions to understanding God.

It is important, I believe, for all people of the Abrahamic faiths to become very knowledgeable about each other's faith and not be out to proselytize. I feel that this is especially the case since the beginning of all three faiths is in the story of Abraham, Sarah, and Hagar. This story was written before any of the three faiths were founded.

For many, the question of "If there is but one God, then why not but one faith?" comes up. I address this question later with the Tower of Babel story.

Abraham, Sarah, and Hagar

In the times of Abraham, many different gods were worshipped. Polytheism was common, but monotheism was beginning to take hold. An interesting aspect of worship at that time was the common practice of worshipping idols. Idolatry can be defined as worship of a physical object or objects, as a god or multiple gods.

A story comes to mind about Abraham and his father's idols. Abraham's father made idols as a business. Abraham offered the idols food, but none of them moved. After no movement, it is said that the Spirit of God came upon him. He took an axe and hacked all of the idols to bits except the largest one. He then placed the axe in the hand of the largest idol and went away.

Abraham's father heard the noise, and upon seeing the destruction, immediately called for Abraham to give an explanation. Abraham said that he had offered food to the idols. He suggested that the idols had quarreled over the food, and the largest of them hacked the lesser ones into pieces. Abraham's father retorted for Abraham not to deceive him, as the idols were images of wood and stone, fashioned by the hand of man.

Abraham asked if that was the case, how can the idols eat the food offered to them daily? How can they answer your prayers? Upon no forthcoming answer from his father, Abraham took the axe and proceeded to hack the remaining idol to pieces.

I like this story because it shows how beliefs can change over time. Abraham preceded all three monotheistic faiths, but is revered by all of them. The message coming from that time – that there is one God, and this God cares for all his children – is still as valid as ever.

The Tower of Babel

The Tower of Babel was not a figment of someone's imagination. Evidence of the great tower still exists today, though just the base remains. It is said that Alexander the Great wished to reconstruct the tower, but with all the resources available to him, he was unable to duplicate such an impressive achievement. During the building of the great tower, there was an enormous strain on the resources available since the tower required a tremendous amount of raw materials. The labor required was also large.

The purpose of the tower and the city is sometimes said to have been to dictate a single language and culture among the people. This also allowed the concentration of power under a single leader and facilitated enforcement of a uniform religious belief.

However, one conclusion that can be drawn from the tower and the city's demise is that humans were not yet ready for a single language, culture, and religion. God dispersed the people and gave them multiple languages so that they could not readily communicate.

Where Does This Take Us?

I have heard, especially from the Christian community – rhyme and verse – as to why they firmly believe that believers of the other faiths are not worshipping the same God. Yet, there is plenty of evidence of common roots that God was ordained in the faiths. There is so much in common that the three faiths appear to be standing together, especially when compared with the differences of Buddhism, Hinduism, and many other religions.

If one looks at the developing view of any religion over time, you can see that there are changes in the understanding of God. There are changes in the understanding of the practice of the religion. We need to allow room for our own views to evolve, as well.

As an example, look at the time when the same approach to using scripture was taken about the Earth needing to be the center of our solar system. The logic of the time was that if God created man, and man was his most important creation, the Earth had to be a very important place. If Earth was a centrally important place, then it had to be the center of the known universe (well, the solar system was pretty much the known universe, other than stars being points of light out there).

The supporters of the need to keep the Earth as the center of creation in all regards used bible verses to support their points. Yet, you would be hard pressed to find any significant number of people who now believe that the Earth is the center of our solar system!

The important point is that our understanding of scripture and our understanding of God changes over time. Each of us likely has a different view of things than we did earlier in our lives. Hopefully, we are advancing our understanding as we move forward in our lives.

The principal bible verses used to support the idea that the Earth was the center of our solar system are as follows:

Psalm 93:1
The LORD reigns, He is robed in majesty;
The LORD is robed in majesty and armed with strength;
Indeed, the world is established, firm and secure.

Psalm 96:10
Say among the nations, "The LORD reigns."
The world is firmly established, it cannot be moved;
He will judge the peoples with equity.

Psalm 104:5
He set the earth on its foundations;
It can never be moved.

1 Chronicles 16:30
Tremble before him, all the earth!
The world is firmly established; it cannot be moved."

Ecclesiastes 1:5
The sun rises and the sun sets,
And hurries back to where it rises.

I point this out because holy book verses are used by many to make the case that believers of the three faiths are not worshipping the same God. It has been estimated that only two-thirds of the Jewish, one-half of the Christians, and one-third of the Muslims accept parity of the three faiths.

Historic Consequences of People
Defying Religious Structure

History is filled with examples of people suffering severe consequences for expressing a view contrary to the prevailing view of their time and place. Consider the consequences for these people who defied the religious structure of their time:

Aristarchus of Samos (310 BC-230 BC) seldom gets more than a few lines in historical accounts. However, this Greek astronomer is actually the first person known to have written that the Earth rotates on its axis and revolves around the sun. Most people at the time ignored this theory, thinking that it was ridiculous. Who cared? It was not a religious issue during the time of Aristarchus.

Copernicus (1473-1543) identified the concept of a heliocentric solar system, in which the sun, rather than the Earth, is the center of the solar system. This Polish astronomer became a symbol of the brave scientist standing alone, defending his theories against the common beliefs of his time. At least Copernicus had the sensibility to wait for his death bed before the book containing the final version of his theory was published.

Galileo (1564-1642) knew the Pope personally, and felt confident he could just blurt out that he observed the Earth was not the center of the solar system. His views appeared to attack the Pope, thus alienating him and the Jesuits, who had both supported Galileo up until this point. The Church ordered Galileo to publicly renounce his beliefs in the Copernicus theory and of the Earth being in motion. He was tried by Roman Inquisition, found "vehemently suspect of heresy," forced to recant, and sentenced to house imprisonment with no visitors allowed for the rest of his life.

Giordano Bruno (1548-1660), who was a friar and astronomer, stated that not only was the Earth not important, but neither was our solar system. The reward for this brilliant and prescient awareness was that this Italian philosopher was burned alive at the stake. His ideas went against Church doctrine.

Until fairly recently, scientists thought that the universe was static. They now understand that it is expanding in all directions at an increasing velocity. Scientists are reworking their understanding. Religious people find it seemingly impossible to make the same kind of changes, especially when they have the bible verses to support their case.

Putting It All Together

Why make the effort to have a change? First, at the core of each of the Abrahamic faiths is this simple message: There is but one God, and this God calls us to practice a radical level of love. Second, just imagine if members of the three faiths actually practiced what God is calling us to do.

The three Abrahamic faiths – Judaism, Christianity, and Islam – represent 55 percent of the world's population. Picture what it would be like if all of those people were so convinced that God is real and they actually practiced what God calls us to do, i.e., love radically. Not only did God create our universe, but God then told us all about it as evidenced in the Creation Story, the Story of Abraham, Sarah, and Hagar, and the Story of the Tower of Babel – all detailed in the Book of Genesis.

The one recurring message from "out there" to down here on earth has been the calling to love but one God. Accordingly, this one God calls all of us to love what is the most amazing creation of this one God, i.e., our fellow human beings – no matter what their beliefs are. The one God who Abraham worshipped clearly calls all believers to love: Love God above absolutely everything and love your neighbor as yourself. Over and over, prophets and mystics have delivered this very clear message.

God did not ordain us to have "one way" to do things. The last Genesis story, the Tower of Babel, shows us why we should embrace, not be fearful of, the differences between the three Abrahamic faiths. In addition, even a brilliant scientist, such as Albert Einstein, who did not embrace a personal god, saw the hand of God. God is calling all of us to be His agent by reaching out and making His loving presence known to each other. It is you and me who are charged with making this world a better place one day at a time, one person at a time, starting immediately. Today the catch phrases "doing random acts of kindness" and "paying it forward" are common. However, are we only paying those expressions lip service?

Donella Meadows was another pioneering American scientist, environmentalist, teacher, and author until her untimely death in 2001 at age 59. She unexpectedly died after a two-week battle with bacterial meningitis. As stated on the back cover of her book, *Thinking in Systems: a Primer* (2008), she was one of the world's foremost systems analysts, winner of a MacArthur Foundation "genius" award, and Pulitzer Prize nominee for her long-running newspaper column. *Thinking in Systems* offers insights for problem-solving from the personal to the global scale.

In Part 3 of Meadows' book that is titled "Creating Change – in Systems and in Our Philosophy," she urges the following:

- Expose your mental models to the light of day.
- Honor, respect, and distribute information.
- Use language with care.
- Pay attention to what is important.
- Stay humble – stay a learner.
- Celebrate complexity.
- Expand the boundary of caring.

- Don't erode the goal of goodness.

When you consider how to show love to your neighbors, picture a stream of water coming down a mountainside. This stream is potentially life giving. However, if it becomes dammed up completely with no water leaving, instead of life giving, it stagnates and is then life depriving. What is the solution? Put a dam hole in the whole dam. Our time, treasures, and talents can be life giving if given freely to love our neighbor, or they can stagnate if we horde them for ourselves.

The solution is simple: Let loose of the things that are not really yours in the first place and allow them to flow from you to help others, especially when the others are different from you. Those people are God's creation too. Our treasures do not really belong to us. God entrusted us with them, and requests that we be good stewards. The true measure of what you really own is what you take with you after you die. Those are the things that really belong to you. Everything else belongs to God. God is simply entrusting us to use them to help our fellow human beings.

The goal of Operation Genesis is to primarily motivate the youth of Jewish, Christian, and Muslim faiths to do the following:

- Understand the basic tenets of the other Abrahamic faiths without proselytizing.
- Understand that God is real and calls us to love.

There is another chilling aspect to the Tower of Babel story. Jewish writers documented the issue of the value of bricks, and what if a brick fell and killed somebody? The person responsible for the brick was punished for the loss of the brick, not the loss of human life. When you think about it, is it not astonishing that they could place the value of a brick above that of a human life?

Do you think that we are any different today? Remember how someone dies of starvation every three seconds today because of an equally distorted value system. Is it really any different state of mind from way back when the Tower of Babel was being built?

My chapter in this book that you have now finished reading is not to solve the world's starvation problem. It is meant to solve the condition of the heart that allows for starvation to happen. Once the heart is changed, then a lot of other equally pressing problems can be eased, such as the lethal animosity between the three faiths that profess to believe in the same God who Abraham worshipped – the very

God who calls each and every one of us to love.

Now go out and be an agent of God's love. Love your neighbor as you love yourself. Most of all, love God above all else.

***

Putting It Into Action
as described by Bonnie Conger

In June 2012, Conrad Pearson established the God of Abraham Foundation, a 501(c)(3) organization. One of its programs is called "100 STRONG." Conrad and I implemented it in August 2014. It is based on the principles of love God above everything and love your neighbor as yourself. Participants pledge to go out into their communities to find a person, family, or organization that needs assistance on the second weekend in August.

Similar to the annual SOLVE fall and spring Oregon beach cleanup campaign, it is envisioned that by the year 2020 one hundred communities in Oregon will hold similar events in their own neighborhoods or towns on the second weekend in August by doing loving acts of kindness and reach out to help people in need. The focus will be on children of the Jewish, Christian, and Muslim faiths working together in the name of the God who Abraham worshiped and all three of these faiths revere.

How Does "100 STRONG" Work?

There are two ways participants help:

1. They might do a good deed or loving act on their own, which requires no money.
2. They accept two $50 bills—one for themselves and the other to give away in keeping with "love your neighbor as yourself." However, they may choose to pay forward all $100 to someone or an organization in need of support. If their hearts are moved in the spirit of love, they may even decide to go above and beyond by adding money of their own to the $100 they receive and passing it on.

There is no obligation or any strings attached if a participant accepts the money. However, it is hoped that participants, who accept the money, will choose to take part in a four-year helping/giving program. Here is how it works:

- Year 1 they accept two $50 bills. They may keep $50 for themselves or decide to give all $100 away to help someone or an organization in need.
- Year 2 they raise $50 on their own, and that $50 will be matched to do the same as above.
- Year 3 they raise the full $100 on their own and use the money to help someone less fortunate.
- Year 4 they raise $100 to give away, in addition to $100 of their own money, in order to start the process over again by encouraging and/or mentoring another person to help others.

Although anyone can reach out to help their neighbors, the money program is aimed at encouraging middle and high school students to use their imaginations and come up with creative ways to help others who are less fortunate than they are. Young people are our investment in the future of this country.

The program is funded largely through anonymous donations and matching money. A short time after the inaugural event in August 2014, 100 STRONG was recognized by the national television series, "Moving America Forward" hosted by Emmy Award Winner William Shatner. He thanked those involved in 100 STRONG for leading this effort to help make America better. For details and to view the 15-minute interview, please visit the 100 STRONG website at www.au-standard.org.

Why Did "100 STRONG" Begin in Aurora, Oregon?

The 100 STRONG program was born in Aurora, Oregon, after Conrad and Barbara Pearson moved there in the fall of 2012. The ideals of the Old Aurora Colony of the mid-1850's were based on The Golden Rule and focused on cooperative effort, as well as concern and care for its neighbors. The 100 STRONG program wants to take the memory of the spirit of Aurora, adapt it to modern circumstances, and have it work again—not just for Aurora, but as a model for other communities in Oregon and even in the United States. Hence, that's the 20/20 vision.

"Au" is featured in the 100 STRONG logo. While it could represent Aurora, "Au" from the period table of chemical elements stands for "gold." While this project began in Aurora, it is hoped that 100 STRONG will become the gold standard for other communities locally, regionally and nationally to emulate.

Where Do We Go From Here?

Helping someone does not need to cost money. Anyone can do random acts of kindness all year round. The projects do not need to be big or major, nor do they need to cost any or a lot of money in order to make a difference in someone's life.

As is readily recognized, the world is far from perfect. It needs more and constant help to improve it. Peace and goodwill on the macro level cannot be achieved if it doesn't exist on the micro day-to-day human-to-human level. It starts with one person at a time. It starts with each of us in our own neighborhoods and communities.

In the words of Ralph Waldo Emerson:

"You cannot do a kindness too soon,
for you never know how soon it will be too late."

Now go out and love your neighbor. Change the world. It starts with you. It starts today!

———————————

"Injustice anywhere is a threat to justice everywhere."
~ Martin Luther King, Jr. ~

"You cannot further the brotherhood of man
by inciting class hatred."
~ Abraham Lincoln ~

———————————

Chapter Eleven

In the Land of Blood, Honey, and Oil...

F. J. Nanic

F.J. Nanic was born in Sarajevo. Currently in Oregon, he has lived and worked in Holland, France, New Zealand, and Australia. He has authored and self-published several books, including two photo books. He has also been teaching French and serving as an Interpreter to Bosnian nationals in three different countries. Recently, he has become a member of the Bosnian-Herzegovinian American Academy of Arts and Sciences. An author of several books, his most recent is titled *Third Country.*

Faruk's Journey

As I was putting together this chapter about my immediate response to 9/11/2001, and my thoughts concerning the event and its aftermath: the way it's affected me, my family and my relationships — I received an email from a good American friend that hit the nail on the head...

"I wonder how Bosnian Muslims in the West, such as yourself, can become overwhelmed by 9/11, where 3000+ were killed, when tens of thousands of Bosnian Muslims were wiped out in Bosnia a few years previous - while the West stood by, watching passively? Is American blood worth more than Bosnian blood? Is any blood more important than another's blood?"

Terrorism reared its grotesque head in Bosnia, just as it did in NYC. Yet, following the Bosnian atrocities, the world went about its business of making and buying more stuff... until 9/11. Perspective, proportion, and compassion are the issues here.

Basically, North America is an island. Island people tend to live their lives disconnected from the non-islanders. Only when the islanders

137

feel threatened or are attacked do they become concerned with global realities.

9/11 is a window for Americans to do a lot more than react with a "global war on terrorism." 9/11 has provided all of us with the opportunity to self-reflect, and look out at the world without the distortions of arrogance and privilege. North American islanders consume 40% of the planet's produced goods, even though they comprise just 5% of the planet's population. Clearly, something is out of balance. The back story to 9/11 is America's conduct in the world that supports this inequitable globalized economic system, and the compartmentalization and selective perception that blinds us to horrific atrocities like Srebrenica.

Thirty years ago, everything seemed different in Bosnia. Thirty years before that, too. A hundred years ago, World War I started there. Yet history repeated itself... again and again. Are we condemned to rehash it because we didn't learn some valuable lesson from it? Or, is it that we just don't remember our history? According to one prominent writer, Chuck Palahniuk, history is just "patterns within patterns." Another writer, Julian Barnes, believes that history is "just burps," depending on the political diet of the moment. We are what we eat, so what are we feeding our brains? Fat or facts? And is it always going to be about deflecting the aggrieved and reassuring the comfortable?

Thirty years ago, I didn't know what I know now, and I still know very little. It's all mis-mashed information. An acquaintance said, "We need a crap-detector." Big time. Most of our planet has been wasted from human abuse, yet the abusers tell us we need to regulate the consumption of our resources.

In the meantime, another "little" war breaks out, like a zit on the face of the world covered in red marks. Loaded with explosives, a college-educated engineer boards a plane, ready to detonate his underpants. What in the world is going on? We don't seem to be teaching our children well. Rather, we're blithely telling them lies about history, or muddying the waters with latent hypocrisies that cause an unbridgeable rift between their senses and their awareness of actual reality.

"To be, or not to be?" is not the question anymore. Rather, it's to have, or to be. As Erich Fromm said, "Economic behavior is determined by ethical principles... Greed and peace preclude each other."

I grew up in a socialist country, a communist society. In our schools, we didn't have to learn the Catechism. According to most of our teachers, God didn't exist. But our grandparents were believers. Some would-be communists believed, too, praying behind closed doors. In public, instead of Jacob's Ladder, they were climbing the career ladder. One was not to mix religion and politics.

I was thinking then, even if there is God, why were there so many faiths in one Maker? The quiet truth was that, instead of being a communist or would-be columnist, I was already on the path of becoming a globalist – One God, one world, one faith. We used to sing "One Love" for a while, then Bob Marley died. Next thing you know, "Tainted Love" became a hit. Slowly but surely, we were skidding towards 9/11, like a landslide making its way downhill.

Not in my wildest dreams could I have imagined that my flight to Australia was going to be canceled, and that I was going to remain stuck in Ol' 'Frisco. Not a bad place to be stuck in, really. But I'll never forget that September morning, watching the frantic news, when everyone was beside themselves not knowing what to do. It felt like the end of the world as we knew it. As if we all needed a Big Brother to take our hands, and help us find our true home.

A lost flock of sheep, but where was the shepherd? Would we have recognized him even if he appeared in a Starbucks or a gas station? What would he look like? Long hair, white robe, olive skin? Would we recognize his radiating compassion? But, how could we, if we forgot the meaning of the word? Would we feel his love? But if we don't feel love in our hearts, how could we recognize it in another?

It was not 9/11 that propelled me into these questions. I was already primed by a so-called "civil war" in my country. Apparently, we went tribal, while elsewhere people just went postal, or viral. The equation was simple. We were not allowed into the EU because we had only one party – Communist, as opposed to the regular birds that sported wings left and right. Freed from the yoke of communism, we eagerly created a three-party-plus system, in which there were three major contenders for power, plus one or more minor parties who were able to win seats but not control the government. Maybe it would have developed into a nice little capitalistic democracy, if it were not for the fact that our three major competitors represented our three major faiths. Imagine Ireland, England, and another side involved in a war of religions. The more the merrier, indeed.

Until then, we lived in peace. Whether we were communists or not, we were free to wander into any church, mosque, or synagogue in our neighborhood. The moment we came up with three different religious parties, all hell broke loose. The power mongers, who initiated all this in the first place, knew what they were doing. They did the same thing in 1877, when the Bosnian uprising was nipped in the bud. They did it again, a mere hundred years later. Who was there to remember our history? Apparently, we were doomed to repeat it... Historia magistra vitae est.

But why?

It's really quite simple, actually: follow the money. See where it comes from, and where it flows. Who pays whom to do what? Who gets to play boss? One would have already flown you to the Moon, if it weren't so damn expensive! We could launch tons of garbage into space, if it didn't cost about $10,000/pound. Global capitalism needs cheap energy and cheap labor. Furniture made by inmates. Oil from Iraq and Caspian Sea, stuff and more stuff made in China, post-war Vietnam, Bangladesh, to fill our garages and provide fodder for our yard sales...and the insatiable war machines, of course.

In Bosnia, what money comes in, and what flows out? None, I used to believe. All of Sarajevo had hoped that America wouldn't wait four long years to intervene. But, we knew intuitively, "If we had oil, he'd already be here..." Toward the end, the entire Bosnian population began to shrug it off. They were beaten and hollow. They recognized their own insignificance, and they accepted it.

Begrudgingly, I have to admire whoever was behind this devious agenda. Because there are plenty of facts, even goddamn interviews, proving that oil was found in Bosnia before this shameful war. No one was able to connect the dots, though. When identity & dignity — your ID — is destroyed, you stop caring altogether. When your wife is raped in front of you, and your nose is cut off, and you're made to hopscotch like a rabbit to avoid snipers on your turf, can you really care about the crude oil that lies under your feet?

In besieged Sarajevo, people needed something to eat! They were not going to have Motor Oil soup for lunch. Although in some Serb-run death camps the detainees were forced to drink dirty engine oil, or their own urine. Thus Bosnians stopped feeling like real people. They stopped feeling human. They needed their dignity back. They didn't give a dime about the alleged tons of oil buried under the ground. Even if they did, they had no way to dig it up.

But when they come in – the Oilbusters, they'll dig it out, and ship it out. In other words, they'll have it and maybe even eat it, too.

And my Bosnian brothers will be content with the leftovers, slaving their life away, as always, and waiting for another opportunity to knock on their door. But they're tricky, those opponents of yours, always two steps ahead! They don't use doors anymore. Now they call them portals, the mighty shape-shifters who seem to be walking through walls. Now you see them, now you don't.

Of course, my personal journey started when I was born, but, as if my umbilical cord was clamped, I cut it when, as a young man, I headed west, leaving my country behind. Migrating was already in my genes. My grandfather, a true pilgrim, led half of his family to Turkey. He was a true believer, and he simply couldn't bear living where, officially, God did not exist. Istanbul was the closest on the map, going east, where one could find a suitable place under the sun, and start from scratch. It's what drew the other members of the family each year. While my father drove through the rolling hills, I sat in the passenger seat watching the Balkans go by. Ever since, it became my designated spot. Life is a scenic drive, and I'm always in the passenger seat on a bus, train, or plane. Sometimes I drive, too, mostly alone, connecting the America's highways and byways. Thus, way before the 9/11, I was already pretty much on the road. As mentioned above, my flight to Australia was canceled that day. So, how in the world did I wind up "Down Under?" (This chapter won't have enough room to answer this one, and I have already written a few books elaborating upon the topic.)

When it came down to being a Muslim, I must admit that the most comfortable I have felt is in Oregon. At the trail's end, no one seemed to be worried about my faith before the events of 9/11. I was perceived as an exotic bird, I guess. The more the merrier. In the state of Oregon, there were only about three million people. The state's regular foreigners were from California and Mexico. Bosnia was definitely unheard of.

However, the infamous siege of my hometown, placed me right up there on page one. Upon hearing the magic word Sarajevo, there was always at least one person in need of an explanation. What exactly went on there? What are the differences between the Bosnian Muslims and Bosnian Serbs? And so forth. Each time I'd be in a mild state of shock, realizing how somewhere someone was undergoing screaming tortures, while elsewhere, a world apart, another someone didn't have a clue (including not knowing what exactly went on in his own backyard).

I figured that I knew too much. We were taught a lot at school. TMI — as they'd call it here. I knew way more about history, and the grammar, too, than my American peers. But that didn't help me in the great race for money and stuff. It just made me stand out more — like a sour thumb. I hurt, but no one knew why. I was not a tough-enough cookie to just brush it off and say something like, "It's no skin off my nose."

I was compassionate, but that didn't pay, unless I was a professional caregiver. Of course, it was more important to be nice than important, but there was too much accent put on congeniality. It followed the simple rule: if you were not nice, you were rude, and that was unforgivable. If you don't smile as needed, even though it's aching, you're considered as impolite as a stale french fry. Needless to add that I had already spent a few years in Paris, where the most common portrayal of Americans was that they're "loud" and "boastful."

It's uncanny, but in France I felt less comfortable being a Muslim than in America. As my name sounded slightly Algerian, I found myself quietly discarded in the Algerian social basket. My girlfriend's mother complained that, on the phone, I even sounded "comme un beur," like an Arab. And that was before 9/11, mind you. France's then-president, Mitterrand, together with Major and Bush, didn't help us. So that was already enough to wipe the Bosnian smile off my face.

I came to America directly from Paris (a French social boot camp). It took me years to learn how to smile again, and I still haven't acquired a permanent care-dealing grin. Smiling with my eyes and lying through my teeth was never my forte, though I remember that even back home some people were born into it. It seems to be a common trait of every snake oil salesman anywhere in the world.

In Australia, it almost felt like being in America, but, lest we forget, almost also means not quite. Australia was more like America still under the Brits. A warm Canada of sorts. "Lest we forget" was a big thing Down Under. For the Aussies, it was as if time had stopped at Gallipoli. The more I watched that movie, the more I'd just sit there heartbroken. All those young men throwing themselves on the enemy's bayonets, the same way our people did fighting the Germans. One million and seven hundred thousand souls perished in my country. America hasn't lost that many people in all of its wars combined. Only the Soviets, during the WW II, suffered more fatalities. They got caught with their pants down early on: 13,684,692 civilians dead, according to the Russian Academy of Science. They had to throw everything at the enemy, the same way we did, and losses were commensurate with that commitment. The philosophy of a war for survival makes a few thousand Australian casualties seem somewhat irrelevant, considering that they fought on the other side of the world, in the name of the British Empire, to affirm their own national identity. Every time I'd see "Lest we forget," during the Anzac Day anniversary, I was reminded of my homeland, and the freedom that we paid for in so much unnecessary blood.

Being a Muslim in Australia didn't even cross my mind until my Australian girlfriend started wondering aloud why no one responded to my job applications. "It must be because of your name," she concluded as if pragmatism actually needed defenders. Once in the street, a few drunken Aussies called my friend and me "bloody Turks." It was a funny situation, though. My friend couldn't understand their slurred speech, and he was Macedonian. He'd rather run a gauntlet than be considered a Turk. Later, when I told him, he wanted to go back and start a fight.

I definitely didn't want that. If I had the power, my vision for a better world wouldn't have the word "fight" in it. But then we would have to come up with a better term when "fighting" for survival, I suppose. Maybe that's the first issue we need to address: why do we fight at all? Is it really about our survival, or is it about something else?

As far as the world goes, as we know it, I sense the nonobvious presence of a hovering virtual world that has an invisible power over the minds of humanity. According to my understanding, this virtual world is controlled by and benefits an elite class concealed behind a curtain of propaganda and disinformation. If Global capitalism is our raison d'etre, then we will need more cheap labor and energy. If our principal motivation is to exploit the opportunity for immediate profits, turning us all into slaves of modern technology — if that's what we have lived and died for these past two thousand years, then human life on Earth has been a sad joke.

But if our policy is placing the interest of entire world above those of individual ownerships and nations, then perhaps the pursuit of cosmopolitanism is our purpose. Only when one's identity transcends geography or political borders and economic systems will there be any hope for entire mankind. The global human community needs to be inter-reliant and holistic, and to be in this club, one needs to have a peaceful and universal heart of compassion that is "neither of the East nor of the West."

Epilogue
In case we pass on before achieving such a subtle heart, WE MIGHT WANT TO CONSIDER WHAT WE COULD BE REBORN AS? Hmmm, let's see… With all of the nanosized aluminum dust being sprayed into the atmosphere to control the weather, the chances are we might come back as an airplane or, at least, an aluminum soda

can. But the good news for all those sunbathers and climatologists complaining about ultraviolet radiation and scorching temperatures is that pretty soon we won't need sunblock. While we are busy being congenially distracted by social media, geo-engineers are trying, literally, to block out the sun.

About Faruk's most recent book: *Third Country*

As if by a conspiracy of fate, Faïk leaves Bosnia a few months before war breaks out. He embarks on a five-year journey, venturing across three continents, and eventually reaching Australia. Meanwhile, the rest of his family winds up in Oregon. In France, Faïk serves as an interpreter to Bosnian refugees who survived the Serb-run death camps. After the war, they are scattered around the world, relatively situated and brought back to "normalcy." The hanging question one confronts is whether those people will ever be able to adapt to their new lives in the West. Twenty years later, Faïk is shocked at learning that Omarska, the notorious death camp, also a producing ore mine, is now owned by Arcerol Mittal, the world's largest steel company, and that oil was "recently discovered" in Bosnia! Tormented by war, the poor victims had no choice but to accept "the dominant paradigm" — the only reason why nobody bothered intervening sooner, saving innocent lives, was because Bosnia had no oil! The legend became fact last year, when the Bosnian government started talks on oil exploration concession with Shell, ultimately deciding to grant it.

In America, immersed in democracy subverted by corporatism, Faïk can't help but notice and feel the difference. Back home, never a communist and shunning the uniformity of any system, he soon discovers that America's independent individualism is the flip-side of the same coin. People are officially free…physically. Mentally, they are enslaved by materialistic fantasies and the desire for gadgets. Faïk begins to sense the non-obvious presence of a hovering virtual world that has an invisible power over people's minds, and which is controlled by and benefits an elite class concealed behind the curtain of propaganda and disinformation.

"The belief in a supernatural source of evil is not necessary.
Men alone are quite capable of every wickedness."
~ Joseph Conrad ~

"Where no one intrudes, many can live in harmony."
~ Chief Dan George ~

"Nothing in all the world is more dangerous than sincere
ignorance and conscientious stupidity."
~ Martin Luther King, Jr. ~

Chapter Twelve

The Battle From Within
(A veteran's philosophy)

Brian "Bush" Bashant

Brian "Bush" Bashant (on the right with Juan F. Rosas) is a United States Army veteran, owner of "Fallen-Not-Forgotten" apparel and President/CEO of the "By My Side" foundation aimed at bringing one-on-one support to every hard-working American that has just reached a complicated obstacle and needs a little boost. Brian has had multiple jobs in various states and countries allowing him to experience some of life's "craziest adventures." He has fought in war and fought against natural disasters. He's fought in the cage and fought for love. He lives for the moments of laughter and unity and is completely dedicated to creating a positive environment for not only his near surroundings, but for a nation.

9/11/2001

I was in eleventh grade. It was second period. I had been up all night hanging out with friends so my head was on my backpack. The door flung open with the voice of a former student telling the teacher to turn on the news that something bad had happened. In panic, she stormed across the room and turned on the television. One of the twin towers was on fire with the news anchor speaking words of terror. My eyes opened and I felt nothing but ache and shock. Students who had family in New York bolted to the hallway to place phone calls in desperate need of their loved ones' voices. Our nation had been attacked. Tears fell to the floor and questions on who could commit such chaos and terror, and then another plane struck the remaining tower.

This life has a lot to offer and over the past 30 years I've endured multiple life changing experiences. From a variety of jobs to airborne infantry serving 15 months in Iraq, to veteran traveling the journey of entrepreneurship, my voyage has gifted me with attributes for my future experiences and has taught me many valuable lessons. I don't claim to know everything, but below are the outcomes of my mistakes and the results of my lessons allowing me to contribute these opinions towards our nation's greatest battle, the battle from within.

Reality Check

War - 15 months out of country, 100-plus degrees, 400+ missions, high quantity and high value targets captured and caches seized, too many brothers taken. The lessons from war were valuable and they changed my outlook forever. I now understand how short life truly is. How valuable each day really is. We only get one body and one time frame to travel and accomplish as much as we can. There are no do-over's or take-backs. It's mysterious to me that when I was young my parents and surrounding mature figures would always give me advice and most of the time it would end with, "Trust me, I've been there before." I always think to myself that if I would have listened where would I be today? What if I took in their words and trusted their advice? Would I have deployed overseas? Could all of this been avoided? I always say that being sent to war was my punishment for not taking the right paths and listening to others when I should have. Our lessons just come in mysterious ways. Unfortunately in war, along with other occasions, there are sometimes no lessons, just results that you're handed and told to deal with.

I've always been an outgoing guy and making friends has never been an issue, but because of being so outgoing I think I have a flaw in allowing others in easily. "Best friends" is a term I rarely use. SPC Todd E. Davis was my "best friend." The whole first half of my military career it seemed like he was with me every day. It was probably 4:30 in the morning and I was pulling guard duty on a balcony in Iraq. It must have been 30 degrees outside. I had my sleeping bag pulled over my body with the zipper broken in the middle, so my M4 and eyes would be of use. My shift had come to an end and I was so damn excited to get inside and get warm. I opened up the door, stormed in shivering, expressing how freezing it had been outside. The room was silent and the brothers were putting off a vibe I'll never forget. My squad leader looked at me and without hesitating he swallowed his spit and said, "Hunter element was hit last night, Bashant." I immediately knew that that was Davis' crew and without a pause I asked, "Is everyone okay?" He said, "It's all bad," and then a voice came over the radio stating our fallen brothers' names. He was the third name to be mentioned out of seven. The whole house blew up with all our brothers inside it. I couldn't breathe. I couldn't feel my body. I turned and went back out the door. It was in that moment that I realized how painful life can really be.

In that case I never actually accepted what really happened and, in all honesty, I don't know if I ever will, but I carry around the event. It's such a detrimental moment that I feel it destroyed certain areas of myself, and I don't know if I'll ever be the same again. A full soul if you will. Of course, after my discharge, I realized how different I was than (seemingly) everyone else. I have always been like that, but back then it was not in a way that I looked at myself as being different. It was the pain of loss and the adrenaline that was instilled in me that I carried around daily. That mix made for a very confusing mindset. For years I dug deep seeking a cure for my "injury." Labeled with PTSD, handed a bag full of pills, and consistently reminded that people (VA) were there to help me while statistics preached 18-25 veterans kill themselves daily, I denied all approaches coming from the outside. I knew that if I wanted to heal up and find peace again I was going to have to gain victory over the battle from within.

Heal up and Pursue all!

I knew that the adrenaline fast pace lifestyle would die down over time, but I also knew that the pain would last forever if I did not treat the injury properly. I tried to overcompensate my depression with love. It only brought me more pain. You cannot truly love someone if you don't even love yourself. I tried to go out with as many friends as I could, hide the pain, and have as great of a time as possible but it left them uncomfortable and me drunk. I lost the ability to smile and everyone I met could see it. Even if they didn't, it felt like it and on a day to day basis I was reminded what rock bottom felt like. I kept telling myself how unfair it was to step up and become a man that ended up leaving me feeling like I was a burden to society. September 11, 2001, struck this nation like the loss of my brothers struck me. A moment that had no lesson, just a tragedy that we were faced to deal with. We never really accepted our loss and we never really accepted the pain it caused us. We sent our troops into foreign territory thinking that war was the cure to heal our wounds. We now see that it's only causing more chaos and still to this day we lie here in pain while guaranteeing more to come. We need to shut out the outside and heal from within like I once had to.

A lot of nights I would catch myself feeling so down with a massive chunk of my once-had confidence missing. It's all I used to run off of was confidence. I looked every challenge in the eye and took it on with the pedal floored. It's amazing how important confidence is for myself. Now that I look back at the days of suffering, I see how easy I used to submit to things that I would never usually allow to happen. In a way it was as if I gave up on myself and didn't really care what would happen to me. I was already at rock bottom so what else could possibly happen to me? That thought really makes me feel upset now. How could I allow myself to give up on the one thing that is the most important thing, myself? How could I not see that when I gave up on myself, I gave up on my family, my friends and ones that wanted to be a part of my future? I was wasting everything valuable!

I look at our nation now as the same as I was during that time. We got hit so hard that we think we can't get out of this. We are at rock bottom, and now we are just being pushed around and could care less about what is happening to us because there is just no hope. We are forgetting how important our confidence is. We are forgetting that throughout history this nation has been hit before and the reason we were never separated is because we were unstoppable from within. You couldn't break our pride and love for ourselves as a nation. No one messed with who we were as a nation and what we were as a nation, and the world knew because there was no way they couldn't know. You can't wake up one day and say that it's time you changed. You have to start small and gradually heal. The skin when cut doesn't just heal at once. It slowly heals from the inside and works its way to the outer surface until it is completely healed properly. Each individual needs to gain their own confidence and build outwards. You can't tell others what to do while you do the complete opposite and without confidence in one's self, no one will follow.

There are a few different types of breeds in our society. I always say that there are "Creators" and there are "Maintainers." This nation was not built on people who maintained a normal living. America was built from the ideas and creations of people who saw something different/new and took the risk in creating it. You have to take the risk if you want the gain and to better yourself. Becoming a better person is not from staying the same or staying where you are. You have to pursue the "better you" or advance past something that wasn't working for you. As a society we will never advance if we just maintain what our ancestors gave to us. We need to contribute. We need to take risks in bettering ourselves as human beings and as a society.

It's not hard to look around and realize that our ancestors broke their backs to give us what they had and witness us just living off of their hard work. We are the laziest that we have ever been. Our mind-sets are just off the charts. I think many are so easily happy with being handed everything on a silver platter, and it is because it provides them with a "comfort zone." Every time a challenge presents itself or there is opportunity to advance, we instantly push it away because it might force us to leave our "comfort zone." I've been comfortable many times and have had the opportunity to live in a "comfort zone," but I couldn't feel a sense of accomplishment living off someone else's success. You have to want to build that success for yourself and for your family. It's time to get to work and put those God given talents to use. Our nation was not built by those living in their "comfort zone," and I feel a huge part of our downfall right now is because of too many people living off of others' hard work. Get out of that "comfort zone" and use your past experiences to assist you in entering the future. Without a will to pursue a goal or dream, it leaves you to wander. When you wander, you will cross areas and paths that you don't belong in and now you are just affecting other people's objectives. You in a way are being a bother to others pursuing.

Right now we are faced with the act of minimum wage increasing because people think that those minimum wage jobs should be able to support their lifestyle. Since I was 5 years old I've always known that I could not make a living at a minimum wage job. That's why they are called "minimum wage" jobs. They are for our youth and immigrants to establish a work ethic and the ways of business. Once you are comfortable with all of those understandings you apply for the "career" jobs and you leave that "comfort zone" to better yourself and your pay grade. I understand tough times are ahead and I know life hits so hard that it drops us down to nothing in only moments. It is in that time where our measures are truly tested. What we do when knocked down is what the true meaning of living truly is. If it were easy, everyone could do it, and if everyone were to be handed freebies every time they struggled, this nation would not be what it is today. This debate displays the mindset of our nation as of right now and shows how used we are to just getting what we want instead of going out and working for it. Don't want the life of handouts. Want that fight to gain everything you've always imagined. Have pride in yourself and leave your "comfort zone" as much as possible until you are happy with what you've created.

"Our deepest fear is not that we are inadequate. Our deepest fear is that we are powerful beyond measure. It is our light, not our darkness that most frightens us. We ask ourselves, who am I to be brilliant, gorgeous, talented, and fabulous? Actually, who are you not to be? You are a child of God. Your playing small does not serve the world. There is nothing enlightened about shrinking so that other people will not feel insecure around you. We are all meant to shine, as children do. We were born to make manifest the glory of God that is within us. It is not just in some of us; it is in everyone and as we let our own light shine, we unconsciously give others permission to do the same. As we are liberated from our own fear, our presence automatically liberates others."
~ Marianne Williamson ~

Confused?

I'd like to cover something that when I realized it, drastically assisted me in bettering myself. It gave me such a perspective, one I thought I'd never understand. As covered before, there are moments that we experience that change the ways we look at life and the people surrounding us. We start to think deeper into the situation because of those experiences. It's a blessing and a curse I always say, but, in all honesty, it's all made me realize how contradicting life is. We are to make money to survive, but money doesn't bring us happiness. We are to live every day like we could pass tomorrow, but be patient and get a job. The Lord said to be fruitful, but don't commit adultery. Help as many as you can, but take care of yourself. Don't hurt others, but defend yourself. It seems like with direction and guidance like that we would all be standing around with our hands up asking what in the hell are we supposed to do if we can't go that way and we can't go this way, but go we must. We do head down a certain way in order to see, and we do make mistakes in order to learn, and we do ask for forgiveness, but then do it again. I think of the word "contradicting" and I relate it to life and it seems so difficult, but then I think of my journey and the paths I've walked so far. Life is so very difficult. Life

151

has been so hard on me. Life is so absolutely beautiful. Life is so full of peaceful moments. We are gifted with the greatest challenges and with the most effective assets in overcoming those challenges without being told how long we have to do so. It is one big mystery and the ultimate challenge. Don't waste any time wandering, and spend all your time going in the way you know is true to your heart. Understand that it is in the grey of life's contradictions where the truth to life really lies, and once you realize that, it should make you want to go after everything imaginable and just enjoy the journey becoming as much as you can become with the greatest people to your left and right. I wish nothing more for you.

"Final Look"

One day I went up to a brother (name to not be disclosed) to bum a smoke from him, he handed me a cigarette, I slapped his ass and asked him (jokingly), "Whatever happened to us?" and I told him that I hated that we didn't spend more time together (it's a military thing, don't judge). We laughed and then loaded up into two separate trucks and rolled out. The day was beautiful until 20 minutes later he took a shot to the head. I sprinted over to him, grabbed his hand while Doc was treating him, and started to speak to him (100% serious now) about the moments we all spent together, and that after he recovered we would create some more. He held my hand with a tight grip and then was lifted to be placed on the med-evac chopper. They wouldn't let me go with him. He died a few minutes after being apart. I thought deep that night. I wished I could have continued to reminisce with him and keep him focused on staying alive. The time that we had before he passed was his "Final Look." He was able to go back and see all the great times he/we had and all the fine memories he encountered. It is in that moment that I realized that when my time comes and it's my turn to be lying there listening to someone remind me of my past that I would not let there be one second of silence. I don't want to look back and say, damn it was great just sitting around doing nothing my whole life. I always thank my fallen brothers through prayer for saving me and showing me that life is to not be wasted. We perfect ourselves and gain that confidence we need to pursue new heights and then we share it with our youth to make sure they have that same drive and determination. What is your 'Final Look" going to be like?

"I firmly believe that any man's finest hour, the greatest fulfillment of all that he holds dear, is that moment when he has worked his heart out in a good cause and lies exhausted on the field of battle - victorious."

~ Vince Lombardi ~

UNBREAKABLE!

Along with the prior messages the military gave me a powerful insight that will forever be the backbone to my beliefs in unity and guide my vision for my foundation (By My Side foundation). After meeting so many people with all different traits (education, strength, common sense, confidence levels) and told that we would all be working together as one, I said to myself there is no way we could all perform on the same level and get the job done! In a short period of time after consistent focused training, we were all unstoppable. There was no distance we couldn't travel and no objective we could not accomplish. It was powerful to witness. It made me want to grasp the understanding of controlling such a massive organization that was clearly made up of people from all different places of the world and so organized and powerful.

It all came down to the ways we operated as individuals that were operating as a whole. Each section had a leader and those leaders were carrying out orders for one leader, all working towards the same main objective. All the judgments (race, gender, etc) that we see in society did not exist once we all put that uniform on. It was like those negative emotions that one would have on the outside towards another never even came across our minds. They are not even brought up. They just didn't exist because we realized how low level it really was to waste your time even thinking that way about others. I absolutely love and miss that dearly. I watched it day in and day out and it all came down to a system; everything and everyone operating as told and carrying out their purpose. If one thing went wrong it would affect the entire objective and we all knew that. Even though we were not the leaders and we were always being told what to do, we all believed in the objective and all egos were pushed aside. We were forced to max ourselves as individuals both physically and mentally for months but when our training was done and we all linked up as one, it was the assembling of a massive structure that was unbreakable. It is so important to understand the true meaning of unity and how easily any obstacle can be overcome if we work as one. If this nation all had the same core values and as individuals pushed away all those ridiculous ways to cause separation amongst each other, 80 percent of this nation's issues would be fixed almost overnight. I know it's got to be so hard to stop hating people because of where they are from, what color they are or what they believe in though, right? Stating an opinion of hatred towards another removes a portion of the best parts of yourself. By hurting someone else, you actually hurt yourself along with others who heard what you said. Stay positive and understand that you are judging someone for absolutely no reason. Making comments on someone's race, religion, etc. is like judging them for what toothpaste they use. That's how small you are for doing so.

Our Business

I can't think of one class in my younger days in which I wasn't an absolute pain in the ass. I would say anything that came to my mind, and all I wanted to do was get everyone else to laugh. I wanted attention and I wanted people to like me. It's in everyone, but there are some that are disciplined enough to do it respectfully. I didn't do anything respectfully, and while the whole class wanted to listen and learn, I was disrupting that and causing confrontation. One day the teacher dragged me outside and straight up gave it to me. She said how disruptive I was being and how unfair it really was to all the other people trying to learn. I'll never forget this. She said that she wanted me to imagine that I was back in the class making everyone laugh and all were paying attention to me; she then said that would never ever happen and it's not reality. What's really happening is that I was being an undisciplined kid who was ruining the class for everyone. I was taking away their time to get an education and learn new things.

The terrorism, the racism, the hate and chaos that is massively affecting our nation right now is nothing more than an obnoxious child in our classroom. Our teacher (president) needs to step up and put them in their places. You do not stop in the middle of class and get on the same level as the child and start a debate with him/her. That brings you down to the same level as the child and still ruins the learning period for the others around. Not only that, it is actually teaching them to argue and act in the same manner. You definitely do not take it out on the class and say this is their fault either! Right now this nation (our classroom) is filled with obnoxious little shits (excuse my language). There is so much arguing and complaining going on and no authority stepping up removing the ones causing all this chaos and our teacher is in the corner doing nothing. We are by far the most powerful nation in the world and we set the standard for this world to live by.

Yes, we get disrespect thrown our way a lot and our actions are sometimes not seen so clearly, but we are disciplined enough to step up and do what needs to be done on a much higher level than most can grasp. We are the nation that makes the executive decisions, and we do not have time to be dealing with such childish behavior and debates. If we cannot have at all times a leader/teacher in position that can maintain an organized and united nation then he/she needs to be removed. There are 300+ million people in our America and it is unacceptable to allow someone who is failing in keeping our country physically and mentally healthy for the remainder of their term (years). This nation no matter how you look at it is a business and if this business is not bringing in profits and treating its employees with respect, it will become disorganized and a punishing chain of events will take place until the doors close. We cannot allow that to happen. Would you keep a manager of your business in charge if he was ruining everything? Take a person from the ghetto and place them in another ghetto they would probably care less, but take a person of wealth and remove all of his privileges and place him in the ghetto, he would be a mental wreck. He would lose his hair line.

The ones who have led in the past and the ones who want to lead now, the ones who work hard day in and day out to give half of their earnings away, the ones who are tired of the media smothering them with negativity are losing their hairlines. We are mental wrecks right now because these "obnoxious children" will not be "scolded." Our president is trading with terrorists. Our teacher let five of the most obnoxious children in the world into our classroom in front of the classroom. It's time for the grown-ups to step in and set everyone straight. Unacceptable consistent decision making, no profits or gains, unorganized employees...you are fired! No one person should ever have the power to run our business into the ground, and at no point should one not be able to be fired on the spot. We should never allow this business to get this bad. We have not fought and broke our backs to live in such a pathetic way. This is so small and dangerous that we must never let it happen again. We are the greatest business in the world. We are the greatest nation in the world. We pay for proper leadership and direction in our country. If we don't like it or where it's going, then we need to get together and fire him/her. We are this nation. God bless America and God bless you!

"Find the greatness within you. Share it with others and help them to find theirs in themselves. Lead from the front, never give up and always keep the faith."

~ Brian "Bush" Bashant ~

In loving memory of the victims of Sept 11th

In loving memory of my fallen brothers:

> SSG Sean M. Gaul
> SSG Jonathan K. Dozier
> SPC Todd E. Davis
> SGT Chris Sanders
> SGT Zachary McBride
> SFC Matthew I. Pionk
> SPC William Sullivan
> SGT Jonathan Gilbert
> SGT Shawn McCann
> CPL Wayne M. Geiger

And to all of our Nation's bravest who sacrificed so much for what we have today. Both civilian and veterans, we miss you every day.

Forever will the pack remain… WOLFPACK!

"Together we can, together we will!"

Website - www.Fallen-Not-Forgotten.com
Email – Fnforgotten@gmail.com
Facebook – Brian M. Bashant
Twitter - @FNForgotten

"Ideology separates us. Dreams and anguish bring us together."
~ Playwright Eugene Ionesco ~

"What is it in us that seeks the truth? Is it our minds
or is it our hearts?"
~ John Grisham (from *A Time to Kill*) ~

"It's easier to con someone than to convince them
that they've been conned."
~ Research points to Mark Twain ~

Chapter Thirteen

Iberia, Islam, and International Relations: My Journey in a Post 9-11 World

Timothy L. Christopher

Timothy L. Christopher is a writer and researcher of religious and ethnic conflict, warfare, foreign policy and politics. A veteran of the United States Navy, Tim has traveled throughout the Mediterranean, Caribbean, and West Africa, where he participated in Operation Sharp Edge, evacuating embassies and foreign nationals during the Liberian Civil War. He holds a Bachelor's of Science in Philosophy, Politics, and Economics from Eastern Oregon University, and a Master's of Science in Political Science from Portland State University. Tim has researched and written about counterinsurgency, religious and ethnic conflict, foreign affairs, and the geo-politics of Africa, the Middle East, and Asia. He is currently researching the strategic doctrine of various terror groups and the strategic implications for the United States, as well as the historical development of state-sponsored terrorism in South Asia and its impact on regional and global politics. Tim lives in Oregon with his wife and four children.

"Grief can be the garden of compassion. If you keep your heart open through everything, your pain can become your greatest ally in your life's search for love and wisdom."
~ Rumi ~

9/11/2001

Two days prior to the terrorist attacks on the United States, I had boarded a ship in Los Angeles as a newlywed, sailing along the western coast of Mexico for an eight-day vacation. When I awoke on the morning of the 11th, I had no idea what was happening in the skies above the East Coast, or how dramatically the course of my life would change. Forty-eight hours into my honeymoon, I was watching United Airlines Flight 175 slam into the South Tower of the World Trade Center. The images of billowing black smoke, massive piles of rubble, and innocent Americans plunging hundreds of feet to their deaths would change the course of my life.

On board the cruise ship, the atmosphere was a mixture of disbelief and panic. Passengers sat in silence, either glued to the televisions broadcasting news reports and images of the attacks, or begging the ship's crew to pull into port and allow them to go home to their families. Returning home was, for the moment, impossible. All air traffic was grounded. All ports were closed. Like everyone else that had boarded the ship two days earlier, I was trapped at sea with no way home.

Once the government ended the nation-wide lockdown, the ship was allowed to enter port in Los Angeles, and all the passengers set about finding a way home. Once I arrived at the airport, it was a ghost town. It was almost completely empty. All scheduled flights had been cancelled, and many travelers were too frightened to board a plane and instead made a mad rush for the rental car desks. I was one of forty-eight passengers on standby for a flight from Los Angeles, California, to Portland, Oregon. At that time, there was so little air travel that all forty-eight passengers that were on standby found seats on our flight, with a third of the seats still empty.

It was when everyone had boarded and the plane was taxiing that I was aware of the first of many changes that were to occur in the post 9-11 America. Over the course of the previous few days, details had emerged concerning the hijacking. Once in our seats, I realized that every seat on the aisle was filled with a male passenger, with all female passengers in the middle or window seats. It was an oddly unifying feeling. Every man on that flight, myself included, sat in the aisle with the full intent of stopping anyone who planned a repeat of the hijackings that had destroyed the World Trade Towers.

When I first returned home, my initial response was to return to the military, something that my then wife and her family could not understand. No one in their family had ever served in the military. In contrast, I had gone into the Navy straight out of high school. My great uncle had fought in the South Pacific; my father had been in the Army, had then transferred to and retired from the Air Force. As a veteran, I felt an obligation to come to my country's aid when it was attacked. I felt I had a skill set that would be useful in the upcoming war in Afghanistan. As I tried to reenlist over the course of the next few months, my family and friends repeatedly told me that this was not my war, that I had done my part, and that I had nothing left to prove. Deep down I knew they were wrong, but after the constant pressure to stay out of the war, I relented. I gave up on returning to the military.

As the country realized that the objectives in the war in Afghanistan would not be attained as easily as promised, I decided that if I could not help fight terrorism with the military, I would find another way. I began to read everything I could get my hands on that I felt was relevant to the war the United States found itself in: U.S. foreign policy, military history, counterinsurgency, terrorism, Islam, Special Forces, geography, comparative religions, anything and everything. I read books by Andrew Bacevich, Ahmed Rashid, David Kilcullen, Gen. Rupert Smith, and Robert D. Kaplan, along with dozens of others. I would make my mind into a weapon with which to fight, or so I thought.

As the years passed, I continued to read as much as I could. But while constantly reading about the far off and dusty places, I had developed a desire to see the world first hand, outside the constraints of my military service. While in the U.S. Navy, I had been deployed to the Caribbean, the Mediterranean, and West Africa during the Liberian Civil War. But I wanted to see the world as the people who lived in the areas I was reading about did. How did they work? How did they eat? How did they view the world, and is it that different from the way I saw things?

In November of 2006, I had saved enough for a round trip ticket to Spain. I had decided to backpack rather than stay in hotels, avoiding reservations, and using the Internet to find available lodging. I rejected the large hotels, resorts, and restaurants where I would find more Americans than I would Spaniards, and sought out hostels where I could avoid familiarity and experience a foreign country. I bunked with Spaniards and other travelers, eating where the locals did. I went to Spain for Spain.

My first few days in Spain were spent in Madrid. I walked the streets, practiced my Spanish, and soaked up the newness of an ancient city. The cobblestone streets, sun-baked doors with peeling paint, fountains, crowds, sounds and smells; all of it was incredible. Huge legs of cured Iberico hams hung in windows, scooters and motorbikes were everywhere, and everyone drank wine, regardless of the time of day. With old buildings, bullfighting posters, and the arid climate, I felt as though I was on the frontier of Europe, vaguely familiar but distant and far away. After spending a few days exploring Madrid,

I arrived at the train station and, with my growing Spanish speaking abilities, purchased a train ticket to Valencia. The winding route from central Spain to the Mediterranean coast took the better part of the day, much of which I spent with two Spaniards, conversing in my "adequate" Spanish language skills and enjoying a long but pleasant ride.

When I arrived in Valencia, the train station I stopped at was across from the Plaza de Toros de Valencia, the grand bull fighting ring built in the 1850s. The massive structure loomed above me in the bright Spanish sun, and made me feel like I was in another world and another time. There it stood, surrounded by blossoming orange trees. The ochre masonry and repeating arches were like nothing I had ever seen in the States.

As beautiful as I had found the cities of Valencia and Madrid, it was in Spain's southern territory, in the cities of Granada and Cordoba, where I found the reason I had travelled across the Atlantic. Here, in Spain's dusty and sun-drenched south was Andalusia, the once Moorish Kingdom of Al-Andalus, and the Islamic Caliphate of Cordoba. Known as Hispania under the Christian Visigoths, the region was conquered in 711 by the Islamic General Tariq ibn Ziyad, and would be under Islamic control until the fall of Granada in 1492 during the Reconquista. The 781 years of Islamic rule and influence the region produced art, architecture, and food that symbolized the conflict and cooperation between Muslims, Christians, and Jews in the Iberian Peninsula. In the post 9-11 world, I felt that this history in particular was again repeating itself.

In Granada, I visited the Alhambra, the 14th century Moorish fortress set in Spain's Sierra Nevada Mountains. Islamic poets described the fortress as a pearl set in emeralds, referring to the bright, white washed color of its buildings and the myrtle forests surrounding them. But the name Alhambra itself is a reference to the red clay soil from the surrounding countryside that was used to build the massive structure. I walked the grounds of the fortress, amazed at the gardens, pools, art, and architecture. While Europe had languished in the Dark Ages, Islamic Spain had exotic animals, rose gardens, orchards, pools, fountains, and sewage systems. This massive fortress was so lush and ornate, and such a far cry from where the Islamic world seemingly was now, I didn't know what to make of the current state of international affairs.

From Granada, I took a two-hour bus ride northwest to the city of Cordoba. Set along the Guadalquivir River, Cordoba had been the capital of Hispania Ulterior during the Roman Republic, and later the capital of Hispania Baetica during the Roman Empire. After the Moorish invasions of Spain, Qurṭubah was the capital of the Islamic Caliphate of Cordoba, which ruled most of the Iberian Peninsula. Al-Hakam II, who secured peace with the Christian Kingdoms of Northern Spain, ruled the region from 961 to 976. The Caliphate of Cordoba became famous for the resurrection of the writings of Aristotle and Maimonides, paving the way for Thomas Aquinas, along with a massive 400,000-volume library, and groundbreaking advancements in medicine, mathematics, astronomy, and philosophy.

The mixture of Islamic and European influences was exemplified in the Great Mosque of Cordoba, or La Mezquita. A stunning example of both Christian and Islamic art and architecture, the Great Mosque boasts the great prayer hall, a massive room with over 800 columns and arches of jasper, onyx, marble, and granite, much of which was salvaged from ruined buildings from the Roman Empire, including the Merida Amphitheatre from the province of Lusitania. There was gilded Arabic script surrounding the mihrab, or prayer niche, as well as ornate domes, minarets, mosaics, and carved wooden screens alongside a towering European organ carved in wood and accented with gold leaf. Outside, the rectangular courtyard was lined with orange trees where the magnificent bell tower covered what was once the minaret. Here I found ancient Rome, Medieval Islam, and Renaissance Europe converging in one building, and it would affect me in a way I had not expected.

When I returned home from Spain, my experiences stayed with me. All of the history, art, architecture, and religion that I had seen were constantly in the forefront of my thoughts. While I had thought that by traveling abroad I would find answers to the questions I had been asking, I realized that I had only more questions. How had Islamic culture created such magnificent structures like the ones I had seen while Europe languished in the Dark Ages? How had the modern Middle East seemingly lost the advancements in science, architecture, and mathematics that it had developed over the centuries? And why had not the Middle East experienced a resurgence similar to the one it had centuries prior? Was the answer simply that European colonialism and American interference wreaked havoc throughout the region?

The idea that the West was at fault for the decline and fall of the Middle East simply did not answer the question for me, and left me wanting more information. The reasons I heard and read explaining the attitudes of Muslims towards the U.S. ranged from interfering in domestic politics to the Israeli-Palestinian crisis to oil companies to military bases. None of these seemed to me to be sufficient. I wanted to develop my own answers to the questions of Islam, the West, and international affairs. One month after I returned home from the Mediterranean, I quit my job and returned to college.

After a few courses at the community college near my home, I was accepted to Eastern Oregon University's Philosophy, Politics, and Economics program. There, I studied philosophy, religion, law, and Islam, as well as public policy, politics and media, economic theory, and terrorism. I found that I was continually drawn to courses and research where politics, religion, and conflict intersected. When I researched the role of the media in the Rwandan genocide, I knew I had found the path I wanted my career and my life to take. While ethnic Hutus had used the media to ferment violence against the Tutsi population, the Clinton administration had used the media to avoid involvement in the genocide, with the assistant press secretary using the media to debate the legal definition of the term genocide, allowing the administration to sidestep any political or military commitment in the conflict.

Once I completed my senior thesis on Lashkar-e-Taiba, one of the most active, violent, and dangerous terrorist groups operating in South Asia, I realized that all my studies again raised more questions than it did answers. The ethical and moral considerations of war and foreign policy interested me greatly, but just how those considerations affected American politics overseas was a topic I wanted to know more about. Did the United States really want democracy abroad? Did the Islamic world really despise America's freedoms? What were the ethical considerations of the wars in Iraq and Afghanistan? Dr. Andrew J. Bacevich, author and professor of history and international relations at Boston University had been gracious enough to speak with me and, after conversing with him, I decided to apply to graduate school to study political science and international relations, with the hope of finding more answers to the questions that had been pressing me since 9-11.

I was thrilled when I was granted entrance to Portland State University's Political Science graduate program for fall term 2010. I was offered the position of research assistant to Dr. David Kinsella, chair of the political science department, a position that I happily accepted. Being a research assistant allowed me to earn a small stipend while working towards my Master's degree, but more importantly, it would allow me to work much more closely with the professors at the university and learn to do top tier research in my chosen field. I had a lunch meeting with Dr. Kinsella where we discussed the direction of

my studies and how he thought I should develop my ideas, after which
I enrolled in my first term of coursework. Over the course of my graduate program, I studied International relations, law, and organizations,
as well as the comparative politics of the Middle East, North and Sub-
Saharan Africa, and civil and ethnic conflict. I read about the theories
of international relations that hoped to explain the occurrences of war
or peace, economic prosperity or grinding poverty, in regions as diverse as China, Sweden, Botswana, Jordan, Germany, and Iran. Had
someone told me that four years after traveling to Spain I would be in
graduate school studying international relations, ethics, and conflict, I
wouldn't have believed them, but there I was. It was heaven.

But there were also challenges and controversy. The invasions
of Iraq and Afghanistan were still hotly debated, and the reasons and
motives behind the World Trade Center attacks were just as contested.
During seminars and debates, theories that U.S. interference, encroach-
ment of Western ideas, colonialism, and lack of democracy across the
Middle East always seemed to be default explanations. When explaining terrorism, the Western nations had essentially brought these gruesome attacks on themselves.

But under a bit of scrutiny, these explanations just did not hold
up. If colonialism and Western interference were the reason behind terrorism and lack of development across the region, then other regions
with similar experiences would produce similar results. The French
colonized both Vietnam and Algeria, but the outcomes for these countries are vastly different. Vietnam has no radicalized terrorist networks
and has an economy that continues to grow and develop. The same can
be said when comparing British rule in its colonies, comparing Malaysia and Egypt or Palestine under colonialism. In fact, British rule in
Malaysia was much more oppressive than most places in the Middle
East, with a war and counterinsurgency lasting over 10 years.

If the answer was simply European colonialism, there would be
more evidence of religious extremism and terrorism in Vietnam and
Malaysia - as there is in the Middle East. What is most interesting is
that when there is religious extremism in Southeast Asia, much of it
can be traced to the influences of the Middle East or Pakistan. Colonialism alone cannot explain the violence that originates in the Middle
East or elsewhere in the region. Countries such as Ethiopia and India,
and the island of Bali, have little or no history of colonialism. They
have more often than not been victims of colonialism rather than the
beneficiary, yet are targets of Islamic militancy.

The lack of democracy across the Middle East could not

sufficiently explain what has happened in terms of extremism, violence, and terror in the region either. Many made the argument that once democracy is implemented across Middle Eastern countries, violence will stop. The belief was that since the violence and extremism stemming from the region is a by-product of crushing repression of authoritarian leaders, democracy and self rule will produce a more equitable, and thereby a more peaceful society. There are few other words that contain the emotion and the promise to remedy every political wrong other than the word democracy.

Former Pakistani Prime Minister Benazir Bhutto claimed in her book, *Reconciliation: Islam, Democracy, and the West,* that Islam and democracy are compatible, and that democracy is the preferred form of government for Muslims across the Greater Middle East. Given the opportunity, a vast majority of Muslims want the rule of democracy rather than a religiously motivated form of governance. But when held to the light of analysis, these claims did not quite hold the promise of a peaceful and equitable society in the Middle East. There was, and is, a difference between how the people of Middle East and the West view democracy, what it entails, and what democracy's perceived benefits might be.

The 2003 Foreign Policy article "The True Clash of Civilizations" illustrates this dilemma. Examining interview data from the World Values Survey, the article finds that democracy means vastly different things for individuals in Western societies than it does in predominantly Muslim ones. There are some similar views of democracy between the Middle East and the West. Both see the structural components of a democratic government as a positive. Democracies are considered to be the best type of government for maintaining order by a vast majority of respondents. Most people also believe that the democratic form is the best type of governmental system, and places restraints on leaders in the form parliaments and elections are a positive.

Aside from the similar attitudes with respect to the structural aspects of democracy, there are vast differences when comparing the idealistic aspects of democracy. While Middle Eastern societies want to adopt the Western institutions that they believe will bring about stability and accountability to government, the support for liberal social stances that Western societies take for granted do not exist at the same level in Middle Eastern societies. For example, support for gender equality is almost 30 percentage points lower in Middle Eastern countries as it is in the West, and while these numbers have steadily risen in the West, gender equality in the Middle East has remained almost stagnant since World War II. These divergences are even more dramatic when examining issues of divorce, abortion, gay rights, and religion in politics.

With the "Islamic State" (aka: ISIS/ISIL) cutting a violent swath east of the "Levant" in Syria and Iraq, and the recent shootings at the Charlie Hebdo office in Paris, asking tough questions about Islam, militancy, and democracy are more important now than ever before. An interesting observation concerning militancy and global jihadist movements in Islam is the apparent lack of indigenous extremist groups outside of Arab majority countries. The countries of Kosovo, Albania, Bangladesh, Malaysia and Indonesia are all majority Muslim countries, with Bangladesh and Malaysia having Islam as the official religion of the state. While it may be a contributor to militancy, Islam is not the primary contributor, although it undeniably plays a part.

The militancy that does exist in countries such as Malaysia or Indonesia more often than not originates from outside the region, coming to these countries from the Arabic countries of the Middle East. This is not to say that indigenous militant groups exist, it is a fact that they do. Yet those that are the most violent and global in their aspirations predominately originate in one specific geographic area, the Middle East. It is an uncomfortable question to pursue in public discussion, but remains important.

At the end of February 2015, ISIS stormed into museums in Syria, taking sledgehammers to some of the most precious pieces of art representing ancient Assyrian culture in the world, destroying priceless artifacts and shocking the international community. As disturbing as it is, there is another example in recent years of Muslim extremists destroying relics of previous cultures that do not fit into their notion of a pure and historic Islamic Caliphate. The Taliban set on and nearly destroyed the Buddhas of Bamiyan in Afghanistan. The two Buddha statues, 58 and 38 meters respectively, were the largest examples of a standing Buddha until their destruction in March of 2001, with the Taliban using anti-aircraft guns and artillery, eventually resorting to high explosives.

The Taliban were an example of how cruel and ruthless religious extremism can be, both regionally as well as on its own domestic populations. ISIS, with its destruction of ancient Assyrian artifacts, has shown itself to be just as violent and dangerous, both domestically and internationally. ISIS began to ethnically cleanse communities in Syria, attacking both religious and ethnic minority communities, killing men, women, and children in some of the most gruesome and horrific ways imaginable.

I completed graduate school, writing my thesis on counterinsurgency theory, religious and ethnic conflict, and foreign policy strategy, but my journey since 9-11 continues. Finishing graduate school was not the end of my journey, but the beginning of a new chapter if you will, and I continue to ask tough questions. Is Islam more violent than other religions? Is their something about Arabic culture that has turned Islam violent, or is it simply a reaction to authoritarian regimes? Why haven't other religions in oppressive states turned as violent as Islam seems to? Answers I thought I had come to simply brought about more questions, many of which were, and still are, uncomfortable to ask.

But remaining comfortable dulls the mind and hampers the body, both literally and figurative. Yet to truly understand Islamic culture and history, and Islamic militancy's place in it, we are forced to asked tough questions, uncomfortable as asking these questions is. This is what I hope for the future: a desire and forum for individuals to ask these tough questions of others and themselves. We need to be able to have these discussions without lambasting one another as racist, bigoted, hypocritical, or imperialist. Stifling these types of conversations ultimately harms free societies and helps no one. As I continue with my own research and writing, I remind myself that lives depend on asking these questions. As Ernest Hemmingway once wrote, "The world is a fine place and worth fighting for."

Recommended Reading:

Out of the Mountains and Accidental Guerilla; David Kilcullen
War on Sacred Grounds; Ron E. Hassner
Treading on Hallowed Ground; C. Christine Fair, Ed.
The Ends of the Earth: A Journey at the Dawn of the 21st Century;
      Robert D. Kaplan
Learning to Eat Soup With a Knife; Lt. Col. John A. Nagl
The Utility of Force; Gen. Sir Rupert Smith
Children at War; P.W. Singer
God's Terrorists: The Wahhabi Cult and the Hidden Roots of Modern Jihad; Charles Allen
The Savage Wars of Peace; Max Boot
The Arabs: A History; Eugene Rogan
Taliban; Ahmed Rashid
Jihad; Ahmed Rashid
Descent into Chaos; Ahmed Rashid

A Peace to End All Peace; Peter Fromkin
Pakistan: A Hard Country; Anatol Lieven
Afghanistan: A Short History of Its People and Politics; Martin Ewans
Afghanistan: A Military History; Stephen Tanner

"If your actions inspire others to dream more, learn more,
do more and become more, you are a leader."
~ John Quincy Adams ~

"Racism is man's gravest threat to man –
the maximum of hatred for a minimum of reason."
~ Abraham Joshua Heschel ~

"The future belongs to those who believe in the
beauty of their dreams."
~ Eleanor Roosevelt ~

Chapter Fourteen

The Colors of My Dreams Post 9/11

Hina Anwar Ali

Hina Anwar Ali comes from Lahore, Pakistan, and graduated from Georgetown University, Washington D.C. in International Affairs and Religion. Earlier she did her BBIT from Curtin University, Australia. She spent the last ten years working in the development sector as General Manager in Architectural & Engineering Consulting, M/S Anwar Ali & Associates in Lahore, a premier consultancy firm she established with her father. She has been active in advocating for youth affairs, gender and human rights causes while representing the Government of Pakistan and the United Nations for more than a decade. Hina has also been closely associated with different non-profit organizations in Pakistan working on the above issues. The depth and breadth of her research publications address issues of human rights, gender, contemporary Islamic Thought in the Muslim world, non-violence and youth leadership. She plans to continue further studies in Islamic law and work in the areas of Islamic political thought, religious pluralism, women emancipation and human rights development.

Believers, uphold justice. Always bear true witness, even if it be against yourself, your parents, or your relatives—and regardless of whether the person against whom you are speaking is rich or poor. God is close to people regardless of their material circumstances. Do not be led by emotion, as this may cause you to swerve from the truth. If you distort your testimony, or refuse to testify, remember that God is aware of all your actions.
~ Qur'an, An-Nisa, Surah 4:135 ~

169

9/11/2001

Realities of living in Pakistan after 9/11 have become so intolerable and bleak that all I can paint now are the colors of my dreams. How many people get the opportunity to paint their dreams? This chapter is thus the colors of my dreams. It entails an active withdrawal from a reality that has turned hostile. I want to greatly hold on to the rare mood of jubilance and optimism. I know withdrawal into one's dreams can be dangerous. I reflect, and in so doing I know that maturity is the capacity to endure uncertainty.

I distinctly remember seeing the horrifying clippings of the attack on the World Trade Center on 11 September 2001 at home in Lahore. The days that followed involved a lot of television as I tried to make sense of the events. Switching between local news channels, CNN International and BBC, I could manifestly note how different the coverage was... heightened drama, emotional rhetoric, uninterrupted speculation. There were repeating videos of the attack on CNN versus more comprehensive analysis on BBC and other local news channels. Afterwards, I felt drained and tired, and out of sorts all day.

The TV shows after the staggering event were flooded with news analysis from both sides as a relatively unknown public figure, Osama Bin Laden, the mastermind behind these attacks, emerged. Pakistanis were shocked and a national debate started, which included people from all walks of life. I was hearing stories from various angles as journalists were reporting, from investigating and exploring the possibilities of 9/11 being a hoax - to the deep sadness at the death of innocent lives, to the beginning of a "war on terror." When more such information became available with varied conspiracy theories, seminars and talks were organized in Lahore and other cities about why 9/11 happened, how to perceive it and how USA will deal with the consequences of the first major foreign attack on its soil in the last 200 years.

There is no doubt that it was a catastrophic attack of poetic yet horrifying symmetry, and that New Yorkers would never be able to see their city in the same way again. Coming from a ménage of architects and buildings design, I was in shock and disbelief at seeing the buildings collapse, each in 10 seconds, something that has never happened in the history of tall buildings in the world. This was sheer totality of destruction, creating a 16-acre burial ground that the world witnessed - especially since the context and cause was not a natural disaster.

At the same time, I find it impossible to ignore the pain of Americans. These good people lost their loved ones in a tragic, horrific way.

Their pain is universal. To cut ourselves off or to build a wall in our hearts to keep their pain away from us is a mistake. It makes us less human. And it makes us more human when we acknowledge that what happened on 9/11 was a blow to the families of three thousand people. Yes, there have been greater natural disasters. Yes, America killed and maimed hundreds of thousands of people in Japan with the atomic bombs. Yes, people have died of starvation and war for millennia. At the same time, watching a woman cry as she reads the name of her child or husband at the podium after 9/11 should not leave you un-moved. Showing your toughness, being blasé about this pain because you do not like American foreign policies, refusing to admit that 9/11 changed the world forever in a terrible, innocence-robbing way, is not an appropriate response for today. Not for me.

I wasn't "there" on 9/11, but I feel for those who were. Later, as the entire world tried to make sense of this man-made disaster of col-lateral damage, I was fortunate to connect with intellectuals, teachers, businessmen, civil society activists and army people to hear their take on the event. The Pakistani nation was shocked and in a state of disbe-lief like Americans, and strongly condemned the attacks. For many it was shocking to witness the tragedy that set USA on a completely dif-ferent historical course afterwards, and the US national narrative that followed. It was also perturbing to note the construction of the fear of the 'Other' (i.e. Muslims) that was formed and indoctrinated into the American public psyche. The entire narrative was fueling the clash of civilization discourse. The American leadership assuaged its acquittal by pre-emptive military strikes within a month on Afghanistan and, surprisingly, the public supported the global war on terror. After 9/11, nostalgia engulfed the American society. What Americans longed for was unclear to me. Was it was a time for unquestioned dominance? Of safety? Of moral certainty?

All the known political paradigms of our world changed after 9/11. Pakistan was at this time under the rule of a military dictator, General Pervez Musharraf. It was soon determined that Al-Qaeda was behind the 9/11 attacks, and that Osama Bin Laden was stationed in Afghanistan. The American government sought the support and coop-eration of Pakistan for their retribution. The Pakistani leadership was told that you are either "with us or against us" in this war against ter-ror – soon launched against Al-Qaeda. The then Taliban government in Afghanistan was sheltering Al-Qaeda. Hence, Pakistan became the frontline state in this USA Jihad/retribution against Al-Qaeda in Af-ghanistan.

171

The Pakistani Army and its leadership supported and facilitated the American War on Terror and still are paying the price for the war in Afghanistan - in terms of the loss of more than 80,000 [1] deaths of its civilians to drones, various episodes of bomb blasts and collateral damage. Nearly 40,000 Pakistani civilians have been wounded. There are about 1.4 million refugees or internally displaced Pakistanis affected by the war on terror.[2]

Over the last decade, the United States steadily used its support of counter-insurgency campaigns by the government of Pakistan through direct military aid and training, and compensation for assistance to the US war in Afghanistan. The US has also used Pakistan as a major supply route for weapons, fuel, and material into Afghanistan, and additionally launched cross-border attacks into Afghanistan from Pakistan's territory.

This increased US support resulted and coincided with a dramatic escalation of the conflict between local Pakistani insurgents groups and their government. Most of the fighting is concentrated in the Northwest, near the border with Afghanistan, but the bloodshed exceedingly affects civilians throughout Pakistan.

And then, in 2004, the US began its semi-covert campaign of drone strikes to kill Al Qaeda and Taliban forces based in Northern Pakistan after fighting them in Afghanistan. These strikes were obscured by secrecy and are of questionable legality. There is a debate about who and how many have been killed in these strikes. According to the highest estimates, these strikes have killed between 2,000 and 3,800 people as of early January 2015.

As a young Pakistani, I wonder how do you calculate the human costs of the U.S.-led War on Terror? Whether or not it is a just war? The proportionality of its success was measured or the US just got itself into all this mess? Some reports conclude that this number is staggering, with at least 1.3 million lives lost in Iraq, Afghanistan, and Pakistan alone since the onset of the war following September 11, 2001. As such, under-reporting of the human toll has attributed to ongoing Western interventions, whether deliberate or through self-censorship, has been key to removing the 'fingerprints' of responsibility. I wonder when I contemplate all of this - isn't it ironic to note that

1 *The Tribune,* Newspaper Story, 80,000 Pakistanis Killed in US "War on Terror': News Report, URL: www.tribune.com.pk/story/860790/80000-pakistanis-killed-in-us-war-on-terror-report/ (29, March 2015)
2 The Watson Institute For International and Public Affairs, Costs of War, Pakistani Civilians, URL: http://watson.brown.edu/costsofwar/costs/human/civilians/pakistani (April 2015)

none of the attackers of 9/11 belonged to Pakistan or Afghanistan? Yet these two countries have seen more blood than what America witnessed on the fateful day of 9/11. However, Afghanistan is the ground from which essentially an "Arab" army is battling America. We are not officially at war with anyone, but we've been fighting the Taliban for years, and this has had a profound effect on life in Pakistan, pretty much driving Pakistan straight into the ground. Today, the country is more battered and broken than I can ever remember it being before.

Some intellectuals affirm that the 21st century will be the century of Islam. What they mean is that Muslim civilization will be central to understanding where we will be moving in the future. Considering the fact that despite regional, ethnic and historical peculiarities, the contemporary Muslim world, approximately 1.6 billion people, roughly one-fifth of mankind inhabiting about fifty-five Muslim-majority independent nation states; plus roughly 43 million living as minorities in many western countries... I see all of this as marked by three common characteristics: (1) the growing assertiveness of Islam and its culture in most of its followers' activities, (2) the fight to defy the label of "Terrorist" from being applied to all Muslims, and (3) aspirations to overcome the relatively underdeveloped socioeconomic conditions that tend to exist in most Muslim countries. At the same time, the Muslims in the West are making an impact on the social, political, and economic life with a religion that comes with commitment and passion. And, of course, one of these nations, Pakistan and its nearly 185 million Muslims, also being a nuclear power.

As I see it, understanding Islam is therefore imperative to anyone wanting to make sense of living in the 21st century post 9/11. The most powerful weapon is an informed mind and my contention is emphasized when you switch on television or pick up a newspaper. There is an Islamic faith or Muslim culture story reported or talked about from one or another part of the world at just about any hour, almost dominating the 24/7 news cycle on any given day. Now the fact that the 9/11 airplane hijackers were Muslims has put Islam under a microscope. The world witnessed all sorts of theories, comments and inferences deducted in the media after 9/11. Remarkably, everyone seemed to have formulated an opinion on Islam, yet at the same time Islam was an unknown commodity in the West - especially in the USA.

What a lot of people don't understand is that Islam is a mosaic, spread over the globe, with different societies, languages, distinctive political cultures, yet at the same time Muslims are aware of their unity of faith and singular vision. Islam, thus, can only be understood in its diversity. The world tends to emphasize difference and in doing so forgets that Islam is embedded in the Abrahamic tradition and shares the same religious message contained in Judaism and Christianity. The idea of an omnipotent, merciful, transcendent God and the chain of Prophets with similar biblical names, i.e. Abraham, Moses, Joseph, Jesus - are the same in Islam. Yet, despite the almost innumerable similarities, the differences in our faiths were magnified in the West after 9/11. A lot of people were only talking about the clash of civilizations instead of striving for a meaningful dialogue among the civilizations.

Politics have never been a secondary issue for Muslims, in contrast to the Christian religious experience. I do understand that most people in the West do not seem to equate their identity with religion, but it is an essential part of a Muslim's outlook of who he is. For example, for Muslims salvation does not mean redemption from sin, but the creation of a just society in which all individuals could more easily perform their respective religious duties and dictums in total existential surrender to bring fulfillment. Nonetheless, it is also not true to think that Islam makes it impossible for Muslims to create and live in a modern secular society, as if the idea of secularity is different for Muslims. Thus, the idea of democracy is not inimical to Islam but actually facilitated in Islamic law. Islam shall always remain important to Pakistan's identity and is ubiquitous in our public life, but it still does not, or should not, affect realpolitik.

As we all know, the brunt of the war on terror came onto Muslims. I am a young woman from Pakistan, a country that is predominantly Islamic. A Muslim myself, I have been deeply committed to the ideals of human rights, cross-cultural and religious dialogues, sustainable development, democratic pluralism and the sharing of experiences across historical spaces. The information and technological revolution that now influence the lives of people all over the world makes it more of an imperative now than ever before to attempt to achieve the ideals I have just stated, as the world is increasingly interdependent and whatever happens in any region of the world is bound to affect the welfare of people in other regions of the world. We are at a time when every well-read and 'thinking' individual is disturbed about terrorism, world peace and sustainable development. We are also living in times when relationships and supporting each other are essentially required to be made whole; and for the healing process to begin there has to be a dialogue of sharing and understanding one another.

Identities changed after 9/11, the divisive narrative against the extremists turned the paradigms for how the world looked at Muslims.

My first identity is that I am a female, then a Pakistani and then a Muslim. But all of a sudden, my identity as a Muslim woman became the most important parameter through which the world judged me. The special checking and calling me aside in international airports has become a norm which is indeed disrespectful, especially when they see that I am a Muslim and belong to Pakistan. For a long time, I could not understand during my international travels that even though Pakistan is a US ally in the war on terror, my passport is not looked at with respect. From where I come, in our culture, we respect our friends and neighbors perhaps more than our relatives. But this treatment that is meted out to Muslims, both male and female, sets the stage for the discrimination on religious, racial and social grounds.

Sacrifice, Surrender, and Submission

When it comes to relationships, these are the values that society teaches us to follow as our moral guideline. Ironically, a relationship built upon this kind of foundation is as deadly to a man's spiritual health as a dose of cyanide is to his physical. For a healthy relationship, man must first free himself from all sources of dependence and acquire a sense of self. To acquire a sense of identity, a practical man must live with reason as his only moral guideline, yet since man can only reason by using his own mind and his own faculties, living morally presupposes that one acts independently from the influence of others. A logical relationship is thus not one of sacrifice, surrender, or submission, but one of voluntary association, fair exchange, and mutual respect. I believe that people never give up their liberties unless they come under some delusion. Education can be enlightening as a progressive discovery of our own past (and present) ignorance.

Fundamentalism is not unique to Islam

We are living in an age dominated by fundamentalism which has brought in its wake violent extremist groups. The western media exceedingly gives the impression that fundamentalism is purely an Islamic phenomena. That is not true. Fundamentalism is a global fact and has surfaced in every established faith in response to the problems of modernity. There is fundamentalism in Judaism, Christianity, Hinduism, Buddhism, Confucianism and even Atheist. We must be aware that fundamentalism is not a monolithic movement; each form of fundamentalism, even within the same tradition, develops independently and has its own symbols, narratives and motivations. Yet its different manifestations all bear a family resemblance. It is also a historical fact

175

that among the three monotheistic religions, Islam was in fact the last (or only most recent) to develop a fundamentalist strain.

However, a renewed interest in Muslim mysticism is visible too, which has been interpreted as a reaction to fundamentalism. Yet this is cultural, as the defining articles of and pillars of Islam constitute the essential teachings. This interest in mysticism has given birth to the idea that a movement should be launched for the revival of Islamic mysticism which hopefully will act as an antidote to fundamentalism and its repercussions. But is it possible to review a long-dead movement which is now a part of history? I think the key lies in our understanding of Islam - first and foremost.

Islam has brought comfort and peace of mind to more than a billion men and women in the world. It has given dignity and meaning to drab and impoverished lives. It was the first religion to give women rights unheard of in human history. Islam is a highly egalitarian religion, an empowering call for people who felt powerless. It has taught people of different faiths and races to live in brotherhood, and people of different creeds to live side by side in mutual co-existence. Islam has inspired a great civilization in which others besides Muslims lived creative and useful lives, which enriched our present world. Well into the 1950's for example, Jews and Christians lived peacefully under Muslim rule. In fact, Bernard Lewis, the pre-eminent historian of Islam, has even argued that for much of history religious minorities did better under Muslim rulers than Christians. So the pertinent question is what went wrong in the world of Islam as we came into the 21st Century?

Muslim leadership has failed to implement human rights and are, in fact, going backwards by now rejecting as un-Islamic the UN Declaration of Human Rights that was adopted in 1948. I do not accept this position. My desire is to understand the issues and to raise awareness about Human Rights related issues among the up and coming generations in the Muslim world. I have always believed that frontiers are an invention of the mind. We set boundaries for ourselves and others by what we choose to see as reality and by what we choose to value. But men and women are social creatures, and individual behavior is subjected to the control of widely shared social values. These boundaries that define the limits of acceptable behavior also tend to reflect and reinforce limits on acceptable thinking.

As Islamic legal scholar and academic, Jasser Auda argues that Islamic law is fundamentally a way of addressing these challenges, but at the same time he believes that many policies currently labeled

"Islamic" in fact fail to adhere to the fundamental values of Islamic law. Many jurists have adopted the approach of continuing to adhere to classical opinions, which according to a Maqasid approach would no longer be relevant for the present context. The word "maqasid" is the plural of maqsid, a word that means purpose or objective. The concept of Maqasid is ideally suited for the modern era but it is not a new concept, with its origins dating back to the classical period of Islamic thought. In fact, to the extent that these rulings enforce injustice, they fail to achieve the maqasid (purposes or objectives) of Islamic law.

"Shariah is based on wisdom and achieving people's welfare in this life and the afterlife. Shariah is all about justice, mercy, wisdom and common good. Thus any ruling that replaces justice with injustice, mercy with its opposite and common good with mischief or wisdom with nonsense is a ruling that does not belong to the shariah even if it is claimed to be so according to some interpretation."
~ Ibn al-Qayyim (d. 748 AH/1347 CE) ~

There is no doubt in my mind that Islam has so much to contribute to this century. Islam's ideas of justice, compassion and tolerance can contribute to a world desperately seeking the ideals stated above. But it can only be done when Muslims and non-Muslims work together in a spirit of mutual respect and understanding. The first step, however, for Muslims, is to begin the process of understanding (and practicing) Islam in its true spirit. Of course, this must also include a proactive and vigorous condemnation of those shouting "Allah u Akbar" (God is Great) as they commit atrocities against all of humanity - wrongfully in the name of Islam.

Although not statistically quantifiable, rising religiosity within the Muslim world is a universally recognized phenomenon. This assertion can be supported by the following evidence: (a) the literary output of scholars and journalists during the last two decades on "Islamic fundamentalism", "militant Islam", "radical Islam", "resurgent Islam" and so on, despite the implied distortions, simplifications and prejudices in content, has become a nominal index of this universal recognition; (b) the number of international conferences held almost routinely in both Muslim and non-Muslim worlds to study issues relating to Islam and its adherents as well as the mushrooming number of organizations and institutions that have adopted the banner of Islam

177

and Muslims since the dawn of the 1970's indicate a growing Islamic assertiveness; and (c) the Muslim penchant for building new and ostentatious mosques during the last two decades, the ever-increasing personal commitment to regularize daily prayers and other obligatory religious practices, and the broadening of dawah work to include social and educational activities. If the contemporary Muslim is said to be passing through a period of "creative tension" it is the quest for a religio-cultural identity that is the main contributor - especially post 9/11.

It is a serious topic, more moving and powerful than I expected, but in a more subtle way. Instead of celebrating the strength of the "American Exceptionalism," it is a sober reflection on how the rest of the world has been impacted by the 14 years following 9/11. America's role in the world now seems more to me that of seeing all other nations as toddlers trying to get along on the playground, with only America trying to keep the peace. And yet it has silver threads of hope — hope that the war will end, that the world can still redeem itself, and that literature can illuminate the areas of darkness that these last 14 years have engendered. We know that the causes of illusion are not pretty to discover. They're either vicious or tragic. Palestine, Iraq, and Afghanistan have suffered more as a result of American policy in this past decade than any other time in history. Extremism is not only an Islam problem, but an Arab and often culture-driven problem. If Muslims are unable to understand and rationalize their shortcomings, America should not be blamed. US is following her interests which are purely political and will use any trick to achieve them. If Muslim governments are willing to become tools for implementing the US policy, then the fault lies with them.

I believe that central to the building of strong, healthy and inclusive communities and nations is the active participation of young men and women. So often this participation is adult defined, led and structured. In reality, it is quite tokenistic in terms of the scope and level of youth responsibility and leadership. Few questions more clearly preoccupy our age than how to facilitate civil, free, and democratic interaction among the citizens of plural societies - plus economic and social emancipation. In recent years, the importance of this challenge has become globally apparent.

Therefore, I aspire to build a world of expanding freedom, opportunity and citizen responsibility, a world of growth in diversity and in the bonds of community; and initiating a system that is conducive for the people of my country and the global community in broad-spectrum. I wish to preach not the doctrine of ignoble ease and mis-informed ignorance, but the doctrine of the strenuous life. We already hear too many high-sounding words - and too few corresponding actions.

The expectation of life depends upon diligence; the mechanic that would perfect his work must first sharpen his tools. The person who gets the most satisfactory results is not always the one with the most brilliant single mind, but rather the one who can best coordinate the brains and talents of his associates and colleagues.

I, at my diminutive level, seek the mission of peace, happiness and prosperity to help bring sustainable global development, political empowerment, and peace by changing perceptions of what develop-ment and peace is - and how to build it, by revealing the power of the often-unrecognized work of our youth, peace-builders and social lot. I do not wait for extraordinary circumstances to do good; I try to use ordinary situations as I could no longer delude myself that the harsh realities a world away are without real consequences for my own people.

If you never take responsibility for yourself, and you're never required to take responsibility for yourself, then countries are like peo-ple, they are kept in sort of a state of permanent immaturity where it's quite easy to convince them that their distress is caused by someone else's success.

Man's capacity for justice makes democracy possible, but man's inclination towards injustice makes democracy necessary. When all is said and done, we need to develop such workstations where we can cater and address the issues that afflict our generation and our modes of thinking.

From my point of view, "Victory" depends upon four things:

- First, we have to win the fight we're in, against terrorist (networks) that threaten us today.
- Second, the wealthy countries have to spread the benefits of the twenty-first century world, and reduce the risks so they can make more partners and fewer terrorists in the future.
- Third, the poor countries themselves must make internal changes so that progress for their own people becomes more possible.
- Fourth, all of us must develop a truly global consciousness about what our responsibilities to each other are, and what our relationships are to be.

So we have to be sensitive to the fact that there are objective reasons for people to be concerned, and that we have to work very hard to eliminate the gaps that exist between the East and the West. For this concise matter I have always adhered to the facets and contributed in manners that are substantial for bringing a positive change in this dynamic world of ours. As a youth activist I have also stood up against injustice, obstacles to peace, and discrimination against women through my volunteer activities, the formation of my NGO, "The Awareness Network," as well as participation in student government activities and trips to India as Peace Ambassador. I believe the young should lead the elders.

Today's intertwined global connections assume many forms and, in this trend, these various kinds of global relations emerge, proliferate, and expand. The world needs to recognize the potential of youth, to celebrate their achievements, and plan for ways to better engage young people to successfully take action in the development of their societies. It presents a unique opportunity for all stakeholders to rally together to ensure that young people are included in decision-making at all levels. I believe that young women and men everywhere can and do work towards national uplift. We are valuable and committed partners in the global effort to achieve the Millennium Development Goals, including the overarching goal of cutting poverty and hunger in half by 2030. We remain at the forefront of the fight against HIV/AIDS. And we bring fresh, innovative thinking to longstanding development concerns. Approaching the mid-point of the race to achieve the MDG's, the world needs our participation more than ever. I deem our energy and idealism can help make up for lost ground, and achieve our development goals in full and on time. In turn, the "older and wiser" world must fulfill its obligations to youth.

Societies of all kinds are held together by complex networks of rights and responsibilities. They define what the members of society can and cannot do. And they define the relationship between individuals and the state. In so doing, they define the underlying nature of the society: whether a society is benign or despotic depends on the nature of its network of rights and responsibilities.

As societies evolve, rights and responsibilities change in response to a combination of political, economic, social, cultural, philosophical and technological development. It is not surprising, therefore, to see that with increased information and interconnectivity around the world, there also needs to be an expanding awareness among all people that includes a continuous reassessment of individual and organizational rights and responsibilities.

There have been welcome exceptions to this pattern, of course. But too often, one step forward has been accompanied by two steps back, especially in my Pakistan. Hope for the future has often meant hope for survival, not hope for progress. The old order yielded its place, but a new world was not ready to be born. Today, this sense of frustration is compounded – both in rich and poor nations – by a host of new challenges. They range from changing weather patterns to mutating viruses, from new digital and bio-genetic technologies to new patterns of family life and a new intermingling of cultures.

Too often, disappointment has been the dominant story. And too often the dominant response to disappointment has been to embrace false hopes — from dogmatic socialism to romantic nationalism, from irrational tribalism to runaway individualism. Another response has been to revisit past glories — contrasting them with contemporary setbacks.

Presently, I am a graduate student at Georgetown University. As a member of this prestigious institution, I am fashioning our common vision for the shared future and our common ways of fulfilling them. But as we all play our role, I hope we will honor the values of our teachers, seers and mentors. For the one ingredient which holds particular promise in the search for fulfillment, is our inherent curiosity and the search for knowledge.

To me, education has always been about overcoming my weaknesses, and about knowing oneself. For me, a part of learning and gaining respect is being able to say, "I don't know." My academic years have been filled with a moral purpose. Standing for something and having a moral compass. I think that I don't have to agree with someone to respect their ethics. My emphasis was upon building relationships built on trust, mutual dialogue, respect and openness with my teachers and peers - especially where areas of conflict were identified, worked on and resolved. I was fortunate to study in institutions where I was able to co-mingle with people from various stratum of Pakistani society. Empathy and listening were the key qualities I developed early in my academic life. The various degrees I was privileged to accomplish in the short span of time endowed me with the ability to work under pressure as well as in unfavourable conditions. This helped me out during the initial years of developing my own family consultancy business. I try to remain committed to excellence for myself, my peers and employees. In my work, I have always tried to be the source for the enabling of an atmosphere that breeds creativity and sincere devotion towards the professional goals. I am disciplined enough to be focused in achieving my short- and long-term work, education and personal goals.

Moreover, my ethics and beliefs keep me focused. My overriding commitment, to myself and others, is to follow-up on everything and accept responsibility when things fail to fully achieve the intended result. I am cautious towards not breaching other people's fundamental rights, and therefore possess a higher degree of tolerance towards people of different colour, race, gender, religion and/or culture. I try not to let go of opportunities to help others and feel responsible to assist them, whether it is to grow self-discipline, leadership skills, provide key input or some level of "expert" advice.

Do not wait for extraordinary circumstances to do good; try to use ordinary situations. Courage is not the absence of fear, but rather the judgment that something else is more important than fear. I have a higher degree of courage and motivation to now pursue my vocation by establishing The International Intellectual Exchange Initiative (IIEX) in DC that will try to bring a scholarly voice to explicate the several dimensions through which Muslim social and cultural identities are constructed, challenged and lived. That will promote public awareness of scholarship in the fields of Middle Eastern and Islamic Studies and their relevance to contemporary American policymaking by adapting and making them accessible to a broad audience. That tries to deepen understanding of and appreciation for and connection to contemporary Islamic thought. An organization that will encourage reconciliation among communities around the world by participating in and establishing peacebuilding programs. It will seek to empower learners to think critically, question freely, share openly, and engage in an ongoing exploration of issues affecting our world. It will be a platform that will cultivate the leadership role of young people in sustainable peace, religious dialogue, and human rights advocacy both in the communities of their practice and in the nation as a whole. Just taking the first step in faith, I don't have to see the whole staircase.

The envious nature of men, so prompt to blame and so slow to praise, makes the discovery and introduction of new principles and systems almost as dangerous as the exploration of unknown seas and continents. Yet, I am animated by that desire which compels me to do whatever might prove to be, in the end, for the common benefit of all. I have resolved to open a new route, which has not yet been followed by anyone, and might prove difficult and troublesome. At least attempt to get across the untellable. What redeems it is the idea only. An idea at the back of it, not a sentimental pretense but an idea; and an unselfish belief in the idea—something you can set up and bow down before, and offer a sacrifice to.

Earlier, through my participation as the official Youth Ambassador from Pakistan in various International forums, I have tried to accent the moderate voice of Islam - as lived and experienced in Pakistan.

I am particularly proud to have been beside my father, when he decided to have his own Architectural and Engineering consultancy firm. He was in his early 50's in 2006. I remember that my two younger brothers where finishing school and I was there to support him in every way. From the inception of the entire organizational processes to business development, dealing with clients, accounting and taxation I was looking after everything.

We started our firm from a single room with me, my father and a draftsman. In the early years, I used to work 24/7 and had decided that no matter how much hard work, commitment and dedication is required, I will be there with my family. I was so consumed with the passion to make our firm a success. Now, by the grace of Almighty, we have our offices in three cities of Pakistan and a dozen projects of national importance worth billions of rupees. Not many young girls in my culture get this opportunity to give something to their parents since they are usually married off early. I feel humbled to be among the few who got the opportunity to give something back to her family.

Practically in all societies, all over the world, women are quite marginalized. I have been keen to explore the question of their plight, their rights and how to foster solidarity among women to ameliorate their conditions and, at the same time, uplift humanity in general. It is my hope that I can, with my background, education and organization, contribute in a modest way to bring about a greater understanding and acceptance of not only the plight and rights of women in Muslim Societies, but non-Muslim as well.

In this journey, I intend to focus my energies in acquiring new knowledge and friends that will make me a better person as well as a useful and responsible citizen of the world. On balance, I would like to dedicate myself to a mission of interfaith dialogue, peace, of sustainable global development, the uplifting of women and achieving effective levels of solidarity.

One of the defining characteristics of my personality has been "God consciousness" or "God awareness." I was blessed to go for Pilgrimage to Mecca in 2012 and was immensely moved by the phenomenal spiritual experience as well as the opportunity of meeting Muslims from every corner of the world – and of so many different sects. I also recognized the image problem facing Islam, misrepresentation and misinterpretation of its message, exploitation by radicals to justify violence and curtail human rights, including women's rights across the world. They are wrongly blending Islam with their own politics, culture and tribal norms for their own selfish agendas and interests.

My request to readers is this: Do not believe in anything simply because you have heard it. Do not believe in anything simply because it is spoken and rumored by many. Do not believe in anything simply because it is found written in your religious books. Do not believe in anything merely on the authority of your teachers and elders. Do not believe in traditions because they have been handed down for many generations. But after observation and analysis, when you find that anything agrees with reason, and is conducive to the good and benefit of one and all, then accept it and live up to it. These are the foundational beliefs and the paths I walk.

But, first, we must acknowledge what it is that we do not yet know — committing ourselves to continued learning and accepting the fact that useful knowledge will often be found by reaching beyond the traditional barriers of both geography and culture.

God is so near to us that nothing can be nearer. The eminence of His position has not placed Him further away from His creatures, and His nearness has not brought them up to His level. Unfortunately, we are passing through times when the majority of "worldly" people seem to think that hypocrisy means wisdom. They lead the uneducated masses to believe that dissimulation is the best form of sagacity. The Idols that beset human minds lie deep in human nature itself and in the very community of our race. It is incorrectly claimed that the human sense is the measure of things. Rather, the case that all of our perceptions, both of our physical senses and of our minds, are reflections of man, not of the universe, and the human understanding is like an uneven mirror that cannot reflect truly the rays from objects, but distorts and corrupts the nature of things by mingling its own form of "nature" with it.

From the 20th century we have to learn this lesson that in vain we try not to use the leftover vocabularies of a tradition whose ambition it was to define the unity, or even the essence, of the social. Our problem is to define difference and to mark off a space in which we can observe the emergence of order and disorder. Breakdown can create breakthroughs!

If we briefly look at policy structures, what are the main benefits of the modern world? The global economy has lifted more people out of poverty in the last twenty years than at any time in history. It's been great for Europe and the United States and, in a similar manner, it can work for us as well.

At this time the great blessing of the global age is the explosion of "democracies," in various forms, and the liberation of diversity within the democracies. You can argue that those changes make all these other good things possible. This is the first time in history that more people live under governments of their own choosing than live under dictatorships. It has never happened before.

Global poverty – well, half the people on earth are not part of that new economy I talked about. Half the people on earth live on less than two dollars a day. A billion people must get by on less than a dollar a day. A billion people go to bed hungry every night and a billion and a half people - one quarter of the people on earth - never get a clean glass of water. One woman dies every minute in childbirth. So you could say, "Don't tell me about the global economy. Half of the people aren't part of it. What kind of economy leaves half the people behind?" We now live in a world without walls that we had worked so hard to make. We have benefits, we have burdens, we have to spread the benefits and shrink the burdens. Social emancipation, therefore, will unfold its most important features if we keep in mind the economic, political, social and cultural barriers to it at the beginning of the 21st century.

As the world economy integrates, global migrations are reaching record levels. Immigrants now account for two-thirds of the population growth in the 30 developed countries of the OECD. Once homogenous societies are becoming distinctly multi-cultural.

Meanwhile, the gap widens between rich countries and poor. Populations explode and the environment deteriorates. The nation-state itself is newly challenged by the influence of non-state forces—including global crime and terrorism.

In the mid-20th century, one of humanity's worst periods, politics were about what we could become. Two collectivist ideologies about destiny claimed to be scientific. Marxism-Leninism was based on inevitable, universal laws of class development and conflict; Nazi-Fascism proclaimed inevitable laws of racial and biological development for one race alone.

Today, we think less about what we could all become. Instead, we worry more about how to live together as individuals in community.

The whole world is on the move, migrating and hoping.

The rich world, above all Europe and North America, faces the rising determination of a hundred latecomer nations who were once silent under the blanket of colonialism and backwardness.

How do we learn to live together, and at three levels: in an international system, in individual nation-states, and – most immediately and intimately – in western cities which are increasingly the goal of migrants from those "delayed" parts of the world? The rich world's current answer to this question is multiculturalism. I argue that this ideal, although it is well-meaning and an improvement on previous recipes, has grown obsolete and is losing its relevance. "Multiculturalism" presently dominates political discourse.

In the condition of plural democracy, people are invited to choose sides, to identify what divides them rather than what unites them. In societies where there is no network of free local institutions, no civil society had been allowed to develop. The first difference which often comes to mind is not wealth or class or social function, but ethnicity.

Why does the sense of freedom translate into the wish to be free alone – without the "Other?" As yet, no sociologist has a satisfying explanation. But all over the world, and especially in the last fifteen or twenty years, there has been ethnic separation as minorities have been driven from their homes. Unhappily, this is going to continue. The world is full of countries where governance has never been anything but arbitrary and in which the experience of liberation, or democratic revolution, or whatever we might choose to call it, is yet to come.

Policy changes, large or small, are not the heart of the struggle we all face. The vital component to this predicament is the need for a visionary cross-cultural strategy. The US, being the only world power, in good faith, must somehow help Islam enter the modern world. If the West can help Islam enter modernity in good faith, peace and dignity, it will do more than achieve security for all against the radical Islamists. It will surely change our world.

So that's what I want to think about and do. It's great that my kids will live to be ninety years old, but I don't want it to be behind barbed wire. It's great that they will have all these benefits of the modern world, but I don't want them to feel like they're emotional prisoners. And I don't want individuals to look at people who look different from them and see a potential enemy instead of a fellow traveler. I believe that we can make the world of our dreams for our children, but since it's a world without walls, it will have to be a home for all our children. May our lives preach more loudly than our lips.

———————————

"May the stars carry your sadness away,
may the flowers fill your heart with beauty,
may hope forever wipe away your tears"
~ Chief Dan George ~

"When you talk, you are only repeating what you already
know; but when you listen, you may learn something new."
~ Dalai Lama ~

"Don't believe everything you think."
(bumper sticker)

———————————

Chapter Fifteen

Understanding Revenge without Condoning It

Tom Tripp

Tom Tripp, Ph.D, is a Professor of Management at Washington State University/Vancouver Campus (WSU-V). Professor Tripp is an internationally famous expert in workplace conflict. For the past 20 years, he has published dozens of scientific papers on workplace conflict, and especially on workplace revenge and forgiveness. He is co-author of the 2009 book, *Getting Even: The truth about workplace revenge — and how to stop it.* At WSU-V, he teaches business courses in leadership skills and in negotiation skills. A popular teacher, Tripp has won numerous teaching awards, including the Business School's top teaching award three times, and the 2010 Sahlin Faculty Excellence Award for Instruction, which is WSU's top teaching award for the whole university. Tripp earned a Ph.D in Organizational Behavior from the Kellogg School of Management at Northwestern University, and a B.S. in Psychology from the University of Washington.

9/11/2001

I study revenge. As a business school professor, I study how employees seek revenge in the workplace. I don't mean the kind of workplace violence that makes headlines when an employee "goes postal;" rather, I study the nasty little things that employees do to each other and to their employer when they feel they have been unfairly treated, and the ways disgruntled customers deal with a firm who has not served them as promised.

So, on 9/11, as I watched these horrific events unfold on TV, like everyone else I asked, "Why?" Why would someone think attacking the USA with hijacked airplanes is a reasonable and just thing to do? Wracking my brain for possible answers, I immediately thought of three maxims I've learned in my studies on revenge:

1 - Evil people don't think they're evil
2 - Lightning doesn't fall from a blue sky
3 - Ethics is the luxury of having multiple means

Let me elaborate on each.

Evil people don't think they're evil

As every police detective knows, one doesn't get very far understanding a crime only by judging the act as evil; rather, the detective must get inside the mind of a perpetrator, to see the situation from the perpetrator's perspective. If all the detective does is judge the perpetrator as unethical, criminal, crazy or evil, the detective will not understand the perpetrator's motives or the perpetrator's way of thinking. And the detective must understand all this to have an accurate working theory of the mind of the perpetrator, and in the case of serial crimes, to predict the next such criminal act. Only by predicting the next act can the next act be prevented.

By the way, for months afterward, much public sense-making of 9/11 actually made it very hard to understand the hijackers and Al Qaeda. I clearly recall one TV pundit, Bill Maher, pointing out how idiotic another pundit's comment was when the other pundit called the hijackers "cowards." Maher replied, "They may be a lot of things, but they are not cowards." After all, the hijackers had sacrificed their lives in pursuit of their cause. But the public backlash against Maher made it clear that nobody dare say anything publicly that might shed light on who the hijackers were and what they wanted – not if it sounded like a defense of the hijackers or a small point in the hijacker's favor (e.g., being brave rather than cowardly). No comments about these hijackers could be positive, not even in the slightest.

Fortunately, detectives are smarter than TV pundits. No detective would be so stupid as to insist on a completely one-sided view. Profiling criminals requires empathy. (That's empathy, not sympathy nor sympathizing.) All that's needed is understanding how the criminals think, including why they might believe their cause is just and their actions justified; it does not require that we agree with the criminals' conclusions.

So, back to the maxim, evil people don't think they're evil. At the time someone deliberately commits an act that harms others, the harm-doer believes, at least at the moment, that the act is justified, that it is the morally right thing to do. What is clear from the research on revenge is that avengers, who normally believe that revenge is an unacceptable act, believe that this time justice demands it. I've found it not so useful to assert that revenge can never serve justice; instead, I just want to understand how the avenger came to believe that an injustice occurred, that the injustice was not rectified, and that revenge is the best or only option available to restore justice. I don't need to agree with what they think, but I must know how they think.

So what did the hijackers think? What was their cause, and why did they believe their cause was so just, that it was morally acceptable to kill thousands of people? Why did they believe that they had no other acceptable options, and that giving their lives was necessary? We have to adopt their perspective, if only temporarily, to answer these questions.

Lightning doesn't fall from a blue sky

Before lightning strikes, skies darken, storm clouds gather, rain usually falls. There are always warning signs that lightning might be coming. However, if we pretend that lightning is a sudden, totally random phenomenon, then we'll never be able to predict it, and thus less able to protect ourselves from it. Fortunately, good weather forecasters monitor the gathering storm, issue warnings and issue effective precautions against lightning.

But not every context has such good forecasters. In the context of on-going, tit-for-tat feuds that I've studied, the participants are terrible forecasters. In such feuds, when a victim suffers an unkind act by another coworker, the victim often concludes that the unkind act came "out of the blue," without warning. The victim doesn't stop and ask oneself the very useful question, "Why might a caring, competent, well-meaning coworker commit such an act?" Instead, the victim often jumps to the conclusion that something is fundamentally wrong with the coworker — the coworker has bad intent, bad skills, bad morals, or bad personality — and that the unkind act is totally unprovoked. Further investigation often reveals that the unkind act was not some unprovoked aggression or crime, but rather is an act of revenge against something the victim had done earlier, but had forgotten about, or didn't think much of. Thus, the victim may mistake a provoked act of aggression for an unprovoked act of aggression.

When victims attribute the wrong motives to their aggressors — e.g., attribute the aggression to bullying or jealousy, which is unprovoked, when the motive is really revenge, which is, by definition, provoked — then victims often choose the wrong response. For instance, such a misguided victim may choose to retaliate in order to even the score, when a better response would be to not react and let the other side believe that its earlier act had evened the score. After all, when each side is keeping a different scorecard, it's impossible for both sides to ever agree when the score is even; at any moment, one side will always feel behind. Thus, tit-for-tat is the wrong response in a different-scorecards scenario.

Actually, it's worse: tit-for-tat backfires in a different-scorecards scenario. Instead of settling the conflict, tit-for-tat escalates the conflict as each side believes it must strike once more to even the score — that is, to have the last word to achieve justice and deter future conflict. Tit-for-tat escalates here because each side believes the other side "started it," and therefore further believes that one's own acts of aggression are righteous attempts to even up the score, and the other's acts of aggression are unprovoked escalations.

I suspect that such a "different-scorecards scenario" occurred between Americans and Al Qaeda. 9/11 was not a lightning bolt from a blue sky. The Al Qaeda storm had been gathering for years. Also, Al Qaeda does not believe it took the first shot with 9/11. In its view, America took a first shot before 9/11 when it, for instance, put its troops on holy, Saudi Arabian soil and kept them there. Al Qaeda, sees a long history where America has 'bullied' the Muslim world, "dictating to its rulers," and "terrorizing its neighbors." Again, the point isn't whether Al Qaeda is right. One doesn't have to agree with Al Qaeda that America deserved 9/11 to recognize that America's previous actions, right or wrong, made 9/11, or some similar terrorist attack, more likely.

Understanding how Al Qaeda believes America fired the first shot helps us understand how they might believe 9/11 was justified, and also how they might believe that 9/11 might deter future American activities in the Muslim world. Why Bin Laden's prediction that 9/11 might deter America was so incorrect? Perhaps because, in part, Bin Laden likely believed that America "knew" America took the first shot, and thus Americans would see 9/11 as a form of retaliation as opposed to an unprovoked, unjust attack. (Note that Bin Laden also hoped that if America were not deterred, that it would over react by going to war against Muslims, spending more money on war than the American economy could withstand.)

191

Ethics is the luxury of having multiple means

This is a point that renowned community organizer Saul Alinsky made in his book, *Rules for Radicals*. Alinsky made this point while criticizing as myopic the cliché, "the ends never justify the means." Alinsky argues that, at least from the aggressor's point of view, the ends sometimes do justify the means, and that if people uttering this cliché would stop and think about it, they would realize that they do not really believe the cliché. One reason he lists that people don't really believe the cliché is that being able to make ethical judgments about means – i.e., that a particular means (e.g., killing someone) is unethical – only occurs when one has multiple, effective means to choose from. That is, only when one has many means of accomplishing a very important objective does one compare the ethicality of various means, rejecting those means that do not meet certain moral standards. But if one has only one effective means to achieve a very important objective, then, Alinsky argues, one does not reject the means for not meeting a moral standard. In short, one believes that the means is justified because "I had no other choice."

For instance, is it ethical to shoot someone who is physically attacking you? The answer in part depends on (and the legality of it in many US state laws depends on) whether escape is possible. If the victim can escape, then the victim has two effective options to avoiding harm: (1) shoot the attacker; or (2) run away. When the victim has two effective options, then there is a legal and ethical debate about whether the victim can shoot the attacker. However, if shooting is the only effective means of avoiding harm, then there is little debate.

Alinsky argues that those of us with multiple effective means often conveniently forget how few effective means our opponents have. Because of our selective memory, we then judge our opponents' means as unethical (or unprofessional, or inhumane, and so forth). We claim we would never "stoop so low." That's right: we wouldn't, but only because we have other, more ethical means to accomplish the same ends. We forget or dismiss that our opponents do not.

America has multiple effective means to accomplish its international objectives. We have economic might to apply economic pressure; we have a seat on the UN Security Council to influence its deliberations; we have the military hardware and soldier training to fight wars in accordance with Geneva conventions. What means does Al Qaeda have to accomplish its international objectives? (If their objectives were legitimate, which Al Qaeda believes they are.) It has no economic might to create economic sanctions. It has neither seat on the UN Security Council, nor any representation in the UN whatsoever given that Al Qaeda is not a nation state. It has very little military hardware and insufficient resources to recruit large armies and train them well. Thus, Al Qaeda cannot play by the United States' rules to achieve its objectives. And Al Qaeda knows this — but many US citizens do not consider this constraint at all when judging Al Qaeda's guerrilla tactics. It is ridiculous to expect Al Qaeda meet us head-on on the open battlefield; they would be slaughtered. Al Qaeda did the only thing it could do to gain more power to achieve its objectives: it used guerrilla tactics, using its enemy's resources (i.e., airplanes) against itself to destroy infrastructure and kill people.

In sum, we conveniently do not acknowledge that Al Qaeda can't fight like America can fight. Once we acknowledge this simple fact, it is illogical to criticize them for choosing the means they did when they had no choice. Of course, they could have simply not fought at all, giving up their important international objectives. Would we do the same regarding our important international objectives?

In the judgment of means and ends, Alinsky makes another crucial point that applies to Americans reactions to 9/11: how harshly one judges an unsavory means in part depends on whose ends the means serve. To apply Alinsky's principle, consider the following question. How should we judge guerrilla tactics? Are they never acceptable? Is that really what most Americans believe? No, not really. To illustrate, examine the labels people use to describe guerrilla tactics (e.g., "resistance," "terrorism") and the people who employ them (e.g., "freedom fighters," "terrorists"). Which guerrillas are terrorists sabotaging public order and which are freedom fighters resisting tyranny? When such guerrilla tactics serve our ends, we label those who use them as "the resistance" (e.g., the French blowing up bridges and cafes in WWII under Nazi occupation) or freedom fighters (e.g., those Nicaraguans trying to overthrow the Sandinista government in the 1980's). When the very same guerrilla tactics serve our opponent's interests, we label those who use them "rebels" (e.g., those El Salvadorians trying to overthrow their government in the 1980's) and terrorists (e.g., Al Qaeda). Perhaps the most blunt example is the Taliban fighters in Afghanistan: when they were trying to overthrow Soviet rule, we approved of their tactics; when they tried to overthrow American rule 20 years later, we disapproved of those very same tactics. In sum, whether one is a "terrorist," "rebel" or "freedom fighter," is not defined by the use of guerrilla means, but by whose ends those guerrilla means serve.

Summary

I study conflict. I am frustrated with and worried about the hypocrisy that escalates so many conflicts – that our side is all shining virtue and our cause (and means) are just; our opponent's side is evil and/or crazy, their cause (and means) are unjust. They are the aggressor, we are the victims. They started it, so we shall finish it.

Even if we aren't to blame, even if their cause violates our values – and on a personal note, make no mistake, religious extremism violates my values; I want no part of a Taliban utopia – they believe they are in the right. If we hope to influence them toward a more peaceful approach, we have to understand their beliefs, grievances, and ensuing motives. We don't have to agree with them, but we do have to understand how they think -- why they think they might be right, why they might perceive that they are victims and we are aggressors, and why they think their cause is just. Only then can we influence them effectively. Alternatively, we can soothe ourselves by insisting that the Al Qaeda did it because "they hate our freedoms," because they can't stand our virtues, and not because they can't stand our vices.

Since 2001 – My Evolving Vision

Since 9/11, my view on revenge has grown even more dismal. In the 1990's, I'm on record as stating that revenge is sometimes a good thing. For instance, revenge looked good when employees used it to right wrongs that management refused to address. My colleague, Robert Bies, and I stated this, in part because we were annoyed with the one-sided "managerial perspective" that permeates so many organizations and business schools. According to the managerial perspective, when employees act aggressively, such misbehavior is unjustified, committed by "deviants" who should just get back to work and do their jobs. Our and others' research told us that such employees did not act aggressively so much because they had 'deviant' personalities that compelled them, but rather, such employees saw injustice and sometimes felt they had little choice, that revenge was their only effective means. But this second, employee perspective was getting little notice. Now that the employee perspective has received much more notice over the last 15 years, and our research has turned to the finer mechanisms of workplace revenge, we now are struck by how revenge is such a crude, imprecise, and sloppy instrument of justice. That's why modern society substituted government-operated legal systems for revenge as the primary means of restoring justice. Both research and history make clear that when victims serve as police detectives, judge, jury and executioner, the victims' biases, cognitive fallibilities, and limited resources often create more injustice than they restore.

The editor of this book, Dan Sockle, asked for ideas for a vision for a better tomorrow. To me that means ideas for how to reduce revenge and the misunderstandings that fuel it. I base my ideas mostly on workplace conflict research, hoping that what works in modern organizations might work, at least partially, on the world stage. I have two basic ideas: reduce misunderstanding of motives to reduce conflict, and use the rule of law to manage the conflicts that still occur anyway.

Reducing Misunderstanding

I agree with musician Roger Waters, who points out that much conflict, insanity, and lack of empathy is caused by "the problem of us and them." Our tribal nature makes it too easy and common to create what psychologists call, "in-groups and out-groups." As recent research and long history both show, labeling another as being in the out-group makes it easier to ignore them and not try to understand their concerns and how they think. If the outsiders won't let us ignore them, then the in-out group boundary makes it so easy to vilify them, or at least consider them sub-human. Decades of psychology research shows that we judge members of "outgroups" much more harshly than we judge members of our "ingroup." This includes misunderstanding their motives.

Consider a recent study that examined the motives for aggression that rival groups assign to each other (Waytz, Young and Ginges, 2014). Studying the feuds among Democrats and Republicans, and among Israeli's and Palestinians, they found that people tend to attribute their own aggression much more to ingroup love than outgroup hate, while attributing their rival's aggression much more to outgroup hate than ingroup love. Ingroup love means that one aggresses to protect one's own community and its central values. Outgroup hate means that one aggresses because hatred compels one to destroy the outgroup. The study found that Israelis support violence with Palestinians more because they love Israelis' than hate Palestinians, but the Israelis did not grant Palestinians the same motives: Israelis also believed that Palestinians supported the violence more because Palestinians hate Israelis than because Palestinians love Palestinians. The Palestinians reported the same asymmetry of motives, but in the opposite direction of course. The same asymmetry of motives was found among Republicans and Democrats.

195

It is clear that we need to overcome these ingroup and outgroup boundaries, but how? That's a difficult question that many people have tried to answer. A partial solution is for Americans to travel more and interact with people who are vastly different. The more we interact, the less subhuman and incomprehensible others will seem. To get inside the mind of our "enemies," we need to talk to them first, obviously. Another benefit that may arise from travel is more humility. I'm always amazed at people who are certain their country is best, when they've never visited another country. How could one know, unless one has gotten to know multiple cultures? George Bernard Shaw was right: patriotism is about believing one's country is best simply because one was born there.

Reinforcing the Rule of Law

The overall germ of a solution is the rule of law. Stephen Pinker, in his book, *The Better Angels of our Nature,* makes an exhaustive, convincing case that world violence has dropped dramatically over the long run – both inter-group violence (e.g., wars between nation states) and individual violence (e.g., crime), and not just over the centuries, but even over the last few decades. A major reason for this decline he argues is the rise of governments as Leviathans. That is, once government took over violence, the number of wars decreased (WWI and WWII notwithstanding as recent outliers to the trend) and as government-operated justice systems made revenge, now implemented by the court systems, much less sloppy and less likely to inspire acts of counter-revenge.

Why do these government systems reduce violence, including vigilante vengeance? Research by psychologists over the last few decades on citizens' interactions with legal decision-making systems, and similar research by organizational scholars on employees' interactions with organizational decision-making systems, reveal why these systems create peace and justice instead of violence and chaos. This research answers the question of what citizens and employees do when authorities say "no" or rule against them. Indeed, when do people accept unfavorable decisions from authorities, and when do people instead disobey, or even revolt until they get their way?

The short answer, shown repeatedly (at least in the developed world), is that as long as people perceive that the decision-making procedures are fair, they will tolerate and accept unfavorable decisions rather than rebel or seek revenge. They may not like the unfavorable decision, but they will accept the decision and move on, continuing to follow the authority. This is what the world needs – a decision-making body that the whole world perceives as procedurally fair. Not every nation or group will get what it wants in this world of such diverse interests and scarce resources, but it will accept the occasional unfavorable decisions as long as it believes the procedures used to make the decisions were fair. People do (at least in the developed world) distinguish between outcome and process fairness, and believe that the latter should buffer against the former.

Fair Process

All this begs the question: are there features of fair decision-making procedures that everyone agrees on as fair, and if so, what are they? Forty years of psychological research has made clear that there are such features that everyone perceives as being necessary and sufficient for decision-making procedures. (Note: This is about what regular people perceive as fair, not about what esteemed philosophers or legal scholars might argue should be fair.) Here, in brief, are the main five procedures:

1. Consistency. People believe that rules that govern allocations and judgments should be consistent. That is, the same rules should be consistently applied across people and across time. So, every person is bound by the same rules. Nobody is "above the law." Also, rules should be stable over time. If instead the rules change too frequently, then for all intents and purposes there are no rules, at least no rules around which people can make plans.

2. Voice. People believe they should have a voice at the table. People believe they have the right to give input to authorities who make decisions regarding their fate, and these authorities have the duty to listen, and listen sincerely.

3. Accuracy of Information. All decisions are based on information. People believe that fair decisions are based on accurate and relevant information. They believe information is more likely to be accurate when facts are documented, rumors and gossip are excluded, and experts weigh in on complex and subjective matters.

4. Bias Suppression. Everyone is biased, including the authorities who make decisions. Fair decisions suppress such biases. The most pristine way to suppress a large bias is for an authority figure

who has a conflict of interest (e.g., the judge is friends with the plaintiff; the Senator has stock in the company she is conducting a congressional investigation of) recuse oneself from the decision.

5. Correctability. Fair procedures are those that allow bad decisions to be corrected. Such correction can be as informal as revisiting a decision once new evidence arises, or as formal as appeal systems.

Note: People care about procedural fairness not just because such procedures give them some influence on authorities' decisions. They also care because they infer from the presence of such procedures that they have standing and can trust authorities. That is, if an authority goes through all the trouble to set up these procedures, then the authority must care about those in its dominion. And if the authority cares about them then they can trust the authority's motives. Inference of another's motives is a huge component of trust, and a huge predictor of revenge.

But none of this works if the procedures are not transparent. What matters in terms of people accepting unfavorable decisions is whether people perceive that the procedures are fair. If they don't know much about the procedures, then they assume the procedure follows the outcome: if the outcome is favorable and fair, the procedure must have been fair; conversely, if the outcome is unfavorable and unfair, the procedure must have been unfair. So, it's not enough for a government to believe it uses fair procedures; they have to look fair to those they govern.

Fair Process on the World Stage

How could America (and other major powers, too; but I'm an American so I'll focus on my country) follow such principles on the world stage? Here are five, quick, crudely-formed thoughts:

First, America needs to behave more consistently. That is, we should treat everyone else by the same set of rules. We violate this principle when we, for instance, treat one dictatorship more favorably than another (while claiming we support only democracy, no less) for no official reason. That then leaves others to speculate what the "real," unofficial reasons are (e.g., one dictator has oil and the other does not).

Second, America needs to keep offering other countries voice. Our leaders do listen to the rest of the world, and our government allows opinions critical of it to be shared openly. This is a big start. Even better might be if average Americans, and not just the intelligentsia, knew more about the rest of the world. Americans are vilified internationally for knowing so little about world affairs that their own government so dominates. With a free, 24/7 media, we should be much better informed than we are. Maybe then, the rest of the world would feel like their voices were heard.

Third, America needs to keep basing decisions on accurate information. Again, the American government has amazing intelligence gathering abilities that do just this. But because so much of it is secretive, the rest of the world may not know what information feeds American policies. Remember, these five principles of fair process are all about perception — can affected parties see these principles in action? There also is the perception that while the Executive branch of government may have accurate information, the public, and perhaps Congress, does not. A polarized media and congress give the perception that American factions accept only the information that confirms their beliefs and preferences.

Fourth, America needs to reduce its biases. The world won't trust America to be its police force as long as the world sees America enforcing mostly those laws that favor American interests. One way for America to temper its biases is to act more often through the UN. The UN was intended to be the fair arbiter of international behavior. Unfortunately, the structure of the Security Council is flawed. The biggest players on the world stage, including America, all have and exercise vetoes of any action that does not serve their own interests. This creates huge conflicts of interest. Until it is solved, I can't see the UN having any teeth, or being seen as procedurally fair.

Fifth, America needs to keep admitting when it is wrong, when it has made a bad decision, and is correcting its course. Making this task more difficult than it should be, however, is that individual politicians are not allowed to admit mistakes and change their minds and policies. While having an open mind is usually a virtue among normal people, among politicians it is a vice. Politicians who change their minds are punished with labels like "flip-flopper."

Implementing these five principles of fair process may work for America as they work in smaller organizations. I say "may" and not "will" for a couple reasons. First, many complications occur when scaling up from the organization level to the national and international level. Second, it's not clear yet that all other cultures value fair process like North Americans and Western Europeans do. Perhaps, those who have more experience with the rule of law better appreciate the importance of fair process.

Conclusion

These are my thoughts on 9/11. They are formed mostly by my experience as a social psychologist who studies workplace conflict, and, of course, by my American address. They are short, incomplete thoughts. I do not intend in this chapter to suggest simple solutions for such complex problems and expect them to work without further development and detail. I am reminded by H.L. Mencken, who said:

"For every complex problem, there is a solution
that is neat, simple — and wrong."

"There are as many opinions as there are experts."
~ Franklin D. Roosevelt ~

"I do not agree with what you have to say, but I will defend
to the death your right to say it."
~ Francois-Marie-Arouet ~
(better known as Voltaire)

"Travel is fatal to prejudice, bigotry,
and narrow-mindedness."
~ Mark Twain ~

Chapter Sixteen

9/11: A Personal Journey from
Insular Islander to Cosmopolitan Globalist

Abdullah Craig Walker

Abdullah Craig Walker – Writer and education consultant, Abdullah Craig Walker is based concurrently in Bellingham, Washington and Lahore, Pakistan. He has an extensive professional education background, having taught political science and international relations at the college level, pioneering the development of inclusion programs for special needs students, and creating several alternative programs for at-risk youth. Prior to accepting Islam, Abdullah served in a Christian lay ministry program working with homeless adults. He lived and worked in Kuwait, and traveled extensively throughout Asia and the Middle East. In Kuwait, he worked for a major English-language newspaper, and helped launch a cross-cultural education program under the auspices of the Kuwait Grand Mosque. Abdullah and his wife are working on a model school development project in Lahore, serving out-of-school children from impoverished families. Abdullah is co-author of Jewish-Muslim Relations – the *Qur'anic View,* published in Kuwait and the U.S. His forthcoming book, *Globalization, Culture and Faith,* examines the impact of the forces of globalization on culture and faith on Pakistan's Muslim-majority society.

Introduction

This narrative documents my post 9/11 transition from a typical provincial American – insular islander -- to a cosmopolitan personality who is at home all over the world, and not limited to just one part of it. My story also describes my transition to globalist, with views and attitudes that place the interests of the entire world above those of any individual nation.

A Wake-up Call

"Craig, wake up! They're attacking New York! It's on TV!" A
family member had burst into my room on the morning of 9/11 to
wake me up with the news of the attack in New York. I rushed into the
living room in time to see live coverage of a jet plane crashing into the
North Tower of the World Trade Center. The South Tower, 2 World
Trade Center, had been hit by another hijacked airliner a half-hour earlier, and collapsed at 9:59 am. Then, at 10:28 am, 1 WTC, the North
Tower, collapsed. Later that day, 7 World Trade Center collapsed at
5:21 pm from fires that had started when the North Tower was hit.

The confusion and fear that swept across the nation like a tsu-
nami in the aftermath of the attack affected everyone, myself included.
I was a child in WW II when my father served in the Army. The news-
reels of the war that I watched with my grandfather in a theater on
Hollywood Boulevard apparently had made an indelible impression
on my psyche. Because on 9/11, I was overwhelmed with 60-year-old
emotions of childhood fear and helplessness that caught in my throat.

My classes were cancelled for a few days following 9/11. I managed an alternative education program for students at-risk of school
failure. On 9/11, I was a couple of years shy of my planned retirement.
I am well educated, by western standards, having earned a master's
degree majoring in international relations, and have held teaching
licenses in elementary, secondary, and special education. I was also
well traveled – Europe and the former Soviet Union in the 60's, three
months in Nigeria with the Experiment in International Living, and
teaching in Rio de Janeiro. Ironically, my first contact with Islam was
in Kano, in the northern region of Nigeria, where I lived with the Muslim mayor and his three wives for a week.

However, with all of these globalizing credentials and experiences, I must admit that I was a clueless North American "islander" on
9/11 when it came to knowledge of the Middle East, Islam and Muslims. I couldn't even name or locate the countries of the region then.
I was stuck in the old paradigms that focused on Russia, China, and
Southeast Asia, when it came to understanding international relations.
Also, I was preoccupied with personal and professional demands, and
gave minimal time to politics and international affairs. I was a busy
wage-earner, divorced parent, and consumer, like a majority of Americans. I had cool Infinity wheels, enjoyed Oregon's beaches and mountains with my children, and was a devotee of the Portland jazz scene.
Life was sweet, relatively speaking.

In the past, I had been more engaged politically, but my life went in a different direction when I became a parent. 9/11 changed all of that in a single explosive moment, and I started to wake up... again. I suppose you could say that I'm the proverbial 'cat with nine lives.' I administered a rural Community Action Agency in the 1960's under the U.S. Office of Economic Opportunity. I lead the CAA in organizing Hispanic migrant farm workers who worked under terrible conditions for peasant wages in northern California vineyards. Cesar Chavez even trained my staff in community organizing. I participated in the civil rights movement with the Student Non-Violent Coordinating Committee, and marched in every Vietnam anti-war demonstration I could get to. Later, I became involved in planning and directing comprehensive manpower training programs for federal agencies, serving low income people in major U.S. cities. I also was involved in politics for awhile, working as a press aide in the California state legislature, and on a couple of Congressional campaigns. I witnessed the machinery of domestic American politics from the inside.

I served my time in the trenches, working the political scene in major U.S. Cities, a state legislature, and the U.S. Congress, where I discovered that most political events are scripted, i.e. contrived and managed. The problem is that most Americans believe political events occur randomly, spontaneously, or by chance. From my experience, this was never the case. Political power and control are hand-in-glove. I'm a trained academic researcher, political historian, and writer. If I require a label, it is "rational empiricist." My interest in political writing is about uncovering and revealing the facts and alternative narratives behind the spin and disinformation that passes for news and political "truth" in America – and around the world.

The 9/11 Narrative

This leads me to 9/11, and the government's narrative explaining the catastrophic event. I witnessed the live TV coverage of the collapse of all three World Trade Center buildings. At the time, I was perplexed by one clearly observant characteristic of the buildings' collapse. They each pancaked and fell straight down into their footprints on the ground. As I watched repeated reruns of the collapsing towers, I also noticed that the collapse of each floor of the skyscrapers was preceded by explosive puffs of smoke, pulverized cement and debris coming from various parts of each floor immediately prior to the floors' collapse. I was struck by the similarity of the WTC towers' collapse with a controlled demolition of a 14-story building in Los Angeles that I had witnessed years earlier with my father, who filmed

it as part of a TV show he was directing. I didn't pay much attention at
the time to what I witnessed on 9/11, however. The significance of my
observations would become apparent later.

Within months of 9/11, it was clear that the government's official narrative was insubstantial. The evidence gathered by numerous
national and international architects, engineers, physicists, fire and
building demolition experts revealed that the three WTC skyscrapers
were brought down in controlled demolitions. Their research is freely
available through the internet, videos, books, and academic papers to
anyone who is interested, and willing to explore the subject. Further,
according to the instructors in Florida who trained the Saudi terrorists
to fly the jet airlines they hijacked, the Saudis lacked the skills to accomplish what they are alleged to have done, namely execute precise
hits on the Twin Towers and the Pentagon.

We may never know what actually happened on 9/11. We only
know that the hijacked planes were not the reason why the three World
Trade Center buildings collapsed. In addition, we really don't know
what crashed into the Pentagon, since there are no photographs available of the plane's remains at the crash site. We only know that there
was a gapping round hole in the side of an unoccupied wing of the
Pentagon, and that several Pentagon employees were killed.

To this day, few people seem to be aware that 7 World Trade
Center also collapsed, even though it was not rammed by a plane. 7
WTC was damaged by debris when the nearby WTC North Tower
collapsed, igniting fires on lower floors of the building. 7 WTC was
the first tall building – 47 stories – to have collapsed primarily due to
uncontrolled fires, and the first and only steel skyscraper in the world
to have collapsed due to fire. The collapse of 7 WTC in just six seconds received minimal coverage in the 2002 report issued by FEMA,
the Federal Emergency Management Agency, that endeavored to explain the collapse of the WTC buildings. Apparently, 7 WTC was an
"inconvenient truth."

What actually happened? Who did it? Why? How? The answers
to these vexing questions put us in the realm of speculation. There are
no conclusive answers because the information is not available. Nonetheless, 9/11 is a conspiracy by definition, and the official narrative, at
the very least, does not reveal all that is known about the event. Today,
14 years after the 9/11 attack, more than half of the American people,
according to a wide range of credible public opinion polls, believe
that the government is withholding information about 9/11, and is not

204

revealing the truth about what actually happened.[1]   It is not possible to discuss 9/11 and ignore the evidence that challenges the official government narrative.

The significance of the government's 9/11 disaster narrative, and my reason for referencing it here, is that it laid blame for the attack exclusively on a handful of naive Saudi-Muslim religious fanatics. The narrative convulsed Americans into a fit of anti-Islamic paranoia and hysteria that gave us two wars, the subversion of the Bill of Rights by the Department of Homeland Security, and mega-data spying by the National Security Agency that has eroded the privacy of every American, as well as anyone else in the world of interest to America's intelligence agencies.

The War in Iraq

By the time I took early retirement from public school teaching in 2003, I had become immersed in examining the 9/11 attack, as well as the 2001 war to push the Iraqi's out of Kuwait, and the invasion of Iraq led by the U.S. in 2003. I had a book in mind, and I wanted to be closer to the story. When I learned that Kuwait was looking for western-trained special education teachers in response to a spike in school-age severely handicapped Kuwaiti children, I secured a position with a British school there.

In Kuwait, I investigated and reported on the Iraq war and the political decisions that brought it about in columns written for two English-language newspapers, and my online column, Common Sense in Bilal al-Hejaz. I discovered evidence, for example, that Bush's PR team, led by Carl Rove, had masterminded a brilliant campaign of fear to conjure up support for the invasions of Afghanistan and Iraq, as well as the HSA and NSA. I learned, also, that the backstories to the wars in Iraq and Afghanistan were about hegemony over the world's oil supplies, and that the two wars, together with the Iran sanctions, were intended to forestall the replacement of the U.S. dollar as the world's primary reserve currency. Indeed, the stakes are high in the Great Game that is being played out in west Asia and the Middle East in the 21st century.[2]

The classic shell and pea game is an appropriate analogy to describe U.S. Middle East policy. The rules of the game were revealed in

---

1   For links to more than eight reputable national and international public opinion polls regarding 9/11, see: https:en.wikipedia.org/wiki/Opinion_polls_about_9/11conspiracy_theories
2   See excerpts from the *Silk Road Journal* article, Appendix B

a candid interview with an unnamed senior adviser to President Bush, by Ron Suskind, former senior national-affairs reporter for the *Wall Street Journal:*

> "He [the White House advisor] expressed something that at the time I didn't fully comprehend -- but which I now believe gets to the very heart of the Bush presidency. The aide said, "Guys like you are in what we call the reality-based community," which he defined as people who ''believe that solutions emerge from your judicious study of discernible reality." I nodded and murmured something about enlightenment principles and empiricism. He cut me off. ''That's not the way the world really works anymore," he continued. ''We're an empire now, and when we act, we create our own reality. And while you're studying that reality -- judiciously, as you will -- we'll act again, creating other new realities, which you can study too, and that's how things will sort out. We're history's actors... and you, all of you, will be left to just study what we do."

It was my habit in Kuwait to go across the street from our apartment building to a bachalla to get a cup of tea before heading to my classroom. There, I was confronted with a rack of daily newspapers displaying grisly front-page color photos of the atrocities of the Iraq war that had occurred the previous day. Occasionally, smoke from burning fires across the Iraq border, located just three hours by car north of Kuwait City, could be seen from our 7th floor apartment. In America, we sanitize and distance ourselves from war with academic terminology, political shibboleths, doublespeak verbiage like "collateral damage," and redacted news photos and video clips that rarely depict the bloody human carnage of war. We don't get hit in the gut with the horrifying reports and images of war that I was experiencing daily in Kuwait. One morning, the Egyptian shopkeeper and I were staring at a particularly unsettling front-page photo of a grandmother holding the mutilated body of her grandchild following a bombing. I looked down at the newspaper, spilling my paper cup of tea. "Why they kill children?" he asked, almost rhetorically. I had no answer, of course. No one does.

"What we see and do in war, the cruelty, is unbelievable.
But, somehow, we gotta make some sense of it.
To do that, we need an easy-to-understand truth,
and damn few words..."
(From the film: "Flags of Our Fathers")

"Operation Iraqi Freedom" was the official code name for the war in Iraq. I even have a U.S. Army cap with this engraved on it. All the coalition military guys wore 'em. However, the code name belayed the facts; "freedom" was not in the equation. From "shock and awe" bombing to Abu Ghraib, the war was devastating for the people of Iraq, and a shameful waste of lives and property on all sides, compounded by a shocking waste of U.S. taxpayer dollars.

. . .

"Life is What You Do While Making Other Plans"

Although I went to Kuwait in September 2003 with plans to be there for just a year, my guiding planets apparently had other plans. I became a close friend with a Kuwaiti philanthropist and executive in Kuwait's national oil company. He mentored me in my quest to understand and know more about Islam. While I haven't mentioned it earlier, I had become what might be termed a "spiritual seeker" over the previous few years. I was active in a local Christian church, and did volunteer work at the church's homeless shelter. In Kuwait, I naturally became interested in Islam, which I knew nothing about. I was attracted to the personal discipline imposed on Muslims by their faith, and the merit of praying regularly together five times daily. I wasn't that attentive as a Christian, and wanted to experience Islam for myself. I began to study in earnest, and read a few translations of the Qur'an. I discovered the linkages between Judaism, Christianity, and Islam, which the Qur'an refers to as the "Religions of the Book", and that the followers of the three faiths are referred to as "people of the Book" in the Qur'an.[3] I found that accepting Islam involved a relatively seamless transition, in view of the fact that Islam is grounded in the teachings of the Biblical Prophets, as well as the Gospels of Jesus the Christ, whom Muslims refer to as a Prophet of Allah.

During this time, I met a wonderful woman from Pakistan who was a special education teacher working at the same school where I taught. We became good friends, and realized one day that we didn't want to be apart. My experiences with marriage and divorce had soured me on the very idea of marriage. However, suddenly, as if a light had been turned on in a dark tunnel, I realized that I didn't want to be apart from her. She felt the same, and we decided to marry.

Accepting Islam, marrying a Pakistani woman, and immersing

3 See Appendix A for excerpts from the book, *Jewish-Muslim Relations – A Qur'anic View*, co-authored by myself and Jihad contributor Arif Humayun.

myself in Middle East and west Asian culture was a sea-change in my consciousness and understanding of the world. But these experiences were not the only ones that put me on a fast-track to becoming a cosmopolitan global citizen. I started working part-time for a prominent Kuwait English-language newspaper, where I was able to access sources of news and information unavailable to me in the U.S. My knowledge base began to expand dramatically. In addition, I was exposed daily to reports of the war in Iraq covered and written by Arabs, both Sunni and Shi'a. My closest friend at the paper was a long-time, well-educated Egyptian reporter, who also was a history teacher in a Kuwait high school. My re-education was now in high gear.

A year after our marriage, I started working part-time for the Kuwait Grand Mosque on a project to improve communication and mutual understanding between westerners living and working in Kuwait, and Kuwaiti citizens. My office at the Grand Mosque overlooked the entry to the main mosque, where I prayed daily. It is an exquisite building evidencing the finest qualities of Islamic design and craftsmanship. I was now immersed in something far more profound than politics. My education and experiences became a pathway to a kind of personal enlightenment, of sorts.

My Post-9/11 Journey Continues in Lahore, Pakistan

The next chapter in my post-9/11 cosmopolitan journey began when my wife and I decided to spend the greater part of each year in Lahore, Pakistan. We recently completed a lovely home there in a well-kept residential colony located a block from my wife's parents' home. We dedicated the second floor of our home for our free school, which my wife launched last year for children of the workers in our colony and nearby who are extremely poor, and can't afford to send their children even to public school. It's been quite successful, and we plan to expand it this coming year. We also are running a special education clinic for children who are experiencing difficulties in their private schools, or who are unable to attend school at all due to their disabilities. I am engaged in teacher training, attempting to transfer my experience and knowledge to teachers in public and private schools in Lahore. Our work is profoundly rewarding.

Living closely within Pakistani family culture is unlike anything I have experienced before. The learning curve has been steep, as I was raised in a culture of individualism. Pakistani culture is family-based and tribal. The preferences and needs of the individual are subordinate to the needs of the family, or group. For me, it has been a sea-change in thinking and behavior. I learn something new daily. I have come to see how loneliness and alienation, common to many in America, simply is not possible in the closely bound family culture of Pakistan (which also includes Asia and the Middle East). Americans pursue meaning in their lives as individuals. Pakistanis find meaning in their lives through their relationships with others. Unfortunately, many Americans self-medicate into psychic numbness in their attempts to cope with the stress and emotional pain of their daily lives. While life is extremely tough for most Pakistanis, they don't resort to drugs and alcohol. Most important is their Islamic faith, which provides structure and guidance in daily living. In addition, there is always someone in the family close by to lend an ear, comforting advice, a helping hand, or a loan if needed. The sense of social-emotional security within this system is palpable.

I have grown well beyond my relatively provincial pre-9/11 consciousness. The journey has been a long one. Yes, I am still an American citizen, and proud to be so. With all the mayhem and pain America causes in the world, we also are doing a world of good through our foundational principles of governance, advocacy for human rights, education, and public and private humanitarian aid. The plethora of U.S. Agency for International Development programs in Pakistan, for example, are keenly appreciated by all Pakistanis, and a source of pride for me as an American. While anti-America political narratives are common, America's international relations are not black and white, by any means. Nor do the negative narratives attach to the Americans who live, work, and travel in Pakistan.

I have encountered only respectful and helpful interactions with Pakistanis and others in our travels throughout the Middle East. I have yet to experience a single negative social interaction in Pakistan in the 10 years I have been visiting and living there. My wife has had the same experience in the States. She is always treated with utmost respect and kindness by my family, friends, and our neighbors. There is immense curiosity about Americans and life in the States. Wherever we travel, I am continually bombarded with questions. My wife, also, frequently has to answer questions from our American friends and family about Pakistan, her family, her culture, and what it's like being married to an American. Significantly, in America, we have never encountered a single negative comment about Islam, or my decision to accept Islam. When invited to dine with family, friends, and neighbors, our dietary preferences are always respected. It seems that everyone, both in the U.S. and Pakistan, is curious about us. Of course, we are always happy to share our experiences and insights. It seems that our principal contribution to inter-faith and cross-cultural relations is our physical presence in both the U.S. and Pakistan. Negative stereotypes and prejudice cannot abide where interpersonal cross-cultural connections, friendships, and transparent dialogue exist.

I am not a Pakistani, of course, although I am married to a Pakistani and immersed in Pakistani culture several months each year. However, my values and awareness have grown beyond the confines of any one culture or society. I am now an amalgam, a mixed brew of ever-expanding experiences, ideas and values that extend across cultures, religions, and political borders. I define myself as a cosmopolite on the cutting edge of an emergent global society.[4]

I'm not alone, by any means. People like me with similar experiences and sensibilities are found everywhere throughout the world. We are, first and foremost, human beings -- one in the awareness and spirit of our common humanity. Our differences -- and they are many, of race, culture, class, language, education, religion, et. al. -- are integral to who we are. Nevertheless, the defining characteristic of a cosmopolitan globalist is tolerance and respect for the uniqueness and differences of others. The guiding principle is acceptance of others as they are, while abstaining from any attempt to make others into one's own image.

A renowned teacher, Meher Baba, has articulated succinctly the spiritual root of this emergent cosmopolitanism:

"Start learning to love God by loving those whom
you cannot love. The more you remember others with
kindness and generosity, the more you forget yourself.
When you completely forget yourself, you find God."

---

4 Cosmopolite [noun]: a person who is cosmopolitan in his or her ideas, life, etc.; citizen of the world.

"Stand up for what is right –
even if you're standing alone."
~ Suzy Kassem ~

"The only thing necessary for the triumph of evil
is for good men to do nothing."
~ Edmund Burke (1729-1797) ~

"Evil brings men together."
~ Aristotle ~

Chapter Seventeen

Events That Shape Our Lives

Alan Bazzaz

Alan Bazzaz, born in Baghdad, Iraq, received his BSEE from College of Engineering at the University of Baghdad. He worked as an engineer in the private sector in Baghdad for a few years before deciding to pursue his postgraduate studies in the US. He received his MS degree in Computer and Information Science from the University of Oregon in 1980. Unable to return to Iraq due to the war with Iran, Alan joined a startup company in Eugene, OR, building automation equipment for sawmills and plywood companies. Later, he acquired ownership and became the company CEO. In 2001, Alan sold the company, and retired in 2006. He currently lives in the Portland, OR, area with his family. Alan is an active member, and past president of his local Rotary Club, engaged in local and international humanitarian projects. Alan speaks Arabic and Farsi.

9/11/2001

On the morning of September 11, 2001, my wife woke me up telling me to come downstairs and watch what's on TV. I didn't see what was so important for her to wake me up, knowing that I had arrived the night before from a long flight from Melbourne, where I had been on a business trip. I attended a conference on Wood Technology, during which I gave a talk on the latest technology available from our company. My body was still numb from sitting on the transcontinental flight, while my head was still buzzing from the sound of jet engines. I dragged myself downstairs and saw the horror of the first tower with a hole ripped into it from the plane's impact. At that time it wasn't clear whether it was an accident or something else. Then the news of the second plane hitting the second tower. TV images are now fuzzy in my mind, but I remember the knot in my stomach coming from

212

the feeling of loss of lives and the destruction we were watching on screen.

Over the next few hours and days, and as the story unfolded, the sadness for some 3000 people who perished that day gave way to a mix of fear and concern. Fear of the American public's reaction towards people from the Middle East, and especially Arabs. There were several incidents of harassment and intimidation throughout the US towards people of darker skin. One incident was against a Sikh who was mistaken for a Muslim, confirming my fears and apprehensions that we, Americans of Middle Eastern descent, are entering a new phase in the American society. Most of my concern was for my wife, who wears a headscarf, and our three children who were in various public schools in Eugene, Oregon.

Images on TV and the Web continued to show the aftermath of the attacks in the days and months following. The pain of the families that lost loved ones stayed vivid in the mind of most Americans, including our family. We ruled out flying in the near term. The only problem is my job required me to fly both domestically and overseas. On my first post-9/11 flight to Chattanooga, Tennessee, I was nervous and looking over my shoulder, thinking someone is watching me. No one was, at least to my knowledge. And, our family did not receive threats or angry letters, as we did in 1979. Then, Iranian students had just taken over the American embassy in Tehran and held 50 hostages. We received a threat note, mistaking us for Iranians, which we turned over to the police.

A year before the Hostage Crisis, and specifically in August 1978, my wife and I, along with our 2-year old son, arrived in Eugene, OR, from Baghdad, Iraq. We had gotten married only 3 years earlier in a suburb of Baghdad called Kadhimiya. Coming to America to study was a dream come true for me, while my wife was hoping we would go back as soon as I finished my Master's degree at the University of Oregon. She missed her family terribly, and her life was focused on our young son. It didn't help that I was burning the night candle studying at the library and the university computing center, while she was at home, with a child, feeling lonely, in a strange land and little knowledge of the English language.

Spring term 1980 was one of the hardest periods in our family's lives. Just before Iraq declared its war on Iran, the government rounded up Iraqis with Persian heritage, and sent them to camps at the border between Iraq and Iran. My parents and siblings were amongst the half a million Iraqi citizens that were exiled to Iran under hard conditions. Some families had the misfortune of having their sons taken away to later clear mines at the war front. My family made it safely to the camp but not before giving up all their wealth and vital documents. While we were tormented by the news of their exile, we ourselves were facing an uncertain future. What will happen after graduation, a couple of months away? Our Iraqi passports were now invalid. Our support system (our families) are now themselves in need of support, and we were in no position to help. These serious distractions led to difficulty concentrating on my studies, threatening not just my school work, but graduation as well.

I joined the American workforce immediately after graduation with the hopes of obtaining US citizenship through work. Success through work did eventually help me attain citizenship, and travel the world. The technology company I was working at manufactured equipment to automate and optimize the production of lumber and plywood. My travels took me to places where forests and wood were an important part of the economy. Australia and New Zealand rely on wood products heavily. The company has many installations in New Zealand's forestry companies. The demonstrations and discussions at that conference in September 2001 were vital to the business for that region, and American technology helped their industry to become more efficient and competitive world producers of wood products.

In the Middle East, the skepticism and conspiracy theories were plentiful after 9/11/2001. America's military and intelligence capabilities were appreciated, and sometimes exaggerated in the region. Through my discussions with people in the region, I got a consistent sense of disbelief that a few Saudis could evade the American security apparatus and execute such a gigantic crime. At times, America is seen as having God-like powers. As such, there must be another untold story, they asserted. Perhaps the American government, or agents in the CIA, had planned this whole thing, their argument goes. No matter how many examples I gave as to errors and mistakes the American government has committed around the world, and even at home, people in the region adhered to other explanations, rather than just plain mistakes.

Another example of the sentiment that American power and intelligence is infallible came through people in Baghdad discussing the situation during the insurgency. They could not accept that American soldiers killed by roadside bombs were the act of a few men with simple tools. "It could be that these bombs are planted by Americans themselves," or "Americans want to see an unstable Iraq to justify their stay," and so on the rumors go. And they accept no other reasoning.

There is a deep-rooted suspicion of government and its actions amongst Iraqis. My father told me that during the 1940's and 50's, while Iraq was ruled by a proxy British government, the saying went, "If you see two fish fighting in the river, the Brits must be behind it." This should come as no surprise. The Brits ruled the region through a well known policy of "Divide and Conquer." In fact, the word "Politic" (in Iraqi Arabic pronounced "Peletika") has a common usage to mean a trick. That is to say, people never took government action at its face value. There is always a hidden motive, a well thought out conspiracy, the result of which may not be evident for years to come. To think that an action had a straightforward reason, is to say the Brits were naive, and that was not logical to Arab thinking.

It is my belief that America's invasion of Iraq was doomed to fail no matter what the American administration did. Of course, it didn't help that the Bush administration made some awful errors during the occupation, at the top of which is disbanding the Iraqi Army. But the deep suspicion of any foreign rule in Iraq by Iraqis creates a difficult environment to operate under.

Personally, I was for the invasion as long as the American forces would leave very quickly after handing the government to an Iraqi strongman, and schedule elections in a few years. I lived through four coup d'états in twenty years. Each time, a new military man would take over the reins and eliminate heads of the previous regime and those who may constitute a threat to the new regime. They were all successful in the sense that a period of relative stability was enjoyed by the citizens until the next coup. The army was always a key factor in stabilizing the new regime. Disbanding the army after the invasion did not make sense to me then, and it doesn't now. The analogy I use is one of moving a beehive. Once the bees are smoked, the hive is safely picked while the bees are disoriented. Disbanding the army is a kin to hitting the beehive with a stick, and then chasing the bees one by one. Generals, captains, and low ranking military personnel were out of jobs overnight. Many kept their weapons and some looted weapon caches on their way out. Many of these soldiers turned to Al-Qaida desperate for work, and they found plenty. For some of the high ranking officers, there was a hope to take over the government and lead the country themselves. Such officers could not even think of such an idea during Saddam's regime – fearing their "heads would be chopped off."

Saddam Husain built a security apparatus that was second to none in the Middle East. Several independent security organizations were operating at the same time, in separate areas, and some of them spied on each other. It was a very complex, but effective system. Of course, the regime did not hesitate to eliminate anyone suspected of conspiracy against the regime, including Saddam's own family and friends. This system kept Saddam in power for some 30 years. Iraqis, including myself, could not foresee a way to dislodge Saddam from power. In fact, he was making arrangements to become a king, so Iraq could be ruled by his kids after his death. That's the reason I was happy to see American forces move to dislodge Saddam from power. Saddam's regime had committed so many atrocities against its own citizens, and the world did not hear about them, or didn't care. The brain drain was so bad that the government prohibited engineers and doctors leaving Iraq, even for a vacation. Due to Saddam's regional adventures, over a million people were killed during the war with Iran, and more died during the first Gulf War after the invasion of Kuwait. In the 1990's, at the height of the economic sanctions imposed by the West, while Iraqi's were dying for lack of medicine, Saddam was building palaces for himself throughout Iraq.

In 1980, Saddam declared war on Iran, despite the fact that Iran had more resources and territory. He made his bet due to a weakened Iran military after removal of the Shah. Iran was at the beginning of its revolution and volunteers arrived by the thousands wanting to "defend the revolution." Many were children as young as 15 years of age, and had no training in combat, but that didn't stop them. Some of these kids cleared landmines, including my brother-in-law, who was injured by such a device. Prior to the start of the war, Saddam's regime rounded up some half-a-million Iraqis of Iranian ancestry and sent them to Iran without documents or notices. My parents and three siblings faced the same fate.

"I was in my office in the morning, when two security officers arrived and asked me for my papers," my father recalled. "After they examined them, they confiscated them and demanded the keys to the office and other establishments, which I handed to them" He continues, "They took me to the Security Office and interrogated me for hours and had me sign documents agreeing to give up all of my assets to the government." They told him he should call home and tell his wife (my mother) to get ready for a trip. My dad, accompanied by two security officers, arrived at the house in a minivan. My mother and siblings were scrambling to gather a few belongings in a couple of suitcases. They were stuffed in the minivan and headed to the Iranian borders. They were dropped about a mile from the Iranian post, and were told to walk. Later, they were picked up by an Iranian border convoy, and were taken to a tent camp where many earlier arrivals were staying. The camp was erected near the Iranian border post, in an open field devoid of vegetation or water. The camp was meant to serve as a temporary shelter until the war ended and people could return back to their homes. As we know, the war lasted eight years, and these people never had the chance to see their homes and businesses until some thirty years later, in 2003, when the U.S. invasion of Iraq took place.

Iran and Iraq

Early after Mohammed's death, the caliphs sought to expand the new faith to the region and beyond. After dominating the Arabian Peninsula, the Muslim army looked to conquer the area then called Mesopotamia, part of which was under the rule of the Persian (Sasanian) Empire. The latter was at its weakest after years of bloody wars with the Roman and then the Byzantine Empire. The Muslim army did not face a significant resistance and were able to sweep into today's Iraq, and later into Iran.

Back in Mecca, Mohammed's death created a controversy as to who should be the successor. Ali, Mohammed's cousin and son-in- law, had received clear support from the Prophet at his last speech to Muslims before his death. However, other Muslims thought there were more eligible candidates, and in a hastily put together meeting assembled at the time of Mohammed's burial, it was decided that Abu Bakr should succeed him. Abu Bakr started the Caliphate rule, and Ali became the fourth caliph. In his reign, he was challenged by Muawiah, the governor of Shamm (today's Syria), but Ali couldn't silence this challenge before he was assassinated. After Ali's death, Muawiah became the defacto caliph, and, with that, the Amawiat dynasty started.

Shi'a (meaning the followers of Ali) never accepted the succession of the caliphate, especially after Ali's death. They believe Ali should have succeeded the Prophet, followed by his descendants. Since the death of Ali, the Shi'a, led by the eldest of the descendent of Ali (imam), continued to challenge the caliph in power, and for that these imams were imprisoned, kept under strict watch, or simply assassinated. The Shi'a movement stayed underground, and as a result it splintered into many factions such as the Alawites, Zaidis, Ismailia's, etc. The Shi'a movement gained steam during the Abbasid dynasty,

217

especially in Iraq and Iran. In the Safawid's dynasty, Iran almost completely converted to Shi'aism and remains today. One reason Shi'a movement survived is the structure of its religious hierarchy and money flow. Sunni scholars and leaders have been, and still today, are paid by the Caliphate or the government. As such, the religious establishment is at best reluctant in criticizing the government. Shi'a scholars (Ulama) receive money directly from followers through a form of tax, called Khums. This structure freed the Ulama to challenge the government, as happened during the Shah's last few years. It also happened in Iraq for over a hundred years. In a recent instance, Mohamed Sadiq Al-Sadr (father of the current Muqtada Al-Sadr) was murdered, along with his sister, at the hands of the Baath regime for refusing to follow Saddam's orders.

What's interesting is as Shi'a leaders can challenge the government, they themselves are not allowed to run the government. The pure Shi'a government combines executive powers and legislative powers, based on Islamic laws derived from Koran and interpretations of it. It is believed that no ordinary human can do this job. As such, the head of government must be an Imam. Imams are infallible, descendents of Ali, and there are twelve of them in the Shi'a Twelvers (less in other factions). This is important, as Shi'a can never claim a caliphate, as Sunnis can. The supreme leader's role in Iran is akin to our Supreme Court. He has the final say, whether a certain law, or indeed government action, is in line with Islamic laws. In practice, however, the supreme leader has been more influential in day to day government affairs.

I was born into a family who believed in the Shi'a doctrine. We lived in the town of Khadamia, where one of the imams is buried in a beautiful shrine with gold-gilded minarets. The town is a suburb north of Baghdad, where the majority of residents are Shi'a. My grandparents had settled in this town at the end of the 19th century, coming from Iran to live close to one of the revered Shi'a shrines.

My parents were not strict. They wanted their kids to be pious and understand the moral teachings, but not necessarily the nuts and bolts of the theology. I knew the Sunni's have different beliefs, but never to think they're bad, only different. During childhood I felt discrimination from those who knew I came from an Iranian ancestry. During high school and college, Iraq was going through a nationalist movement, and religious tolerance was at its best.

However, in the early 1970's, and with the rise of the ruling Baath party, a new slice of society started rising to power. They were mostly Sunni, tribal, and especially from the region where Saddam was born. By its nature, the regime marginalized the Shi'as in Iraq, and eventually took concerted measures to limit them. During these times, I felt discriminated twice. Once for being a Shi'a and another for being of Iranian descent. That went on until I had the opportunity to leave the country in the late 1970's.

Full Circle

Living in the United States was such a relief at first. It was a fresh start in life. No one will treat me differently because I'm Shi'a or of Iranian descent, I thought. That feeling didn't last long, however. The hostage crisis in Iran brought all those feelings back, albeit in different colors. Since then, every criminal act by a Muslim individual, group, or country made me and my wife worry of more discrimination. It's as if I wanted to apologize to the people for these acts, simply for the fact that I was a Muslim. I wanted to say to the world, these are bad apples, criminals, who don't believe in what I believe. It is unfortunate that they're labeled as Muslims, but they don't belong to the Islam that I know and grew up with.

One of the main tenants of Islam that I was taught in my childhood explained in a verse in the Koran that says "If you kill one innocent person, it's as if you killed all of humanity." That verse is so clear and indisputable. One cannot justify killing an innocent human being. Collateral damage does not exist in the framework of this verse. How then do some, who call themselves Muslims, get around this powerful law? The answer is obviously complicated, but has much to do with people who, in the pursuit of power, wealth, and dominance, can justify anything. Later in life, I learned everything is subject to interpretation when the desire for power grab is strong enough. History is full of examples of kings and vagabonds alike, advancing their interests despite their own opposing religious or moral teachings. In fact, some even go as far as doing so in the name of that religion. When King Henry VIII could not divorce his wife, he changed his and his kingdom's religion to reach his goal.

My American friends have keen interest in understanding the region, the religion and culture, in small bites so they can digest the situation quickly and easily. We are a culture of simplifying and solving problems quickly and efficiently. Unfortunately, this approach does not apply very well to events that are based on thousands of years in a complex mosaic of interdependent religious, ethnic and cultural forces. Our quick solutions tend to become a patchwork of imported western methods that have no roots or buy-in from the various sides in the region. On the other hand, my Iraqi and Iranian friends feel that Americans are imposing heavy-handed solutions that are not consistent or fair. The nuclear issue with Iran is the most recent example of this American behavior. While Israel has hundreds of nuclear bombs and the means to deliver them anywhere in the Middle East, Iran is not allowed to even do advanced research in the field. Citing Israeli democracy is not an acceptable answer to most in the region. Most argue that Israel's democracy has not prevented the harsh treatment of Palestinians and occupation of their land. Acquiescence by the US is just another example of the hypocrisy of American policy in the region.

What is the solution then?

I have pondered this question for years. How can we bring stability to the region? What role should the US play to bring about such stability?

We must first assume that it's to the interest of the US to see the area stable. Most people in the region would not agree with this assumption. The belief is it is better for Israel's security to have the countries surrounding it weak and fragmented, so there would be no chance in assembling an army that could invade Israel as it happened in 1948, and then in 1967.

Whatever the reality is, I believe Israel has much to gain by having stable neighbors with which they can trade and coexist in the region. With its advanced technology and stable government, Israel to the Middle East can be as Germany is to Europe.

Devoid of any real change in the world attitude regarding the Middle East on the horizon, I choose to adopt the philosophy espoused by Rotary International: "Service Above Self." For through service and good will we can achieve a better and more lasting Peace than any other way. The region is in real need of economic development. Most of the population in the region are below age 40, and the youth are looking for opportunities to better their lives. We witnessed the eruptions by the youth in Tunisia, Egypt, and other places, demanding a different course. More eruptions are boiling under the surface in most countries in the region.

The Peace Corps work is an excellent example of such effort. Going into the country with no agenda, no strings attached, and real intent to better people's lives can have a profound impact on people's impressions of the US. Work by NGOs and humanitarian organizations will eventually build goodwill with the people of the region. It may take a generation or two, but we must be patient and persistent. No more instantaneous results and quick solutions. Having said this, the larger the effort, the faster the results.

I joined Rotary as a channel to give back. For living the American Dream, my intent was to give back to my local community by doing projects to help the less fortunate. My passion has been in the areas of peace and education. Peace allows for a stable environment without which education and economic prosperity are not possible. My Rotary Club has installed "peace poles," and is sponsoring an anti-bullying camp for kids in the community. The peace focus by Rotary International today can apply anywhere, and is not only beneficial to the local community. Rotary, with its 1.2 million members around the world, is the perfect organization to start or facilitate projects with grass root organizations in the Middle East and elsewhere in the world.

Growing up in Baghdad, I used to listen to Voice of America, enjoy the news, and programs such as jazz music. My family had an American car, American made appliances, and followed the news in the U.S. My generation spoke fondly of America and America's way of life. We dreamt about studying in one of the fine US schools. It's only after decades of schizophrenic American foreign policy that people in the region have lost faith and gained mistrust. I believe the American people can restore this trust, especially if they distance themselves from US foreign policies while engaged in projects and aid to the communities they serve. This is not a foreign concept to most people in the region, as their own government's policies rarely represent their will.

Wouldn't you agree?

"Sometimes even the smallest step in the right direction
ends up being the biggest step of your life.
Tiptoe if you must, but take that step."
~ (unable to confirm origin) ~

"Life is ten percent what happens to you
and ninety percent how you respond to it."
~ Abraham Lincoln ~

"Alone I can go fast. Together, we will go far."
~ African Proverb ~

Chapter Eighteen

The Need for a Forward-Looking Ijtihad in the Contemporary World

Farzana Hassan

Farzana Hassan is an author, a freelance writer, women's rights activist, musician, M.A., MBA, Ed.D, Farzana Hassan, also known as Farzana Hassan-Shahid is a well known writer and commentator on Islam and Muslim issues. Though based in Canada, her opinions, particularly on women's rights in Islam and Islamic terrorism are sought worldwide. Farzana received her early education at Sacred Heart, a missionary Catholic school in Lahore, Pakistan. She went on to complete her Bachelor's degree from the Kinnaird College for Women, also in Lahore. Farzana went on to complete her Master's in Political at the University of the Punjab back in Lahore, her MBA from the University of Massachusetts and her Doctorate in Education from the University of Phoenix. She has been actively involved in ecumenical and interfaith dialogue for the past nine years. Farzana is an author of two books and numerous articles and opinion pieces, and she has made media appearances all over the world.

9/11/2001

9/11 was undoubtedly a catalyzing event in the lives of Muslims across the world. Their faith under constant scrutiny after the tragic events, many turned belligerent, while others recoiled and became overly defensive about their faith. Some of us took to activism, which forced us to undergo a thorough examination of our religion. I too began a journey of intense introspection and reexamination of my faith. What I had previously accepted as Gospel truth, was now open to critical scrutiny, often with unpleasant realizations. The most troubling aspects of my faith involved the treatment of women and minorities in Islam, but I shall confine this discourse primarily to women's issues.

There is currently much debate on Islam's treatment of women.

Some assert Islam favours women, while others disagree vehemently
with that position, suggesting that in fact it marginalizes them greatly.
Certainly, hadith and some verses of the Quran are highly controver-
sial in this regard. The messages one gets from examining the literature are inconsistent.

For example, the Quran states: "Cherish the wombs that bear
you." The mother is to be loved and respected more than the father.
It is reported that the prophet always spoke fondly of his biological
mother Amena, as well as his foster mother Haleema. Mohammad
also advised his companions to treat their wives kindly, to not beat
them, because they were "crooked" as they were created from Ad-
am's rib. The Prophet of Islam also urged his companions to treat their
daughters the same as their sons, that they be educated in the same
manner. A well-known Hadith says: "If any of you would raise your
two daughters the same as your sons, he would be close to me in paradise." Islam's advent also put an end to the custom of burying female
children alive—a practice that was not widespread, but one that was
nonetheless repudiated by the founder of Islam.

But while this domestic ethos exhorting kindness toward wom-
en is a reality within Muslim communities, it is equally true that it
exists only within the strictures of the countless legalities that marginalize Muslim women. Also worth mentioning is the superior status of
men in Islam and that they are placed in a position of authority over
women. The latter must, at all times, obey the former. (Quran: 4:34)

There is hence an obvious problem with gender equality in
the Quran. The orthodoxy uses what has come to be known as the
"complementarity" argument to justify this inequality. It rests on the
notion that the rights of men and women are indeed unequal, but that
somehow this inequality is justified for the overall good of society. It
further includes the view that the rights accorded to women are commensurate with their role and obligations in society.

Male authority, too, is thus justified. According to Dr Jamal
Badawi of Queen Mary University Nova Scotia, the allowance for a
husband to beat his wife, for example, is in the overall interest of the
family and a desirable course of action. He writes:

> "…in extreme cases, or wherever greater harm such as di-
> vorce is a likely option, it allows for a husband to administer a gen-
> tle pat to his wife that causes no physical harm, nor leaves any sort
> of physical mark. It may serve in some cases to bring to the wife's
> attention the seriousness of her continued unreasonable behavior."

Wife battery and other inequities in the Muslim cultural ethos are thus justified in the interest of "the higher good of society." This begs the question: Is such justification warranted, and are the fundamentalists wrong in their continuing support of religious edicts that render women vulnerable to abuse? How, for example, can a husband monitor his rage and exercise necessary restraint in administering a "light beating?"

Let us also look at Islam's inheritance laws to evaluate their fairness in modern times. Though Islam's inheritance reforms were laudable fourteen hundred years ago, they must be revisited for further reform, as women's circumstances have changed drastically over the centuries. Societies today are vastly different from the communities of seventh century Arabia when these laws were enacted. While women at the time may indeed have been the financial responsibility of men, modern women are just as burdened with financial commitments and responsibilities as men. Islam's clear cut demarcation between the rights and responsibilities of men and women which informs the so called complementarity argument is no longer valid. Often Muslim women are the single breadwinners for their families. Women, therefore, cannot be discriminated against based on laws that may or may not have been fair even in the seventh century. They must be entitled to equal shares in inheritance. In modern civilized societies, laws must not discriminate on the basis of race, ethnicity, creed or gender whether they are laws inspired by religion or secular ideology.

The rationale for justifying polygamy must be similarly scrutinized. What is puzzling about the conservative Muslim narrative is the zeal with which many Muslim women defend polygamy not only as fair, but desirable and virtuous. Female theologian Farhat Hashmi is one such example. These traditionalists contend that men have a greater sexual urge than women. Liberal Muslims on the other hand wonder why God would cater to the basest of human urges while ignoring the tender sentiments of women, if this rationale were indeed true. What about love between men and women? Why should this be about sex alone?

The conservatives often respond by stating that such questions have been addressed through Islam's strict condition of fairness. Muslims, therefore, accept polygamy as a social institution worthy of being preserved for posterity, as holistically speaking for them; its advantages far outweigh its disadvantages.

But if one looks a little closer, the Quranic condition of fairness imposed on men seems a bit superfluous. Due to its very nature, an institution which is inherently unjust cannot accommodate fairness. An arrangement where one man is shared by several women is intrinsically unjust, no matter how much care he exercises in maintaining "parity" among them. It is as absurd as telling someone to commit murder with kindness. Polygamy also causes extreme emotional distress not only to women, but also to children who must often endure great disruptions to their lives. For me, polygamy is simply adultery in the guise of sanctimonious piety.

While polygamy and other Muslim practices may cause women daily frustrations, it is reports of stoning for alleged adultery in countries like Pakistan, Iran, Afghanistan and Nigeria that cause the greatest consternation to human rights activists. Many a time, agencies such as Amnesty International have had to intervene in such cases to have the sentences reduced. Amina Lawal of Nigeria narrowly escaped sentence, while a teenage girl in Somalia by the name of Aisha Ibrahim Duhulow suffered the most brutal fate of being stoned to death for alleged adultery.

The problem with deeming adultery a crime is also tied to the issue of polygamy. A man can have sexual relations with more than one woman under some guise or another and not be accused of adultery, as these would be considered religiously sanctioned unions. A woman under Islamic law has no such privilege.

A husband's second, third or fourth union is considered legally and morally acceptable as it enjoys "divine" sanction. His sexual encounters with multiple women would therefore not be considered adultery. If a woman, on the other hand, were to fall in love with and have intercourse with another man, she would immediately be considered adulterous. Fewer men would be considered adulterous because they would already have access to other women "legally."

But even if the law established culpability equally to both sexes, one must answer a very basic question about the resulting punishment. If adultery is seen as a crime (and medieval punishments seen as civilized), the provision of one hundred lashes to both the adulterer and adulteress is hardly fair when one considers the privileged sexual opportunities Muslim men enjoy.

In light of such inequality, which imposes the charge of adultery on a woman much more easily, equal punishment must be seen as utterly unfair. Jurists and other modern exegetes of the Quran have failed to recognize the injustice. The terminology has simply been manipulated to legalize men's multiple unions while criminalizing the same for women.

I therefore no longer accept polygamy, wife battery or the mistreatment of religious minorities. But as a spiritual Muslim, I am equally convinced there are answers to be sought from within the ideological framework of my faith. The answer lies in a revamping of the concept of ijtihad and its applicability for modern times.

Traditionally, Ijtihad is defined as free or independent thinking to arrive at a juristic ruling for issues on which the Quran and Hadith are silent. The efforts of the eighth and ninth century doctors of Islamic jurisprudence such as Imam Shaffi and Abu Hanifah came about as a result of such ijtihad, as these exegetes were exercising independent reasoning to interpret legal sources by responding to the changing conditions of society. Consequently, they came to formulate elaborate rules of conduct for Muslims that would govern both their private and public life according to prevailing circumstances.

Though the need was widely felt to undertake ijtihad in the form of juristic rulings, earlier tensions among emergent juristic schools suggest there were differences in methodology over how such rulings were derived. There were some who insisted that rulings would have to conform to the text of the Quran and Sunnah, thereby discarding the notion that Ijma (Consensus) or Qayas (analogy) were legitimate sources of Shariah. However, what crystallized as the Usul-ul-Fiqh or the classical theory of jurisprudence, positioned the Quran and Hadith as the primary, and Ijma and Qiyas as secondary sources of Islamic law. The secondary sources would have to conform in principle to the two primary sources.

Unfortunately, rulings deduced through such meticulous adherence to the Usul-ul-Fiqh, led to discrimination against women and other disadvantaged groups in Muslim countries. Less commonly known is the fact that such an eventuality was forestalled by early exegetes of the Quran, particularly those who belonged to the group of scholars known as the "Ahl Ra'aay," who considered rationality and the principle of Istihsaan (juristic preference to arrive at the most equitable solution) a paramount principle in deducing religious law. Their objective was to achieve a just society that would accommodate the rights of all, while paying special attention to the rights of the weak and underprivileged. Regrettably over time, the principle of Istihsaan was abandoned and the doctrine of Taqlid or blind following of established juristic schools gained ascendancy among Muslims.

Any forward looking ijtihad must revive the concept of Istihsaan as a first step towards delivering justice and equality to all in Muslim society. It must also take into consideration the difference

between the Quran's time-specific societal injunctions, its broad normative principles and its overall objective of creating a just society
that would treat members with equality and fairness.

The Quran's overarching principles of justice and fairness or
Adl and Ihsaan, have been consistently ignored due to excessive adherence to the temporal legal injunctions of the Quran. Whether it is in
the application of Shariah law in Pakistan, unequal inheritance rights
for women, unjust dispensations of cases involving alimony, child
custody, divorce, and polygamy due to an obsession with conform-
ing to specific seventh century expressions of Quranic principles, the
result has been the repression and marginalization of Muslim women
and minorities living under Shariah law.

My approach to Quranic exegesis is holistic. One must look
at the principles behind Quranic edicts which exhibited fairness and
compassion towards the weaker sex. It is these principles of fairness,
compassion, justice and equity that need to be expressed as greater
equality under the law for women in the contemporary context, where
notions of gender equality, peace, tolerance and harmony have been
refined to a point where such rights are considered inalienable and
inhering in every human being. The Quran, through planting the seeds
for such reform within the social context of its own revelation, showed
the path for future reform and progress towards universally recognized
human values.

According to this holistic approach to the Quran, I would reiter-
ate that any forward looking ijtihad must of necessity conform to the
principles and objectives of delivering a just society the Quran itself
propounds, rather than being excessively preoccupied with their seventh century expressions and manifestations that resulted in disparities
between the rights of men and women.

Here the issue of "gender equity" verses "gender equality" must
be examined in greater detail. Gender equity is premised on the argument that the roles of men and women in society are complementary;
therefore, their rights must be distributed accordingly. Men, for example, are the breadwinners, they are the "protectors and sustainers"
of women – hence it is only fair they are apportioned a greater share in
inheritance. While this argument may hold some validity in theory, it
has to be examined against the reality on the ground. The ground reality is vastly different from the ideal envisioned by Muslim jurists and
calls for a reexamination of such anachronistic justifications for unequal shares in inheritance or unequal rights generally. The fact is that
conditions justifying such inequalities no longer exist. Women nowa-

days are often the sole breadwinners for their children and families, many of them live below poverty lines and a significant population of rural women in impoverished Muslim countries work like slaves in the fields, only to come and play slave to their husbands at home. Where is the justice in unequal shares? One cannot therefore use the contexts and scenarios of long ago to continue justifying unequal rights. The "complementarity" or "gender equity" argument, though it enjoys wide currency among Muslims, now needs to be looked at afresh, as it entails far too many justifications for the continued discrimination and marginalization of women. It is preventing young Muslim women from recognizing their own secondary social and legal status in Muslim societies. Because of the complementarity argument, Muslim women believe there is no discrimination against them within Shariah law, but they are sadly mistaken on these issues. They must realize that equality must be conceived as an absolute if progress is to be achieved in Muslim societies.

There are at present, in my opinion, three distinct discourses within Islam on women's rights. The first is the one vigorously promoted by Dr. Farhat Hashmi which attempts to render women invisible and anonymous by enshrouding them in Burkas, endorsing polygamous marriages and upholding the uncontested leadership of the husband over the wife. Ironically, such a discourse claims to be progressive, once again based on the "complementarity" argument, this time applied to the letter. The second, a slightly more progressive discourse, does not envision the subjugation of women to the extent of compartmentalizing them in gender specific roles, but nonetheless emphasizes the need for reclaiming the "rights Muslim women enjoyed under Islam many centuries ago." This is dangerous in my opinion, because it will not lead toward progress; it will instead lead toward seventh-century norms and applications of those norms which are by no means desirable in this day and age, given our vastly transformed societies. This is by far the prevalent discourse among Muslim women who are self-proclaimed "feminists" out to reclaim their rights. In my opinion, it is no longer enough to simply reclaim these rights. While such reclamation will certainly improve conditions for a segment of Muslim women in some societies, it will fall hopelessly short of modern standards of gender equality under the law. To summarize:

1. Ijtihad for them would have to be applied unfettered by the Usul Fiqh and conform to the Quran's broad principles of justice and fairness or Adl (Justice) and Ihsaan (the doing of that which is

beautiful), rather than to the specific manifestations of these principles that may have worked within a particular cultural framework

2. Islam's social regulations represented progress in the context of
   seventh century Arabia. It is that precedent that must be upheld for
   future reform. What has happened is precisely the opposite, which
   is in direct contravention to the precedent set by the Quran. When
   reactionary Muslims urge renewal of a pristine Islamic society,
   they fail to acknowledge that they are violating the fundamental
   principle on which the Quran enacted certain laws; the ameliora-
   tion of certain conditions for the underprivileged.

3. The Quran's moral code conforms to other ethical systems. It is
   this commonality that must be recognized and fostered. What is
   considered permissible or prohibited in Islam is also universally
   recognized as such.

ADDITIONAL AUTHOR INFORMATION: For Farzana's efforts
in promoting interfaith harmony, the National Christian/Muslim Liaison
Committee of Canada gave her their annual service award in 2004. As a
prominent member of the South Asian-Canadian community, she has headed
a number of Canadian organizations including the progressive Muslim
Canadian Congress. Her literary achievements include a third place poetry
award for her poem entitled "The Loner." The award was conferred by Bakers
Books in Dartmouth, Massachusetts in 2000. Farzana is also a public speaker.
She has presented papers at several national and international conferences. In
January 2009, she represented Canada as part of a three-member delegation
to Syria to promote citizen diplomacy and peace-building among Jews,
Christians and Muslims in that country. She also addressed a conference held
at Capitol Hill, Washington D.C. on "Women's Rights in Islam" in July 2009.
As a member of delegations to various UN workshops on women's rights,
she presented a paper on female education in Pakistan in March 2010.

Farzana is very well known to the media. Her international media
appearances include participation as a speaker at the world famous "Doha
Debates." Media appearances also include interviews with BBC World
Service, Al Jazeera, The Voice of America, Le Monde, "The Agenda with
Steve Paikin" and the Canadian Broadcasting Company.

Her several articles and opinion pieces have appeared in the *Montreal
Gazette, Toronto Star, Globe and Mail, Calgary Herald* and the *Huffington
Post*. Farzana is also a regular contributor to *Thara-E magazine*, the largest
English publication on women's issues in Syria. She has previously authored
two books on religion. Her most recent publication, *Prophecy and the
Fundamentalist Quest* (McFarland & Co, 2008), is a comparative study of
Christian and Muslim apocalyptic religion.

"War doesn't determine who is right –
war determines who is left."
~ Chinese Proverb ~

"Before you embark on a journey of revenge,
dig two graves."
~ Confucius ~

"We can easily forgive a child who is afraid of the dark;
the real tragedy of life is when men are afraid of the light."
~ Plato ~

Chapter Nineteen

Life as a Doctor's Son – and Afghan Refugee

Baha Jangzapuly

As a young Sunni Muslim Afghan displaced by seemingly continuous conflict and death, **Baha Jangzapuly** completed his elementary and high school education in Pakistan as a refugee. He then went to a private medical institute in Afghanistan. Highly motivated by the chaotic world around him, and influenced by his family, Baha found himself working with numerous national and international humanitarian organizations. He has also been a good will ambassador to the expats with whom he worked, always striving to project messages of peace. Baha Jangzapuly has both seen and endured many hardships in his relatively young life, and believes that this has become a gift through which he can most effectively help those who have experienced so much suffering at the hands of others. Baha hopes to work for the marginalized and to oppose the tribal system that, for too long, has been a major obstacle to education, peace, security and economic development of both his community and the country. He is now in his final year of studies, interning in hospital in India.

9/11/2001

The situation in the world today, after 9/11, actually started a little earlier in my life as an Afghan. It must have been 1993 when I started primary school in my native village in Afghanistan. It was shortly after we returned to our home from Pakistan, because the Russians were defeated and the Mujahedeen were now ruling Afghanistan. We preferred to live in autonomous Afghanistan, no longer living in Pakistan as refugees. After a short time, civil war broke out between two tribes, innocent people were murdered, and houses were burned. Our home was looted, but not burned, because my father was a doctor.

Back then, like now, it was warlords who were behind this war. The reasons then were much like what has happened in Afghanistan following 9/11. The two tribes were fighting against each other, but the key players behind this were Mujahedeen who won their Holy title by fighting against communist Russia. Only this time, they were killing innocent Muslims who were Afghans, who believed the same religion and even spoke the same language.

Each warlord wanted to capture the state's land and to become wealthier and more powerful. This capturing of state land continued under President Hamid Karzai for all or most of his governing after 9/11. This time, without civil war, the same warlords were accommodated in Karzai's regime, and they continued to become wealthy without engaging others in civil war. Now they had the advantage of America's "war on terror" providing the distraction from their misdeeds.

When I say the situation started in my life before 9/11, I mean that I have experienced the situation in my district long ago. Back then, between the Soviet withdrawal and 9/11, there were no outside invaders. Both the killers and the victims were of the same religion. There was no issue of Muslims and non-Muslims. We, as a family, were again displaced to protect our lives. Pakistan was the only safe haven to accept us as refugees, but, this time, not as victims of the non-Muslim communist invasion by USSR, but of our own people. These Mujahideen had earned their holy title by doing Jihad for a holy reason to expel communists out of Afghanistan, but they had no such honorable basis for expelling innocent people like us. There was nothing holy or noble in how they were now taking both private and state land to increase their own territory and power.

After a lot of struggle, and living in poverty, we finally settled and rented a house in a Pakistani neighborhood. After a few months, the civil war between the warlords back in my district and other parts of Afghanistan was stabilized by the emergence of the Taliban. This planted another seed of hope among Afghans for the re-development and restoration of our homeland.

Of course, similar hopes had been germinated by the tree which was planted by Mujahedeen - which later turned into a civil war. Mujahedeen is plural for the Arabic word mujahid, which means one that struggles for the sake of Allah. Mujahedeen who struggled to defeat communist rule (Soviet Russia) fell into two groups: (1) those who abided by the holy justification, then put their guns away and started living peacefully; and (2) those who became greedy for power. It was this latter group, i.e. those who became greedy for power, who fired artillery and rockets at Kabul. They seemed to forget the Holy reason(s) they fought, giving rise to the Taliban.

Taliban is also plural for the Arabic word Talib. Talib means a student. People were very hopeful again, but soon those living in Afghanistan were hit by extreme poverty. Afghanistan under the Taliban was an abandoned country - which later became a haven for Osama bin Laden and Al-Qaeda.

We had left Afghanistan because of civil war and were once again living as refugees in Pakistan. The majority of Afghanistan was under Taliban control. Although their rule was oppressive and poverty prevailed, it was nevertheless a welcome period of peace for my country.

An American ex-patriot friend and humanitarian worker told me during Taliban time he would openly drive, often traveling to remote districts of Afghanistan, and there was no concern of abduction or the killing of foreigners. Sadly, in Afghanistan post-9/11, this safe freedom of movement is now unimaginable - even for me as a citizen of my country who believes in the same God as those who would kill me. The threat of being killed or abducted is very high in my part of the country – especially if you are educated and working in Afghanistan. This is Afghanistan after 9/11.

In medicine, the importance of preventative or prophylactic treatment is far above clinical treatment. Prophylactically, you can stop serious fatal diseases more easily by preventative measures and on a smaller budget. But, if you let the disease happen, then it will bring lots of destruction and it will be difficult to regain control.

I don't know why America didn't take preventative or prophylactic measures when they gave billions of dollars to the Pakistan and Afghan Mujahedeen to defeat their common enemy, Communist Russia. After the Russians were defeated in Afghanistan, America abandoned Afghanistan, displaying no compassion for the millions of refugees. America even stopped their humanitarian assistance. If America and Western powers had only taken prophylactic measures, Osama bin Laden and al Qaeda would not have gained the opportunity to stay in Afghanistan. With no investments or reconstruction efforts, Afghanistan was simply forgotten by the rest of the world. Osama would have not have enjoyed safe refuge in Afghanistan, and Afghans would have not gone through another fifteen years of violence. American troops would not have lost their lives in Afghanistan, and the thousands of American civilians would not have been killed by those planes in the 9/11 attacks.

I know American people to be the most generous in the world who donate a lot to good causes across the globe, but I do have one complaint about your government. You helped us defeat the Russians, but you should not have left us afterwards. Those warlords who defeated Russia were not mature or equipped to take care of their homeland. Worse, they have turned the guns and Stinger missiles on their own people – the same weapons America once gave them to defeat Russia and bring the end to the Cold War.

In my opinion, this was the root cause leading to how so much has gone so wrong for both America and the rest of the world. Whatever is happening today, especially in Pakistan, Iraq, Syria, Yemen, and other places now threatened by ISIS/ISIL or other offshoots of al Qaeda, the source for much of this infectious radicalism got its start in Afghanistan.

I think it has taken me a little longer to come to my story of 9/11. When 9/11 was close, there was peace in Afghanistan. But there was also extreme poverty during this time, which kept us living in Pakistan.

Even though we were living as refugees, we made sure we had a room for our guests who would come to Peshawar, Pakistan, from Afghanistan for education or medical treatment. Our door was always open for our fellow countrymen.

I have not yet traveled to the "developed world," but have worked with some international organizations and ex-pats. I can confidently say that Afghans are the most hospitable people in the world, but our hospitality and rich culture are not generally known to the West. Most of the media seems to portray Afghanistan as a rugged, dangerous and belligerent country. That saddens me.

During Taliban rule, Afghans were not allowed to watch TV. For those Afghans who would come to Pakistan for different reasons, watching TV or some Indian movies on VCR, was a special treat. One evening, just after 9/11, we had guests from Afghanistan and had arranged a TV for them in the guestroom. One of the guests suddenly jumped from their KaTT (an Afghan type bed), and said, "Now Afghanistan will develop this time!" His reaction was to the news he just watched about the World Trade Center being attacked. He later explained, "America will say to Afghanistan you have attacked me - and now I have to take my revenge - this way America will enter Afghanistan and will bring a lot of money."

As a young kid who had already experienced various kinds of conflicts and political instability, I could not believe that attack on a building would be such a history-changing event.

Even at that time, America had not attacked Afghanistan, but our guest's prediction was right. This relative of ours later started to work in construction when America entered Afghanistan. He has been among those fortunate enough to have economically benefited in a large way from America's response to the 9/11 attacks.

We were now hearing a lot of good stories coming from Afghanistan after the defeat of the Taliban. Now people were allowed to shave their beards, watch TV and girls have started to go to school. We, as a family, were now tired of living in refuge and had lived in eleven different locations. We also wanted to go back to our homeland, have our own house, which doesn't leak while it rains, and to live free of the fear of a Pakistani house owner telling us to leave his house - no longer being called Muhajir, or refugee.

In Pakistan, no matter how good the person, an Afghan refugee was his identification. "Refugee" was a taboo word. Having been called Muhajir (refugee) for many years I can feel the pain a black person experiences when being addressed with the "N-word." This was one of the reasons I quit a Pakistani school and would travel for two hours every day for seven years to an Afghan school in an Afghan community where only Afghan students study. Here, there were no Pakistanis who would call me "Muhajir" any more.

My father still wanted to wait for a few years to see if Afghanistan would stabilize, because, by this time (2003), America had also invaded Iraq. Afghanistan was disturbed again by the return of insurgents - this time bloodier than ever. Years passed and we could not decide whether to leave our leaking ceiling and "Muhajir" identity in Pakistan to return to our own homeland which might have represented a better future for us.

We could not decide on our own, but our decision was forced by the emergence of Mangal Bagh in Bara Khyber Agency, a leader of Lashkari Islam - a Pakistani Afridi tribe and militant group. Many people in our village in Peshawar said that Mangal Bagh was supported by Pakistani ISI. This time, the situation for us was a little different. Now a dispute between two groups started in Bara Khyber agency, which was very close to where we lived. Sadly, we were now experiencing something in Pakistan which, until now, we had only experienced in Afghanistan.

The conflict now was between an Afghan Islamic scholar, Pir Saif ur Rahman, and another Pakistani Islamic scholar, Mufti Muni Shakir. Now that my father couldn't go to work in Pakistan any more, he preferred to live his remaining years of life in Afghanistan. He has spent his youth, and I my childhood, in refuge and war - which still continues for both of us.

I would like to mention here that I am not an Islamic scholar. I am but a simple Sunni Muslim. Both of these scholars were claiming to be Muslims and, in Islam, it is strongly prohibited to kill a human being, but still they, and many more today in the world, have been killing innocent human beings in the name of religion like Pakistan, Afghanistan, Iraq, Syria, Libya, Somalia - you name it.

When I look at this situation, I personally don't understand their logic. I am only left thinking that there is something serious going on in this world that is difficult for simple people like me to understand.

These people are claiming to be working for Islam, but, in reality, they are destroying the image of Islam throughout the world. Many people in the West may ask, "Then why are they doing it?" I would simply say that the evil in the world is easily seen - but the good that exists can hardly be seen. There are thousands of humanitarian workers from all faiths who help others, but the media is not talking about them. I come from an Islamic family. My parents have never told me that I can go to heaven by killing innocent people. But we do pray five times a day, recite from the Holy Quran, fast in the month of Ramadan, and live by Islamic laws. And we understand if we have a poor hungry neighbor from a different faith come to our door, according to our faith, we would be accountable for not feeding any fellow human in need.

So we went back to our home in Afghanistan, which we had left before the civil war. Things were okay for a few years. My father found a job which paid him $600 a month and we were happier than ever. Soon after, the Taliban got stronger again, because now the American troops were leaving Afghanistan. It was becoming increasingly dangerous for educated Afghans to stay in districts far from the city.

Our struggle for a better and safer life has not stopped yet.

Now it was time for another move within our country. The good side of America's presence this time was that now we would move our home on a paved road from our district to the largest city of eastern Afghanistan - relatively much safer for educated people.

Before the civil war, we could not imagine that this road would ever be paved. Many people would seldom travel to the city. The sick and pregnant would either die or get to the city with more serious complications.

I still remember how severely sick and vomiting I was when my father was bringing me to the city to see a dentist. I told my father I would rather live with the toothache, than be subjected to traveling to the city. The road was a bumpy dirt road which connected our small village with the city and was five hours drive in the only one public bus. But by now, the Americans had paved the road for us. What had once been a grueling five-hour ordeal, now only took about forty minutes to escape from our village to the safer central city. While driving on this road, I still had the pain, but this time it was an emotional reflection that continues even today.

We have now started living in the largest city in Afghanistan. My father had lost the job with an NGO that was working to support the Health Ministry - because the international aid had been decreased.

During America's presence since October 2001, Afghanistan has become a very corrupt country. The wealth America and NATO countries brought radically changed the life of some who must have been cherry picked. These people became billionaires, bought properties in the UAE, and some even looted banks. These relative few were accommodated during Karzai's government. I don't want to be all negative. Ordinary people's lives have also changed for the better. Children started to go to school, and almost everybody has a cell phone now in Afghanistan. I still remember when we lived in Pakistan how we hosted families who came to Pakistan only to make a phone call to their loved ones who were seeking asylum in far western countries.

This was also another unimaginable situation that American influence also brought Afghanistan its own telecommunication system. One no longer needed to travel to other countries to make a phone call. You know this wasn't only helpful to call your family in other countries, but also in keeping eye on your loved ones who still live in Afghanistan.

The tragedy of 9/11 has been a little kind to us to give us a cell phone which is the first thing an Afghan will need when there is 9/11 like attack in their hometown. When I hear a bomb explosion or the western media calls it an IED (Improvised Explosive Device), the first thing I do is to check on my father and brothers with the cell phone I have. I get immediate relief to hear that every male of my family is doing okay and have not been the victim of an IED. Usually in Afghanistan, women stay at home. The bombing victims are mostly people trying to go about their normal lives. Often, after the phone calls, I do realize deep inside that while the IED has not killed my father or brothers, someone like myself may have called - but his findings were different than mine.

Life now in the city continues for us but every single day we hear bad news coming and coming. I believe the world has also become unfairly biased toward Afghanistan. Just last month, on February 10, a female member of provincial assembly, Ms Angiza Shinwari, was assassinated. She was a school teacher teaching girls and was a role model in eastern Afghanistan for women's rights. As a teacher for over fifteen years, she had been fighting for the same rights to education as Malala Yousufzai. Fifteen years, which was even more than the age of Malala when she was shot. When Malala was shot, she was taken to a good hospital in the UK, but when Afghan Angiza Shinwari was shot, she was taken to local hospital where she lost two limbs, and later died of sepsis.

Nangarhar: Afghans pray during the funeral ceremony of Nangarhar provincial council member, Angiza Shinwari, who was wounded in a blast on Feb. 10 and later died. Nangarhar province, eastern Afghanistan, Feb. 16, 2015. (Xinhua/Tahir Safi/IANS)

This is but one example of perhaps an unintended ignorance or form of discrimination going on with Afghans. Pakistani Mulala Yousufzai was given the Nobel Peace Prize, but Afghan Angiza Shinwari was not even mentioned in western media.

Recently, there was an international student festival in Norway about corruption. More than 450 students from around the world gathered to share their stories, and join hand in hand to fight it. I was also one of the 450 selected from over 5000 applicants to share my voice. Afghanistan is the most corrupt country today and I can attest to lots of hardship because of corruption as a student. Unfortunately, I was denied a Visa by Norwegian authorities. Why? Because I am an Afghan and I come from a country in a conflict, I wasn't chosen. I am not a terrorist.

I am a victim for having lived in situations of physical problems like living in refugee camp, living in a house with a leaking ceiling, living in poverty and limited food, and plenty of physical and mental stress arising from a lack of security and chronic lack of peace.

I would like to tell the readers that living with physical challenges in a safe environment is far better than living where there is an almost constant lack of security and peace. I would give everything to get peace in Afghanistan, because I cannot enjoy my life there - nobody does in Afghanistan. I sleep and wake up with fear of losing my loved ones. My mom's heart beats rapidly when we go out of the home. I am not afraid of being killed, I do fear what will go through my parents' hearts for having struggled to educate me in such harsh conditions, who always taught me to do the right thing even in the most tough situation. I regularly fear for my parents' and siblings' safety and survival.

If you are living in peace anywhere in the world, do not take this for granted. You have to appreciate it. If that peace is taken by force, by the blood of someone else, it will not last. As they say, "Drop by drop fills the tube." If each one of us does a little good in this world, our world will be a better place soon.

Again, do not take your life for granted…

Baha would like to share his favorite Pashto proverb:

خ به حساس د چا اودونه يوز وي چ يو پ زوند وي خل زربلي نه وي.   چ چي پ هپ زوند وي خل زربلي نه وي.

Translation: How can one feel the pain of someone's tears when he himself has never grieved?

Baha hopes to work for the marginalized and to oppose the tribal system that, for too long, has been a major obstacle to education, peace, security and economic development of both his community and the country. He is now in his final year of studies, interning in hospital in India. He believes peace between Pakistan and India is the most important step for peace, prosperity and, ultimately, the successful recovery and development of Afghanistan. Baha was raised a Sunni Muslim. He is living his life intent upon doing his best for all of mankind.

Below is a poem by the most famous and philosophical Afghan poet, Rahman Baba, translated by Robert Sampson and Momin Khan:

~ Sow Flowers ~
Sow flowers so your surroundings become a garden;
Don't sow thorns, for they will prick your feet.

If you shoot arrows at others: take it from me
That the same arrow will come back to hit you.

Don't dig a well in another's path;
In case you come to the well's edge yourself.

You look at everyone with contemptuous eyes;
Though you will be the first one whose body turns to dirt.

Humans are all one body;
Whoever tortures another, wounds himself.

If you don't look for faults in others,
Everyone will keep your weaknesses concealed.

The farmer doesn't sow the upland field;
Be humble – so that your wasteland becomes a garden.

The sound of a broken pot will never ring true;
Everyone's behaviour is divulged by their speech.

Follow the straight path now by the bright light of day;
For all of a sudden morning will become pitch darkness.

Don't consider any sin too small, however minute;
For when the small are put together they become a lot.

If another does you harm, do him good;
For every tree that bears fruit is harvested.

Harm from the evil ones inevitably reaches the good;
As worms destroy soft wood.

The heart that is safe in the storm
Is the one that carries other peoples' burdens like a boat.

May no sin be committed by his hands, and if so;
May all of Rahmān's sins be forgiven

241

"What we do for ourselves dies with us. What we do for others
and the world remains and is immortal."
~ Albert Pine ~

"Whoever undertakes to set himself up as judge in the field of
truth and knowledge is shipwrecked
by the laughter of the gods."
~ Albert Einstein ~

"In a time of universal deceit,
telling the truth is a revolutionary act."
~ George Orwell ~

Chapter Twenty

Encouraging Thoughtful Connections, Cultural Consciousness and Geographic Understanding in a World of Learning

Heather J. McAfee

Heather J. McAfee is currently the Chair of the Department of Geography at Clark College in Vancouver, Washington. She identifies as a geographer, instructor, and researcher in her professional life. She is also a blogger, poet, passionate global citizen, and outdoor enthusiast interested in proactively participating in the world. Between 2006-2009, in support of Operation Iraqi Freedom, Heather directed the daily operation of a regionally-focused research team supporting requirements generated from primary customers deployed to combat theaters of operation. Her team provided support for short and long-term Requests for Research (RFR) from collaborative government and non-government sources. Heather developed, produced, edited, and managed timely, operationally-relevant socio-cultural research and analysis. She designed, implemented, and executed a "Reach-Forward" analyst exchange between the US-based Reachback Research Center (RRC) and deployed teams which included her own travel into the Iraq theater of operations for interaction with most of the deployed teams. Heather remains engaged in conversations about conditions of displacement, homelessness, violent political landscapes, poverty and, ultimately, the expansion of geographic education in U.S. schools.

"I look at struggle as an opportunity to grow. True struggle happens when you can sense what is not working for you and you're willing to take the appropriate action to correct the situation. Those who accomplish change are willing to engage the struggle."
~ Danny Dreyer ~

243

Who am I now?

I suppose, at first glance, I would like to think I am like any other country girl who grew up on the Great Plains of Colorado. Dig deeper, you discover a geographer and global citizen who sees the world spatially and appreciates *why of where* questions. I am also a feminist who is passionate about the complexities of identity, culture, power, and how those simultaneously produce and are produced from our sense of place. As a feminist academic and researcher, I believe that our lived experiences should not be silenced or simplified by stereotypes or heteronormative power structures. Feminists from many different disciplines work hard to avoid "flattening" and facile explanations of our world. My hope is that more people recognize humans on this planet have many ways of being, and also consider that no single "way" may be the right one. This chapter is an invitation to participate in conversations about cultural consciousness, geopolitics and education today from the perspective of a feminist geographer focused on the production and sense of place. I argue that by learning how to make thoughtful connections at different geographic scales—individual to the global—we are able to engage in successful and transformative struggles for change.

I engage in this struggle for cultural understanding and change as a college instructor in my day-to-day life. I deeply appreciate how my father puts it: "I teach humans, not a subject." These humans are two-year college students with an eagerness to understand their own boundaries and explore the world, typically in reverse order. Students are offered the opportunity to expand their vocabulary by using the language of geography, and I work to provide respectful spaces for them to give themselves permission to think critically about... well, about the world they want to explore. By using geography to invite expansive conversations about cultural awareness in my classroom and throughout this chapter, I encourage people to try to articulate how the world is organized and filled with different perspectives, which, no matter how different, are not necessarily in opposition to their own. While seemingly unfiltered and universal, at the core of this objective is the feminist principle of consciousness raising: how are we in this world together? How do we broaden this world to allow for equitable experiences regardless of social position? And, perhaps more importantly in the United States at this time, how does my personal experience and sense of place hinge on the success and/or oppression of others?

Learning to ground concepts like population, migration, power or politics in humanistic and cultural geographic discourse, in tandem with feminist approaches of the space of the everyday, the notion of a sense of place and views of landscape has been empowering for me. This offers me a framework to invite real-world examples of sense of place and identity for better situating many of the social and geopolitical questions with which we all struggle. We are in a time where feminist theories about knowledge and subjectivity, intersections of power and the varying facets of the geography's masculinism, are influential approaches to instruction as argued by many in the discipline (Rose 1993; Nelson & Seager 2005). There is vulnerability in such openness as a researcher. I offer students and you, the reader, a dialectical space to thoughtfully unpack complex ideas at different scales, from the individual to the state, the region, and across all cultural boundaries. By framing this chapter and parts of my pedagogical approach on the recognition that humans construct the world through emotions (Anderson & Smith, 2001), I align myself with discourse arguing that emotional geographies do exist and are useful in identifying how to bring about change across these scales (Koskela 2000; Nash 1998; Smith 2000; Widdowfield 2000). I suppose anyone can teach culture as a subject; it is my intention to construct sound spaces where thoughtful connections and cultural consciousness can unfold on the page, in the classroom and lives of humans I interact with.

My hope is that anyone who walks into my classroom, sits next to me on an airplane, or reads this essay, recognizes how easily they can make their own connections and challenge their personal barriers in the context of today's world. So, the decision to take part in this project allows me the opportunity to come together with individuals who want to continue making progress through discussion of the current human experience. In other words, instead of shutting down conversations about Islam, the Middle East, or the past decade of war, with narrow "answers" that only reinforce the status quo, we want to encourage more people to freely engage. Being a feminist geographer means creating a space where we can all participate in honest conversations about gender and space. This book is an example of a space where people with different opinions are open to having their worlds changed by empirical encounters with privilege, success, oppression and inequality. As Dreyer's opening quote asserts, we are often moved by those who choose to engage in actions, which may help us all unite in addressing situations that continue to perpetuate the "othering" or erasure of people on this planet. My hope is that readers are motivated

245

by the thoughtful-minded individuals on this project to struggle with hard topics, to become vulnerable readers. I chose to be part of this project because it re-aligns who I am fundamentally, contextualizing my own personal journey from being just another American girl to a conscious global citizen.

"Travel is fatal to prejudice, bigotry, and narrow-mindedness."
~ Mark Twain ~

Who was I before 9/11?

The initial seeds beckoning me to participate in the struggle were planted while experiencing Europe in 1992. Within days of graduating from high school, I traveled abroad in order to find myself and see the globe. There were many nay-sayers confused by my decision to fly away from the small rural county I grew up in. My journey brought me to places where a "wall" had recently been torn down, and many diverse nations of people were emerging from this "curtain" that divided them. Creating and recreating the new old world appeared to be a geopolitical journey for Europe, and highly visible on the cultural landscape. While skirting the former Cold War landscape, I listened to how the people of the Yugoslav territories were struggling to carve out their piece of the pie. Turns out, they weren't the only ones! For the first time, I found myself in conversations that weaved the complexities of culture and politics in a way I had never really participated before. I, too, was attempting to find a sense of belonging, a sense of place. As I said previously, I was never taught to see the world geographically; I had no idea we were so interconnected.

Naively, I thought global borders and boundaries were enforced and reinforced by distant, apathetic or fearful minds in the U.S. I returned stateside excited to question what I had experienced, but no one wanted to talk about it. I began to observe how media reports "flattened" the many different voices and spaces seeking refuge in the places they called home. By "flattening," I am referring to the ways in which geographically-distant voices are transformed into one voice, while the spaces they compete over are transformed into one thing— Gaza, for instance, becomes a "war zone" rather than the warzone/ home/Holyland/Christian space of Muslim Imperialism/Muslim space of British Imperialism/Jewish struggle for home/countless un-named conflicts all structured around different and competing ideas about space and its meaning. Recognizing this, I quickly appreciated that

I was an American who never needed to worry about that struggle. Little by little, I realized most people did not "think global" in order to "act local," because they were too busy living at the scale of survival. It became clear to this girl fresh out of high school that few people I knew were going abroad, and, for that matter, I was not equipped to unpack the religious, ethnic or political events in the Balkans or former Soviet States. Still a teenager back home and unscathed, for the first time, I started thinking about college and 'those people' on the other side of the world.

"History shows that there is nothing so easy to enslave and nothing so hard to emancipate as ignorance, hence it becomes the double enemy of civilization. By its servility it is the prey of tyranny, and by its credulity it is the foe of enlightenment."
~ Lemuel K. Washburn ~

No longer just another "American girl"

Half a decade later, while living as a military dependent in Italy, the Kosovo "conflict" again provided me with another opportunity to view the world. I witnessed religious-ethnic conflict, as well as internal and external displacement, at a multitude of scales and locations. Separating me from the violent political landscape, the deep blue of the small Adriatic Sea reinforced a pleasant military family existence, but, in reality, I was a conversation killer at the gatherings for enlisted wives. After reading about the sheer magnitude of the displacement caused by the conflict, I wanted to get involved and volunteer, but instead, I was urged to just be glad my husband came home to eat the dinner I should be preparing every night. Fairly quickly, I stopped going to baking night or the bowling alley for lunch get-togethers. I started seeking ways of emancipating myself from the feminized and irrelevant prison house of wifely space, and in turn, I soon found myself jumping from the frying pan into the fire!

As an uneducated American girl volunteering to collect and distribute aid to refugees, I did not realize how many "Muslims" lived in Europe. Heck, even though my father always tried to provide me with books about philosophy and world religions while I was growing up, I really had a shallow understanding of Islam. There I was, armed with my small-town history lessons and the impression that this landmass was a "white Christian" space. Oh, how I struggled to

247

understand the ways aid workers used positionality and language to separate themselves from the devastated population seeking refuge from the violence. Language relieved us of a sense of responsibility—as an occupying force—so that we might feel good about the aid work we were doing. Silently, I wondered if language, religion and cultural understanding could ever be factors in peaceful resolutions instead of continually promoting difference? But when I talked to friends and family back home, they did not see the same headlines or articles as our European newspapers, and their opinions—if they had any—were vastly different. So many of them had no idea of the Kosovo/Serbian atrocities taking place. It slowly became evident that the language of the American media framed the geopolitical events in a way that created distance rather than global interconnectedness. What has fundamentally altered my perspective, to this day, was the question: Why didn't the American people want to know what was going on in the world? It seemed clear to me that it had to do with the power our media had over what we consume as Americans. The geographic distance from the rest of the world was simply too great for some to even navigate in their own minds. Personally, I just had no idea how to bring about any change.

In 2000, I returned to the U.S. seeking—no, appealing for—an opportunity to educate myself so that I, too, could participate in conversations about global cultural and political differences. At this point, you might be feeling a bit lost as to how this all relates to America's jihad or provide a takeaway in your own life. Truth is, each of us can bring about change in our own life and make a difference in the world. Even this "small-town American girl," struggling with doubt and life, knew it, but often quieted that message in her own mind. I had barely been living in the U.S. a year when 9/11 happened. I was in the middle of a divorce, nearly homeless, and applying for the same jobs that so many refugees, immigrants and marginalized people were trying to obtain. I had it "better than" many, "worse than" others; war was breaking out, and I—like many Americans—let go of the idea that I was I going to help anyone at the global scale when I could barely help myself. And this is the problem! I fell back into the trap of being isolated from the world that existed on the other side of oceans, which was easy to do considering that mainstream news rarely took me there for more than a few seconds.

"It is easy to blur the truth with a simple linguistic trick: start your story from "Secondly." Yes, this is what Rabin did. He

simply neglected to speak of what happened first. Start your story with "Secondly," and the world will be turned upside-down. Start your story with "Secondly," and the arrows of the Red Indians are the original criminals and the guns of the white men are entirely the victims. It is enough to start with "Secondly," for the anger of the black man against the white to be barbarous. Start with "Secondly," and Gandhi becomes responsible for the tragedies of the British."
~ Mourid Barghouti, *I Saw Ramallah* ~

How did 9/11 change it all for me?

This infamous question is where the conversation starts; although, to begin with September 11, 2001 is to begin with "Secondly" as Barghouti asserts. Yes, like so many, 9/11 changed me.

The day the Twin Towers fell, I was living stateside after a number of years residing abroad. I learned it was not the first time the Towers had been a target—who knew?! Which I ask because students walking through the doors of my classroom still don't know this critical detail. I suppose I am one of the many global citizens who would say the "attacks" did not seem very "holy" either time.

The truth is, the violent political landscape of New York City over a decade ago is a far-reaching reminder that we Americans too often lack the ability to see our global interconnectedness and humanity's struggles at different geographic scales. Today, we have the ability to reflect upon the elements of culture, politics, economics and geography revealed in the narratives and aftermath of that event. As stakeholders in global peace, I urge we keep ourselves in check by not continuing any 9/11 discussion with careless "secondly's." I am a stakeholder in this discussion: when I reflect on how I ended up in Iraq in 2009, it's because of the events of 9/11. And when I am asked why I teach geography, it's because of the events leading up to 9/11 and beyond.

I believe Americans need to expand their geographic vocabulary in order to become more culturally conscious. The clearest way for me to argue this is to leap-frog through my life and share my own emotional story of being geographically illiterate for a bit of anecdotal evidence. The terrorist attacks that occurred on U.S. soil were dramatic, and the cultural and political response in the aftermath of the event continues to be quite emotional. So, in order to understand why fundamentalists become extreme, why people (re)act differently around the world, why "they hate us," shouldn't we try to make sense of diverse narratives and ways we have all constructed our identities around the world? Yes, there are stakeholders from various locations and at multiple scales; again, I consider myself a stakeholder, every contributor on this project is a stakeholder, and you, dear reader, have a stake in this too.

> "The attacks of September 11th were intended to break our spirit. Instead we have emerged stronger and more unified. We feel renewed devotion to the principles of political, economic and religious freedom, the rule of law and respect for human life. We are more determined than ever to live our lives in freedom."
> ~ Rudolph W. Giuliani, December 31, 2001

In the aftermath of the event...

Moments after the event, nationalism and patriotism boiled to the surface of my identity as an American. I was not scared, instead, undertones of loyalties to my brothers and sisters in the New York Fire Department tempted me to jump in a volunteer truck, drive east, toward 'Ground Zero,' as it was now known. Why didn't I go? I stayed in Colorado, struggling to put food on my table and a roof over my head, reflecting on the fact that I was a soon-to-be divorcée lacking the credibility of a tertiary degree. The reality is, thinking of myself as just another American country girl, I felt like I was sitting on the sidelines as the weeks passed and the world talked about "terror" on our soil. It became very clear I consumed data about the tragedy in a dramatically different fashion than my local community members. Conversations were myopic, fear-based, America-centric and lacked thoughtful geographic awareness. I was shocked to hear how some of my more "educated" friends could not even distinguish the national identities of the extremist Saudis on the planes from the millions of moderate Muslims living in our country and around the world. I changed; the cultural landscape of Colorado Springs changed; and We the People prepared for war.

Like most Americans my age, until September 11, 2001, my exposure to violent conflict had been limited. As a child of the 70's, I had questions about Vietnam, watched some Gulf War headlines, and felt the shockwaves of the Oklahoma City Bombing carry across the Great Plains. My father, a middle school teacher and former U.S.

Army officer, did his best to provide resources for explanations on topics such as: religion, history, politics, and current events, to name a few. Most mornings, I woke up to National Public Radio (NPR) and went to bed hearing the three or four nightly news reports broadcasting throughout the country. Still, I have no recollection of ever owning a globe, looking at maps in the classroom, or really being taught in school how to respect and link unique aspects of culture to locations around the world. A number of my teachers had never traveled beyond the coastlines of North America. By the time I was seventeen, I knew Oktoberfest originated in Germany and "The Wall" running through Berlin was being torn down, but prior to traveling to Europe after graduating high school, I had few reference points forged to build global awareness.

Like many who remember that day, the events of 9/11 have stayed with me, yet not necessarily in the way that I would have expected. I found myself struggling to understand how I would engage in dialogue about 9/11 and its aftermath when so few of my peers had lived overseas and so many people could not see beyond "someone paying" for the tragedy. I now recognize the true impact of those airplanes hitting those buildings, and, subsequently, the less obvious means through which they altered the United States and our world. As geographers, we must confront how humans are environmentally/culturally/economically/politically organized and intertwined (Murphy, 2004). It both saddens and motivates me that so few of my students can identify the dots as dots, much less connect them. If we cannot negotiate the lines of connectivity, how is the average American expected to understand the global, national or local significance?

Kay Anderson and Susan Smith argue, "At particular times and in particular places, there are moments where lives are so explicitly lived through pain, bereavement, elation, anger, love and so on that the power of emotional relations cannot be ignored (and can readily be appreciated)" (2001). That infamous day changed the cultural landscape of New York City and our diverse multinational state, but it also changed the rest of the world by setting in motion yet another wave of the systematic 'othering' of groups of people living here and across the globe who are identified as a "threat" to "our way" of life. These forms of othering—strong American heroes confronting evil head on, creating or exacerbating stereotypes of sneaky, cowardly and evil Muslims attacking vulnerable people rather than fighting like "real men"—hinge on a long history of gendered imaginings of spaces and the people that occupy them (Said 1978). Marginalizing people for being different is not new, but it is problematic, so maybe we should all view this struggle as an opportunity to revisit our beliefs and cultivate our minds.

It's easier now to recognize how Giuliani's references to "rule of law" and "religious freedoms" are integral to appreciating how the United States is not merely a location on this planet but a place of meaning to be targeted by "outsiders." I did wonder, years ago, if the American Dream was actually a tale built as tall as those towers, symbolically constructed to fall like a delicate house of cards. Looking back, I now question if we do have a "respect for human life," as Giuliani suggests. Until the towers fell, I suppose my take on freedom was that it was pretty much free, envied by the outside world and built on what we learned in our history books. Sadly, this continues to be the modus operandi for many of my current students.

In the aftermath of September 11, I wanted to read and talk about the why's, but all I heard was fear and blame. That year, I wanted to understand how people in other countries viewed and lived with "acts of terrorism" or "extreme" actions taking place around the globe, but the hunt for one man and his religion took center stage. In the years to follow, I chose to be motivated by the fact that I simply did not have access to all the answers. I had a desire to visit the Middle East and wanted to meet "those people" in order to ask "them" how they felt. Today, nearly fifteen years later, college students enter my classroom with a similar kind of muted angst and condemnation that I would expect from a disengaged community fed stories that start with Barghouti's "secondly" and end with unimaginative patriotic jargon built on the words of political campaigns and big business.

"From the halls of our schools to the highest reaches of our government, the evidence suggests that Americans have only a vague understanding of how the world is organized politically, economically, culturally, or environmentally."
~ Alexander B. Murphy ~

Engaging in the struggle was a struggle!

During the early 2000's, my personal struggle and patience paid off. I attended community college with the very same people I was applying for jobs with; veterans of Desert Storm, Bosnia, Kosovo, as well as immigrants and refugees from all over the world, sitting next to me. Funny, so many of them had degrees from their home countries, but we, the People of the U.S., did not recognize their academic achievements. My classmates worked in hotels, restaurants and department stores during the day while attending classes at night. Without asking, I assumed their lives were "better" because the People of the United State had opened our doors to them—I mean, apart from those terrorists on 9/11, everyone loves the U.S, right?

When I graduated from university, our soldiers were already in Afghanistan and Iraq. Life in the military was never for me, so instead, ironically, I became a contractor with the U.S. Department of Defense (DoD), working on a project called the Human Terrain System (HTS). Now this project was an incredible idea on paper. In fact, it was actually motivated by the political desire to create a doctrine of peace and intercultural understanding, and not the intelligence unit its opponents claimed. In the years following 9/11, I listened to politicians, the media and my college professors all describe what was happening in the world in different and often conflicting ways. I realized HTS was my chance to join the conversation. I believe soldiers, civilians... all humans need to start with an opportunity to hear diverse stories of an area and its inhabitants.

The Nigerian writer, Chimamanda Ngozi Adichie, urges us to seek out all the stories of a people in order to stop "single-stories" that result in stereotypes or narratives that malign and dispossess (2009). I felt working within the HTS and DoD would allow me to tell stories with and not just about our world, hoping we would utilize cultural analysis to prevent loss of life before, or as, we engaged in the conflict of a given location. So, I joined the struggle from my desk in Fort Leavenworth, Kansas. I consumed anything and everything I could read about Iraq and the people of the "Middle East" (ME) region. Interestingly, many ME "experts" loosely defined regional boundaries and rarely distinguished between the uniqueness of its people beyond reinforcing the construction of an "us vs. them" binary. I tried to make connections with past, present and future "Iraq" any way possible. I found myself frustrated that I had never really learned about this region or its people in any classroom. Bottom line, I was geographically ignorant and it angered me.

Now, of course I grappled with the logistics of living in and serving a country while remaining true to who I am fundamentally as a global citizen of peaceful resolve. This is my culture, my identity... who I am. I would sit around with the HTS analysts and ask, how do you plan on approaching peace in the Middle East when we continue to lack an understanding of conflicts at our own family gatherings or on the streets of urban America? People at home wanted the war headlines to fade away and the "enemy" to stop killing our soldiers. I ask you, the reader, do you have a stake in local, national and global peace, or do you just accept there will always be people to deal with war? Written over a decade ago, Alexander Murphy's article, "Awash in a Sea of Geographical Ignorance" challenges us to question if it's important that decision-makers and the voting public, with the power to exert "an unprecedented influence in global affairs," actually "understand the geographic context within which events are situated" (2004). How many people in your community knew that the Iraq-Afghanistan wars were not one-in-the-same? Murphy goes on to argue, "The United States is the only country with a significant international political and economic influence where it is possible to go from kindergarten through university without a single basic course in geography" (2004). Does this quote shock you? Well, it shocked me as I read it late one night in 2008, in my containerized housing unit) (CHU) on Forward Operating Base (FOB) "Justice" in Baghdad, after having a discussion with soldiers who were convinced their families "couldn't even pick out where [they] could up and die" on a map. And they were right! Armed with my spatial frustration, I wasn't exactly a "geographer" by trade, but after that moment, I do believe I was destined to become one!

> "The word 'jihad' has nowhere been used in the Qur'an to mean war in the sense of launching an offensive. It is used rather to mean 'struggle'. The action most consistently called for in the Qur'an is the exercise of patience."
> ~ Maulana Wahiduddin Khan ~

Maybe "jihad" is a displaced American "struggle?"

After midnight, if I remember correctly, I was sitting at a desk in our makeshift office on FOB War Eagle in northern Baghdad, and I'd just received the news that my interpreter's paperwork, seeking refuge in the U.S., had once again been denied. She had called asking if we could exchange information "just in case" she "made it out of Iraq alive." I sat there, wondering what we were "fighting for" and she said, "... for a peaceful and democratic Iraq, Habibi!" The phone was silent, then, stoically, she whispered something like, "Honestly, I want to live in my country with my children, not yours... but... if I am let in... it will be because I fought alongside of you and your soldiers after your towers fell and Bush decided to change my world. This is what I struggle with... like my personal jihad, and Insha Allah (a few long seconds passed) . . . I will have the patience" (Personal Journal/ Interview Notes, 2008).

So often is the case that a word used out of context is subject to cultural misinterpretation. Even though I had been to this area of the world multiple times, even though I was a trained analyst, I paid little mind to how the word *jihad* was used within its social and cultural geographic context. As Adichie conveys, I had a "single-story" of jihad and that story emanated from 9/11. For a brief and ignorant moment, I thought my interpreter was expressing her disenfranchisement and would come to "hate all Americans" in a way that threatened my way of being. Boy, was I ashamed.

Careless or deliberate use of words to identify and frame the extreme actions of a few can result in "single-stories," 'othering' and maligning groups of people. In time, it has become apparent that I am not alone in my concern that linguistic misrepresentation of the word *jihad* by the Western world is inherently problematic. Is it too bold to suggest that the word *jihad* has been hijacked by the media and popular culture just like those planes that flew into the Towers and Pentagon over a decade ago? As it pertains to the continual misunderstanding of many cultures' ways of being, I would argue yes, and yet, we do it over and over again. Somewhere in the middle of all this, I realized we teach misunderstanding in our homes, classrooms and through popular culture. As interconnected as we are in the world today, this struggle was bound to become someone's jihad!

I chose to leave Iraq and HTS and return to school once more—this time, I found the language of geography was definitely my way of engaging in the global discussion. In 2009, I set out to become a geographer and better understand post-2003 Iraqi refugee narratives of identity in the United States. My research attempted to unpack the intricacies constituting the establishment of 'home' in the country that remains an occupying force within their native land. The project provides insight into the lived experiences, feelings of belonging, and resettlement of Iraqis in two U.S. cities. I employ work by geographers and the widening body of literature on Diaspora, refugee studies, and resettlement in other related disciplines to frame important and challenging questions about refugee identity, homemaking, and sense of belonging.

Looking back at the year 2001, I know now that on September 10th, I felt as at home and safe as any American on U.S. soil.

255

However, twenty-four hours later—eyes and ears fixated on the media and the smoking ruins of those buildings—things changed. I set forth on a journey questioning and engaging in global conversations that were inherently spatially nuanced. I believe we can draw from our own personal experiences in order to "take the appropriate action to correct the situation," as Dreyer argues. I sat at my desk, on the phone, listening to a woman, mother, an Iraqi/Coalition Forces interpreter… my friend, who happened to be Muslim. She was not the "enemy," she was a fellow global citizen affected by the events of 9/11. Today, the situation is that we are still in Iraq and Afghanistan, yet we are no closer to winning the so-called "War on Terror" or the "hearts and minds" of an increasing body of people within and beyond our borders.

"As a single footstep will not make a path on the earth, so a single thought will not make a pathway in the mind. To make a deep physical path, we walk again and again. To make a deep mental path, we must think over and over the kind of thoughts we wish to dominate our lives."
~ Henry David Thoreau ~

Understanding different ways of being in the world . . . and in the United States?

Upon returning to graduate school, my intention was to expatiate on the topic of the resettlement of refugees and their struggles creating 'home' here in the U.S. This body of discourse is extensive; nevertheless, I wanted to tell this story from the perspective of those people who experienced—not analyzed, not politicized, not wrote policy about—displacement following the military invasion and/or occupation of their country by my own, the United States of America. As a feminist geographer, protecting human subject participants is as central to their well-being, trust and voice as it is to my research. All my respondents/participants have suffered through so much, they related to my experiences in their country and wanted their stories to be told. During our meetings, in the comfort of their homes in the United States, they were just as vulnerable and openly-honest as I am in the classroom and here in this chapter. It is in the depths of field work where I learned the most about culture and different ways of being.

Today, each term, I tell my students these were the spaces where I was invited to understand the day-to-day struggles of a Muslim or Non-Muslim/Sunni or Shi'a/Arab/Iraqi/educated or not according to

Western "standards"/man or woman/hetero or homosexual human being. These were the spaces of emotional geographies for myself and the participants in my research, and a whole world of understanding opened up to me. In turn, I'm now able to thoughtfully create assignments that expose students to "difference" while reminding them that vulnerability is also a lesson in the negotiation of our own personal boundaries as global citizens.

Throughout the research process, Muslim and non-Muslim participants, directly and indirectly, referred to the word *jihad* in different contexts. Although an analysis of the word *jihad* was not central to my exploration of identity-making and creating 'home' by Iraqi refugees in the United States, many participants expressed their conviction that culturally, jihad was "a personal struggle" for "their people," no matter what they "believed." They often wanted to clarify that I accepted jihad was like a "campaign" or "crusade" for a principle within the context of their identity, and is an intricate part of living and growing up as a Muslim, family member, friend, employee, citizen, member of a nation of people, or spiritual human being. It became apparent, early on in my work on the topic, that in only a few instances did the Iraqi refugees refer to the word jihad as a "holy war," and always in the context of referring to Western media's use of the word. Furthermore, concerned for their safety living in the U.S. post 9/11, participants worried that they would be targeted as "terrorists" if they even spoke the word in public, so they refrained from using it in mixed company (Participant Interviews 2010-2012). A Muslim-looking person saying the word "jihad" was a terrorist, my participants easily deduced from the representations they saw of themselves on the news—representations that were flat—flattened in exactly the same way the spaces of Afghanistan and Iraq were flattened.

I struggle with this perpetual flattening of people's identities, cultures, languages and political ideologies. In the classroom, I give new human geography students two to three minutes to free-write who they are without any pausing. Unpacking the phrase "Who am I," according to great philosophers and theologians can be an impossible task for some and quite liberating for others. Knowing our own identity is a way we can embrace our agency within the power structures of the world. I have learned that knowing other people's identities changes the whole conversation. The meaning of jihad to a singular definition of "a holy war against unbelievers" in Western media and the uninformed masses complacent with the way we are spoon-fed news in America. From where I stand, knowing Muslims who partake in this personal struggle has allowed me to become more culturally conscious and make thoughtful connections that go far beyond the events of 9/11. Knowing Middle Easterners' views on such words brings my understanding back to a history of many ways of being, geographically located and spatially nuanced.

So I ask, is it our intention to continue to flatten—and vilify—the moderate Islamic communities living in the U.S. and around the world? How I engage in the 'struggle' is by making changes right here, in the heart of America. I began with not accepting stories that start with "secondly" like the "failed" Iraqi or Afghan states. I ask my students to recognize the individuals who have undertaken the time to express their personal struggles in devotion to Islam in moderate and reflective ways. It is our responsibility to ensure they feel 'at home' in the United States. There are hundreds of thousands of people who align with our geopolitical effort to rid the world of "Osama bin Ladens" and the oppressive Hussein regimes. There is an unending cycle of displacement leaving people in distress, crossing borders and seeking a safe space to call home. Each one of these humans carry with them their culture, language, political ideology and all of them have narratives that can teach us about their many stories and ways of being.

Although parts of my research focuses on Iraqis who have obtained refugee status or Special Immigrant Visas (SIVs) in the U.S., my conclusions could be applicable to the experiences of wider groups of refugees, particularly those displaced by, or stemming from, U.S. military action. Simultaneously, however, I would like to discuss how my research on immigrants has uncovered a set of unique questions about the complex ways that 'home' and identity become meaningful in the disparate contexts of Iraqi refugees. Iraqis, as well as many other refugees and exiles across the world, have witnessed the physical destruction of their home and their homeland caused by the impacts of the Iraq war (Blunt 2005a, 2005b; Blunt and Dowling 2006). Through their experiences of 'extreme domicide' —or "the deliberate destruction of home" by war—displaced people are traumatized by acts of overt violence often "in the pursuit of specified goals, which causes suffering to the victims" (Porteous and Smith 2001: 12).

As a result, post-2003 Iraqis, now living in the U.S., are varied in the degree to which they see their host country, in this case the United States, as home (Al-Ali et al. 2002, 2005; Blunt and Dowling 2006), and the extent to which they share a sense of "domicide." This confirms the observations of Portes and Rumbaut (2006) and Valenta

(2009a) that immigrants' experiences vary both across groups as well as within particular migrant communities such that broad generalizations obfuscate, rather than clarify, living conditions. What does this mean? I argue, there is a clear and unique Iraqi component that involves the "putting up with" or "dealing with" the frustrations associated with being displaced because of fighting alongside American troops. After all, troops represented the promise of liberating and democratizing their country. This emphasizes the critical differences in how Iraqi refugee communities see the U.S. from other political refugees—as a liberating force and as 'home.'

Iraqis' notion of home, then, is undoubtedly bound up in notions of security and insecurity, crucial to ideas of home and identity-making in the context of militarization (Walters, 2002). The concepts of security and insecurity are also held by the U.S. as the host country with legal authority, and thus become "bound up with themes of mobility," resulting in immigration policies and a politics of homeland security that "depend upon, and perpetuate, a normative assumption of the nation-as-home" (247) for some individuals and not others. What I discovered is, for Iraqis displaced by the U.S. militarization of the Middle East, negotiating a new identity and creating a sense of home is not as difficult as looking at their 'successes' or 'failures' under resettlement policy-making or agency support. Instead, an examination of this issue also requires deeper understanding of how Iraqis negotiate the systems of privilege and oppression generated through homeland security policies (Horst 2004; also see Blunt and Dowling 2006). The notion of home for Iraqi refugees, I am suggesting, is bound up in legal and symbolic negotiations—that is, socio- and juridico-cultural systems (Foucault 1981, 1986; also see Lemke 2010). I am not suggesting that I speak for all refugees, nor all the moderate Muslims living, belonging, and identifying as "_____-Americans;" I suggest we recognize the ways in which we, at the grassroots level, can develop and extend a sense of community to all who now call the United States their home.

The post-2003 Iraqi refugees' experience is shaped by past memories of living under an oppressive regime, contested spaces (Cohen 2001, 2010), as well as the stigmatization associated with the post-9/11 Euro-American world that acts as the new host society (Valenta 2009a, 2010). At times, the subtlety of being labeled "refugee," "Middle Eastern," "Muslim," or unambiguously being associated with 9/11 terrorism, is traumatic at a personal level and is also often viewed as problematic for both the host country and the refugees resettling there

(Al-Rasheed 1994; Valenta 2010; also see Silva 2010; Sharma 2010). On the other hand, refugees and asylum seekers are simultaneously rendered visible and invisible as they negotiate the laws of homeland security vis-à-vis legal identification, a process in which they occupy positions of non-recognition and 'over-recognition' (Humpage and Marston 2006; also see Potts 2011). I reason that these types of studies are significant because they provide a space for advancing research and debate about refugees by highlighting alternative arguments concerning home, identity, belonging, and resettlement (Hiruy 2009; Su 2012), both as an intellectual and policy endeavor. For this book, America's "Jihad," I hope my research and personal narrative encourages conversations to deepen and widen spaces for change.

"The aim of education should be to teach us rather how to think, than what to think—rather to improve our minds, so as to enable us to think for ourselves, than to load the memory with thoughts of other men." ~ Bill Beattie ~

I teach humans: the language is geography

Five years ago, I asked myself, how can I help teach humans to see the world spatially and make thoughtful connections that won't shut down conversations? I came to the conclusion that I must be my authentic self in front of the classroom, every term, day in and day out. Wow, what a concept! I get to be me to the humans I teach! I don't have to put up some kind of the-professor-knows-all academic front or require students to regurgitate the "facts" and nothing but the facts. Unlike many classrooms, my students are provided ways of discussing the events of 9/11 through multiple lenses, such as culture, economics and geopolitics. By recognizing the different ways of framing such events, students can tap into their own emotional geographies and explore personal boundaries and subjectivity. Anderson and Smith (2001) argue, "Emotions are an intensely political issue, and a highly gendered one too." Reading this discourse, I realized there continues to be gendered bias in the production of knowledge which is "probably a key reason why the emotions have been banished from social science and most other critical commentary for so long" (Anderson and Smith, 2001). The world feminizes this approach. In other words, it isn't the expected or dominant way of teaching humans, so it is not embraced.

The reality is too many students entering my classroom are unable to make local to global connections beyond the superficial spaces in which they operate every day. Sure, many of them can talk about 9/11, and some can flesh out details regarding the road to war in both Afghanistan and Iraq. The message is that the threat of terrorism lingers on the distant horizon—Oklahoma, New York City, the streets of Boston—but they are apathetic after those words spill from their lips. They shrug their shoulders and wait for the "lecture" to commence. I often wonder who is not numb to those thirty-second sound bites fed to us on the anniversary date or when another "threat" arises. Conflict, war, and so-called peace-keeping missions continue to take their toll on human lives, creating disenfranchised people, while stories starting off with "secondly" are told by leaders and teachers alike.

Still, we live in a geopolitical world where, "thinking emotionally is implicitly cast as a source of subjectivity which clouds vision and impairs judgment, while good scholarship depends on keeping one's own emotions under control and others' under wraps" (Anderson and Smith, 2001). Phrases like "who am I?" are important to us all. These are the spaces for thoughtful connections to be explored and navigated. Who am I? Well, I am nobody to important people and somebody to my community; I am a stakeholder. When asked how 9/11 changed me, I respond emotionally because who I am today includes that moment in history. It also includes the moment in my classroom when a self-identified, tattooed "ex-con, I guess… Christian white boy" introduced himself to, and set out on a journey in becoming a Syrian Druze refugee's close friend.

As the years pass, I continue to communicate with Iraqis who reflect not as a generation of powerless stakeholders; instead, they embody strong undertones of apathetically plugged-in-but-helpless frustrated emotions. Funny, they—like my American students—are disconnected and living apart from the world beyond, streaming stories seeping with the same old stereotypes and reeking with "secondly." Literature pushes us to recognize that we can no longer marginalize research investigating human emotion and spatial interaction. In doing so, it promotes the distorted status quo that researchers are detached, objective and rational. Not all of us in research and academia feel we need yet another generation of educated people believing, without question, that they are objective and rational. Which is exactly why I challenge my students (and you) with calls for more "engagement, subjectivity, passion and desire" to interact with events around the globe. This way of thinking has been "devalued, and frequently feminized" (Anderson and Smith, 2001). Valuing a type of research and analysis that perpetuates the norm did not make me a geographer, global citizen or culturally conscious. And it certainly doesn't help students in my classrooms make thoughtful connections in their own lives: maybe the norm is not working in classrooms across America.

Many questions arise as I continued to grapple with issues of refugee status in the context of militarization, America's geographic ignorance, and the ability to create spaces for thoughtful connections to somehow bring about a nuanced cultural consciousness in the world. Mahatma Gandhi said, "Be the change," right?! As a former human terrain analyst with the U.S. Department of Defense, I have first-hand experience with war zone contractors and indigenous support personnel who became refugees when their lives were threatened if they stayed in Iraq. This taught me a great deal about the distinct issues that surround Iraqi resettlement within the U.S— a state to which many of these refugees feel patriotically attached, but a nation that also implicitly denies them a sense of belonging. I am continually challenged as to how U.S. discourse about homeland security affects diasporic notions of home and belonging for Iraqis during escalated times of military intervention in Iraq. Let's be clear: for Iraq, the conflict is not over. As Iraqis continue to struggle with post-war atrophy across their social, cultural and political landscape, the so-called Islamic State (IS) digs in for the long run. And where are we? Far, far away from the multitude of tragic stories unfolding in the world.

Participants in my research gave credence to what they thought were the cultural and political principles driving the invasion of their country. The question is: now what do we do? Field-based experience, on site, in Iraq, helped launch my exploration of issues such as Iraqi home, identity, and refugee resettlement within the larger context of academia and policy-making circles, but the surface has just been scratched. After examining post-2003 Iraqi refugee narratives of identity in the United States and the intricacies constituting the establishment of 'home' in the country that remains an occupying force within their native land, I am left with more questions. After all, these people fought for the liberation of Iraq, and in return, they were displaced. Which is exactly why they continue to believe in democracy and the freedoms upon which America was built, while, at the same time, they struggle to construct new lives in a land that affords them limited opportunity to do just that. freedoms upon which America was built, while, at the same time, they struggle to construct new lives in a land that affords them limited opportunity to do just that.

Only time will provide us with insight regarding the ongoing struggle with the highly organized and funded IS/ISIS/ISIL in both

Syria and Iraq. As the words flow across the bottom of our screens, we must not wane in our critique of those who continue to appropriate language for inflammatory headlines or attention grabbing. Knowing the news and misuse of language alienates a portion of our own population while detracting from the opportunity to question what is not working in geopolitics today; we must take this opportunity to engage in the conversation. Considering that the long journey since 9/11 has no end in sight, I believe this is our time to constructively "engage the struggle" and extend the conversation.

This chapter is dedicated to my dear friend, fellow geographer, mentor and "brother," Doug Foster. Thank you for filling so many hearts with incredible joy and a lifetime of memories.

And to my parents, "Where thou art, that is home." ~ Emily Dickinson

Works Cited and Suggested Reads

Adichie, C. (2009). "The Danger of a Single Story." Speech. TED: Ideas Worth Spreading. Ted Conferences, LLC. Oct 2009. Web.

Ahmed, S., Castaneda, C., Fortier, A., & Sheller, M. (Eds.). (2003) *Uprootings/Regroundings: Questions of Home and Migration.* Berg: Oxford.

Anderson, K. & Smith, S. (2001). Editorial: Emotional Geographies. *Transactions of the Institute of British Geographers* 26: 7-10.

Blunt, A. and Dowling, R. (2006) *Home.* London: Routledge.

Bond, R. (2006). "Belonging and Becoming: National Identity and Exclusion." *Sociology,* 40(4), 609-626.

Butler, J., & Spivak, G. (2007). *Who Sings the Nation-State?: Language, Politics, Belonging.* London: Seagull Books.

Cohen, S. (2001). "An Absence of Place: Expectation and Realization in the West Bank." In A. Murphy & D. Johnson (Eds.), *Cultural Encounters with the Environment: Enduring and Evolving Geographic Themes* (283–303). Lanham, MD: Rowman & Littlefield Publishers.

Cohen, S. (2010). "Revisiting Territorial Pragmatism in the Palestinian-Israeli Conflict." *Eurasian Geography and Economics*, 51(6), 733-743.

Connolly, W.E. (2002). *Identity\Difference: Democratic Negotiations of Political Paradox.* Minneapolis: University of Minnesota Press.

Dudley, S. (2008). "A Sense of Home in Exile." *Forced Migration Review,* 30, 23-24.

Gupta, A., & Ferguson, J. (1992). "Beyond Culture: Space, Identity, and the Politics of Difference." *Cultural Anthropology,* 7(1), 6-23.

Hollinger, D. A. (2004). "Identity in the United States." In, Keywords: *Identity: For a Different Kind of Globalization*, 27-45. New York: Other Press.

Interview with Edward Said, Professor of English and Comparative Literature, Columbia University, on Democracy Now! Pacifica Network broadcast, Apr. 24, 2003.

Massey, D. (1996). "Space/Power, Identity/Difference." In A. Merrifield and E. Swyngedouw (Eds.). *The Urbanization of Injustice*, 100-116. London: Lawrence and Wishart.

Khan, M.W. (2002). *The True Jihad: The Concept of Peace, Tolerance and Nonviolence in Islam*. Delhi: Goodword Books.

Morley, D. (2000). *Home Territories: Media, Mobility, and Identity*. New York: Routledge.

Murphy, A. B. (2003). "America Rejecting Geography at Its Peril" *Minneapolis Star Tribune*, Nov 11, 2003, p. A21; Reprinted in Ubique, 23 (3), December 2003, pp. 1, 2 and 4 under the title "Awash in a Sea of Geographical Ignorance."

Nelson, L. & Seager, J., Eds. (2005). *A Companion to Feminist Geography*. Massachusetts: Blackwell Publishing Ltd.

Rose, G. (1993). *Feminism & Geography: The Limits of Geographical Knowledge*. U of Minnesota Press.

Said, E. (1978). *Orientalism*. London: Routledge & Kegan Paul.

Sporton, D., Valentine, G., & Nielsen, K.B. (2006). "Post-Conflict Identities: Practices and Affiliations of Somali Asylum Seeker Children." *Children's Geographies*, 4(2), 203-217.

Valentine, G., Sporton, D., & Nielsen K.B. (2008). "Language Use on the Move: Sites of Encounter, Identities and Belonging." *Transactions of the Institute of British Geographers*, 33(3), 376-387.

Valentine, G., & Sporton, D. (2009). 'How Other People See You, It's Like Nothing That's Inside': The Impact of Processes of Disidentification and Disavowal on Young People's Subjectivities. *Sociology*, 43(4), 735-751.

Walters, W. (2004). " Secure Borders, Safe Haven, Domopolitics." *Citizenship Studies* 8 (3):237-260.

Yuval-Davis, N. (2004). "Borders, Boundaries, and The Politics of Belonging." In S. May, T. Modood, & J. Squires (Eds.). *Ethnicity, Nationalism and Minority Rights* (214-230). Cambridge, England: Cambridge University Press.

"Peace cannot be kept by force. It can only
be achieved by understanding."
~ Albert Einstein ~

"Anything war can do – peace can do better."
~ Desmond Tutu ~

"In the End, we will remember not the words of our enemies,
but the silence of our friends."
~ Martin Luther King, Jr. ~

Chapter Twenty-One

My Personal "Jihad" - Striving for World Peace

Al Jubitz

Al Jubitz joined Rotary in 1977 as a third generation Rotarian and is Past President at the Rotary Club of Portland. Al believes that Rotary is uniquely capable of turning the world toward nonviolent conflict resolution, ultimately leading to a world beyond war. Al has been invited to speak at more than 60 Rotary clubs, conferences and community events over the last three years to share his vision that peace is possible and that Rotarians can play a leading role. A native Oregonian, Al received his BS degree from Yale University in 1966 and earned his MBA from the University of Oregon School of Business in 1968. Al retired from the family business (Jubitz Corporation) after a career spanning 34 years. He also served as a director of two private start-up companies. Al is President and founder of the Jubitz Family Foundation which directs funding to organizations that foster peace building, environmental stewardship and early childhood education.

9/11/2001

Perhaps it was a blessing we were in the South of France on 9/11. Celebrating our 35th wedding anniversary, we were checking into our hotel when the lady behind the counter stated, "I am sorry what happened to your country." Unaware, we asked for an explanation and hurried to our room. The next two days involved too much television and not enough touring as we tried, like most Americans, to make sense of the events. Switching between CNN and BBC I soon learned how different the coverage was... endless speculation and repeating videos on CNN versus more in depth analysis on BBC and not the repetitive video of the planes hitting the towers. On the second day, I asked the Concierge to contact an officer of the local Rotary Club as

266

I would like a European's perspective on what had occurred and, more importantly to me, why? Within a few minutes a nice Frenchman was on the phone and we had a 15-minute conversation - but without any groundbreaking insight. The blessing of being out of country on that fateful day meant I didn't feel the shock that most Americans felt... I was viewing events from afar and with a welcome degree of insulation that comes with distance.

By December, my Toastmasters group was willing to talk freely about the event and analysis - although with surprisingly little introspection into "why they don't like us" or "what did we do to hurt them?" What was a profound moment, however, was when a WWII veteran gave a "table topic" of less than a minute as he derided Americans' reaction to this being our generation's "Pearl Harbor." He stated that the Brits lost multiple buildings every night during the siege of London and here we had only lost 4 planes and 2+ buildings and we're behaving as if this is the end of the world. He asked us to put the events into perspective, the loss of life notwithstanding.

When my turn came to give a speech I called it my September 12th speech as President of the United States. This is the speech I wish our President had given instead of the one he did. Mine focused on challenging all Americans to become energy independent by switching to renewables and to build out high speed trains so as to be less dependent upon airplanes and, while we were focused on that, he (the President) would seek out the culprits and bring them to trial.

Instead, a regime of fear, offense and war was promoted, aimed at humans fitting a certain profile in a far off land. It was hard to contain our fears or suspicion of others when flying. In short, America became afraid and over-reacted predictably employing its military might as the preferred tool of response. Over the past 14 years we have paid a horrendous cost financially, morally, intellectually and spiritually. I am saddened by the lack of creativity and innovation that informed our response. I write it off as an overall immaturity within our society that is reflected in our US-centric view of the world, if not our belief in "American Exceptionalism."

Since these early days of shock, war, deficit and debt I have taken a much more circumspect view of events by forming my own rationalization of how the world works. Is it because I have touched the seven continents? Is it because I am a member of Rotary International? Is it because I love nature? Is it because I am the middle child? Or is it just because I have read and thought and felt and lived - that I am not afraid? I consider myself a Planetary Loyalist (a relatively new term inspired by Historian Kent Shifferd) which is closely associated with modern day Humanism. It is hard for me to hate, and it is hard for me to cut down a tree or to squish a bug. Mosquitoes are an exception, of course.

I recognize my birth luck and, during the past decade, decided I must give back in some meaningful way that honors this great fortune and the resultant opportunities and success that came with it. I am of the ilk that believes I had a lot of help along the way, from those I know who mentored me to those I don't know but contributed to my well-being via college scholarships, infrastructure investment, basic education and social supports. Being born white, male and to educated parents in America during the 20th century puts me in the most privileged one quarter of one percent in the world. What will I do with this privilege? Will I pay my good luck forward by helping others? What will my fourth quarter of life contribute to the common good?

Much earlier in life I decided I wanted to be a leader (vs. a follower) when my father observed some immature high school behavior. One day he pulled me aside and, after stating he noticed who I was hanging out with and what mischief I was up to, he told me that I had a choice in life... to be a leader or a follower. It was that simple. I thought about that conversation for several days and decided that I would have to change my friends. That simple mid-course correction was profound in the outcomes it had. So today I value leadership. It is hard for me to do nothing in the face of need or to say nothing in the face of indisputable evidence. I have become passionate to make a difference in the world whether I will see results during my lifetime or not. A few years ago I heard a definition of leadership which has stuck with me and it goes like this; "Leadership is understanding reality AND taking action." I could not live the rest of my life as an armchair intellectual or closet academic. I had to take action...what was I going to do? Did I have the stamina to see it through? What was I good at and what did I need help with? I knew I was a better entrepreneur than a manager so I would need the right people around me. But what was the mission and did I have passion for it?

In contemplating my life, I realized I joined two remarkable groups, both in 1977. I was 33 years old. Old enough to have some confidence and young enough to reform some ideas about how the world worked. The organizations were Creative Initiative Foundation (CIF) of Palo Alto, California, and Rotary International (RI) with headquarters in Evanston, Illinois. CIF was founded by Harry Rathbun, a beloved Stanford philosophy and religion professor. Rotary

International was founded by Paul Harris, a lawyer who moved from Vermont to Chicago and wanted to network with others. Both these men understood that there are far more similarities than differences in the human family. Both encouraged education and service to others. Little did I realize that CIF would launch a project called Beyond War in the early 80's to educate Americans about the excesses, including irreversible consequences, of the arms race. Nor did I realize Rotary International was the world's preeminent peace group with a long history of contributions to good will, humanitarian service and fellowship worldwide.

While my activities in the Beyond War movement waned in the mid-to-late 1980's, my participation in Rotary continued. By the year 2000 I still had little idea of the rich and robust history Rotarians played over their first 95 years as an organization. Then, in 2002, I received a shock. Rotary International announced it was investing in the education of 70 students each year who sought a Masters Degree in peace and conflict studies. Fully paid scholarships including tuition, room, board and travel expenses were to be funded by The Rotary Foundation. Administratively, Rotary decided to highlight a distinct subset of its long standing Ambassadorial Scholars program. This new group of scholars would be called Rotary Peace Fellows. Once again I was amazed at the wisdom and foresight of the Rotary Board of Directors and the Foundation Trustees. Their announcement rekindled my interest in peace education and I began to think that maybe, just maybe, Rotary could play a large part in actually getting the world "Beyond War."

Coincidental to 2002 our family business had just sold the division I was running. Part of the overall transaction was to set up a family foundation to 1) advance the lives of at-risk children, 2) to steward the environment and 3) to promote world peace. My cousin, Ray Jubitz, was hired to run the foundation. After nearly a decade of operations the weakest of the three legs of the foundation was the peace leg. We were not attracting enough funding requests. Ray suggested we hold a weekend gathering at our mountain house. We called it the Parkdale Peace Gathering. Invited were senior local Rotary leaders, religious leaders, academics from the University of Oregon and Portland State University and leaders of peace groups operating in Oregon. Ray's suggestion was brilliant. The peace movement needed leadership and the family foundation was providing it.

Out of the first Parkdale Peace Gathering was formed a project of the family foundation called the War Prevention Initiative. Patrick

Hiller, PhD in Conflict Studies, was hired to direct the initiative. Soon thereafter we co-founded the Rotarian Action Group for Peace. Action Groups represent a new structure within Rotary which recognizes Rotarians' desire not only to meet as members of their club but also to align with other Rotarians around a common interest, in this case peace. It was ideal timing for me personally as I had fully retired from the family business and had this continued interest in promoting peace on earth. In short, the stars were aligned to set an end of life goal to prevent all war by 2030. The more I learned about the peace movement, peace science, and the 28 Trends of the Global Peace System (Shifferd, 2011) the more I felt this goal possible. But, to achieve it by 2030 would require the help of Rotarians worldwide, and also of the Board of Directors of Rotary International.

But was Rotary really ready to lead in Peace? Little did I realize in 2002 how ready and willing Rotary International was. Nor did I understand the deep commitment to peace, good will and understanding Rotarians carried since the early days of Rotary. When the Rotary Foundation announced that a special subset of its long standing Ambassadorial Scholarship Program for post-graduate study would focus on Conflict Resolution, I was surprised. Candidates wanting a career in peace and conflict resolution would be awarded full two-year scholarships to study in one of seven peace centers around the world. The peace centers amounted to a contractual relationship with Universities on five continents with stellar programs offering a Master's Degree. Rotary also announced a three-month "certificate" program at Chulalongkorn University in Bangkok, Thailand. In total, over 100 deserving students would graduate each year and join the growing cadre of Rotary World Peace Scholars. Now, over a decade later, the world is seeded with competent, committed early or mid-career individuals that understand what peacebuilding and non-violent conflict resolution is all about.

A decade later, in 2012, our Rotary District 5100 had a committed and visionary Governor by the name of Mike Caruso. He had the foresight to make our district a "Peacebuilder" District, which was a new special designation by Rotary to encourage districts to support the Peace Centers Program. While Mike was an early adopter of this idea, he went one step further and pioneered the concept of Peacebuilder Club by encouraging individual clubs within the district to set up Peace committees and also to support the district's peace efforts. These creative actions have contributed vastly to an overall growing culture of peace in our region and it has motivated scores of Rotarians to work for peace in their own communities. When I think of the vision of Mike and others within Rotary I am struck with the notion that today's peace movement is not my father's peace movement. Today's is more sophisticated, broader and deeper in the knowledge of peace scienc,e which is a new and growing discipline throughout the world.

Also in 2012, I began speaking to any Rotary Club that would invite me. I would cover the nuclear weapons risk, Rotary's deep history in peace and human rights, and the modern peace movement as evidenced by the Global Peace System (see Shifferd, From War to Peace, 2011). At the end of meetings, I would often receive well-wishers who obviously had an interest in peace. How would I corral this sincere interest? The answer soon became clear.

For decades many Rotarians have participated in what is called fellowships. Fellowships can be described as groups of Rotarians with a similar hobby or activity like flying, fishing, golf, traveling or reading. These provided an avenue to share common interests. But the fellowships were typically not doing humanitarian service work. Something new was needed. Hence, the invention of the Action Groups, now collectively referred to as Rotarian Action Groups. They came at a good time as Rotarians were tiring of the seemingly endless effort regarding polio eradication. Some thought we were losing a generation of Rotarians and we needed a new structure to organize around service, not just hobbies. So the new action groups provided a perfect vehicle to harness the interest in peace I had been seeing in the various clubs I visited, and at conventions. The Rotarian Action Group for Peace (RAGFP) was born, and today has over 2000 "members" and a robust website featuring databases of both human and academic peace resources.

Once again, in 2012, the Rotary Foundation decided to focus its grants in six "Areas of Focus:" the first on the list was Peace and Conflict Prevention/Resolution. The others were (2) Water and Sanitation, (3) Basic Education and Literacy, (4) Maternal and Child Health, (5) Economic and Community Development, and (6) Disease Prevention and Treatment. While all six contribute to peace, the first directs its attention to preventing conflicts and resolving disputes, skillsets that come naturally to many Rotarians.

A final word about Rotary in the 21st century. The now 30-year effort to eradicate polio appears to be near completion. The project took a decade longer to realize than originally thought, and that fact speaks to why Rotary is a wonderful partner. It is called staying power, continual funding and leadership. These are the three major factors

Rotarians bring to the table. And we learned how to partner with the World Health Organization (WHO), with the United Nations Educational/Scientific/Cultural Organization (UNESCO), and major funders like the Bill and Melinda Gates Foundation and governments around the world. I believe that what we, as an organization and as a collection of individuals, have learned over the past 30 years prepares us for our next major opportunity… creating a world beyond war. What greater contribution to humanity and the planet than to set a goal to prevent all war by 2030. We have the vision, we have the growing number of Peace Fellows, we have the global "Polio-Plus" experience, and we have the respect of the world's leaders.

"America's Jihad." We are at a turning point in our post 9/11 dialogue as a country. Our struggle is to define who we really are and to act upon those convictions. Are we warriors who want to dominate the planet as modern day neo-colonialists with over 900 off shore military installations under the justification that we are protecting our national interests? Or are we moral leaders of individual freedoms promoting the rule of law and universal human rights while opening our borders to the oppressed from other countries? Which way America leans may depend upon our tolerance for risk and our attitude towards fear. When terrorism strikes it is difficult to keep the carnage in perspective. Yes, a coordinated "attack on America" was executed on 9/11/2001. Or was it an attack on our symbols of power and influence beyond our borders? The Pentagon was attacked, which was arguably an action against our bloated and offensive military footprint around the world. The World Trade Center was attacked, which is a symbol of our economic prowess and domination. And maybe the White House was a target which symbolizes our freedoms and democracy which may offend the perpetrators stuck in religious or dogmatic law. Was this an attack on America or what America represents and projects? When considered in the context of the WWII vet, it was a criminal attack on four buildings utilizing four airplanes and, yes, it killed over 3000 innocent civilians, a number far smaller than we kill every year in our reactionary wars.

There is so much to say about the futility of fighting fire with fire or responding to terrorism with drones which are more terrifying than a sneak attack as they hover overhead day and night threatening everyone who lives below. Are we so afraid of occasional criminal acts and loss of life that we must become the world's most feared terrorist ourselves? Are we unwilling to take risks and therefore subjugate others to a life of fear and hatred towards the big bully from

272

North America?

I believe it comes down to our tolerance for risk and our attitude toward fear. Will we risk death to maintain our free and open society or will we arm ourselves and "wall and gate" ourselves to reduce the risk of living and understanding the "other." How we answer this question will determine whether we will construct a prison in which we live fearful lives or, alternatively, will those with power over others construct prisons for them to inhabit under the illusion this will make us safer. Either choice will condemn us all to a life of fear and retribution. This is not our forefathers' notion of freedom or the pioneering spirit. This is our challenge in the 21st century. I, for one, choose to play the odds which still are very much in favor of living life as it should be in harmony with all living beings and the life support systems provided by nature. Yes, I will lock my doors, but no, I will not live in a compound out of fear of others. I will smile at people of all colors as they approach me rather than walk to the other side of the street. I will carry love in my heart and risk the random sociopath who may want to do harm. I will not carry a weapon in fear of others as I believe the vast, vast majority of others wish no harm upon me. I will wear my Rotary pin with pride and the commitment to work with others to build a world beyond war. This is how I choose to live. My wish for the planet is that all humans choose the same.

Recommended Resources:

Rotary International Peace Fellowships:
https://www.rotary.org/en/get-involved/exchange-ideas/peace-fellowships

Rotarian Action Group: http://www.rotarianactiongroupforpeace.org/

War Prevention Initiative: http://www.warpreventioninitiative.org/

Al submitted the application for the Rotarian Action Group for Peace (RAGFP) to Rotary International with these objectives:

- Enable Rotarians in every community around the world to initiate peace service projects
- Involve Rotarians in nonviolent conflict resolution training
- Train Rotarians to monitor and report hot spots around the world as a vital first step in an "early warning" system to prevent escalation to violent conflict
- Provide leadership to Rotary International in adopting a world-wide goal to prevent all wars by 2030
- Engage Rotary Peace Fellows to support these objectives and play an active role in promoting nonviolent conflict resolution

In addition, Al currently serves on the board of the United Way of the Columbia-Willamette. In 2010, Al and his wife Nancy were recognized nationally by United Way with the Tocqueville Society Award for their ongoing commitment and support. He is a Senior Fellow of the American Leadership Forum of Oregon, Class 20, and also serves on the Leadership Councils of Yale University School of Forestry and Environmental Studies, Portland Children's Museum and the National Advisory Board of Environmental Defense Fund. He is Director Emeritus of Morrison Child and Family Services and an emeritus trustee of Outward Bound Wilderness School. Al and his wife Nancy have been married 46 years. They have three grown daughters and four grandchildren. Al believes that Rotary is uniquely capable of turning the world toward nonviolent conflict resolution, ultimately leading to a world beyond war.

"Imagination is more important than knowledge.
Knowledge is limited; imagination encircles the world."
~ Albert Einstein ~

"I do not think much of a man who is not wiser today
than he was yesterday."
~ Abraham Lincoln ~

"There are millions of Christians who do not take all portions
of the Bible literally… a strong belief system is a very good
thing if your faith helps you and others. But if you're
judgmental and demand that others believe as you do,
that's a very bad thing…"
~ Bill O'Reilly ~

Chapter Twenty-Two

Respect Through Understanding

Brian J. Adams

Brian J. Adams, Ph.D, is the Director of the Centre for Interfaith & Cultural Dialogue (ICD) at Griffith University, South Brisbane, Australia. As a former Rotary Peace Fellow, Brian is primarily focused on promoting respect and understanding across cultural, religious and organisational boundaries. This work is supported by a Ph.D. (political science) in deliberative dialogue and two Master degrees in community development and conflict resolution, respectively. Brian's 20+ years of work in Africa, Europe, North America and the Asia-Pacific certainly brings a compelling international perspective to the ICD. His background in mediation, conflict management and dialogue facilitation strengthens the Centre's ability to address some of the great challenges facing the world today, while his fluency in English, French and Swahili allow him to expand the work of the ICD to marginalised groups in Australia and to troubled regions across the globe. Brian is also the proud father of five children.

> "The natives are unintelligent.
> We can't understand their language."
> ~ CHINWEIZU ~

9/11 and finding a new life path

As the attacks on the World Trade Center and the Pentagon were taking place on Tuesday, September 11, 2001, I was on a bus at Michigan State University. It was the first semester of a Ph.D. program and I was settling in at a new school and social life, wondering what opportunities lay ahead. I remember standing next to the driver and enjoying the beautiful autumnal view. At first, in my daydreaming I didn't really hear what the news announcer was saying on the radio, but after a few moments his message woke me from my reverie

276

and shock and disbelief that such a thing could happen hit me. I rushed home from the bus stop to watch it unfold on TV. Seeing the images made it all heart-sickeningly real.

For a few days I felt dazed, unable to process the magnitude of the event. Then, on the following Thursday, my bishop approached me with a request that I speak in our Sunday meetings as part of a memorial service for all who were killed in the attacks. Despite feeling overwhelmed by the magnitude of such a responsibility, this gave focus to my thoughts and my mind began to clear.

Part of the clarity that began to develop was a realization that I did not really like what I was studying. MSU is a fabulous school and I had a great supervisor, but I feel that I was not making the positive impact on the world I desired. And I certainly was not contributing to making sure something like these attacks would never happen again. So, after my first year, I postponed indefinitely my studies at MSU and set out on a new life path.

This path first led me back to work in Africa. My profession up to that point was as a development worker, so I took a step back to figure out how to move forward. I knew this could not last long, because, in my eyes, the development projects I worked on did not make the fundamental contribution to a peaceful world I desired to make. Much of what I had seen in development rarely benefitted the most needy in the land. In fact, it often strengthened elites, pushed a funder's agenda and/or furthered a great power's foreign interests. However, at this time I did realize that one of the great impediments to social and economic development was conflict. Therefore, if I could work to resolve conflicts, this would help establish a foundation on which development could take place.

Thus, the next step on this new life path would be to become knowledgeable and skilled in resolving conflicts. My golden opportunity came in the form of the Rotary World Peace Fellowship. Each year, the Rotary Foundation selects 70 fellows from around the world to pursue a Master-level degree in peace and conflict studies at one of seven centers worldwide. I studied the first year at Sciences-Po, Paris, and then completed the degree at the University of Queensland in Brisbane, Australia. I cannot speak highly enough of this experience, as it allowed me to pursue my professional passion, associate with an impressive cohort of Peace Fellows, and gain invaluable knowledge in the field. But, like most of the Peace Fellows, the theory and

---

1 Applicants are typically very successful mid-career professionals who are looking to add conflict resolution training to their career development.

issues, however interesting, were not where my ultimate ambitions lay. I wanted to be a practitioner, so I began working with one of the top mediators in Australia. And yet, the Master degree did help me see that theory combined with practice can make a potent, mutually strengthening package. So I concurrently enrolled in a Ph.D. program in Political Science where I studied the use of deliberative dialogue as a tool for conflict resolution.

Throughout this journey, inter-faith engagement arose as an integral part of my success in numerous undertakings. I found that far from being a divisive issue, expressing and exploring faith (in a non-judgmental, non-proselytizing way) formed connections between me and people from many backgrounds. This was as true with Methodists in Fiji as with Ibadhi Muslims in Zanzibar and with Greek Orthodox in Cyprus as with Tidjani Sufis in Senegal.

The journey continues. Since 2011, I have been working at a large university as the director of a center for peace through dialogue. Our objective is to build strong, resilient communities by fostering mutual respect. In fact, respect for the differences of another has become the measuring stick against which we judge each of our activities. However, this level of respect isn't always easy to come by. Thus, we try to address important issues through processes that facilitate respect for another and their differences: we **dialogue** instead of debate; we **educate** instead of proselytize; we **collaborate** instead of compete; and we **celebrate** instead of compare.

I have learned on this journey that respect can come in many forms. It can be the simple respect for the other as a human being or even respect for the other as a potential obstacle to a resolution or goal. Respect can be the view of another as a capable contributor to a resolution or goal, or it can be the perspective where all are seen as equal partners in the process/relationship. While each of these forms of respect is legitimate and powerful in the proper context, none is the ideal type for the goal of building a cohesive, resilient community. To strengthen diverse societies in our globalized world we need to be able to respect others as equal contributors and respect them for the differences they bring to the public sphere.

My Vision

My vision for a better tomorrow is one where conflicts are resolved through dialogue, instead of violence; where all religious and cultural traditions are threads in a social fabric woven with respect and understanding.

If I were King of the World, what would I do to contribute to bring this about? Very quickly I would abdicate. Honestly. I would make a terrible king and then I could go back to doing what I am doing right now.

But before abdicating, I would set up a center with the mission to teach people that respect between most people is possible. This would focus on four principles for respectful cultural engagement: courage, integrity, curiosity and humor. Because these principles are the pillars that hold up my vision of a better tomorrow, I would like to take some time to explain them before concluding.

Principle 1: Courage

"It takes a lot of courage to release the familiar and seemingly secure, to embrace the new. But there is no real security in what is no longer meaningful. There is more security in the adventurous and exciting, for in movement there is life, and in change there is power."
~ Alan Cohen

Imagine taking a taxi in Manila. The sun is pounding on the roof and the humidity is high enough to induce beads of sweat that sting your eyes and trickle irritatingly down the back of your neck. Cars and jeepneys press in on all sides, so close you could simply reach out the window and adjust their rear-view mirrors. The air is filled with suffocating exhaust and the screeching of tires. And through it all, your driver is texting somebody on his mobile phone.

Encountering other cultures or religions is remarkably similar to taking a taxi in Manila. For some, it is a scene out of their worst nightmare; simply thinking about it gets their heart pounding, stomach churning and causes all color to rush from their face. For others cultural encounters are exciting adventures they long to take and for which they are willing to plan and pay a large amount. No matter which of the above descriptions fit you, cultural encounters are difficult affairs. While they rarely result in a threat to one's life, they do require courage because they mean that one risks having a carefully created world turned on its ear. Perceptions are stretched. Growth is sometimes painful. And there is a danger that what one had always known to be true, right and the best way to do something is not.

Thus I say that one of the foundation principles to respectful cultural encounters is courage: the capability of facing danger or difficulty without retreating, the ability to endure in times of adversity. It is akin to fortitude, which is a firmness or strength of mind rather than physical bravery.

Principle 2: Integrity

"He who closes his ears to the views of others
shows little confidence in the integrity of his own views."
~ William Congreve ~

It was a lazy afternoon in the village of Kizimkazi on the south end of Zanzibar Island. John was walking in companionable silence with the village schoolmaster, a gentle fellow and a key stakeholder in a project John was developing between that area and a U.S. university. By sheer coincidence, just as we were passing the village mosque, John began to whistle tunelessly as is his wont when feeling content and comfortable. This particular mosque is a regional holy site because within it are found the remnants of an ancient wall that contains Persian writing—the oldest evidence of Islam this far south. After whistling a while John noticed a change had come over his companion. He seemed nervous, uncomfortable and kept glancing around. John pondered on this as he continued his tuneless music making and soon realized his companion's discomfort coincided with the start of John's whistling. So he decided to ask him about it.

"You know, I don't think I have ever heard anyone in this village whistle. Why is that?"

The schoolmaster replied, "It is because many people here are superstitious and they believe that whistling is an attempt to attract evil spirits."

John's face immediately began to glow bright with embarrassment. "Oh [gulp]. So, would people that heard me whistling just now assume that I was trying to call evil spirits to the mosque?"

"Yes," was the simple reply.

Defensiveness or an overblown sense of self-importance can be great barriers to collaborative cultural encounters. In this instance, John could have easily laughed at the silly superstitions of the villagers and felt justified in doing so. He certainly hasn't meant any harm by whistling. But this would have undoubtedly strained relations between him and the schoolmaster, as well as undermined the project on which they were working. Instead, John apologized profusely, was quickly forgiven and he never made that mistake again. The project went forward to the benefit of all parties involved.

Integrity is the second principle in respectful cross-cultural encounters. Someone who has integrity is defined as being whole, undivided. They possess internal consistency and evince moral strength. Everyone knows people who have great integrity, and chances are we admire them for that. But what exactly is integrity? I submit that integrity is best understood as a basket of traits such as honesty, fairness, modesty, open-mindedness, and patience. It is the moral fiber that binds together a person's characteristics. The strength of a person's integrity is then a measure of how consistent they are across a range of traits. Are they consistently honest or do they lie or cheat in certain circumstances? Will they treat their colleague or supervisor with patience and attentiveness, but yell at a waiter or their spouse for an overcooked meal? Do they work diligently when unsupervised? This consistency has particular import in collaborative encounters with other cultures, as you will be challenged by situations and expectations you would never have envisioned.

Principle 3: Curiosity

"Curiosity is the very basis of education and if you tell me that curiosity killed the cat, I say only the cat died nobly."
~ Arnold Edinborough ~

There are plenty of motivators for wanting to engage with another culture. One might fear being left behind in the wake of globalizing forces. One may recognize profitability in the relationship. There could even be pressure from peers or a supervisor. Although normal and understandable, none of these motivators alone will inspire respect between interlocutors. But one motivator that will is curiosity.

Curiosity is simply a strong desire to know or learn something. It is a motivating trait that leads to action. In the eyes of the beholder, curiosity is an affirmative act showing that people and their perspectives are interesting and important. They are worthy of being understood. In the eyes of the curious, there is recognition that one's own view, idea, belief is not the only one available or worthy of attention. Curiosity is the first step in being able to see from another perspective because it is proactively seeking to understand and discover.

Presenting curiosity as an essential principle for respectful cultural encounters may seem problematic, in that it apparently narrows

281

the audience of adopters to those who are curious. One might say, for example, "The French just don't interest me." But this is not good enough for those individuals who, through various circumstances, have to work with the French or get the foot in the door in Central Africa or parts of Polynesia. Because of this, some may find curiosity to be the most difficult of the four principles to foster, for how do you find something interesting about which to be curious where none exists?

I argue that interests almost always exist. In fact, it is extremely rare to come across a cultural encounter in which there is absolutely no interest between the parties. It just needs to be uncovered and fostered. A first step to uncover this interest would be to hearken back to the foundation principles. Remember that courage is the seedbed in which all other virtues grow. A possible inhibitor of curiosity is that one does not feel confident enough to inquire of others to see if something interesting will come up. Or maybe one is too comfortable and does not see the need to stretch out into new spheres. The disinterest may also be a question of the integrity of either party to the encounter. If one is not particularly modest in regards to those whom they encounter, then curiosity will rarely spring up. And if the other lacks integrity, one would not feel secure enough in their responses to inquire. (In this latter case I would strongly recommend finding another party with which to associate.)

If a lack of curiosity cannot be traced to underdevelopment of the foundation principles of courage and integrity, then I would recommend as a second step to recognize what Edward Said presented in his book, *Culture and Imperialism*, when he wrote that "cultures are involved in one another, none is single and pure, all are hybrid, heterogeneous, extraordinarily differentiated, and unmonolithic." [2] (p. xxix). In other words, since cultures are "extraordinarily differentiated," it is unlikely that every single thing about the other culture is uninteresting. Take some time to think about what interests you in your only daily activities. Is it music, sports, fashion, games, politics, literature? Whatever interests you, the possibility is very high that you will find its equivalent expression in another culture.

For example, the most natural way to pique my curiosity is through my belly. I love food and I love to find unique meals (that are tasty). Starting with food allows me to sincerely show appreciation for an important aspect of that culture, because cuisine is often a source

---

2 Said, Edward. 1993. *Culture and Imperialism.* New York: Knopf

of cultural pride. This, in turn, opens other paths of exploration and topics of discussion and exchange.

Principle 4: Humor

"Why do ducks have webbed feet? To stamp out fires. Why do elephants have flat feet? To stamp out burning ducks."[3]

If you found the above quote funny, there is a good chance you are from Belgium, or have spent a significant amount of time with Belgians. I say this because this is the joke Belgians, who prefer surreal humor, found the most funny in a 2002 study by psychologist Dr. Richard Wiseman of the University of Hertfordshire. Dr. Wiseman set out to find the world's funniest joke and, by so doing, understand the psychology of humor. Particularly, he wanted to know if there was scientific evidence behind the common wisdom that there are regional differences in humor as well as between sexes. He did this in an ingeniously simple way by asking people to submit their jokes online and then allowing these jokes to be ranked on a five-point system, eventually collecting about 40,000 jokes rated by over 1.5 million people.[4] Dr. Wiseman not only turned up what might be the funniest joke in the world, but he also found solid evidence that, generally speaking, men's humor differs from women's, children's humor is distinguishable from that of their elders, and the things people laugh at in one country are often quite different from that laughed at in another.

The fourth principle for respectful cultural encounters is humor. Like curiosity, humor is a powerful way of increasing the level of respect and engagement between people of different cultures. Why is this? Humor is a cultural universal as well as a significant cultural marker, meaning that humor is found all around the world and in surprising diversity. There are 'knock knock' jokes (Knock, knock! Who's there? Doris. Doris, who? Doris locked, that's why I had to knock!), 'Yo Mama' jokes (Yo mama is so skinny, she uses a Cheerio for a hula-hoop), puns (Time flies like the wind, but fruit flies like bananas), inside jokes, etc. We even recognize types or subsets of humor within a country or culture group like the genre of movies and entire

---

3 World's funniest joke no laughing matter! By John von Radowitz, Oct. 3, 2002. WalesOnline.co.uk. http://www.walesonline.co.uk/news/wales-news/page.cfm?objectid=12250627&method=full&siteid=50082, accessed December 26, 2008
4 Visit Dr Wiseman's website at laughlab.co.uk for more information on the methods and results of his study.

websites built around 'college humor.' [5]

But most important to our discussion is the simple fact that humor is important to people.[6] Humor is about communication and shared understanding. Seeking to understand another's humor is a great way to increase your respect for another cultural perspective as well as for others to feel their perspectives are and will be respected. In being able to 'get' a joke from another culture, one shows an underlying familiarity with and even acceptance of their thought patterns and assumptions. Therefore, a principle of humor is important for respectful cultural interactions because an attempt at understanding another's humor is an attempt at understanding a deep and broad range of ideas, beliefs and assumptions, many of which are unspoken or unrecognized by the other.

Thus, what often makes a story funny is not what is said. The humor can be as much from what is NOT said—those things about which the uninitiated would have no clue. Universally, assumptions in communication underlie and allow for spoken communication.[7]

Finally, perhaps the most important aspect to remember about the principle of humor is to laugh at yourself often and sincerely. To do so indicates to others that you recognize your fallibilities and that you will not let them stop your efforts at respectfully engaging with them.

Conclusion

I realize the story of my journey since Tuesday, September 11, 2001, is a very university-centric one. A key opportunity came through a university scholarship program. I have made a career as the director of a university center for peace through dialogue. But this does not mean that I think this is the only or best path to resolving these great challenges before us. If we are to create a world where all religious and cultural traditions are threads in a social fabric woven with respect and understanding, then this effort has to be a collaboration between a broad array of social actors. Politicians and lawmakers have to create a legal framework in which this can flourish. There needs to be judicial force behind these laws and policies. And civil society, including university professors, need to interpret and practice these laws and create the social norms that undergird the entire effort.

5 E.g. Weird Science, www.collegehumor.com
6 Stewart Lee, "Lost in Translation" *The Guardian,* Tuesday, May 23, 2006.
7 For other stories with different perspectives, I suggest reading "The Cow-tail Switch and other West African Stories" by Harold Courlander and George Herzog. It's a collection of stories ostensibly for children, but great for all ages.

My argument is that respect is what will make this collaboration possible, especially when built on a foundation of **courage, integrity, curiosity** and **humor.** Building this type of respect takes work, but like many forms of work, it gets easier with practice. And, if practiced, these principles can establish an environment where respect prevails and others feel safe to work with us in building this vision.

"Education is the most powerful weapon
which you can use to change the world."
~ Nelson Mandela ~

"Learning without thought is labor lost."
~ Confucius ~

"Teachers open the door, but you must enter by yourself."
~ Chinese Proverb ~

"Democracies die in darkness."
~ Bob Woodward ~

Chapter Twenty-Three

Awakenings: Teaching Our Younger Generations About World Cultures, Religions and Politics

John Forest

John Forest is a Humanities teacher in the Pacific Northwest and an active member of the Middle East community. You can find him fishing native trout streams or paddling local whitewater when time allows. He assists with an Alpine Ski team and is a shameless admirer of works by Ian Fleming.

9/11/2001

It was a gorgeous day in the "City of Roses" (Portland, Oregon). The sun was shining and the teacher had just cracked the window to allow some of the cool breeze to enter the classroom. Maps and charts covered the space as we were introduced to the expectations of the class. I was already thinking about where we were going to have lunch when an administrator came into the classroom. A television was rolled into the classroom as the whispers had become too loud to ignore. America had been hit. New York was under attack. As the volume of the commentators began to nestle into our ears, the class watched silently in horror.

It Begins

I think the root of my curiosities really started before I was even aware. I remember my time in Cambodia rather vividly, a country that was worlds away from my own and the truth was, "they hated us." I mean that might sound strong, but it isn't. After a few beers, the niceties at a guesthouse or restaurant, there always came the question, "… Why you king of the world? What make you so special?" I had almost gotten used to it; aptly forgetting this was a country that paid

286

dearly for our incursion into Vietnam. Originally I had thought it was because of the generally poor behavior of Americans traveling abroad. Honestly, for what other reason could "rich" white people fly all the way to this mosquito-infested hellhole but for the pleasures of a young girl? The sad truth was that many tourists were here to get away from the trappings of acceptable society, and this meant that the streets and people of SE Asia often received an eye-level view of American intolerance and egotism. That idea that it was "our" behavior made the treatment easy to compartmentalize, the harder reality was the policies of the West toward the third world had been appalling and the poverty and hopelessness left was far greater than a few NGO's and USAID workers could handle. Cambodia needed help, and I was on a working vacation.

So you might ask how the sweat-ridden streets of Phnom Penh and the riverine jungles of the Tonle Sap have anything to do with 9/11, Jihadists, and American foreign policy? My story tends to unfold in unusual pockets and places of the world, but I am getting there.

Questions and Curiosities

My back hurts, I thought, keeping it quietly to myself. It was one of those unseasonably hot days in Eugene, Oregon, and I had signed up for the summer course to fulfill some of my humanities requirements. I, like many others, was staring measuredly out into space. Catching glances of the clock as the hands of the timing device seemed to mock me. The instructor was doing a fair job of providing the entertainment, but my eyes were glossing over as the lids became heavier and heavier. There were nearly one hundred people in the Mackenzie lecture hall, so I was not worried of being caught. My eyes began to gloss over, the pleasures of the dark felt nice: 5... 10... 15... seconds passed as I drifted in and out of consciousness. I remember thinking how stupid it was to have stayed out so late, that last Coors might have been the contributor to this pint-sized migraine I was slowly developing. The dark felt good. My brain slowed, my ears seemed to pick up fewer sounds, and the room's voices began to blend and blur together as if to provide a gentle soundtrack to my power nap. Gently, I succumbed to it.

I cannot tell you how long this lasted, but I can clearly remember the words that ended it. "Ladies and gentleman, this is the reason why they hate us!" It was a powerful statement and I was already regretting my failure to stay awake – damn it, this sounded interesting. I slipped out of the lecture hall as nonchalantly as possible. My head still spinning from a combination of siesta, exhaustion and interest. "They hate us?" I thought. I mean that is a pretty strong word, "hate." I ran home to reflect on my curiosities and my failures as a student. A reflection of this might include: already being asked to leave a business class, constantly switching trajectory and failing a fairly basic set of collegiate math classes. In all honesty, this might have been the first subject that had piqued my interest in the year and half I had already been at the university. After I awoke, an interest peaked and I walked to 7-11 to grab a hot dog and walk down to Smith Family Bookstore to see if I could find anything in the stacks. To say that this bookstore is "packed" with books is a complete understatement. Only the employees can understand the chaotic system in place (and believe me they do). It is packed from floor to ceiling with books. Many have close ties to classes offered nearby and some have found a restful sleep here as professors shamelessly hawk new editions. After asking for some guidance finding sections on political science and the Middle East, I landed in a small corner upstairs; pulling book after book reading author and jacket copy, nothing was grabbing me. I fingered through Israel, WWII, Pakistan, 1947, Egypt, Kennedy, and BAM! - There it was, *The Seeds of Hate*. Without another thought I pulled the book from the shelf, ignored the price or synopsis and proudly marched out as if I had found all the answers I was looking for.

Several sleepless nights, energy drinks, and relentless covert in-class reading sessions, I had finished it. The book had left me with far more questions than answers and I struggled to gain a grasp on the world that seemed to be spinning around me. This Washington State professor had led me down the rabbit hole; Lebanon... American servicemen... Inequality... Islamic poverty... Al-Qaeda... I enrolled in a Middle East studies class the following semester - one which I will tell you took me further into the darkness and folly of American foreign policy. Perhaps fortuitously, I failed that class, and promptly switched majors. It was the most I had ever learned, albeit while passionately struggling for answers. This failure would lead me to continue my studies in the Political Science Department investigating the dynamics of American policy abroad and quickly precipitated a love for the subject; I never failed another class.

The Cambodia Experiment

This same feeling of Jihad, or struggle, would be found years later in the classrooms of a poor English language school off the side streets just beyond the Psar Tuol Tom Poung, or the Russian

Market. In the beginning, my days were spent as a tourist-teacher, sitting around planning the evening's exploits and enjoying libations with international volunteers, sitting around in our house talking politics, great music and playing on our house guitar that was a string or two short. The longer we stayed, the more the conversations drifted to our students, the 4-year-old on the corner who sold us Asahi or Anchor beer, and the open sewers that would run into the streets when the rains would come. This couldn't be how people were forced to live - or could it?

As the weeks turned to months, my connection with the students deepened. I had thought that this would open my eyes a bit, and allow me to check Southeast Asia off my bucket list, and come back to the world refreshed and "cultured." To say that I was sorely mistaken was an understatement. The more I ventured out of the city to rural villages, the more I was reminded of how hatred and resentment are bred in climates of poverty, hopelessness and inequality. Nowhere in the country was this more evident than the shores of Sihanoukville and temples of Angkor Wat. Snotty tourists scoffed at the outstretched hands of children and took pictures with the limbless. As droves of buses cued up to visit the Killing Fields and witness the aftermath of the Khmer Rouge, I pondered how this genotourism affected my students. After speaking to Seangly and Sambo, several of the school's staff, it was clear that learning the English language led to "good" jobs in the tourism industry; jobs paying much higher salaries and tempting the youth who were disillusioned with the Hun Sen regime.

My curiosity continued and drew me further away from Phnom Penh. After visiting Ke, Kampung, Kratie, Kandal, and Prey Veng, I got the courage to venture out to Pursat and eventually Pailin. I had heard about the "Wild West," a place where the legacy of the Khmer Rouge was still very real, rumors of Chinese and Vietnamese dissident movements, gangs and slavery were common themes among sources I had talked to. The van volleyed through mud-drifts on the way into the city; paddy workers plowed with water buffalo. I spotted one of my first signs this might have been a bad idea - a dead woman lay splayed out, her graying body set inconspicuously amongst the landscape. After visiting a few temples and walking the town's market, I sat down for an evening meal at a place suggested to me by the guesthouse owner. I had not seen any foreigners that evening and was quickly invited to sit down with the locals after they saw I was eating alone. The conversation was reminiscent of a horribly dubbed movie; we spoke with hand gestures and facial expression between my limited

Khmer and their limited English. As the sun set and the food slowed to a trickle, I was invited to join them at the nearby watering hole. Out of the view of the public, the conversations turned to frustration, the "old ways," and the exploits that lay outside the city. Gems, prostitutes, communism, and landmines quickly became the topics as we were joined by several others, ostensibly off work, who could speak much better English. As the night grew late and the karaoke tunes louder, I swore I could hear gunfire. I later learned that a soccer match that was heavily bet upon often caused policeman and gangsters to discharge their weapons into the air - either out of frustration or in celebration. After the night had come to a close and I was ferried on the back of a moto back to the guest house, I sat in dizzying reflection on two points: being "Canadian" has its benefits and struggle takes many forms - both historically and ideologically.

Using what extra time I had to volunteer outside the school offered further perspective. As the work took me further up the Mekong to island communities and into rural villages, the will to stay grew. Running low on money, I took a job in a province near Pailin called Battambang and began teaching collegiate level writing and business at a rural university. The money wasn't much, but it offered plenty of time to reflect as there were very few westerners in the city. Between classroom sessions, I had some free time to travel. After running up and down the Vietnamese and Thai borders I wanted to venture a bit further, so I bid my students and staff farewell and bought a train ticket from Bangkok south. No plans had been set, or itinerary, but Malaysia was in the distance. After sleeping on a train platform I was awakened by National Policemen who were combing the station. I later learned that just hours earlier a group of teachers had been assassinated, and bombs had gone off in the heavily Islamic Yala Province. Despite my better judgment, I changed my plans and took a slow mover through Southern Thailand toward Kota Baru on the Malaysian side - right through the Islamic South. The attitudes of those I encountered grew cold and, realizing this was really not a place for a westerner, I continued on to Kuala Lumpur - and left Southeast Asia shortly thereafter.

Three Simple Truths

For me, this trip had galvanized three things. First, disparity might exist in the United States but I had never seen this level of despair. Second, fear, shame, frustration, and poverty, when mixed in equal parts, are an absolutely awful cocktail. Third, the struggle for purpose, growth, hope and survival influences those who would otherwise never hurt others to think of themselves first and to justify violence. Simply put, it was a matter of survival. Docendo discimus (By teaching, we learn).

These questions led to my return to the States to prompt further investigation, and to tempt fate with a career that was deep within my blood. After several short months of odd jobs I applied to a master's program in education. I yearned to explore relevant questions which were deeply reminiscent of the talks I shared with my students just a year before. I believe that one way to combat the problems I had seen was, through education, to share my experiences, and bring the (harsh) world I had experienced into the classroom.

My time at the university brought many questions, but the curiosity I had felt back in college returned. I excelled at my studies for the first time in my life. The literature was fascinating, the methods refreshed, and a sense of reinvigoration finally had come. Although I also studied mathematics education, my passion came through in my social studies and methods classes. Debate, questioning, and analytics were the currency traded by professors and students in a unique economy that truly benefited both parties. The ethics behind student advocacy and teaching quickly became discussions of ideology, of a near religious magnitude. The waliyha (passion) and jihad (struggle) to educate, and to change misperceptions, was very real. As graduation neared, cliché as it is to say, we were indeed ready to go out and change the world. The climate of education was unforgiving, in the news a constant reminder of the failures of our system, unions and salary freezes, the apathy of teachers, and a curriculum that had not changed in nearly 100 years; and here we were armed with revolutionary methods of teaching and an obligation to make our professors proud – ugh! You could say that our first struggle was to get a job, and the second was to prove that we belonged.

The Sandy City

The search wasn't easy. In fact, after months of looking it seemed like this city had little to offer young educators. Then it happened. After nearly an entire day of interviews, resumes, and booths of prospective school districts around the region, I noticed a table with the words, "American Schools of Kuwait." Pondering a line of nearly 100 potential candidates to my left and the rural districts of Alaska to my right, I took a chance. The rest is pretty much history. That summer I landed in Kuwait City to temperatures well above 100 degrees Fahrenheit with a stamped passport, visa and the strong arms of a Pakistani

who graciously took my bags after nearly 30 hours of travel. It was
pretty scary. I was handed a bottle of cold water and informed that I
had several more hours to consume food and water before fasting - it
was Ramadan.

It should be said that the next morning brought one of the scari-
est moments of life. Still holding first place was a river trip in Thailand with a sinking raft and an elephant, but I digress. Completely jet-
lagged and dead asleep, I awoke to a loud sound that can only be truly
understood by those who have heard it - Friday prayers. The sun was
just about up and the muezzin was performing the Adhan, or Muslim
call to prayer. Before I could even respond, I was hiding under the bed
as it came from all directions, "Allah Akbar, ash-shahādah as lā 'ilāha
'ilā-llāh," which I would later learn meant that "God is great and there
is no other but God." In that moment I was in shock - both cultural
and sensory. The Islamic community had asked me to awake and be
grateful and go out into the world to do good - and all I could think of
was the sound ringing through my ears that brought me to movies like
Blackhawk Down and *Rules of Engagement*. His voice felt particularly
militant to me and, as the speech progressed, his vocal chords only
sent me further into contemplation about my decision to fly halfway
across the world.

As my acclimation progressed, and I saw the smiling faces of
my students, it became quickly apparent that everything was going to
be okay. The funny thing is that no matter where you are in the world,
middle-schoolers look and act pretty much the same. My command
of Arabic was limited, but my sixth sense for mischief had made the
flight undamaged. I began working with students on everything from
multiplication to fractions and ratios - the issues I had with students in
pre-algebra in the states were identical to those in my classroom in the
Sandy City. Some truths are indeed universal.

Why They Hate Us

It wasn't long before I fell in love the Arabic culture, my students, and the little Indian pocket of the city we had made our home.
The shisha cafes, coffee shops, endless shwarma and falafel deli's, and
my local barber, all helped to ease my discomfort. I grew to become
a creature of habit, enjoying a ritualistic straight-razor shave in the
mornings after prayers let out. My barber and his son were from Pakistan; both had careers before they left and, upon deeper talks, I found
out he actually had an engineering degree but made more in the Gulf.
It was these relationships that galvanized my belief in the Arab world,

and the Islamic world as a whole. Trust garnered by a man holding a six-inch blade to your throat speaks volumes. It was the looks, smiles and eventually light Arabic pleasantries at my local grocery co-op as I bought olives and cheese - or when the Syrian kebab vendor would hover over my shoulder awaiting approval of my first bite - I didn't feel hate here. And there it was, the question that arose nearly ten years prior had crept back into my mind and was prying away at me. I really didn't know how to approach it. It became worse every day; who could I safely ask? Would I ruin one of these relationships that had brought me such comfort? I eventually had the courage to ask one of the Egyptian teachers over some food I had prepared for her. Sharing bread, ful medames (marinated beans) and shorba ads (lentil soup), we just talked. She remarked about how weird it was that an American could cook... and I asked about Hosni Mubarak, Al Qaeda, and the strong Islamic language that had been pointed at the West in recent years. Here we were, breaking bread, talking like old friends and, besides the occasional Hijab passing in the halls, this really could have been anyone, in any school, anywhere in the world. But she was a beautiful, Islamic, Egyptian Arab, proud mother, teacher and now a friend. She took no offense to my questions on Jihad, nor made me feel bad for equating Islam with violence. In fact, she encouraged other staff members to join; the group grew and conversations deepened. It reminded of the talks with my professors, my colleagues, my fellow graduates. Another universal truth might be that food and tea (or beer) have some pretty magical powers - in universally getting beyond the superficial bullshit and other politically correct 'niceties' that seem to transcend all cultures.

Not all of my time in the Middle East shared the same sense of jubilance and success. Other times it was ugly, confusing, and even scary. The ugly - the Gulf is rampant with migrant workers. In some countries like Qatar, nationals make up only a small part of society. In Bahrain and Kuwait you will find much the same. This modern day caste system means that Sri Lankan, Nepali, Indian and, to some extent, even other Arab expats all play within the lines of indentured servitude. It wasn't long before I began to hear about murder, rape, and workers being locked in closets before they sleep. Some try to escape to their embassies for help, but often they are caught and jailed.

I witnessed one worker beaten within inches of his life (in the street) to further demonstrate the master/slave relationship. Nowhere was this more apparent than in the lines to queue up for health inspections during the permanent visa process: upon entrance to this military-like facility were lines that you followed through to all your health check stations. Upon arrival we were separated. I am not sure if there was an exact science to this process; poorer Gulf Arabs, then Northern Africans and those from the Levant, maybe Afghans, Pakistanis and Nepalis, Indians, and, lastly, Westerners. After being pricked several times incorrectly, with blood running down my arm, I asked the Filipino woman if I could insert the IV needle myself. When I got back in line, I asked another man how the country of Kuwait could have such amazing infrastructure and yet this totally different world was but a 30-minute drive out of the city? The Irish gentleman behind me whispered, "Wasta my friend. You will learn about it soon enough."

Confusion and Uncertainty

This concept of "wasta" - one part nepotism and one part corruption, intrigued me. Rich Emiratis, for example, would be offered the comfort of a nice hospital bed for this previously-discussed procedure. Others would simply skip the whole procedure - knowing that if they were caught or hassled they would throw money, influence or their connections at the problem. This extended to highway police, airport security, even grocery stores or lines at the mall. The entitled would simply walk to the front and speak loudly on their phones with nearly reckless abandon. This even extended into the classroom, at one point I heard a student's parent, who happened to work in customs and immigration, threaten a teacher with deportation if he did not change his daughter's grade.

Greater struggle exists over "Insha Allah," a most common response when it comes to whether or when something might occur - "if God wills it." For example, after your passport has been sent to every office in Kuwait, translated, stamped, perfumed and glittered, the customs "fixer" who has been working on it will never give you a specific date that it will be returned. He will simply say "Inshallah - it is up to God my friend. It could be days, it could be weeks." In many ways this was a courteous "perhaps" veiling a more realistic "probably not." The unrelenting bureaucratic "red tape" created an undercurrent of resentment among many of the expatriates of the country.

A side note: Wouldn't a country that netted nearly 150 billion last year in petroleum be able to provide clean streets and infrastructure for its 1.4 million citizens? Think again, my friends.

Below The Surface

Upon entering the country you are ferried onto the freeway with

294

haste. To enter the Kuwaiti road system is to commit one's life into the hands of God - literally. There are no real speed limits, nobody obeys traffic laws, and road lines are more a suggestion. Automobile accidents make up the majority of all deaths in the country. Some teachers had cars, and the iron-will to take us out into the rural parts of the country to see the Bedouins, the coastline, and, on one trip, up to southern Iraq. We had permission to enter with a team of aid workers and other educators and several foreign journalists. After all I had heard about Iraq the past several years, this was a pretty scary endeavor. Ironically, it was raining, there was some green out, and the townspeople we visited were kind and hospitable to us. The Shi'a south gave way to bombed out villages, evidence of shelling, and communities struggling to rebuild. I asked myself - did we do this? That question again crept into the back of my mind, wouldn't this cause hatred? There were plenty of other scary things that defined my trip: the rape of young boys, angry parents, visa scares, attending Catholic mass in a hotel basement, and alcohol check. Nothing rattled me as much as the evidence of the Coalition Forces' wave of destruction.

My suspicions only grew deeper as I met servicemen and contractors who lived and worked in the region. Between the arrogance of the 'seasoned' expats and the indifference of those serving, I felt an ugliness that turned my stomach. Some were here for the money, others (including private mercenaries) to shoot "sand niggers" and "hajjis," but the majority we encountered seemed to not care how we left the country, or about the state of its people. It was only a select group who really cared about the region's endgame. Those that I met at the embassy were frustrated at the status quo - the ambivalence for Arab self-determination. They conceded that the region was still going through growing pains - many remarked that before "Operation Desert Storm," Kuwait's tallest building couldn't have been more than four-five stories. What many failed to reflect on was the buildings destroyed in Iraq had stood for more than just a few years. Some Iraqis I spoke with told me that their homes, villages, and wells were hundreds, even thousands of years old. Some of the world's oldest laws, civilizations, and rulers hailed from the fertile valleys of the Tigris and Euphrates. Saddam's relentless tyranny on the fertile south exacerbated the ruin by destroying places that just a generation before had used small boats for travel and held immense agricultural power. Of course, much of what was wrong with the Arab world was of their own doing, but the policies that were now shaping the Middle East were not being crafted by the minds of young, dynamic regional politicians. Instead, key decisions were being made by those in Washington and other external governments many of which had formed their opinions of this little "sandbox" years prior. Such opinions were not only misinformed and wrong, they often actually put our interests at home and abroad in danger. We were and are at a point where changing the politics of Washington has to come from a new generation. Shortly after this visit in Iraq, I flew home to take a job teaching World History.

Reshaping Pedagogical Norms

The high school I joined charged me with creating a reinvigorated world history curriculum that addressed changing global perspectives by moving away from a western-centric emphasis. I spent the summer crafting this curriculum to include deeper investigations into the Islamic world, the impacts of poverty, the development of China, and the resurgence of a vocationally focused middle class in India (at nearly a billion strong). My goal was to shift the emphasis from primarily ancient study and provide space for students to discuss and analyze current political situations within an appropriate historical framework. My struggle was to convince students that the content is relevant and essential to intelligently and constructively confront misperceptions and stereotypes. This meant that for any classroom dialogue or interaction to take place, students had to first feel safe and confident - which only knowledge provides. Another challenge was to address a prevailing attitude and thinking that is deeply rooted in a traditional history curriculum with the West and Europe at its center.

The first years in the classroom are difficult no matter who you are or where you teach. Introducing and authoring an entirely new curriculum made my first year doubly challenging. I often felt as if I was standing on shifting sands, not at all confident in my lessons, how they were landing with students or with my colleagues. I continually second-guessed myself. When I began teaching my units on the Middle East, a light went on in the classroom. I saw a change not only in my students but in myself - this was territory that was uniquely meaningful to me and that passion translated to my students. Projects, like the Arab League of Nations, unfolded naturally. Before long, my students were comfortably discussing Syrian politics, the Assad regime, and the events leading up to the "Arab Spring." Students could articulate the difference between Shi'a and Sunni Islam - even that the single-pillared Ibadi Muslims only lived in Oman. The remainder of the this first year continued to underscore the power of engagement – students must have context for their learning.

If we continue to base curriculum on the same bland textbooks, Euro-centric historical perspectives and deemphasize geography and human development, then why as a society are we surprised when students develop and maintain pejorative stereotypes toward the world's poor or lesser developed countries? Contextual knowledge and learning help to prevent assumptions such as: "can't they see we are trying to help them -- they are too backwards or stupid to appreciate it – it has always been like this -- it is their own fault." Clearly, this presumption that we need to impose our own democratic values and ethics upon those with different belief systems from us, creates a damaging neo-imperialist narrative. Our attempt to craft policies and policy makers utilizing this mantra continues to fail and my hope is that the young people leaving history, ethics, and religion classes today have a better understanding and appreciation for the world's complex nuances.

Three years later, I find myself feeling that there is so much more to do. My hope is that my current and past students have a better understanding of the world, the Middle East and the politics that ring the globe in ever-tightening and conflicting spheres of influence.

Moving Forward

As an educator and citizen, I am aware that the conversations we seek to have about the increasingly fundamentalist world around us can be intimidating. Knowledge and awareness erode away the pleasant Western narrative that has comforted us and our students. To ask a high school student to engage in a conversation that willingly shakes the world he or she knows really comes down to trust. With that said, I would like to share three statements that have helped inform my practice as an educator directly from the reflections of my students.

1. **We need to see the picture through both macro and micro lenses.** The Islamic narrative really picks up during the India unit where students learn about the great Mughal conquerors who bring Islam and its mystic cousin Sufism to India. As early conquerors like Mahmud of Ghazni set foot on the steps of the Hindu Kush the legacy of Mother India really begins to change. Through the Islamic Mughals' influences, India would be a land divided by religion; and later through the falsely constructed ethnic lines. Students love the stories of India - they revel in the culture of exoticism, spices, and a mercantilism that would shape the subcontinent. But as we got closer to the time of the East India Companies and British Imperialism they felt that those stories

297

seemed to disappear or were dominated by the colonialist narrative. In exploring strategies to gain a deeper connection for them, I found a photo series by American photojournalist Margaret Bourke-White. Bourke had masterfully captured the 1947 partition of India and set her photographs in the most personal of settings. Allowing students to analyze the settings, faces, and demeanors of her subjects allowed them to connect to the conflict - a realization that brought their emotions to the table. Explaining the migration of millions of Muslims across Pakistan, Bangladesh and Myanmar brought the region into focus, but it was the faces of those traveling barefoot with belongings on their backs that made it most impactful. This personalization made the viewing of the film *Partition* (2007) and the subsequent deaths of hundreds of thousands, very, very real.

2. **Don't just tell us about the problems - involve us in the solutions.** During work on the Middle East unit the news cycles had increasingly shifted toward the relationship between the Obama administration and Benjamin Netanyahu. Students wished to discuss the historic relationship between the two nations and by extension, the background of the Palestinian Territories. They were already familiar with the painful British legacy left during the partition of Pakistan, and it seemed a logical step to explain the imperialist legacies left in the Levant. The further we got into the conflict the more students wanted to insert themselves into the conversation. Against my better judgment, and warnings of my colleagues, I decided to set them up for a structured debate on Israel and Palestine. I divided the class up into teams, gave them potential debate questions and left them a week to prepare for arguments. I nominated student judges to control the floor and dictate scoring, then I simply played the narrator and the students took charge. The passion and conviction with which these students demonstrated their engagement was incredible; to date, I think this might have been my proudest day teaching. What was inspiring was that after a decent amount of sparring, the conversation quickly turned to suggestions for the future - how to move forward and end this ugly conflict. Hence statement #2 - the phrasing is quoted directly from a student's post-debate reflection.

3. **We can handle it but we need time to process.** This approach asks students to challenge their core beliefs and understandings

298

of the world. For many students this is tough and daunting. Several times a year, we stop everything and get into the politics of the world. These are often no test/quiz/homework sessions where students have plenty of "think time" and little to no "work." I have learned that with harder content, more compelling content, and content that leads to raise the engagement - students need more time to process. This year we focused primarily on conflict in Ukraine, Boko Haram in Nigeria, and several films relating to the food, cultures and religions of Israel/Palestine. The themes of these films reflected immense religious hatred, xenophobia, and racism on a scale that many had not witnessed before. The photos, comics, and video clips depicted peoples' rawest emotions. Despite the mature level of content, I found that students wanted to see the real as opposed to an edited or homogenized version of the world. That said, experience taught me that trust between student and teacher is critical and requires processing and reflective time to develop. Documentaries such as, *Real Bad Arabs* and *China: A Century of Revolution,* or videos like *Munich* or *One Day in September* belay incredibly strong imagery and messaging. I lost nights of sleep deciding whether to screen a scene of a brutal beating of a Nigerian Muslim by state security forces and militia members. Ultimately, I decided to screen it, forewarned students and debriefed immediately after the film. Even the cameraman turns away while filming this scene, but not before catching the rage in the perpetrator's eyes. It was this incredibly terrifying gesture that students later reflected was the moment that solidified the lesson.

Without knowledge and context, the world can be a scary place for students and their teachers. I see my role as facilitating tough conversations and creating a safe place for dialog. This will be the first year that I will have to explain to some students what 9/11 meant, and means to this nation. As students grow older the narrative becomes less and less personal for them, the memories altogether distant. My Jihad is real. It starts everyday that I battle to convince kids that the histories are relevant and that their opinions matter.

"An educated citizenry is a vital requisite
for our survival as a free people"
~ Thomas Jefferson ~

Two hundred years later that statement remains relevant. The difference today is that issues of the electorate are broader in context and increasingly complex in scale. Young voters need to understand the world in order to understand the decisions of their own country's leadership – decisions that, sadly, sometimes reflect a disturbing lack of understanding and respect for the people most affected. It could be argued that the failings of poor investment in our K-12 education system have regrettably led us here.

"I ran on the platform of moderation and won the election by a large margin. By virtue of the strong mandate that I received from the electorate, I am committed to operating in the framework of moderation, which calls inter alia for a balance between realism and the pursuit of the ideals
of the Islamic Republic of Iran."
~ Hassan Rouhani (President of Iran) ~

For students to understand the power of Rouhani's statement in the context of today's world is undoubtedly complicated. While many U.S. states struggle to fund their educational budgets, the Islamic Republic is increasing their investment surpassing (by World Bank statistics) U.S. graduation rates by a significant percentage.
It makes you wonder if our priorities might need to shift a little…

———————————

"There can be no keener revelation of a society's soul than the way in which it treats its children."
~ Nelson Mandela ~

"It is easier to build strong children than to repair broken men."
~ Frederick Douglas ~

"If you want to end war, instead of sending tanks, send books."
~ Malala Yousafzai ~

———————————

Chapter Twenty-Four

One Rotary Club's Response to 9/11:
Starting with a School Project* in Jalalabad,
Afghanistan

Stephen R. Brown and Fary Moini

Fary Moini and Stephen Brown among Afghan students

*San Diego and Jalalabad established a Sister Cities relationship in November 2004, and formed a Foundation shortly thereafter. Many of the activities described herein were undertaken in collaboration between the La Jolla Golden Triangle Rotary Club and the San Diego~Jalalabad Sister Cities Foundation.

Fary Moini - After the tragedy of Sep 11, she was inspired to work as Rotary volunteer at two Afghan refugee camps in Peshawar, Pakistan. Fary holds a Bachelor of Science degree in Nursing from the University of Tehran, Iran. She held the position of Chief Nurse at the Iranian Medical Center in Dubai. She was Rotary International's representative to the U.S. National Commission to UNESCO, a Rotary Foundation Volunteer at the Don Bosco Boys School in Nairobi, Kenya, and one of the Medical team members to Gondar, Ethiopia. Fary is the recipient of numerous awards including recognition by the White House as a "Champion of Change" in 2012; Lifetime channel's Lifetime Achievement Award as a "Hometown Hero." She has also been recognized by the Lt. Governor of California, and Soroptimist International of Rancho Bernardo, California. Fary resides in La Jolla, California, and is president of Moini International Consulting.

Stephen R. Brown - Motivated by the tragedy of September 11, Rotarian Steve Brown has traveled to Afghanistan twelve times during the last thirteen years working with Rotarian Fary Moini on various programs of the Rotary Foundation and other partnering organizations to carry out educational and humanitarian programs in the City of Jalalabad. Steve was a partner in the San Diego law firm of Luce, Forward, Hamilton and Scripps from 1972 until retirement several years ago. He has been a member of Stanford Law School's Board of Visitors. He received the Eleanor Roosevelt Human Rights Award from United Nations Association of San Diego. A Rotarian since 1986, he has served the Rotary Foundation as vice chair and trustee. Steve has been involved in Rotary Foundation projects in numerous countries and traveled extensively to support international service through Rotary. He is a recipient of Rotary Foundation's Citation for Meritorious Service, Distinguished Service Award and Rotary International's Service Above Self Award. Steve and his wife, Susan, reside in the Del Mar suburb of San Diego, California.

Shortly after the incidents of Sept. 11, 2001, Rotarian Fary Moini, a relatively new Rotarian to the La Jolla Golden Triangle Rotary club, asked Steve Brown if he could help her work with Afghan refugees. She had just spent two months in refugee camps near Peshawar, Pakistan. Upon her return, she suggested that their Rotary Club should build a school in Afghanistan. Steve was skeptical, but with encouragement from some Pakistani Rotarians and a grant from the William H. Donner Foundation to help pay for the building of a school, Fary and Steve traveled to Jalalabad in November 2002 to explore this idea. This turned out to be the first of thirty-seven (37) trips to Afghanistan over the next thirteen years, and was the beginning of a chain of events neither could ever have imagined.

Upon arrival, Fary and Steve met with the Governor of Nangarhar Province in Jalalabad just on the Afghan side of the Khyber Pass through which they had traveled with some Rotarians from Pakistan. The Governor advised there would soon be many Afghan refugees returning to the Jalalabad area and he would set aside a site to build a school. They went to the site and found two UNICEF tents where boys studied under one tent and girls under the other. Steve and Fary were sufficiently encouraged that they contracted with an Afghan Non-Governmental Organization (NGO) to oversee the work. A groundbreaking ceremony was held shortly thereafter.

Fary and Steve returned in early 2004 for the dedication of the school. It was built in two phases and, with its 20 classrooms, was designed for 1,000 students. As of 2012, there were about 6,000 students running in two shifts - with some classrooms outside under tents and some classrooms just in the shade of its walls.

Pictured above is the school and students lined up on opening day.

In the early stages, Fary and Steve were in touch with a gentleman named Gopa from the country of Oman regarding this school. When he learned about the need for more classrooms, he was able to raise $95,000 from colleagues and businesses in Oman which was sufficient to add six classrooms. He was not a Rotarian, nor is there a Rotary Club in Oman. Yet, when prospective donors learned that Rotary was involved, they expressed confidence that the money would be properly managed and utilized – putting the Afghan people and culture above all other considerations.

Soon it was learned that it was easier to build a school than it is to assure the quality of the education provided therein. For example, one girl could find California and Afghanistan on a world map, but her teacher could not. The typical primary school teacher may have at best only a high school education - let alone instruction on how to teach. It was also learned that girls were not going to go to school after the sixth grade - for lack of female teachers. When asked how many would attend if female teachers were found, everyone raised their hands. For the cost of $600 per teacher per year, eight female teachers were found and hired. The first graduating class of females to have completed grade 12 occurred in 2012. In 2010, the first class of boys graduated.

The club's centennial project provided a clock at the Afghan Rotary School and one at a sister school in San Diego. On one side of each clock is the time in San Diego and on the other side the time in Jalalabad.

In March 2008, Steve and Fary met with the Afghan friends they had developed, and experienced the warm welcome that is traditional among these wonderful people. They also made it a point to meet with the elders while there to be certain that they were comfortable with what was being done to support education.

While working with the local Afghans, they became curious about this Rotary organization. The idea that Rotarians were unpaid volunteers who kept returning to help them was a bit mystifying. However, they soon expressed interest in becoming involved in Rotary. During their trip of January 2005 Steve and Fary helped to charter the Rotary Club of Jalalabad.

Since that time, Rotarians have sponsored two Afghan Group Study Exchange teams coming to San Diego. The first, in May 2005, was made up of college professors, three from the medical school, two English professors and one agriculture professor. The second team came in the summer of 2009, comprised of three English teachers and a Rotarian team leader who is also a neurosurgeon.

During that first trip in 2002, Steve was surprised to see the Rotary logo on a sign in Kabul. As he looked more closely, he saw that the billboard was promoting the polio eradication efforts in Afghanistan. Since that time, a local Jalalabad Rotarian became Rotary's representative for polio eradication in Afghanistan. He had been Director of Public Health in Nangarhar Province and visited San Diego in early 2009.

During one of these trips, their Afghan contacts arranged a meeting of the mullahs to have a discussion about the importance of supporting the immunization efforts. One, a local moderate Taliban leader, talked eloquently about how, under Islam, adults have an obligation to protect children and thus the message must be provided through the Mosques regarding the importance of supporting the polio immunization efforts.

The Rotary Club of Jalalabad and students in our Global Connection and Exchange Program raised $1000 which was donated to the Rotary Foundation for eradication of polio. As volunteers, after two days of training, they went into the community to raise funds and educate the public about the importance of polio drops.

On their first trip to Jalalabad back in 2002, Fary and Steve asked if there was a local university. They were advised that Nangarhar University is one of the top universities in Afghanistan and a visit was arranged. They met with the Chancellor and the various department heads, and were advised that the university had 4,000 students and 250 faculty. Only a few held advanced degrees. They did not have a relationship with any other university; they did not have a single computer and no useable textbooks. The professors taught from lecture notes that were between 20-30 years old. As one might imagine, they asked for help.

When Fary and Steve returned in March 2004 for the dedication ceremony for the Rotary school, there was also a dedication ceremony for a computer lab at Nangarhar University. Fary Moini spent two months in Jalalabad in advance of this visit to help oversee the work needed to be done to complete the Rotary school and set up the

computer lab at the university. For this trip, they also brought Steve
Spencer, a professor from San Diego State University who oversees
some distance learning programs in the Pacific. At the dedication ceremony for the computer lab, he provided a lecture about the Internet
and later helped set up some of the professors with email accounts.
Steve Spencer brought a projector with him, did a web search, and displayed the Quran on the wall of the lab. Later, the head of the Veteri-
nary Medicine Faculty advised that he could bring some Tetracycline
to help with the computer "virus problems" professor Spencer had
discussed. Six months later, Steve received an email from that same
professor, now much more familiar with computer viruses, advising
that through the use of the Internet and email communications, he had
obtained a $300,000 grant for his Veterinary Medicine Faculty.

A few months after that trip, Steve Weber, President of San
Diego State University, learned about their activities in Jalalabad.
After meeting with them, he advised he would like his university to
become involved. Fary and Steve met with a representative of the
World Bank, which had just launched a program to fund partnerships
between universities in Afghanistan and universities in other countries.
They were able to facilitate putting together a partnership between
the Nangarhar University and San Diego State University to build
an English language program at Nangarhar University. The World
Bank provided about $2,000,000 in funding for that partnership, and
later a second partnership between the two universities to build a Civil
Engineering department at Nangarhar University - again with about
$2,000,000 in funding from the World Bank. Related to this, they
were able to assist in obtaining Rotary Foundation Ambassadorial
Scholarships for four professors. Two of these were funded by the
Rotary Foundation through Rotary Districts in Michigan, and two more
were subsequently funded by the Rotary Foundation's Scholarship
Fund Pool for Low Income Countries. One of them received Master's
Degrees from the University of San Diego's School for Peace and
Justice. From time to time, the La Jolla Golden Triangle club has

enjoyed visits from a collection of Afghans who participated in these various programs. Also, two engineering professors received their MA at SDSU, and six engineering professors went to Cracow University and completed their MA in March 2012 thanks to SDSU/World Bank funding.

These collaborations included constructing some buildings at Nangarhar University and furnishing them through Rotary Foundation matching grants. This included a guest house for visiting professors.

Volunteers and professionals additionally designed and built a facility named the "Stephen R. Brown" International Learning Center at Nangarhar University, which became a technology-rich environment used for live video conferencing between the professors at SDSU and NU - among other things.

These buildings were designed by Rick Clark, acting as a volunteer. Rick is an architect and member of La Jolla Golden Triangle Rotary Club.

In 2009, again with partial financial assistance from the William H. Donner Foundation, the team constructed a dormitory for up to 72 females on the main NU campus, and furnished the same with a grant from the Rotary Foundation. Generally, few females attend the university since, in this and many cultures, females are often not comfortable walking alone or being transported without a male relative serving as an escort. This dormitory now allows for more female enrollment and eventually will facilitate developing qualified females to be teachers, engineers, lawyers and professionals in other fields.

The La Jolla Golden Triangle Rotary Club Foundation has been able to enter into a variety of partnerships that have resulted in overlapping programs. Some of these partnerships are with the U.S. Department of State, NATO, USAID and Washington State University. A common theme for all of these partnerships is to use technology to improve the learning experience in education, and to facilitate relationship-building. Different partners provided funding for different aspects of these programs.

For example, the U.S. Department of State provided funding to set up computer labs to serve high school students in Jalalabad. In addition to providing basic computer training, these programs enable students in Jalalabad to communicate through technology through various social media with students around the world. Skype is also used for live video conferencing with the students. Judith McHale, U.S. Undersecretary of State, participated in one of these conferences.

This project has also been able to obtain funding for some small grant programs at Jalalabad area high schools. Some of the funding came from the San Diego~Jalalabad Sister Cities Foundation. The Sister Cities relationship was established through Rotarians in both cities. Examples of small grants projects include a program put on by Afghan female high school students talking about violence against women. The audience includes male and female high school and college students. Other projects included clean up and vegetation planting at a high school. Another example was to build a water cistern at the school. The students need to raise additional funds in the community and obtained in-kind donations from vendors for these projects. Students initially involved in these projects have since initiated follow-up projects. The idea is quite new to take social responsibility for their own schools. Funding from USAID helps pay for Internet connectivity at the high schools and to add additional computer labs at other high schools.

Rotarians in Canada have partnered with the Canadian International Development Agency to undertake a project in Afghanistan. Asked to help find and initiate the project, Fary and Steve met with the Nangarhar Director of Education. He recommended building a school at the Nasrat II School site. There were about 4,000 students attending classes - mostly sitting under trees. The school construction was completed in 2010. The second phase of building a hall for community meetings and three more classrooms is underway. Teacher training is another project which is supported by Canadian Rotarians. Also, as a result of a request by female teachers, a small nursery was established for the children of the female teachers.

The Nasrat II School includes a 6000 square foot computer training facility and auditorium constructed at NU's Faculty of Education and named the Faculty of Education Learning Center. The FELC was opened in December 2011 and contains two classrooms providing computer training. The ground floor auditorium seats 250. A large hall for the community meetings, conferences and high school GCE Program operates upstairs. Also, in November 2011, through a Smart Technology donation, two "Smart Boards" were acquired and installed in this center. These are believed to be the first Smart Boards used in public education in Afghanistan. Through their Rotary Club's Foundation they provide for all the training taking place in the FELC.

With funding from Washington State University, they set up a computer lab at the NU medical school. Also, with USAID funds they brought the Internet to a medical clinic where they set up a telemedicine network involving use of the Internet to distribute imagery to a network of physicians in San Diego. Additionally, a computer lab was established in the university's computer science department.

NATO has arranged to provide Internet connectivity to six universities in Afghanistan, but NATO does not provide directly for setting up the IT system to manage and distribute the Internet signal. They obtained a grant from NATO to finish running fiber optic cables to sixteen buildings on the Nangarhar University's main campus, and subsequently established signal relays that signal to four remote NU campus locations. At these remote locations, they have ongoing programs that are Internet-based. These include the medical school, education faculty, a teaching hospital and computer science department - all affiliated with Nangarhar University.

They also obtained a grant for a program known as "Teen Teach." Through this program, Afghan high school students who participate in the GCEP program taught English to 1,800 grade school students in the summer of 2012. This program was administered by two former Rotary Scholars.

During their trip to Afghanistan in April 2012, Kalyan Banerjee, President of Rotary International (from India), traveled with Fary and Steve for two days in Kabul. There were also several meetings relating to the ongoing polio eradication efforts in Afghanistan. Meetings included representatives of World Health Organization and UNICEF, organizations that oversee the immunization efforts and receive funds from various organizations for polio immunizations. (Rotary International has contributed more than one billion US dollars towards this effort worldwide and continues to contribute millions of dollars to the efforts in Afghanistan and Pakistan.)

These meetings in Kabul were setup by US Ambassador to Afghanistan, Ryan Crocker, with whom the Rotary contingent met at the US Embassy.

The highlight of the two days was meeting with Afghan President Hamid Karzai, who was a strong supporter of the polio eradication initiative throughout his presidency. He re-affirmed his commitment and asked "What more can I do?" He offered to work more closely with religious leaders to advance communications regarding the importance of the vaccinations. Rotary International President Banerjee provided Rotary International's Medal of Appreciation to Afghan President Karzai.

One of Rotary's Presidential Themes was: The Future of Rotary is in Our Hands. Steve and Fary believe that this holds true as Rotarians strive to work in partnerships with other organizations to serve the greater good – especially our children, grandchildren and future generations.

Fary, Steve and their many collaborators look forward to continued work in Afghanistan, focusing on respecting Afghan culture and in collaboration with all stakeholders, including parents from all walks of life – certainly including the Taliban and others who are understandably wary of Western and other outside influences.

"Never doubt that a small group of thoughtful, committed
citizens can change the world.
Indeed, it is the only thing that ever has."
~ Anthropologist Margaret Mead ~

Rotary's 4-Way Test

Is it the TRUTH?
Is it FAIR to all concerned?
Will it build GOODWILL and better FRIENDSHIPS?
Will it be BENEFICIAL to all concerned?

"Rotary in Afghanistan" (video):
https://www.youtube.com/embed/NKOAaujCScc?feature=player_detail-page

---

"Prejudice is a burden that confuses the past, threatens the future and renders the present inaccessible.
~ Maya Angelou ~

"A belief is not merely an idea the mind possesses;
it is an idea that possesses the mind."
~ Robert Oxton Bolt ~

"He who closes his ears to the views of others shows little confidence in the integrity of his own views."
~ William Congreve ~

Chapter Twenty-Five

What Have We Learned?
Where Do We Go From Here?

Dan Sockle

You have now heard from a small, diverse cross-section of fellow human beings. Generally speaking, did you conclude that you have more in common with some than others? Even those that you might have considered to hold views much different from your own, would you not say that you share more in common than there are differences? Did the source for one or more of the quotes surprise you? Any stereotypes broken? Was anyone more "expert" than another? Was anyone's "truth" more or less valid than others – or even the truths you hold dear?

Whatever your faith or belief system, would your future communications not benefit from elevating your effort to achieve at least some level of mutual understanding and respect? Would all parties not benefit from abiding by a philosophy of engagement that starts with the Golden Rule? ("Do unto others as you would have them do unto you.")

Mediators, whether professional or volunteers, set out to help the disputing parties to first focus upon and discuss their common interests and shared values. For divorced or divorcing couples, this is most commonly their children. For many employers it is simply the "bottom line," but for those most successful, that pursuit of profit and growth includes cultivating a collaborative culture where all employees at all levels feel that they are important members of a team effort. Everyone shares in both the successes and the "failures," which, if handled correctly, offer the greatest opportunities for learning, process or product improvement, and growth. Timely and effective damage control where repair and restoration trumps the "blame game" puts on display the talent, camaraderie and character of an organization. "Bad news doesn't get better with age" is a quote and philosophy that

312

I would attribute to those relatively few leaders who really stand out from the rest.

The attacks on 9/11 afforded not just America, but the Western World and, ultimately, all of humanity, the opportunity to study the "Who, What, When, Where, Why and How" of both the attacks and what preceded them. Unlike what many book writers or security entrepreneurs were suddenly selling, as we typically look for quick and easy answers, the causes were multi-faceted, complex, and there was plenty of "blame" to go around in both the "West" and the "East," spanning all of humanity. At the apex of what could or should be are the political and religious "leaders" who have the power, influence and, hopefully, wisdom and humility, to actually lead with genuine integrity, accountability and transparency. Unfortunately, there are too few leaders able to set aside political and personal agendas in favor of simply doing what is right, just and fair.

Everyone has his or her own view of history and the people, organizations or institutions that they consider to be the most credible source(s) on any given subject, incident or piece of history. When it comes to seeking and assessing the best information available on any given topic or issue, at a minimum, the researcher or decision-maker should always seek out at least two sources. Ideally, these sources would not only be independent of one another, but commonly known to have opposing views – whether arising from ethnic, religious, cultural, gender, or political perspectives.

If you want to take the approach of an investigator, applying your own sense of logic or "common sense" in your probative process, you would first consider all of your senses if an eye-witness to the incident. Of course, even eye witnesses see things differently, so the most irrefutable is always physical evidence; i.e. fingerprints, DNA and that which is provable through science. Next-best, and arising with increasing frequency, is the security camera or cell phone camera video recording of the incident. Into all of this comes testimonial evidence that generally comes from victims and eyewitnesses. Hearsay, or that which does not come directly from the alleged original source, does come into play, but is given much less weight as it might go with the preponderance of circumstantial evidence arising from any of a variety of subjects or circumstance – including the application of the age-old "reasonable man (or woman)" theory. At some point, depending upon many legal factors, if there are no admissions of guilt, all of this and more might have to be considered by a judge or jury.

If you want to approach the present and future challenges, you might want to do so as an educator. Let's take education reform advocate Sir Ken Robinson, who has put forth his view on "How Schools Kill Creativity." Here is what he sees as the four primary purposes of education:

- Economic – to become economically responsible and independent

- Cultural – to understand and appreciate diverse cultures

- Social – to become active and compassionate citizens

- Personal – to engage with the world within themselves - and with those around them

I know of no one who does not agree that education is the ultimate weapon against radicalism and fundamentalism – anywhere and everywhere.

No Experts or Magic Bullets - Change Starts With You

The goal of this book is to help you, our reader, to sort out at least a good share of the players, issues and challenges that face us today – through the eyes and hearts of twenty-four very different people, including: Muslim, Jew, Christian, agnostic and atheist; women and men; military and academia; citizens of or with roots in America, Israel, Kuwait, South Africa, Pakistan, Iraq, Iran, Afghanistan, Bosnia, Australia and Canada. What we offer, for your consideration, are our personal journeys from 9/11/2001, when America, and the world, became united in a common cause, to the divisive political rhetoric and "Occupy," "Tea Party," "Black, Blue and All lives matter" movements of today – reflecting a world that arguably has never been so divided, bewildered, misinformed, frustrated, and angry.

Connected, yet Increasingly Disconnected

We live in a time where news and communication is 24/7 from a variety of sources never even imagined less than fifty years ago. But, along with this technologically-unprecedented age that should have us more connected with one another than ever, we are increasingly seeing people wearing ear buds or head phones, or otherwise individually engaged in some kind of hand-held device, many oblivious to the world around them. I would venture to say that, with all of the limitations in the 1950's and 1960's, Americans were generally far more aware of local and national politics than people are now. It is scary how vulnerable especially our younger generations are to quick sound bites that might pop up on their iPhone, iPad, Droid or Blackberry – not to mention Facebook, Twitter and other social media.

Look no further than the "Arab Spring" for the double-edged sword of instant communications – via cell phones or through satellite news like "Al Jazeera," which might, one day, be the "uniter" between the western and eastern worlds, predominantly non-Muslim vs. predominantly Muslim. The greatest challenge will be in effectively identifying and separating the ideals and values between the genuinely peaceful Muslims and the radical Islamists who have hijacked the religion to further personal and political agendas. A dramatically increased awareness of freedoms such as democracy represents helped to bring about this movement, but, once regimes were ousted, the Muslim Brotherhood was best positioned to gain the most votes. Over the longer term, however, either the MB will have to radically moderate their extreme foundational beliefs, or the ever-increasing desire for freedom, jobs and open/fair governance will simply overwhelm those bent upon establishing a global caliphate – an "Islamic State" as currently envisioned and pursued by Abu Bakr al Baghdadi and his followers.

Balancing Individual Responsibility
vs. Organizational Accountability

Having worked eight-plus years specifically in tort claims against the State of Washington, I grew to see our country's propensity for litigation as a uniquely American passion for blame-shifting (aka: "The Blame Game" or "I won the Lottery" culture). Sadly, it seemed to me that Americans had departed from our once strong principle of taking personal responsibility to embracing avoidance and blame. The power of people to rationalize almost any level of misbehavior is out of control. Worse yet, it seemed that this cultural practice was arguably becoming one of our more significant exports – whether through influencing other legal systems or through the various portrayals and influences arising from our "entertainment" industry.

A "Wake-up Call" not just to America,
but to our Educators – at all Levels

On September 11, 2001, Osama bin Laden and Al Qaeda exposed America's Achilles Heel. No, not our compartmentalized and silo-structured law enforcement and intelligence agencies, but our educational shortfalls and isolationist culture that has, for too long, minimized our exposure to foreign language, global history and cultures, and religions of the world. Compounding these shortfalls in our K-12 public education, we have been raised never to discuss religion or politics. We are now faced with global challenges that require knowledge and insights into all of the above. Our education system, K-12 and "higher ed," need to get started soon for better preparing the American people, and our future diplomats and foreign policy decision-makers.

Where have the Heroes and Role Models gone?

As I increasingly lamented the decreasing heroes and role models in our society, and the media's propensity to start calling everyone "heroes," it seemed like perhaps this was the answer, or at least something to explore. Of course, many of those we once looked upon as heroic or greater than life, eventually fell to rumors or documented "flaws" that had somehow gone undetected for all or most of their living years. From Hollywood actors to sports figures, elected, appointed, civilian or military, to religious leaders, once adored individuals were falling hard under the increased scrutiny of our researchers, historians, authors, investigative reporters and, eventually, anyone who had a grudge as he or she got onto the Internet.

Hopes and Dreams

We Americans take hope and dreams for granted. Well, at least most of us used to. In many parts of the world, in places we can't even imagine where the most basic necessities like potable water are scarce, millions of children have no cause for hope or dreams. They, like their parents, are focused on survival, day-by-day, hour-by-hour, minute-by-minute. There is nothing in their stomachs, hearts and minds but the here and now. Their concept of time is so much different from ours. Their vulnerability to exploitation of any kind is so much greater. They might as well be on some other, desolate planet. We can no more conceive of their world than they can of ours. Along comes someone either promising them something more – or creating an enemy upon whom they can place all blame for their endless suffering. In Iraq and Afghanistan, it was easy to see how even good people were enticed to do bad things – if the equivalent of $50 to plant an improvised explosive device (IED) would put food on the table for your otherwise starving family, what would you do? For some, wearing and detonating a suicide vest was their only chance to bring honor to their family.

If children grow up without hope or dreams, would it be any surprise that they might be exploited and controlled by others, indoctrinated and trained to be our next adversary or terrorist?

Which came First – the Chicken or the Egg?

Was America always this adversarial in its "problem-solving?" Did it grow out of our system of laws and a jurisprudence that relies more upon retributive than restorative justice? Is it Hollywood's depiction of America, feeding our hunger for good versus evil, sinister plots, government corruption, or even putting "Robocops" on the streets of Tehran? Has the media adopted that adversarial method exercised in the courtrooms by bringing on the "Point-Counterpoint" culture that prevails today throughout the various talk shows and pundits? Are folks like Keith Olberman, Ed Schulz, Chris Matthews, Bill Maher, Sean Hannity, Ann Coulter and others predisposed to be so politically biased and nasty or are they simply playing to their audiences? Is Bill O'Reilly so confrontational because it is his "Irish" nature or is he truly an independent who is frustrated in trying to restore integrity and accountability in our media and government? Is Glenn Beck a new form of televangelist or is he genuinely trying to elevate the level of constructive discourse throughout politics and the media? It is easy to say, "With freedom comes great responsibility," but, until we take that to heart and revisit "political correctness" as the prevailing answer today, our listening and communication skills are going to continue to deteriorate. Thankfully, we have had the likes of Jon Stewart, Stephen Colbert, John Oliver, and "Saturday Night Live" to poke fun at both the politicians and the news media. Although leaning left, sometimes far left, they have at least helped us to laugh rather than cry over the self-serving greed and hypocrisy that surrounds us in today's world.

What is at the Root of Human Nature?

First, no matter how educated or civilized, we humans seem to be predisposed towards *getting even*. You see it in the story lines of many movies, on television, and our interactive video game industry. Indeed, *revenge* seems to be in our DNA. But that has been addressed elsewhere in the book. Beyond that, I have come to learn that even the most altruistic of volunteers might draw the line at empowering others to help themselves. At a minimum, as the old adage goes, "We must love ourselves before we can love others." Everyone needs to feel important or successful, at some level, in his or her own way. At our foundation, some level of self-actualization seems to be tied to whether

317

or not we "make a difference" in this world of ours – be it within the walls of our home or hut, our immediate family, our community, or beyond. Several years ago, at a monthly meeting of volunteer mediators, I enthusiastically suggested that a local one-page listing of public and private community resources would be an ideal tool to put into the hands of our "clients," i.e. those in some level of crisis and/or dispute. Unfortunately, this group of otherwise terrific and giving people, with no financial stake in the discussion, nearly unanimously rejected this idea – whether at the onset of contact with the mediation center or even at the end of the first mediation session. It took me a while to recognize that they did not want to give up what they held dear – their individual "power" to help people. If they were to empower others with what amounted to a simple piece of paper - that somehow diminished their uniqueness and perhaps even their self-worth. Egad.

"Politics as Usual?" – Is it not Time for a Change?

"Black lives matter" and "Hands up – Don't shoot," "Death to America and Israel" are politically-motivated slogans and "battle cries" intended to get attention, raise money and support, keep disadvantaged, oppressed or suffering people focused on an external "enemy," and sustain campaigns based upon agendas that find more profit in dividing, rather than uniting, any given populace. Alas, on so many levels, conflict remains more profitable than stability and peace.

So long as there are those who promote our *differences* instead of *commonalities*, gaining power and influence that translates to wealth, in a world where the media is only too happy to perpetuate the debate and hate while also profiting from the conflicts and cries of victimhood, we are unlikely to effectively turn the tide on the madness, whether domestic or foreign, in this game of spin and deception.

This is humanity's greatest "jihad" – an internal and external struggle, seemingly without end. It is as if it is our unshakeable curse that came with the creation or "evolution" of humankind.

Has humanity peaked and now finds itself in a downward spiral of devolution, arising not just from ignorance and fear, but driven uncontrollably by our 24/7 news cycle and global expansion of social media, all seemingly dominated by victimhood and a "gotcha" mentality?

Who will prevail in this emerging clash of political correctness, self-serving narcissism and a concurrent resurgence of tribalism?

Politically-speaking, "kicking the can down the road" has become an institutionalized policy throughout our political landscape.

Our elected leaders have no incentive to actually resolve issues, because, if they do, each side loses those particular special interests who keep contributing money into the war chests of the respective political parties to vote their way. Think about it, from healthcare (lawyers on all sides vs. doctors vs. insurance companies vs. government) to immigration (imagine the multitude of interest groups there, including corporations, unions, consumers, and the human traffickers), to "Life" vs. "Choice" (abortion/birth control where arguably only women should be engaged in the discussion), to tort reform (too many attorneys on all sides making money) to just about any other national or local debate you can imagine – those running for political office are almost forced to pick a steadfast position, even create "straw men" about which to accuse and argue. Yes, "politics as usual" has devolved into the most unsavory, unproductive and destructive industry in our country. "Words of Mass Deception" abound, whether arising from a politician or as spun by media bias and profit-driven motives to create or perpetuate the argument or conflict.

Both the "Tea Party" and "Occupy" movements have plenty of grievances to be aired – and arguably have more in common than differences. But it is in the best financial interests of both political parties to keep these two movements apart, perpetuating the accusations against one another – marginalizing and/or keeping these two grass roots initiatives divided - so that they do not unite to possibly become a viable third party that is truly transparent and accountable to Americans, grabbing that moderate, common sense and "independent" demographic that presently is without a party that represents and acts with integrity on behalf of the majority of Americans who are fed up with the two extremes.

> "Let us not seek the Republican answer or the
> Democratic answer, but the right answer. Let us
> not seek to fix the blame for the past. Let us accept our own
> responsibility for the future."
> ~ President John Fitzgerald Kennedy ~

Time for a Reality Check on Our "Leadership"

In January 2015, IraqiNews.com revealed this map alleged to reflect the "Islamic State's" goal relevant to the Caliphate being pursued by self-proclaimed "Caliph" Abu Bakr al Baghdadi. Familiar geography, but with ancient names associated with what Islamists regard as the "Islamic State" that, in their minds, should or could have been several hundred years ago. For the sake of argument, let's assume that this is in fact the goal of al Baghdadi and "DAESH." What is America and the West prepared to do in order to protect not only the Christians, but millions of other non-Muslims in this challenging and most complex part of the world? What are Russia, China, India, Greece, Turkey and the rest of North Africa, the Gulf States and Eastern Europe prepared to do?

While most would probably agree that going into Afghanistan in response to the attacks of 9/11 was justified, or at least defensible, our later invasion of Iraq was arguably based upon flawed and/or selective intelligence, misplaced trust (particularly surrounding the issue of WMD's perpetuated by Iraqi Ahmed Abdel Hadi Chalabi), and a very poor grasp of the country, culture(s) and region. Despite all that, we almost succeeded in our goal to oust Saddam Hussein and turn the government over to the Iraqi people. While a multitude of mistakes were made, they were relatively minor compared to the "debaathification," which led to the total dismantling of key government functions and, as previously noted, the "firing" of the Iraqi military. No matter their true intentions, the Bush Administration and Coalition partners, for the most part, got it horribly wrong.

In my experience, many "leaders" seem most reluctant to

directly confront challenges or significant issues involving some level of personal risk unless or until they absolutely must. Of course, this is most evident in politics, and arguably demonstrated most recently on the world stage by the individual and collective failures to accurately assess and effectively confront ISIS/ISIL as it was still growing in Syria and Iraq. Now, that "JV Team," as initially described by President Obama, has caused the worst refugee and Internally Displaced Persons (IDP's) crisis since World War II – arguably unprecedented. Was it because of faulty intelligence or did the intelligence and related threat assessment run contrary to the preferred politically driven narrative during an election cycle?

Remember the adage, "Bad news doesn't get better with age?" The leader who encourages honest and immediate notification of adverse incidents, mistakes or threats knows that it is always easier to deal with anticipated or "routine" operations and outcomes. Thus, it is much more important that your chain-of-command and all team members, however large or small the organization, feel not only comfortable, but encouraged (even required) to expeditiously report "bad news" to facilitate timely "damage control" – whether involving customer service, a military operation or security-related intelligence. An organization that instead reverts to the "blame game" has the wrong kind of leadership.

The bottom line is that when a political narrative and/or political correctness drives decision-making, many lives might suffer for such a breakdown in leadership. Thus, the timeless words of JFK bear repeating:

"Let us not seek the Republican answer or the Democratic answer, but the right answer. Let us not seek to fix the blame for the past. Let us accept our own responsibility for the future."

Beyond the current circumstance of our two major political parties, or tribes, putting their own interests above the American people, along with a complicit media all too happy to perpetuate and accentuate their often visceral conflict, the United States is also at a distinct disadvantage relative to the rest of the world. We might be an "exceptional nation" in respect to our compassion for our fellow man and freedoms, most notably of speech and of/from religion, but our democratic republic and an election cycle that results in new leadership (in virtually all key positions) every four to eight years, puts us at a huge disadvantage to particularly our adversaries – most notably today, the re-emergence of Russia under Vladimir Putin, who has personally enjoyed positions of power and influence dating back to the Cold War. We have clearly been outmatched and outplayed over at least the past two, if not three, administrations.

I am not suggesting that we dramatically change our system of government, or rewrite the US Constitution, but I am saying, **we** are saying, that Americans need to become not only more self-aware, but particularly better educated relative to the world around and increasingly within us. Our cultural and situational awareness, particularly relevant to world cultures and religions, is sorely lacking. Starting in K-12, but essentially in all of our public and private education, Americans need to increasingly reach out to others, first recognizing the values we share as fellow human beings, respecting our differences, and, ultimately, embrace the richness that will come with higher levels of mutual understanding and respect across our common-yet-nuanced species. Education should enhance our awareness and respect for one another, but the political correctness that currently permeates our schools, inhibiting constructive dialogue, must be seen for its destructive nature having the opposite effect of its alleged intent. Too often, it seems, particularly among the younger generations, we have an ongoing struggle between the Realists and the Idealists. In a conceptual "Continuum of Life," with hard core "Realists" at one end and the most hopeful "Idealists" at the other, I sometimes challenge the audience to see if they can't find their own "sweet spot" somewhere closer to the middle. Whether in business, religion or politics, we really do have to overcome the great divides that result from fixed or extreme positions.

Certainly, at a minimum, "Safe Places" and comparable refuge from hearing opinions other than your own, must be eliminated from institutions of "higher learning."

Why not strive to be a more *idealistic* Realist or *realistic* Idealist, find your common interests, achieve higher levels of mutual understanding and, at the very least, reduce the tension, mistrust or fear to start bridging those divides that likely should not have been there to begin with? This can only come from open dialogue, not by hiding from one another or by providing institutionalized insulation from opposing views.

Today, we have a very real "external" threat in the form of ISIS/ISIL/IS or DAESH, Al Qaeda, Boko Haram and others driven by a radicalized ideology that is inspiring "Lone Wolf" attacks such as we have seen most recently in San Bernardino, Orlando, Dallas and Baton

322

Rouge – against both "soft targets" and police. Whether inspired by Islamism or racism, these attacks are equally deadly. Americans are further shaken by what appears to be the disintegration of our belief in "equal justice for all" as we see so many instances of misconduct, security lapses, criminal transgressions and the "extremely reckless" handling of our country's most sensitive secrets – for which few-to-no pubic servants, elected or appointed, are held accountable.

We Need Inspiring Humanists and Thought-Provokers

Perhaps the truest "Uniter," certainly not a divider, of the past decade, has to be Pope Francis. Whatever your faith or politics, this man is finding ways to build or repair bridges across the many divides. As evidenced by other quotes seeded throughout this book, the Dalai Lama is similarly doing his best to bring the world together in thoughts and deeds – likewise reaching out to those of all faiths or belief systems. Sadly, in 2014, we lost Maya Angelou, equally profound in her poetry, philosophy and messaging.

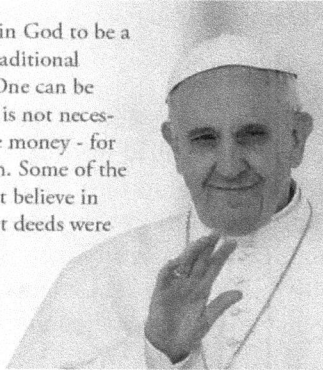

It is not necessary to believe in God to be a good person. In a way, the traditional notion of God is outdated. One can be spiritual but not religious. It is not necessary to go to church and give money - for many, nature can be a church. Some of the best people in history did not believe in God, while some of the worst deeds were done in His name.
-POPE FRANCIS

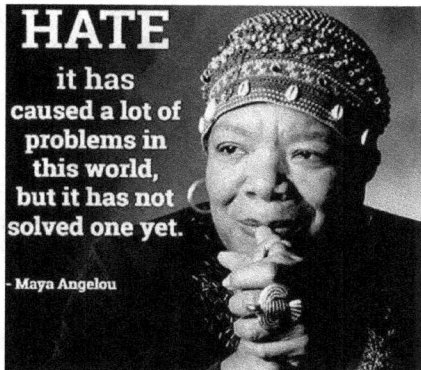

HATE it has caused a lot of problems in this world, but it has not solved one yet.
- Maya Angelou

Appendices

Appendices A/B/F/J have come from Contributors Walker and Humayun, including extracts from their writings and where you can find more about:

A - "Jewish-Muslim Relations; the Qur'anic View" and "The Myth of the Islamic State"

B - "The "Great Game" (compelling piece on the "Durand Line")

F - The Constitution (Charter) of Medina

J - St. Catherine's Monastery, Mt. Sinai, Egypt

Appendix C is Pakistani blogger Sana Saleem's tribute to Nobel Peace Prize recipient Dr. Abdus Salam, of whom the Pakistani people and Muslims everywhere should be extremely proud. Sadly, Islamist-driven decrees declared him to be non-Muslim as a member of the Ahmadi sect.

Appendix D is an overview of an endeavor similar to the Jalalabad Schools project described in Chapter 24: The Green Village Schools (GVS) project, started in early 2001 by Dr. Mohammad Khan Kharoti and supported by Dr. Steve Boyer and others in the Portland, Oregon, area. I urge readers to strongly consider lending their support to this very worthwhile project that is making a huge difference in so many young lives in that very challenging and important part of the world.

Appendix E is an extract describing the "Saqi Shrine and Cemeteries" community outreach project that took place in Kirkuk, 2008-2009; reflecting an example of the efforts of Human Terrain Teams in Iraq and Afghanistan.

Appendix G is the full text of the United Nation's Universal Declaration of Human Rights, a foundational document to which several Muslim countries contributed, as well as Rotary International having a key role back in 1948.

Appendix H is Mohandas K. (better known as Mahatma) Gandhi's "Peace Prayers" that were drawn from the Ba'hai, Buddhist, Christian, Hindu, Islamic, Jewish, Native American, Shinto and Zoroastrian faiths.

Appendix I is especially for educators, offering ideas and supporting resources for more effectively teaching students about world religions and cultures, with some effort to clarify that the most challenging region often simply referred to as the "Middle East" often extends from North Africa to the Far East – confusing and confounding too many different cultures and millions of people by associating them all with radical Islam and the dreaded "Third World" label.

Appendices K is a "Top 10 List" of Ways to Prevent, Reduce or Resolve Conflict

Appendix L - "Peace through Rotary International" – Attorney, Businessman and Rotarian Dave Bateman offers his perspective with a concise overview of where and how Rotarians can contribute to a more peaceful and thriving world.

Appendix A

More about what Jewish-Muslim Relations should be; and The Myth of the Islamic State

The book *Jewish-Muslim Relations: The Qur'anic View,* written by contributors Abdullah Craig Walker and Arif Humayun, reveals the unity of faith that is at the heart of Judaism and Islam; and articulates the common historical and theological ground shared by the two religions. To this end, the book:

- Documents the abundance of references found throughout the Qur'an that venerate Israelites, Jews, Hebrew prophets, and the Torah, and which inform and illuminate Islamic history and teachings.

- Explores the history of Muslim-Jewish relations, including examination of the social, political and religious dynamics in Medina which circumscribed Muslim-Jewish relations when Prophet Muhammad (PBUH) and his followers migrated there from Mecca in 622 C.E.

- Probes the criticisms of Jews found in commentaries in the Qur'an that pertain to three wars that occurred in the 7th Century between Medina's Muslim, Arab, and Jewish tribes.

- Examines the contributions of Islamic scholars and jurists to Muslim-Jewish relations, with focus on the rules of governance concerning non-Muslims residing in regions under the jurisdiction of Muslim rulers.

This well-researched and documented book also discusses the emergence of ethnocentrism and anti-Semitism in Arab Muslim societies following the passing of the Islamic Golden Age in the 13th century, and which persists in more virulent forms in the present era of globalization.

*****

Gateways to this and other works by Walker and/or Humayun can be found at: http://www.circleofpeaceonline.org/

326

Appendix A (continued)

Two Abstracts from Arif Humayun

Jewish-Muslim Relations – The Qur'anic View
Posted on August 13, 2013 by Arif Humayun

The area of Jewish Muslim relations has not been well researched and is viewed through the lens of the current political climate in the Middle East. This paper traces the historical roots of the relationship between the followers of the two great Semitic faiths and documents the doctrinal commonality between them. This paper also traces the evolving relationship between Islam and Judaism, starting from the Holy Prophet's migration to Medina in 622 CE and through the demise of the Muslim Golden Age. To read or download this paper, click the following link:

http://www.circleofpeaceonline.org/?s=jewish-muslim

THE MYTH OF THE ISLAMIC STATE
Posted on December 17, 2014 by Arif Humayun

The Islamic State (IS, ISIS or ISIL) is a Sunni extremist, jihadist, organization who, having captured territory in parts of Syria and Iraq, has proclaimed the establishment of an Islamic Caliphate. The unashamed brutality of IS has terrified governments around the world. The exploitation of Islam for their consolidation of power and popularity in Iraq, Syria and growing has shocked many in the Muslim world. For the complete article, click on the following link:

https://globalengage.org/faith-international-affairs/articles/the-myth-of-the-islamic-state

Appendix B

Excerpts from the SILK ROAD JOURNAL ®

By Abdullah Craig Walker - Lahore: April 2015

THE GREAT GAME AND AN INTERNATIONAL BORDER THAT DEFIES COMMON SENSE

INTRODUCTION - The Durand Line is arguably the most contentious international border in the world today... The 2,640 kilometer-long border, de facto, divides Pakistan and Afghanistan. It was drawn in up in 1893 by the British Colonial Office to serve the geopolitical interests of the British Crown at the time. With no intrinsic geophysical distinctions, it defies common sense, and appears to be another arbitrary "line in the sand"; similar to how the Middle East was partitioned by British and French colonial powers in the 19th and 20th centuries. Comparable to volatile national boundaries in the Middle East, the Durand Line has been a catalyst for violent ethnic and tribal conflicts for more than a century. . .

Pakistan inherited the Durand Line following independence from the British in 1947... While Pakistan and the international community have accepted the Durand Line as the de jure international border separating the two countries, Kabul has not, nor have the tribes and ethnic groups residing in the region. Separatist movements and anti-state militancy along the Durand Line are rooted in the refusal of these tribes and ethnic groups to acknowledge the paramountcy of the nation-state system itself, let alone the legitimacy of political decisions concerning their indigenous lands made in Kabul and Islamabad. As a consequence, neither Pakistan nor Afghanistan has been able to establish its sovereignty in the region. . .

THE GREAT GAME - The "Great Game" referred originally to the strategic rivalry between the British and Russian Empires for supremacy in Central Asia between 1813 and 1907. In the postcolonial period following World War II, the term was resurrected to describe the Cold War conflict-by-proxy between the U.S. and the Soviet Union in Afghanistan. Today, the Great Game references the geopolitical competition among the dominant world powers – the U.S., Britain, Russia, Saudi Arabia, India, Iran, and China -- for hegemony in the oil, gas, and mineral-rich geo-strategic region of the former Silk Road. . .

The game-changer in the Great Game was the Soviet invasion of Afghanistan in 1979. The Cold War conflict played out on Afghan soil in the 9-year war that followed between the Soviet Union and multi-national Muslim insurgent groups known as the Mujahideen. . .

The back-story, however, was not about anti-communism. Following the Soviet Union's withdrawal from Afghanistan in 1989, the focus of the Great Game shifted to oil, and intense competition for access to oil and gas in the Middle East and Caspian Sea Basin. . .

President George H. W. Bush's advocacy for an oil and natural gas pipeline from the Caspian Sea Basin, running through Turkmenistan, Afghanistan, and Pakistan to the Arabian Sea, led to deepening U.S. involvement in the volatile region of the Durand Line. . .

THREATS TO REGIONAL SECURITY AND PEACE - Afghanistan and Pakistan are ranked among the top ten Fragile States on an index of 178 states developed by the U.S.-based Fund for Peace. Fragile states are defined as "weak and failing states that pose significant threats and challenges to the international community." In today's world, with its highly globalized economy, inter-dependent security, and synergistic information systems, the socio-political and economic pressures within one fragile state can have serious repercussions not only for that state and its people, but also for its neighbors and other states across the globe. . .

On the Afghan side of the Durand Line, the prevailing threats to regional peace that are playing out today include the absence of the state's writ in most areas of the country, violent religious extremism, tribalism, communalism, sectarian insurrection, corruption, and the immense drug trade in opium, heroin, and hashish. On Pakistan's side of the porous border, volatile relations with Afghanistan, the ongoing insurgencies in Balochistan and Kashmir, tribalism and communalism, religious extremism and terrorism, the opium-heroin-hashish drug trade, and pervasive corruption have undermined Pakistan's writ in its northern areas, as well as in parts of Sindh, including Karachi. The problems accruing in the region of the Durand Line are spilling over now into all of Pakistan, constituting an existential threat to the nation's sovereignty. . .

TERRORISM - The historic irony of jihadi terrorism is that it evolved out of the Cold War battle between the Soviet Union and the U.S. and its allies that took place in Afghanistan between 1979 and 1988. The Soviet army and its Afghan forces fought against multinational insurgent groups -- the Mujahideen -- composed primarily of Sunni insurgents. They received military training in Pakistan and China, and were supplied with weapons and billions of dollars in aid by the U.S., England, and Saudi Arabia. . .

The Muslim insurgents believed they were fighting a religious war – jihad – against infidel non-believers ...Following the war, the Mujahideen morphed in anti-state jihadists intent upon forcing Islamic political-religious governance upon Afghanistan and Pakistan. The religious-based terrorism and Shi'a-Sunni communalism that is terrorizing the region today is a direct consequence of the war between the Soviets and the western-backed Mujahideen in Afghanistan. . .

Today, the violent jihadist organizations...have morphed into virtual death cults. The men and women who form the cadre of terrorists and suicide bombers awaiting their assignments believe that the ultimate aim of human life is martyrdom, i.e. to die in battle "protecting" Islam ...Now that the Pakistan military is routing the militants from their hideouts along the Durand Line, these so-called "martyrs" are choosing "soft targets" to terrorize and divide Pakistan society. The systematic row-by-row execution of 137 school children in the Army Public School in Peshawar in December 2014 is a recent example of the barbaric acts being committed in the name of religion, which are occurring with increasing frequency on both sides of the Durand Line.. . .

SAUDI ARABIA - Saudi Arabia's contribution to this ideological witches' brew is twofold. Saudi clerics and private donors in the Gulf States fund and support Islamist madrassas (i.e. religious seminaries) in Pakistan and Afghanistan that propagate Wahhabism, a puritanical and intolerant version of Islam that condemns Shi'a, Sufi, and Ahmadiyya Muslim sects as apostates, and non-Muslims as infidels. The ideology promulgated by these madrassas underpins Sunni religious extremism and communalism. The madrassas are an important source of manpower for the militant religious movements that threaten Muslim communities on both sides of the Durand line. Reportedly, they also are a breeding ground for so-called "martyrs", who are taught – some from childhood – that an act of violent jihad against "infidels" is an act for which they are promised "eternal reward" in heaven. In practice, the consequences of this perversion of the Qur'an and the Sunnah have resulted in assassinations and suicide bombings targeting anyone -- Muslim and non-Muslim -- identified as apostate or infidel by the terrorist groups that sponsor the attacks. . .

Saudi Arabia's deepening rift with Iran, which is undermining Shi'a and Sunni Muslim relations throughout the Middle East, is the Saudis' other destabilizing contribution in the Durand Line region. Essentially, the rift is about the pricing and marketing of oil, political hegemony in the Middle East, and the long-term survival of the House of Saud monarchy. Nevertheless, the stage set is the doctrinal Sunni-Shi'a schism rooted in Islam's history. . .

OPIUM - The metaphoric elephant in the room is Afghanistan's multi-billion dollar opium trade. According to the United Nations Office on Drugs and Crime (UNODC), Afghanistan produces more than 90% of the world's illicit opium supply, and is at risk of becoming a "fragmented criminal state". . .

UNODC estimates that the annual revenue generated by Afghan opiate trafficking to and through Pakistan exceeds $1 billion, and that the illicit trade in ascetic anhydride, used to produce heroin, is of a similar value. . .

Opium and hashish production in Afghanistan play multiple roles -- funding anti-state tribal war lords and jihadist terrorist networks, while simultaneously fueling massive government corruption in Afghanistan and Pakistan. The consensus among western counter-narcotics officials is that the global war on terrorism cannot be successfully prosecuted until the terrorist-opium/hashish connection is severed. Nor will it be possible to establish political stability and develop viable democratic institutions in the Durand Line region given existing narco-state conditions. . .

WATER - Barely noted among the more sensational threats in the region are severe water shortages in Bangladesh, India, and Pakistan. Climate scientists predict ever-increasing water shortages in the Punjab due to climate change, threatening agricultural productivity and, in turn, regional political stability. . .

POLIO - Last year, Africa was declared polio-free. In India, with a population almost seven times larger than Pakistan, the disease has been eradicated entirely. However, Afghanistan and Pakistan report a very different narrative. This past year, 86 per cent of the cases of polio reported worldwide – 306 out of 356 new cases of polio – have originated in Pakistan. In spite of hundreds of millions of international donor dollars spent on polio eradication in the two countries, the World Health Organization (WHO)...has declared that the spread of polio in Pakistan constitutes a Public Health Emergency of International Concern (PHEIC) ...Ultimately, the problem at the heart of the failed anti-polio campaigns is the absence of state writ -- the power and authority of the governments of Pakistan and Afghanistan to implement and enforce their national laws and provide security to their citizens in the Durand Line region, which includes Balochistan, as well as Pakistan's largest city, Karachi. . .

NATURAL RESOURCES - Competition and conflict over the region's natural resources plays heavily into the geopolitical narrative of the Durand Line. Oil and natural gas reserves in Iran and the Caspian Sea Basin continue in play ...Of growing significance are the untapped metal and mineral resources in Afghanistan and Pakistan's Sindh province, which are being targeted by state and multi-national interests in India, Europe, the U.S., and China ...The estimated value of the huge deposits runs into trillions of U.S. Dollars ...They include iron, copper, cobalt, gold, and industrial metals essential to modern industry including lithium (the mineral used in Laptop and Cell phone batteries), and niobium (a soft metal used in producing superconducting steel). The strategic deposits, reportedly, are so large that they could transform Afghanistan and Pakistan into the most important mining centers in the world.. . .

INDIA - India's involvement in Afghanistan illustrates the high stakes at play in the Great Game. Under the Taliban regime, Afghanistan became a proxy in the undeclared war between India and Pakistan. The Great Game between China and India is accelerating with China's dramatic entry into west Asia via its proposed China-Pakistan Economic Corridor (CPEC). . .

CHINA - China is emerging as the biggest player in the Great Game. China's multi-billion dollar China-Pakistan Economic Corridor (CPEC) initiative will connect China by land and sea to Central and

South Asia, West Asia and Europe. CPEC proposes to create land and sea transportation routes from Pakistan and Afghanistan to China, as well as underwrite crucial energy and infrastructure projects in Pakistan and other countries impacted by the CPEC. . .

China's overarching strategic foreign policy objective Vis a vis the CPEC initiative – and its crowning move in the Great Game – is to turn its national currency, the Renminbi, into a global reserve currency. The world's financial markets are looking for an alternative to the U.S. dollar as the only reserve currency...The Renminbi is the only currency that has the potential to meet the criteria to become a viable reserve currency in the international monetary system. . .

AMERICA - The geopolitical priorities and elated policies of the United States are infused in every issue and conflict in the region. The vast economic and military power of the world's remaining empire factor into virtually every issue and event mentioned, and underlay America's recent foreign policy "tilt" toward Asia. . .

The U.S. launched its war against the Taliban in October 2001 immediately following the September 11th Twin Tower attack. The declared objective of Operation Enduring Freedom was to dismantle al-Qaeda and deny it a base of operation in Afghanistan by removing the Taliban from power. However, the back-story was about oil. . .

The overarching factor that frames America's involvement in this energy-rich region, however, is the preeminent role of the U.S. dollar in the international monetary system. The dollar is the principal currency in which oil is priced and marketed. Accordingly, the dollar is the world's primary reserve currency and medium of exchange in world trade. The countries of the world must maintain dollar reserves to purchase oil and to engage in international trade, thereby creating nearly unlimited demand for the dollar. . .

However, the current credible threat to the dollar's hegemony in the global economy is not exclusively about petrodollar interdependence. Rather, it is the growing legitimacy of China's Renminbi as a potential alternative reserve currency ... The acme of Great Games between the U.S. and China is afoot, and is being played out on the world's monetary stage . . .

CONCLUSION - The Sunni-Shi'a schism, China's Indian Ocean port and aggressive economic incursions into the region, Afghanistan's calamitous drug trade, jihadi terrorism, climate change and water wars, incendiary communal conflicts and separatist insurgencies in the Durand Line region are daunting, if not flat-out unmanageable. It is an irony of history that has placed the Durand Line at the heart of this geopolitical Gordian knot. . .

Kabul and Islamabad have been unable to establish their writ over the territories that comprise their countries. The ethnic and tribal alienation at the root of this dilemma empower the anti-state narratives of religious militants, further contributing to the volatility and anarchy that prevail in the region. The conflated imbroglio not only threatens the sovereignty of Afghanistan and Pakistan, but also jeopardizes stability and security throughout the west Asian region.. .

The governments of viable nation-states monopolize the use of force to ensure the safety and security of their citizens. While in weak and failing states, criminals and anti-state elements expropriate the use of violence for their own nefarious purposes with minimal consequences... Herein lies the nut of the problem: governance, or the absence thereof, in one of the most volatile and ethnically diverse regions in the world . . .

These multiple crises are compounded by the fact that Pakistan is a nuclear-armed state surrounded by three other nuclear powers, and a fourth – Iran, which most likely will become one in the foreseeable future. . .

The lack of legitimacy of the Durand Line, and the vacuum of power and sovereignty in the two conflicted, strategically located countries, rank with the gravest geopolitical problems of the 21st century, right up there with climate change, nuclear weapons proliferation, and overpopulation. . .

The common denominator in this geopolitical Gordian knot is the Durand Line, where virtual anarchy reigns and the proverbial Dark Force is positioned to ignite a conflagration with the potential to burn down the world. . .

Appendix C

Salam Sahab, we have failed you
Sana Saleem — Published Jan 30, 2012 01:10pm

Mohammad Abdus Salam (1926-1996) was his full name, which may add to the knowledge of those who wish he was either not Ahmadi or Pakistani. The man proudly lived and died as both, and much more, as Pakistan disowned him, in life and in death. The government denied him the honour of a state funeral; the media remained absent from the burial ceremony at Rabwah, which has since been renamed not after Abdus Salam but as Chenab Nagar, just to spite its Ahmadi residents.

Yesterday marked the 85th Birthday of Dr.Abdus Salam, theoretical physicist and the only Pakistani Nobel Laureate. He is not our national hero; his name is rarely ever mentioned; in his life the only befitting 'honour' we could provide him was a life in self exile. In his death, however, we went a step ahead by blanking out the term 'Muslim' from his epitaph. A member of the Pakistan Atomic Energy Commission, a member of the Scientific Commission of Pakistan and the Chief Scientific Adviser to the President, Salam was one of the most prolific researchers in theoretical elementary particle physics. No minister or high government official attended his funeral... He was an Ahmadi.

Happy Birthday Salam Sahab, we have failed you.

Over 5,000 gathered in Rawalpindi yesterday, blaring witness to the systematic hate, prejudice that has been curtailed by a whole series of ordinances, acts and constitutional amendments against the Ahmadiyya community, that had been the cause of Salaam's self-exile four decades ago. Nothing has changed since for the Ahmadis. It has only gotten worse. The rally called out by traders' associations was attended by activists of Jamaatud Dawa, Jamaat-i-Islami, Sipah Sahaba (banned organisation), and Ahle Sunnat Wal Jamaat in Rawalpindi, claimed that a 'worship place' belonging to the Ahmadiya community was built without permission. The irony of protest on land encroachments by parties who themselves have been involved in extortion and land encroachments is immeasurable. But it was not long until the

335

real incentive became clear. A few weeks ago anti-Ahmadi banners appeared in the same area, threatening the residents to leave, claiming their existence was unconstitutional and any restraint from them could lead to 'repercussions.' Terrified, no one spoke. If you are a Pakistani passport holder, chances are you have signed a declaration claiming Qadianis as non-Muslims. This means that you declare them prohibited from calling themselves 'Muslim,' to call their 'places of worship' mosques, to pray in 'Muslim mosques' or 'public prayer areas', to give azaan, to greet others with "salaam," to publicly quote from the Quran – these acts, amongst others, could get one up to three years in prison.

Now they want to take away their right to worship. Through intimidation and hate mongering, speakers at the conference yesterday blatantly announced that there will be 100,000 Qadri's raging against the Ahmadis, issuing an ultimatum to the Ahmadiyya community to stop praying. If they do and if the authorities fail to take action against the open call for aggression and violence, you and I will be responsible for authorising prejudice, for remaining silent in the face of aggression, for letting the hatred breed within our society, for not standing up for one of our own, and for allowing men driven by their convoluted faith to kill in the name of God.

If being party to vigilantism burdens your conscience, voice your concern, stand up and be counted.

Our state reminds me of Faiz's words that he had scribbled in Dr. Abdus Salam's diary when they met at an airport. 'Nisar mein teri galiyon kay aye watan kay jahan Chali hai rasm kay koi na sar utha kay chaley' (My salutations to thy sacred streets, O beloved nation! Where a tradition has been invented - that none shall walk with his head held high) jo koii chaahanewaalaa tawaaf ko nikale nazar churaa ke chale, jism-o-jaan bachaa ke chale (If at all one takes a walk, a pilgrimage One must walk, eyes lowered, the body crouched in fear).

Sana Saleem blogs at Global Voices, Asian Correspondent, The Guardian and her personal blog Mystified Justice. She recently won the Best Activist Blogger award by CIO & Google at the Pakistan Blogger Awards. She can be found on Facebook and tweets at twitter.com/sanasaleem.

Appendix D

~ One of Many Ways YOU Can Make a Difference ~

The Green Village Schools Project
http://www.greenvillageschools.org/

An Overview and Brief History

In March 2001 (before 9/11), Dr. Mohammad Khan Kharoti, an Afghan American physician, began supporting classes for ten boys and six girls in the Kharoti family compound where he grew up in Shin Kalay, a village of 11,000 in Helmand Province of southern Afghanistan. The country at that time was under the control of the Taliban and the education project was undertaken with their consent,

School construction

including instruction for girls. Two literate women from another village were hired as teachers for the girls. Mohammad personally funded the construction of three classrooms within the family compound. But as the demand for classes increased, the teaching space was stretched to capacity. Some students had to remain outside the classrooms and sit or lie on the floor as they worked on lessons.

Back home in Portland, Oregon, Green Village Schools (GVS) was officially recognized as a US charity and, with new funding available, Mohammad met with the elders of Shin Kalay in 2003 to discuss with them the need to build a real school. Construction began immediately on half a hectare of

Class held at family compound

land owned by Mohammad's brother, Habib. In the ensuing years the educational complex eventually comprised eight classrooms for boys on one side of the school and eight for girls on the other, providing space for nine grades. A well was dug and an elevated storage tank, separate latrines for boys and girls, and a privacy wall around the entire complex were constructed. In addition, the complex contained a library which also served as a community center, and a computer lab was under construction.

By 2007, with about 800 boys and 400 girls the school was licensed by the Ministry of Education (MOE) in Afghanistan and they provided some financial support for teachers' salaries. Other support came from a diverse range of community and international partners. The Provincial Office of the Minister of Education records that over 2,400 students had attended the school during its short history. Then, in October 2008, the school in Shin Kalay was destroyed and looted by Punjabi speaking militants with uncertain motives. Over a period of three days, a backhoe was used to destroy much of the structure as unarmed villagers watched from a distance. Most of the furniture, supplies and materials (iron beams) were carried off.

Students in school yard

The school was replaced by mud brick classrooms built adjacent to the central mosque. Construction was financed by Afghan Appeal, a London based NGO, and teacher salaries were paid by GVS through June 2011. After that time the village elders had the responsibility of arranging with the MOE to pay teacher salaries. Enrollment in the mud brick classroom rose to about 700 boys while 170 girls were schooled in private homes because of continued unrest in the area for some time. In 2012 Afghan Appeal offered to finance the rebuilding on the site of the original school and work began with removal of the rubble, recycling of bricks and other material, and construction of new classrooms. The enrollment is up to 1200 boys and 600 girls with 35 government teaching positions. The school has 24 classrooms, several administrative offices, a canteen where students can purchase school supplies wholesale, separate computer labs for girls and boys, and, the most recent addition, a 300 square meter library.

In 2011 GVS, PeacePal (Albuquerque), and Afghan Sister Village Project (Los Alamos) had received a grant through a joint application to set up an Advanced Education Center (AEC) in Lashkar Gah. Mohammad spent five months in Afghanistan setting up the project. The center was equipped with 30 computers and internet access via a

VSAT (very small aperture terminal) system. Afghan teachers were interviewed via Skype and four of them, all university graduates, were hired for computer and English instruction. The English teachers completed a TESOL (Teaching English to Students of Other Languages) course over the internet. The first class of 240 students, almost half of them female, received certificates in June 2012. In the second year of the AEC, we received a smaller grant and enrolled slightly fewer students and when funding ended at the end of the third year, we closed the center.

Our goal at the school in Shin Kalay has long been to add advanced English and computers to the government curriculum. With this in mind, four teachers from the Wahidi English Language and Computer Center in Lashkar Gah, began English classes for 60 boys and 27 Shin Kalay teachers this summer. GVS is paying half of the tuition while parents pay the rest. Girls are not yet involved because the center has no female teachers and the parents are not yet ready to help with tuition for daughters. We want them to have equal access so we are working to solve these challenges. When we closed the Advanced Education Center, we moved the computers to the labs in Shin Kalay. Operation of the labs with access to the internet awaits funding for solar panels. We want the students and staff to be able to communicate with others both inside and outside Afghanistan which requires a reasonable level of English as well as computer literacy. The keyboards do not have Pashtu script.

In the meantime, we have graduated the first 12th grade of boys from the new school and girls' classes have reached the 6th grade level. A large number of boys and several girls from the original school have graduated from high school and gone on to higher education. In fact, three girls are now in their fourth year of medical school. With these role models from the community, the hunger for education among students and parents alike is so strong that additional classrooms are the current highest priority. We are beginning construction on the second floor of the new school with space for an additional 24 more rooms. Again, funding is limiting how quickly we can meet the needs of the community.

School building destroyed in 2008

For more information on how you might help with this extraordinary project in one of the more challenging parts of Afghanistan, Helmand Province, please visit the website below. You will be honoring not only the efforts of Dr. Kharoti and so many brave and determined Afghans, but also the other foreign personnel who have worked so hard to bring a better life to the people of Afghanistan – especially to the children.

http://www.greenvillageschools.org/

Girls' computer class at AEC

Appendix E

Saqi Shrine and Cemeteries
A Community Outreach Project
Identifying Opportunities to Repair and Build Cultural Bridges Across the Human Terrain

"Sultan Saqi" Shrine and Cemetery located on Al Hurria Air Base (FOB Warrior), Kirkuk, Iraq

On November 4, 2008, five years into Operation Iraqi Freedom (OIF), Human Terrain Team (HTT) members inquired about this cemetery and what appeared to be a Mosque located on this joint Coalition Forces (CF) and Iraqi air base. This paper will describe the collaborative effort that ensued with the intent to focus upon this sacred site as a catalyst for a community outreach project. Our ultimate goal was to put the senior-ranking Iraqi Air Force (IQAF) Base Commander in the lead as part of ongoing efforts to legitimize the Government of Iraq (GoI) in the eyes of the Iraqi people – of all ethnicities and religions.

Executive Summary

Is there something on or near your base that might have cultural significance? An important component of preparing for a tour in Iraq or Afghanistan is developing cultural awareness. During Human Terrain training, one of the examples of how this can make a difference for our military forces involved partnering with a neighboring village to repair and restore a damaged Mosque that was located next to the Forward Operating Base (FOB). This was not only well received by the local population, feeling that their culture and religion were being respected by the CF, but was credited with an almost immediate decrease or cessation of incoming rockets and mortars onto the base.

As we more closely partner with the Iraqi Army (IA), Iraqi Police (IP), and any other form of Iraqi Security Forces (ISF), we should all be alert to opportunities where we can actively mentor these forces relative to Civil Affairs (CA) operations and Community Policing practices that deliver not only respect to the population being served, but also various forms of humanitarian aid (HA) and compassion.

This project began with inquiries about what appeared to be a Mosque and cemetery on the Kirkuk Air Base (FOB Warrior). These inquiries, both here in Kirkuk and through our CONUS-based support network, ultimately led to connecting the Kirkuk Provincial Council's Religious Affairs Committee (RAC) with base Chaplains, and enhanced cooperation between USAF, Army, Provincial Reconstruction Team (PRT), US Army Corps of Engineers (USACE) and the Iraqi Air Force. This collaborative journey continues to grow and expand, and now extends to the coordinated distribution of HA from US military families at Yakota AB in Japan to orphanages and single parent (widow) shelters throughout the Kirkuk province.

"To Protect and Serve" is a common motto among many American law enforcement agencies. In years past, under several regimes, Iraqis only saw their military and police as representatives of a government intent upon controlling them through violence and intimidation. The notion of armed ISF actually protecting and serving their communities might take years of actual practice. Here in Kirkuk, thanks to a beloved USAF Chaplain and 11,000 pounds of donated clothing, school supplies and toys from his former congregation in Japan, the connections and relationships developed through this outreach project have facilitated a coordinated distribution of these goods through the 2nd Brigade Combat Team's Civil Affairs elements, working side-by-side with their ISF counterparts. These Iraqi soldiers and police are experiencing firsthand the gratification that accompanies this broader aspect of their roles. By involving the RAC to identify the orphanages, shelters, and their counterparts in the outlying districts, Iraqis are involved in both the planning and execution.

"Nothing succeeds like success" - especially when accompanied by the eyes and smiles of the children and their single mothers (widowed by this conflict) on the receiving end of this truly global and international extension of good will – invigorated by this multi-agency and multi-national partnership to elevate focus on cultural heritage.

Introduction

Among the many challenges recognized early by the Kirkuk HTT was how to best engage the local population without simply being another group of foreigners coming around asking the same questions as those who went before us, writing notes relative to the expressed needs and wants, followed by inaction. "Make no promises" was as important as "do no harm" relative to our mission in support of non-lethal engagements and operations. As we explored what was and was not known about Kirkuk and its very diverse and complex population, we soon realized that relatively little was known compared to the rest of the country. "Success stories" of other teams, shared during Human Terrain training, included the identification of damaged or otherwise neglected Mosques and other culturally sacred sites near or adjacent to Forward Operating Bases (FOB's) and smaller outposts. Once the local populations were engaged and supported in the repair and restoration of these sites, honoring their culture and religion, mutual respect and trust grew. More significantly, incidents of direct or indirect fire (IDF) onto these nearby CF bases diminished or stopped altogether. We hoped that this effort on FOB Warrior would help to develop Courses of Action (COA's) that might have a similar effect, starting with the neighboring population and extending to the rest of the Kirkuk province.

What's in a name? When making initial contact with BG Shihab at his headquarters, it was noted that on the face of his building and on a map inside that our "FOB Warrior" was apparently known as the "Al Hurria Air Base" to the Iraqis. Inquiries about this revealed that "Hurria" means liberty or freedom. However, this name was also associated with Saddam Hussein's regime under which no one felt especially liberated or free. That said, BG Shihab and his staff stated that referring to the base as "Al Hurria" or "Kirkuk Airport," consistent with signage outside gates 2 and 3, would be well received by the surrounding population. This discovery was shared with 18 EN BDE's and then 2/1 CAV's Information Operations (IO) Working Group (WG). As a result, "Kirkuk Airport" and/or "Al Hurria Air Base" now appears on just about every administrative (internal) and IO/PSYOP product – both by the USAF/Army CF elements as well as the Provincial Reconstruction Team (PRT).

Background

The Air Base: It is generally believed that a much smaller Kirkuk air base was established between 1955-1960. We have thus far been unable to determine its original boundaries, and there does not appear to be any record of the basis for its location (e.g. whether or not the ethnicity of the residents was a consideration). In the end, it was the Turkmen of Tis'Ayn and Bilawah who ultimately gave up their homes and property – violently and without compensation. Using the Saqi Shrine and well-established trees as reference points, current Tis'Ayn residents claim that their homes and neighborhood once comprised over one half of the current dimensions of the base.

Demographics: Kirkuk's population today is generally estimated to be approximately 1.2 million. Turkmen were once the larger segment in the city (estimated at around 40% from the last "legitimate" census taken in 1957) before various forms of "Arabization" commenced under President Abd Kareem Qassim, and subsequently under Saddam Hussein.

Note: [First 4 of a 27-page report; reflecting one of many such projects as but one example of the many efforts of Human Terrain Teams deployed to Iraq and Afghanistan]

Appendix F

The Constitution (Charter) of Medina

(Contributed by Abdullah Craig Walker and Arif Humayun)

Prior to the migration from Mecca to Medina in 622 C.E. by Prophet Mohammad (pbuh) and his followers – the Hijrah, the dominant Jewish tribes in Medina allowed the pagan Arab tribe of Banu Qaylah to settle on uncultivated land around the small desert community. The Banu Qaylah was divided into two major clans – the Aws and the Khazraj. Various developments in the latter part of the 6th century weakened the Jewish community's hold on Medina, and the Banu Qaylah tribe became dominant. However, hostility among the Arab clans resulted in continual fighting. The Arab clans had allies among the Jewish tribes, who aided them in their conflicts. In a decisive battle fought just before the Prophet's (pbuh) migration, the victorious Aws clan became the dominant authority in Medina.

Ten years after Muhammad's (pbuh) first revelation on Mount Hira a delegation consisting of representatives from Medina's Arab clans, including the Aws and Khazrai, invited the Prophet (pbuh) to come to Medina. They pledged to protect Muhammad (pbuh) if he would come as a neutral outsider and serve as chief arbitrator for the tribal community, which had been fighting with each other for decades. A few months prior to the Prophet's (pbuh) migration, Jewish converts to Islam from Medina also invited Muhammad (pbuh) to Medina. It is estimated seventy Jewish men and women from Medina accepted Islam while performing pilgrimage in Mecca. The significance of these events was the fact that Muhammad (pbuh) was esteemed and trusted by both Arabs and Jews, and that Islam's message was able to unite women and men from different regions, clans, social classes, and religious beliefs.

In 622 C.E., the Prophet (pbuh) migrated to Medina amid its contentious political environment, prepossessing a symbolic presence rivaling Medina's embattled leaders. Accordingly, his arrival was perceived as a threat to those in power, as well as to those benefiting from the status quo. The Jewish tribes were concerned about the Prophet's (pbuh) intentions, and were divided in their recognition of the similarities of Islam's monotheistic message with their own scriptures. Prior to the Prophet's (pbuh) arrival, Medina's Jewish leaders

345

had spoken out in opposition to the claim that he is the "final" Prophet, and also questioned elements of the Qur'an which they thought contradicted Hebrew scriptures.

The amalgam of the political, social, and religious conflicts in Medina were destabilizing and fraught with danger. Given the terms of his invitation, Prophet Mohammad (pbuh) proceeded to create peace in the community upon his arrival. His efforts resulted in a tripartite agreement between Medina's Muslim converts and those who had migrated from Mecca, the Arabs from the Khazraj and Aws clans, and Medina's Jewish tribes. This agreement, known as the Sahifat in Arabic, is better known today as the Constitution of Medina.

The Constitution of Medina (also known as The Medina Charter or the Charter of Medina) was written and promulgated by Prophet Muhammad (pbuh) on behalf of the ten-thousand multi-religious citizens of the state of Medina in 622 AD. It is a remarkable political-constitutional document and it is regarded by scholars as the first written constitution of human history upon which all the later constitutions were founded.

The Sahifat was based on an inclusive conception of the rule of law, with two basic principles: the safeguarding of individual rights by impartial judicial authority, and the principle of equality before the law. The terms of the agreement recognized the diverse ethnic, religious and secular affiliations of the signatories – Jews, Muslims, Medina natives, Meccan immigrants, the Arab Aws and Khazraj clans, and did not demand conversion to Islam. The community created by the Sahifat became known as the ummah, a term describing the totality of individuals living in Medina who were bound to one another by the Sahifat.

As a rudimentary basis of civil law, the primary purpose of the Sahifat was the resolution of conflicts without violence. Accordingly, blood feuds were abolished, and all rights were given equally to Medina's citizens, regardless of religion, ethnicity or social position. The salient principles of the visionary Constitution of Medina included:
1. The signatories formed a common ummah, or nationality.
2. The signatories were to remain united in peace and in war.
3. If any of the parties were attacked by an enemy, the others would defend it with their combined forces.
4. None of the parties would give shelter to the Qurayshi of Mecca, or make any secret treaty with them.
5. The various signatories were free to profess their own religion.

6. Bloodshed, murder and violence were forbidden.
7. The city of Medina was to be regarded as sacred, and any strangers whocame under the protection of its citizens were to be treated the same as Medina's citizens.
8. All disputes were to be referred to Prophet Muhammad (PBUH) for arbitration and decision.

The Constitution of Medina is the first Constitution of democracy in the history of constitutional rule. Its principles were based on the Qur'an and sunnah. The Constitution expressed that freedom, justice, and equality were inherent to humanity itself. It also made clear that the Jews and Christians, along with the Muslims constituted a political unit of a new type of ummah or community. The Jews were not mentioned as separate tribes, but respectfully as Jews who are 'People of the Book' – as are Christians.

Historians agree that the Medina Constitution was successful in establishing:
- peace and security of the community
- religious freedom for all the community-members
- acceptance of Medina as a sacred place, which included barring all violence and weapons
- security of women
- stable inter-tribal relations
- the parameters for political alliances external to Medina
- a system for granting protection to individuals,
- a judicial system for resolving disputes
- a regulated system for the paying of blood-money

The Constitution established Medina's ethnic minorities as equal to the majority in a brotherhood that formed one community or ummah wahidah (i.e. one nation). The objectives of the rules enunciated in the Constitution were to maintain peace and cooperation, to protect the life and property of all citizens, to eliminate aggression and injustice regardless of tribal or religious affiliations, and to ensure freedom of religion and movement. Indeed, the Constitution of Medina placed the rules of justice over and above religious solidarity, and affirmed the right of the victims of aggression and injustice to restitution regardless of tribal and religious affiliations. The Constitution defined the political rights and duties of all citizens – Muslims and non-Muslims, and created the political structure of the of the first Islamic state as a multi-tribal, multi-religious society. The significance of this achievement today relative to Muslim religious extremism is self-evident.

Appendix G

United Nations
Universal Declaration of Human Rights
Source: http://www.youthforhumanrights.org/

AN INTRODUCTION

On October 24, 1945, in the aftermath of World War II, the United Nations came into being as an intergovernmental organization, with the purpose of saving future generations from the devastation of international conflict.

United Nations representatives from all regions of the world formally adopted the Universal Declaration of Human Rights on December 10, 1948.

The Charter of the United Nations established six principal bodies, including the General Assembly, the Security Council, the International Court of Justice, and in relation to human rights, an Economic and Social Council (ECOSOC).

The UN Charter empowered ECOSOC to establish "commissions in economic and social fields and for the promotion of human rights...." One of these was the United Nations Human Rights Commission, which, under the chairmanship of Eleanor Roosevelt, saw to the creation of the Universal Declaration of Human Rights.

The Declaration was drafted by representatives of all regions of the world and encompassed all legal traditions. Formally adopted by the United Nations on December 10, 1948, it is the most universal human rights document in existence, delineating the thirty fundamental rights that form the basis for a democratic society.

Following this historic act, the Assembly called upon all Member Countries to publicize the text of the Declaration and "to cause it to be disseminated, displayed, read and expounded principally in schools and other educational institutions, without distinction based on the political status of countries or territories."

Today, the Declaration is a living document that has been accepted as a contract between a government and its people throughout the world. According to the Guinness Book of World Records, it is the most translated document in the world.

UNIVERSAL DECLARATION OF HUMAN RIGHTS
Official Document

Article 1. All human beings are born free and equal in dignity and rights. They are endowed with reason and conscience and should act towards one another in a spirit of brotherhood.

Article 2. Everyone is entitled to all the rights and freedoms set forth in this Declaration, without distinction of any kind, such as race, colour, sex, language, religion, political or other opinion, national or social origin, property, birth or other status.
Furthermore, no distinction shall be made on the basis of the political, jurisdictional or international status of the country or territory to which a person belongs, whether it be independent, trust, non-self-governing or under any other limitation of sovereignty.

Article 3. Everyone has the right to life, liberty and security of person.

Article 4. No one shall be held in slavery or servitude; slavery and the slave trade shall be prohibited in all their forms.

Article 5. No one shall be subjected to torture or to cruel, inhuman or degrading treatment or punishment.

Article 6. Everyone has the right to recognition everywhere as a person before the law.

Article 7. All are equal before the law and are entitled without any discrimination to equal protection of the law. All are entitled to equal protection against any discrimination in violation of this Declaration and against any incitement to such discrimination.

Article 8. Everyone has the right to an effective remedy by the competent national tribunals for acts violating the fundamental rights granted him by the constitution or by law.

Article 9. No one shall be subjected to arbitrary arrest, detention or exile.

Article 10. Everyone is entitled in full equality to a fair and public hearing by an independent and impartial tribunal, in the determination of his rights and obligations and of any criminal charge against him.

Article 11.
- Everyone charged with a penal offence has the right to be presumed innocent until proved guilty according to law in a public trial at which he has had all the guarantees necessary for his defence.
- No one shall be held guilty of any penal offence on account of any act or omission which did not constitute a penal offence, under national or international law, at the time when it was committed. Nor shall a heavier penalty be imposed than the one that was applicable at the time the penal offence was committed.

Article 12. No one shall be subjected to arbitrary interference with his privacy, family, home or correspondence, nor to attacks upon his honour and reputation. Everyone has the right to the protection of the law against such interference or attacks.

Article 13.
- Everyone has the right to freedom of movement and residence within the borders of each State.
- Everyone has the right to leave any country, including his own, and to return to his country.

Article 14.
- Everyone has the right to seek and to enjoy in other countries asylum from persecution.
- This right may not be invoked in the case of prosecutions genuinely arising from nonpolitical crimes or from acts contrary to the purposes and principles of the United Nations.

Article 15.
- Everyone has the right to a nationality.
- No one shall be arbitrarily deprived of his nationality nor denied the right to change his nationality.

Article 16.
- Men and women of full age, without any limitation due to race, nationality or religion, have the right to marry and to found a family. They are entitled to equal rights as to marriage, during marriage and at its dissolution.
- Marriage shall be entered into only with the free and full consent

of the intending spouses.
- The family is the natural and fundamental group unit of society and is entitled to protection by society and the State.

Article 17.
- Everyone has the right to own property alone as well as in association with others.
- No one shall be arbitrarily deprived of his property.

Article 18. Everyone has the right to freedom of thought, conscience and religion; this right includes freedom to change his religion or belief, and freedom, either alone or in community with others and in public or private, to manifest his religion or belief in teaching, practice, worship and observance.

Article 19. Everyone has the right to freedom of opinion and expression; this right includes freedom to hold opinions without interference and to seek, receive and impart information and ideas through any media and regardless of frontiers.

Article 20.
- Everyone has the right to freedom of peaceful assembly and association.
- No one may be compelled to belong to an association.

Article 21.
- Everyone has the right to take part in the government of his country, directly or through freely chosen representatives.
- Everyone has the right to equal access to public service in his country.
- The will of the people shall be the basis of the authority of government; this will shall be expressed in periodic and genuine elections which shall be by universal and equal suffrage and shall be held by secret vote or by equivalent free voting procedures.

Article 22. Everyone, as a member of society, has the right to social security and is entitled to realization, through national effort and international co-operation and in accordance with the organization and resources of each State, of the economic, social and cultural rights indispensable for his dignity and the free development of his personality.

Article 23. Everyone has the right to work, to free choice of employment, to just and favourable conditions of work and to protection against unemployment.

- Everyone, without any discrimination, has the right to equal pay for equal work.
- Everyone who works has the right to just and favourable remuneration ensuring for himself and his family an existence worthy of human dignity, and supplemented, if necessary, by other means of social protection.
- Everyone has the right to form and to join trade unions for the protection of his interests.

Article 24. Everyone has the right to rest and leisure, including reasonable limitation of working hours and periodic holidays with pay.

Article 25.
- Everyone has the right to a standard of living adequate for the health and well-being of himself and of his family, including food, clothing, housing and medical care and necessary social services, and the right to security in the event of unemployment, sickness, disability, widowhood, old age or other lack of livelihood in circumstances beyond his control.
- Motherhood and childhood are entitled to special care and assistance. All children, whether born in or out of wedlock, shall enjoy the same social protection.

Article 26.
- Everyone has the right to education. Education shall be free, at least in the elementary and fundamental stages. Elementary education shall be compulsory. Technical and professional education shall be made generally available and higher education shall be equally accessible to all on the basis of merit.
- Education shall be directed to the full development of the human personality and to the strengthening of respect for human rights and fundamental freedoms. It shall promote understanding, tolerance and friendship among all nations, racial or religious groups, and shall further the activities of the United Nations for the maintenance of peace.
- Parents have a prior right to choose the kind of education that shall be given to their children.

Article 27.

- Everyone has the right freely to participate in the cultural life of the community, to enjoy the arts and to share in scientific advancement and its benefits.
- Everyone has the right to the protection of the moral and material interests resulting from any scientific, literary or artistic production of which he is the author.

Article 28. Everyone is entitled to a social and international order in which the rights and freedoms set forth in this Declaration can be fully realized.

Article 29.

- Everyone has duties to the community in which alone the free and full development of his personality is possible.
- In the exercise of his rights and freedoms, everyone shall be subject only to such limitations as are determined by law solely for the purpose of securing due recognition and respect for the rights and freedoms of others and of meeting the just requirements of morality, public order and the general welfare in a democratic society.
- These rights and freedoms may in no case be exercised contrary to the purposes and principles of the United Nations.

Article 30. Nothing in this Declaration may be interpreted as implying for any State, group or person any right to engage in any activity or to perform any act aimed at the destruction of any of the rights and freedoms set forth herein.

Appendix H

Gandhi's Peace Prayers

Very early in his life, Mohandas K. Gandhi began to appreciate the universality of religion. He described religions as highways leading to the same destination. As a mark of his respect for all religions and for all human beings, he incorporated the prayers and hymns of different faiths into his daily prayers. Not only did he observe this respect for all religions, but he influenced millions in India to do the same. All of the following passages have the underlying theme of Peace.

Bahai Peace Prayer
Be generous in prosperity and thankful in adversity. Be fair in thy judgment and guarded in thy speech. Be a lamp unto those who walk in darkness and a home to the stranger. Be eyes to the blind and a guiding light unto the feet of the erring. Be a breath of life to the body of humankind, a dew to the soil of the human heart and a fruit upon the tree of humility.

Buddhist Peace Prayer
May all beings everywhere plagued with sufferings of the body and mind quickly be freed from their illnesses. May those frightened cease to be afraid and may those bound be free. May the powerless find power and may people think of befriending one another. May those who find themselves in a trackless, fearful wilderness – the children, the aged, the unprotected – be guarded by beneficent celestials and may they swiftly attain Buddhahood.

Christian Peace Prayer
Blessed are the peacemakers, for they shall be known as the Children of God. But I say to you, love your enemy, do good to those who hate you, bless those who curse you, pray for those who abuse you. To those who strike you on the cheek, offer the other also; and from those who take away your cloak, do not withhold your coat, as well. Give to everyone who begs from you, and to those who take away your goods, do not ask them again. And as you wish that others would do unto you, do so unto them as well.

354

Hindu Peace Prayer

I desire neither earthly kingdom, nor paradise; not even freedom from birth and death. I desire only the deliverance from grief of those afflicted by misery. Oh Lord, lead us from the unreal to the real; from darkness to light; from death to immortality. May there be peace in celestial regions. May there be peace on earth. May the waters be appeasing. May herbs be wholesome and may trees and plants bring peace to all. May all beneficent beings bring peace to us. May thy wisdom spread peace all through the world. May all things be a source of peace to all and to me. Om Shanti, Shanti, Shanti (Peace, Peace, Peace).

Islamic Peace Prayer

We think of Thee, worship Thee, bow to Thee as the Creator of this Universe; we seek refuge in Thee, the Truth, our only support. Thou art the Ruler, the barge in this ocean of endless births and deaths. In the name of Allah, the beneficent, the merciful. Praise be to the Lord of the Universe who has created us and made us into tribes and nations. Give us wisdom that we may know each other and not despise each other. We trust in Thee, oh Allah, the One who heareth and knoweth all things. We shall abide by thy Peace. And, we shall remember the servants of God are those who walk on this earth in humility and, when we address them, we shall say Peace Unto Us All.

Jewish Peace Prayer

Come let us go up to the mountain of the Lord, that we may walk the paths of the Most High. And we shall beat our swords into plowshares and our spears into pruning hooks. Nation shall not lift up sword against nation – neither shall they learn war anymore. And none shall be afraid, for the mouth of the Lord of Hosts has spoken.

Native American Peace Prayer

O, Great Spirit of our Ancestors, I raise my pipe to you. To your messengers the four winds, and to the Mother Earth who provides for your children. Give us the wisdom to teach our children to love, to respect and to be kind to each other so that they may grow with peace in mind. Let us learn to share all the good things that you provide for us on this earth.

Shinto Peace Prayer

Although the people living across the ocean surrounding us are all our brothers and sisters, why, Oh Lord, is there trouble in this world? Why do the winds and the waves rise in the ocean surrounding us? I earnestly wish that the wind will soon blow away all the clouds hanging over the tops of the mountains.

Zoroastrian Peace Prayer

Oh Hormuzda! We pray to Thee to eradicate all the misery in the world; let understanding triumph over ignorance, let generosity triumph over indifference, trust triumph over contempt and Truth triumph over falsehood.

Appendix I

Teaching the "Middle East"
(And World Religions and Cultures)

Annual Workshops for area educators specifically dealing with the Middle East – hosted by the Middle Eastern Studies Center (MESC) of the Portland State University (PSU). These workshops have led to a significant sharing of innovative ideas and programs in area high schools, colleges and universities. Here is a sampling of the concepts and shared resources that should be of interest to educators everywhere:

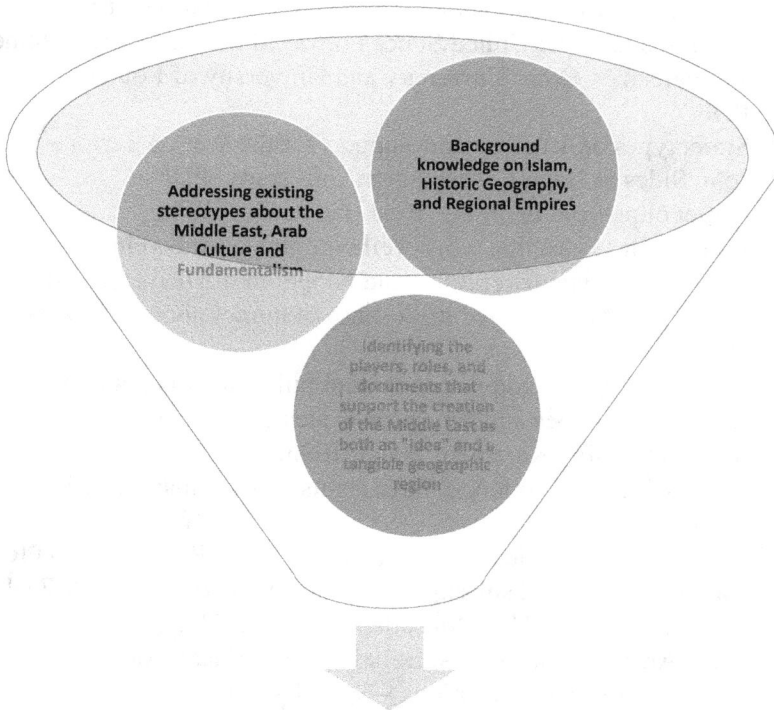

Addressing existing stereotypes about the Middle East, Arab Culture and Fundamentalism

Background knowledge on Islam, Historic Geography, and Regional Empires

Identifying the players, roles, and documents that support the creation of the Middle East as both an "idea" and a tangible geographic region

Arab League of Nations

Appendix I (continued)

Compiled Resource List for Middle East Unit: Primary Source Documents, Research Processes, and United Nations Model

Prerequisite to Unit: Background knowledge on Islam, Historic Geography, and the development of Regional Empires.
Links are provided at www.AmericasJihad.com

Addressing existing stereotypes about the Middle East, Arab Culture and Fundamentalism

- PBS Global Connections – Stereotypes and Realities -LINK
- "The Image of the United States Portrayed in Arab World Online Journalism" – Qatar University and University of Louisiana - PDF
- Stereotypes of Muslims and Support for the War on Terror – John Sides at George Washington University -PDF
- Target clips from the film, "Real Bad Arabs." Wiki
- Films with scenes that work well with this portrayal include: Rules of Engagement (2000) and Kingdom of Heaven (2005)
- TED Talk -Aman Mojadidi: A sense of humor about Afghanistan? LINK
- Using Disney's Aladdin to look at popular stereotypes PDF
- "Arab Stereotypes and American Educators" by Marvin Wingfield and Bushra Karaman, March 1995. LINK
- After 9/11: 'You no longer have rights' – The Guardian UK - LINK
- "Many Arab-Americans Still Perceived As A 'Problem'" – NPR Radio Program and subsequent article about 'How Does It Feel To Be A Problem?' by Moustafa Bayoumi LINK
- What Arabs Think: Values, Beliefs, and Political Concerns – Council on Foreign Relations – Speech – Survey
- Arab and Muslim Perceptions of the United States by Andrew Kohut at the Pew Research Institute -LINK
- PBS Global Connections – Stereotypes and Realities -
- TeachMideast.com – Stereotype Essays -LINK
- http://arabface.us

Identifying the players, roles, and documents that support the creation of the Middle East as both an "idea" and a tangible geographic region.

- "Bringing the United States Back into the Middle East" by Shadi Hamid and Peter Mandaville Center for Strategic & International Studies PDF
- The Map as History – 19 animated maps to explain the Middle East - LINK
- The United Church of God: The Middle East in Biblical Prophecy selected excerpts only: LINK
- "The Creation of the Modern Middle East"
- "A Rising Tide of Arab Nationalism"
- "Fundamentalist Islam Resurges"
- "Anger Mounts Following Gulf War"
- Middle East Research and Information Project -Primer on Palestine, Israel and the Arab-Israeli Conflict -   LINK
- BBC Middle East – "Why border lines drawn with a ruler in WW1 still rock the Middle East" by Tarek Osman LINK MAP S/P AGREEMENT
- PBS Global Connections – Nation States/Formation (lesson plans) LINK
- "Civilization and the Mandate System under the League of Nations as Origin of Trusteeship" Nele Matz, Max Planck Institut Germany PDF
- World.Mic: How the British Screwed Up the Middle East, in 10 Classic Cartoons LINK
- Promises & Betrayals: Britain and the Struggle for the Holy Land (2002)
- British double-dealing during WWI ignited the conflict between Arab and Jew in the Middle East. A disturbing picture of a duplicitous wartime government. 53min IMDb YouTube
- The Cold War's Arab Spring: How the Soviets Created Today's Middle East by Claire Berlinski LINK
- Modern History Sourcebook: Sir Henry McMahon: Letter to Ali ibn Husain, 1915 LINK
- INSTITUTE FOR HISTORICAL REVIEW: Behind the Balfour Declaration LINK
- Yale University: Lillian Goldman Law Library – The Avalon Project, "The Sykes-Picot Agreement (1916)" LINK Library Portal LINK

- Documents Pertinent to Middle East Issues -Mount Holyoke College LINK
- Arab League or League of Nations Project and Supplemental Geography
- What is the Middle East? – TeachMideast LINK
- "Where is the Middle East?" Carolina Center for the Study of the Middle East and Muslim Civilization -University of North Carolina at Chapel Hill
- Use for a timeline of maps LINK
- "INTRODUCTION TO THE GEOGRAPHY AND HISTORI-CAL BACKGROUND OF THE MIDDLE EAST" by Asma Afsaruddin at Notre Dame LINK
- BBC New: Middle East and Al Jazeera News Network
- The CIA World Factbook – Middle East LINK
- "40 maps that explain the Middle East" by Max Fisher LINK
- "Islamist Militants Aim to Redraw Map of the Middle East" – Wall Street Journal LINK
- Arab League Nations – Maps of the World LINK

Appendix J

St. Catherine's Monastery Mt. Sinai, Egypt
by Abdullah Craig Walker and Arif Humayun

Photo by Abdullah Craig Walker

St. Catherine's Monastery, located in Egypt at the foot of Mt. Sinai, is the world's oldest monastery. Its original purpose was to preserve Jewish and Christian sacred texts and historic artifacts, particularly those related to the Prophet Moses, as well as to facilitate access to Mt. Sinai by Jewish, Christian, and Muslim pilgrims. It possesses a huge collection of Christian manuscripts, second only to the Vatican, and claims the oldest collection of Christian icons. The World Heritage Site also is believed to be the physical repository of the "Burning Bush", which is mentioned in Hebrew writings and in the Old Testament.

My wife and I made two pilgrimages to Mt. Sinai. On one visit, we rode camels to the base of an ancient stone stairway, upon which we hiked up to the top. There, we came upon a small mosque alongside a Coptic Christian chapel. A handful of Muslims were praying in the mosque, while a group of Christians knelt in prayer in the chapel. As we descended that evening to a glorious sunset, for which the mountain is famous, we felt uplifted and very much in tune with the unifying spirit of Prophet Moses (pbuh).

When we explored St. Catherine's Monastery, we were astonished to see an original letter dictated by Prophet Muhammad (pbuh) when Muslims controlled the region in the 7th Century A.D. As a result of this letter, St. Catherine's Monastery has remained safe under Muslim protection and open to people of all faiths for over 1400 years. The story goes back to 628 AD, when the Sinai Peninsula was

361

under Muslim control. A delegation from St. Catherine's Monastery came to Prophet Mohammad and requested his protection. The Prophet responded by granting them a charter of rights .

In the context of the intolerant and violent ideologies that plague the Religions of the Book today – Jewish, Christian, and Muslim, the significance of the document cannot be overstated. Muhammad asserts that Muslims "are with Christians near and far," that they are his "citizens" and "allies," and "their churches are to be respected." Although the letter was written in 628 A.D., it protects the right to property, freedom of religion, freedom of work, and security of the person – fundamental civil rights.

Clearly, the document is an inspiration for Muslims to rise above communal intolerance, and appeals to the good will of Christians who may harbor fear of Islam or Muslims.

The letter is translated below in its entirety:

"This is a message from Muhammad ibn Abdullah, as a covenant to those who adopt Christianity, near and far, we are with them. Verily I, the servants, the helpers, and my followers defend them, because Christians are my citizens; and by Allah! I hold out against anything that displeases them. No compulsion is to be on them. Neither are their judges to be removed from their jobs nor their monks from their monasteries. No one is to destroy a house of their religion, to damage it, or to carry anything from it to the Muslims' houses. Should anyone take any of these, he would spoil God's covenant and disobey His Prophet. Verily, they are my allies and have my secure charter against all that they hate. No one is to force them to travel or to oblige them to fight. The Muslims are to fight for them. If a female Christian is married to a Muslim, it is not to take place without her approval. She is not to be prevented from visiting her church to pray. Their churches are to be respected. They are neither to be prevented from repairing them nor the sacredness of their covenants. No one of the nation (Muslims) is to disobey the covenant till the Last Day (end of the world)."

Note: the letter was dictated by Prophet Muhammad, and bears his imprint. However, there is controversy among some Muslim scholars concerning its authenticity.

Appendix K

Top Ten Ways to Prevent, Reduce or Resolve Conflict

1. Take responsibility what you say and do – be accountable

2. Approach all encounters with intent to achieve greater mutual understanding and respect

3. Focus first on your common interests and shared values

4. Whatever your religion or beliefs, practice the "Golden Rule" ("Do unto others as you would have them do unto you")

5. Avoid absolutes such as "always," "never," etc.

6. Avoid fixed positions whenever possible

7. Empathize; Consider the other's perspective

8. Strive first to understand before expecting to be understood

9. Acknowledge the other's anger, frustration, pain

10. Consider Rotary International's "4-Way Test:"

Of all the things you think, say or do:

Is it the TRUTH?
Is it FAIR to all concerned?
Will it build GOOD WILL and better FRIENDSHIPS?
Will it be BENEFICIAL to all concerned?

Appendix L

Peace through Rotary International

Dave Bateman, AB, JD, LLM

These are key points from my working and educational experience over fifty combined years in the USAF/USAFR, criminal and civil law practice, international law, international coffee trade, and Christian missionary work:

Some Root Causes of International Conflict and War

- Land – Expansionist policies to control populations and resources
- Religion – Expansion of particular theologies and belief systems
- Natural Resources - Need for food, water, fuel, minerals, and agricultural growing regions
- Megalomania – Dictator rise to power and subjugation of populations and opposing politics

General Guidelines for Peaceful Coexistence of Nations
and Dispute Prevention

- Nations must agree to respect principles of international law and in particular protect individual and group rights enumerated under the UN Declaration on Human Rights – peace through UN principles
- National leaders should strive to employ the equitable and fair principles of the Rotary Four Way Test in every personal and business relationship within the nation – peace through Rotary principles
- Nations must establish governance based on laws derived from the populace rather than on the dictates of one man or a group of individuals who are not popularly elected, and Nations must treat all citizens of the nation equally under the law – peace through the rule of law
- Nations must treat peaceful foreigners or immigrants fairly under the law which, at a minimum, protect basic human rights – peace through immigration reform
- Nations must respect individual religious freedoms - peace through mutual spiritual respect

364

- Nations should encourage higher education of all of its citizens both male and female - peace through education
- Nations should encourage fair bilateral trade between its citizens and the citizens of other nations and provide a stable economic forum to accomplish this goal – peace through trade

Resolution of Disputes

- Non-binding mediation of international disputes through UN international Peace Tribunals utilizing trained and experienced Rotary Peace Teams led by Rotary Peace Ambassadors and Diplomats. Tribunals would be constituted of neutral third parties experienced and knowledgeable of the area of dispute but not directly involved. Intervening parties with standing and a direct interest in the dispute allowed to participate. For religious disputes, the disputing parties will be referred into the new UN Chaplaincy Program – goal is to frame the issues and to develop the initial positions of the parties
- Binding arbitration through International Peace Tribunal in a more formal legal and judicial setting with formal presentation of evidence under the rules of procedure and evidence of the World Court
- World Court administrative appeal on the record with the court reviewing the record, and hearing concluding arguments from the disputing parties, to make a formal and final ruling on the dispute

Index

People:

251-253, 256-257, 261, 301-311, 314, 316, 320, 332-334, 337-340
Assyria, Assyrian 111-120

B

Baghdad 1, 9, 47-56, 76, 78-79, 112-113, 212-214, 218, 221, 254, 371
Bosnia 137-144

C

Cambodia 286-288
Croatia 3

E

Egypt 40, 164, 220, 288, 361

F

Fort Hood, Texas 41, 67

G

Gaza 246

I

Iberia 158-167
Iran, Iranians 2, 9-10, 45, 164, 205, 212-221, 226, 300, 301, 314, 328, 340-343
Iraq, Iraqis, XII, XV, XVI, 2-12, 27-28, 47-54, 74-84, 100, 111-114, 117-119, 140, 147, 163, 164, 166, 172, 178, 205-208, 221-218, 235-237, 243-263, 295-296, 314, 316, 320, 322, 327, 341, 344, 371
Israel 27, 220, 288, 298, 299, 314, 318, 359

J

Jordan 2, 105, 164

K

Kirkuk 1, 8, 341-344
Korea 15
Kurdistan, Iraqi Kurdistan, Kurds 2, 9, 10, 28, 118
Kuwait 2-3,105, 201-209, 216, 291, 293, 294, 314

L

Lebanon 44, 288

Libya 237

P

Pakistan, Pakistanis 10,16, 70, 35-45, 106, 164, 169-184, 201, 208-210, 223-230, 232-241, 288, 292, 298, 301-302, 309, 314, 328-335, 336
Palestine 164, 178, 298-299, 359
Philippines XV-XVII, 76

S

St. Catherine's Monastery Mt. Sinai, Egypt 361
Saudi Arabia 2-3, 45, 328-330
Syria/Sham 2, 12, 166, 217, 230, 235, 237, 263, 321, 327

T

Turkey 2, 30, 116, 141, 320

V

Vietnam 6-7, 75, 140, 164, 203, 250, 287

Y

Yemen 23, 105, 235
Yugoslavia (aka: Jugoslavia) 2, 6

Quotes:

A

John Quincy Adams 168
African Proverb 222
Maya Angelou 46, 60, 311, 323
Aristotle 211

B

Rahman Baba 241
Bill Beattie 260
Benazir Bhutto 32, 110
Paul Boese 121
Robert Oxton Bolt 311
Les Brown 46
Edmund Burke 211

America's "Jihad"
Compiled and Edited by

Dan Sockle

Most of Dan's career has been in intelligence, criminal and civil investigations. Dan was a communications intelligence analyst and criminal investigator for the US Army, retiring as a supervisory special agent/ CW3 in 1992. He served as a CID agent in the first Gulf War (Operation Desert Storm), and as a Research Manager/Cultural Advisor (contractor) on "Human Terrain Teams" in Kirkuk and Baghdad, Iraq, in 2008-2009. He has taught classes for the Clark College Mature/Lifelong Learning program and conducted numerous presentations, workshops, training and briefing sessions both in the military and later with the State of Washington's Risk Management Division in Olympia, Washington. He has a B.A. in Criminal Justice (Univ. of Nevada/Reno) and Masters in Public Administration (The Evergreen State College in Olympia, Washington). His volunteer work has included coaching youth sports, Kiwanis, Crime Stoppers, community mediation, veteran advocacy and Rotary – where he founded and chaired his first club's "Peace & Conflict Resolution" committee, served two years as the "Service Projects Director" on the club's board, and now collaborates with other Rotary "Peacebuilders" as a member of the new and evolving United Services Rotary e-Club (unitedservicesrotary.com), which was founded with the intent to reach out to veterans and active military throughout the world. Dan is equally proud to serve on the board of the Community Military Appreciation Committee (CMAC website: cmac11.com) supporting veterans and military families in the greater Vancouver/Portland area.

Finally, Dan, as a realistic idealist, believes that a strong military will always be necessary. But, he also believes that our military men and women are the most compassionate in the world, and should be seen as allies in peace-building, conflict prevention and resolution. After all, "No one appreciates peace more than a soldier."

"The challenge of the coming months and years
won't be how to defeat the Islamic State.
It will be how to do so without defeating the future
of the people it has terrorized the most."

~ The Soufan Group ~